About Pfeiffer

Pfeiffer serves the professional development and hands-on resource needs of training and human resource practitioners and gives them products to do their jobs better. We deliver proven ideas and solutions from experts in HR development and HR management, and we offer effective and customizable tools to improve workplace performance. From novice to seasoned professional, Pfeiffer is the source you can trust to make yourself and your organization more successful.

Essential Knowledge Pfeiffer produces insightful, practical, and comprehensive materials on topics that matter the most to training and HR professionals. Our Essential Knowledge resources translate the expertise of seasoned professionals into practical, how-to guidance on critical workplace issues and problems. These resources are supported by case studies, worksheets, and job aids and are frequently supplemented with CD-ROMs, websites, and other means of making the content easier to read, understand, and use.

Essential Tools Pfeiffer's Essential Tools resources save time and expense by offering proven, ready-to-use materials—including exercises, activities, games, instruments, and assessments—for use during a training or team-learning event. These resources are frequently offered in loose-leaf or CD-ROM format to facilitate copying and customization of the material.

Pfeiffer also recognizes the remarkable power of new technologies in expanding the reach and effectiveness of training. While e-hype has often created whizbang solutions in search of a problem, we are dedicated to bringing convenience and enhancements to proven training solutions. All our e-tools comply with rigorous functionality standards. The most appropriate technology wrapped around essential content yields the perfect solution for today's on-the-go trainers and human resource professionals.

Pfeiffer *Essential resources for training and HR professionals*
www.pfeiffer.com

The Global Diversity Desk Reference

Managing an International Workforce

Lee Gardenswartz
Anita Rowe
Patricia Digh
Martin F. Bennett

A Wiley Imprint
www.pfeiffer.com

CONTENTS

LIST OF MODELS, TOOLS,
AND EXERCISES

CHAPTER 2

CHAPTER 3

CHAPTER 4

CHAPTER 8

CHAPTER 9

CD-ROM CONTENTS

CHAPTER 1

What Do You Need to Know?

Diversity Values: How Well Do They Translate?

Global Diversity Strategy Audit

You as a Culturally Diverse Entity

Cultural Dimensions at Work

Three Cultures Model at Work

Building Your Own Business Case

CHAPTER 2

Global Assessment for Inclusivity

Personal Assessment for Inclusivity

Stages of Corporate Development and Global Diversity

Legal Drivers and Implications for Global Diversity

Global Performance Management Audit

Identify Global Diversity Exemplars

Global Diversity Corporate Assessment Tool

CHAPTER 3

Cultural Orientation Questionnaire

Cultural Orientation Profile

Cross-Cultural Communication Style Inventory

Global Communication Effectiveness Checklist

Global Communication Analysis

Use of Interpreters Checklist

Considerations in Planning Presentations

CHAPTER 4

The Impact of Culture on Global Team Performance

Factors That Enhance Effective Global Teams

Achieving Task and Relationship Balance on a Global Team

Expanding Views on a Global Team

Framework for Developing a High-Performance Global Team

Leadership Behaviors on a Global Team

Leadership on a Global Team

CHAPTER 5

What's the Source of the Conflict?

Dimensions of Conflict

What's Your Conflict Style?

Conflict Information-Gathering Checklist

Assessing Your Conflict Competencies

CHAPTER 6

Cultural Adaptability Assessment

Problem-Solving Response Sheet

Blocks to Problem Solving

Essential Characteristics of an Effective Member
     on a Global Problem-Solving Team

Influencing Others: Unimundo Case Study

Group Experience Rating Form

Cross-Cultural Adaptations on Global Teams

CHAPTER 7

Using Social and Professional National Competencies

Global Diversity Trend Assessment

Global Diversity Capability Cycle Appraisal System

Interview Preparations and Analysis

Interviewing Techniques Chart

Global Diversity Interview Review Checklist

Global Diversity Perspectives in Training Design

Globalizing the Training Design Process

CHAPTER 8

Performance Management Quick Check

National and Civilizational Influences
Within the Performance Management Process

Nordic New Co Petroleum Goes Global: A Case Study

Five-Focus Performance Dialogue Model: Nordic New Co Petroleum
Goes Global

SSI Global Diversity Assessment Tool for Nordic New Co Petroleum
Case Study

Global Diversity Performance Management Focus Sheet:
Nordic New Co Petroleum Goes Global

Performance Management and Ethics

Global Diversity Rater Competency Review

Global Diversity Performance Review Outcome Analysis

CHAPTER 9

Actual and Expected Gains and Losses from Change

Corporate Culture Styles and Change

Reconciling Conflicts Based on Different Cultural Responses to Change

Leader Behaviors

Essential Change Agent Behaviors

ACKNOWLEDGMENTS

No book is ever completed without the support of other people. We're lucky to count the following among those who supported us in this project, both personally and professionally:

Janet Bennett

Milton Bennett

Rita Bennett

Jan Bowler

Bill Brazell

Jorge Cherbosque

Monica Emerson

Urusa Fahim

Tony Frost

Anna and Thomas P. Gerrity

Charles M. Hampden-Turner

John Irvine

Bruce La Brack

Michelle LeBaron

Ronald Matheson

George Monagan

Monica Moreno

Claudia Mueller

Angelika Plett

John and Emma Ptak

Maricel Quintana-Baker

Hilde Regnier

Darrell Rowe

Nestor Santtia

Samya Sattar

George Simons

Suzanne Stemme

Harvey Sweet

Fons Trompenaars

Jan Walsh

Donna Zimmer

INTRODUCTION

Globalization has become one of the business world's hottest topics as we begin the new millennium. From news about protests at World Trade Organization meetings to the agendas of conferences of world leaders, globalization and its economic and political implications hit both a nerve and the bottom line. However, beneath the debates and philosophizing lies the complex and demanding reality of managing a multicultural, geographically dispersed, polyglot workforce.

As organizations face stiffer global competition, the need to internationalize continues to increase. Penetrating new markets, accessing cheaper raw materials, reducing wage costs, bringing in specialized skills, and improving technology push organizations to cross borders, continents, and civilizations. A tenfold increase in foreign ventures even in the 1980s, which accelerated further in the 1990s, attests to this evolution in the United States alone.[1] While the increased cultural diversity brought about by global expansion brings the potential for greater creativity, better decision making, and enhanced marketing, it also brings challenges. Conflict, misunderstanding, and diminished performance can also result when organizations attempt to grow and thrive with the diversity that a geographically dispersed, multinational, and multilingual workforce brings.

Success in global business depends on how that diversity is managed, and not managing the global workforce effectively has severe consequences to one's reputation and the bottom line. Organizations can ill afford the negative business

1

impact of incidents such as that experienced by Coca-Cola, an organization that had already faced domestic diversity issues. This time the image blow had global repercussions, as described below.

> Two senior managers of Coca-Cola in Malaysia, both Australian expatriates, have been criticized by the Malaysian Human Resources Minister Lim Ah Lek for showing disrespect to their employees. They have been accused of changing collective agreements with workers, ordering a 10 percent pay cut, altering public holidays, and extending working hours to compensate for the time lost due to Friday prayers. Lek described the actions as "belittling" Malaysia, showing disrespect and demonstrating that "Australians are not fit to work here." Senator Zalnal Rampak, president of the Malaysian Trades Union Congress, has requested that the work permits be withdrawn as the managers showed "no respect whatsoever for local customs, manners, traditions, and religious sensitivities."[2]

Individual companies suffer when their managers are not adept at negotiating the challenging dynamics of global business. In addition, national economies feel the compounded impact. Research by the Australian Industry Task Force on Leadership and Management Skills found that Australian managers were ranked behind managers from competitor countries by Asian managers polled,[3] creating a significant hurdle for Australia to overcome in dealing with its closest trading partners.

Practitioners helping organizations manage these challenges see an increasing need for practical tools, concrete suggestions, and pragmatic methods to help global organizations realize the tremendous potential of an international workforce. Since the Society for Human Resource Management (SHRM), the world's largest human resource organization, established a division of International and Diversity Programs in 1993, it has been inundated with questions such as:

- "We need to roll out our organizational audit process in several countries in Europe—do we need to change the survey instruments?"
- "We have a diversity training process that all headquarters staff in Louisville has completed. The next phase is to conduct the training in Kobe, Japan, at our site there. What should I change or alter in the training?"
- "Our global employees complain that our open resourcing system does not work equitably for many overseas staff. How can we make it more accessible and fair to all?"

While organizations are expanding their reach, the workforce around the world is changing as well. According to a year 2000 survey and report, "In a world in which companies generate 43 percent of revenues outside their home countries, technologically enhanced communications spread both business concepts and the message of globalization. Consequently, it is no surprise that we are beginning to see worldwide consistency in employee expectations and demands as a result of the global dissemination of human resource policies, practices, concepts, and solutions."[4] In Japan, for example, the harmony-disrupting, counter-culture behavior of whistle blowing is slowly growing in acceptance as the population reacts to defective products and tainted food that resulted from unquestioning loyalty. In a nation that has traditionally revered loyalty and seen betrayal as a crime punishable by *Mura Hachibu,* exile from the village, a 2000 Consumer Research Institute poll found that 45.1 percent of people surveyed supported whistle blowing in the public interest.[5]

International operations in the past may have been handled by a few select home-country expatriates. Now the number and mix of employees is growing, as can be seen from a few verbatim comments from a recent global survey.[6]

"We're sending more families, females, and third-country nationals."

"We have been sending more lower-level managers than in the past, where we sent only VPs."

"There are fewer U.S. expats and more third-country nationals."

"I've seen more reliance on local talent for leadership."

In addition, companies are now intentionally increasing the mix. Mobil Oil, for example, has increased the use of third-country nationals by placing managing directors in regions different from their own nationalities. An Australian man heads up operations in Japan, a U.S.-American woman leads in Singapore, an English woman does so in New Zealand, and a Singaporean man is in charge in Australia.[7]

This mix of nationalities, genders, headquarters-based, and locals creates fruitful ground for innovation, growth, and leadership. However, without intentional management, it can also create costly mishaps and counterproductive conditions.

Organizations suffer direct financial loss when they do not prepare employees adequately for international assignments. One major global aerospace firm found that, on average, placing an employee in a three-year international assignment costs the company one million dollars, with a third of that amount covering the cost of moving the employee and family in and out. Each time an individual does not succeed in one of these assignments and needs to be replaced, a third of a million dollars is lost, attesting to the high cost of what one global professional terms the "Roman coliseum school of management."

However, global diversity does not merely have significance for expatriates and headquarters-based executives. Employees in India, Brazil, Thailand, and

Korea who may never work outside their home countries are also part of the global workforce. Their issues and barriers need to be addressed, their cultures, perspectives, and input taken into consideration, and their potential contributions realized for the benefit of the organization.

HELP IN MANAGING GLOBAL DIVERSITY

Managing global diversity is a proactive, strategic approach that leads to business success. This approach is best defined as the capability of an organization and the individuals within it to effectively manage or be managed, using and maximizing the total workforce potential by having the knowledge, attitude, and skills to identify and use alternative cultural styles and behaviors to achieve the business objective with respect to the national culture(s) and the multiple locations in which they operate.

This book provides neither a template nor a list of dos and don'ts for global diversity management. What it does offer is practical information to deal with the complexities of working with a globally diverse workforce. First, it presents conceptual models that provide both insight into the issues and a framework on which to build an effective approach. Second, this book provides tools for increasing effectiveness in managing diversity at three levels—the individual, interpersonal, and organizational. Building individual awareness, knowledge, and skill in managing global diversity is an essential first step for any leader in international organizations. Functioning productively with employees, colleagues, and managers whose global diversity profile is very different is a second area of competence. Finally, creating and aligning organizational systems, policies, and practices with the requirements of an international workforce is critical for success.

As shown in the Managing Global Diversity diagram, information, activities, and tools are focused on (1) increasing your *awareness* about global diversity

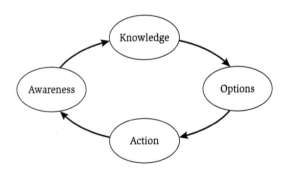

Managing Global Diversity

issues, challenges, and opportunities; (2) giving you *knowledge* to understand the issues, dynamics, and factors at play; (3) helping you enlist the cooperation of others in creating *options* so that you can (4) take beneficial *action* that reconciles differences and leads your organization to success.

The concepts and tools found in this book rest on a fundamental orientation regarding managing global diversity that is best described in the diagram.

Each of the chapters presents information and activities that build *awareness*, increase *knowledge*, enhance the ability to create *options*, and give guidance in selecting suitable *actions* that lead to a process of ongoing improvement.

Awareness

A U.S. presentation team left Korea thinking they had been successful in working with a group of employees from six countries. Only later did they receive feedback that told them they'd ignored cues and failed in achieving their objectives. Rather than being blissful, ignorance is dangerous. What we do not know often hurts us, and lack of knowledge prevents us from taking action that can help. Awareness of obstacles or exclusions is essential to dealing with them. Likewise, recognition of opportunities presented by diversity is necessary in order to take advantage of them. The first step in dealing effectively with global diversity is becoming aware of the challenges and opportunities it offers. Interpreting your Chinese colleagues' smiling, helpful, and gracious hospitality for acceptance, rather than the dutiful behavior as your hosts that it is, probably would be a mistake. On the other hand, showing understanding of the irritation that might be felt by local staff at headquarters-based control and the frequent preference given to expatriates could be helpful in approaching colleagues and staff in those offices with empathy and humility. Each chapter provides tools and activities that raise awareness of differences and recognition of situations that need to be addressed.

Knowledge

However, awareness alone is not enough. Beyond noticing that differences exist, we need information about the situation or issue. Gaining knowledge is a critical next step. What are the different norms of the cultures in the workforce? How does each civilization involved look at the situation? What are the particular sensitivities in each country? How do the national differences involved play out? How do employees understand their roles in the workplace due to differences in race, gender, and age? What factors may lead to conflict? What potential opportunities are presented? Finding ways to gain information about the individual, organizational, national, and civilizational cultural differences as well as the internal and external dimensions of diversity is essential at this stage. Chapters 1 and 2 present detailed information about these differences.

Options

Such knowledge then helps in the next stage, that of generating options for actions to take. What range of actions would help deal with these differences? How can you get help from cultural informants about how different civilizations or national cultures might approach this issue? What steps need to be taken to meet the needs of all parties and accomplish goals? What mutual adjustments and adaptations could be made to reconcile differences? At this point, generating multiple options and avoiding polarized thinking in an either/or trap is critical. Reconciliation requires a sensitivity to others' values, perspectives, and needs on the one hand and a willingness to adapt to the needs and preferences of others on the other. Options that are generated need to take into account the perspectives of the multiple cultures involved, those of the individual, nation, organization, and civilization. Chapters 3, 4, 5, 6, 7, 8, and 9 present a myriad of guidelines and activities that provide options for dealing with these differences and activities that engage others in developing them.

Actions

Finally, action must be taken, and that requires deciding which combination of options will be implemented. Here, too, one must take into account the objectives of the organization and the different cultural and individual perspectives involved so that a mutually acceptable resolution results. The aim at this stage is a reconciliation and utilization of differences that maximizes the diverse contributions of employees and leads to business success. Chapters 3 through 9 offer guidance in selecting the most effective actions for your organization.

ASSUMPTIONS UNDERLYING DIVERSITY WORK

All work is value-based, influenced by the priorities, experiences, and orientations of the individuals, national cultures, and civilizations involved. In addressing diversity in global organizations, it is important to examine this value base and consciously recognize the assumptions that form the foundation of one's approach, the platform from which individuals and organizations leverage diversity.

It has been our experience that there are a few shared, although rarely articulated, assumptions that exist as underpinnings of diversity work:

1. *Diversity has the capacity to add value.*

   While diversity brings the potential for both creativity and conflict, the driver underlying the attention to diversity is a business imperative, because diversity brings the possibility of enhancing and enriching organizations. Differences in perspective, approach, skill, and background can stimulate innovation that leads to progress and improvement. Employees from cultures that value conformity and homogeneity in their own national contexts may find it difficult to embrace global diversity within the corporate structure.

2. *For diversity to add value it must be managed.*

Many individuals dislike the term "manage," as for some it connotes control and harnessing rather than capitalizing on and using. However, most would agree that diversity does not automatically benefit an organization. To reap diversity's potential rewards, organizations must address barriers, create ways to include a wider range of perspectives, and intentionally focus energy and resources on making use of diversity as a strategic business advantage.

3. *Diversity is ultimately about inclusion and exclusion.*

At the most basic level, diversity involves the fundamental issue of who is included and who is not, the dimensions of differences around which we include and exclude others. These differences may be visible and obvious, such as gender, race, and nationality. However, they may also be more subtle, involving aspects such as personality and thinking styles, education level, and civilizational orientations.

In all organizations both formal and informal parameters exist regarding inclusion and exclusion in decision making, problem solving, and information gathering. In addressing global diversity, these patterns of inclusion and exclusion need to be examined and managed to get the best from a worldwide workforce to serve the needs of the company.

4. *Perception is reality.*

Diversity work needs to take into account the perceived realities of a wide range of individuals in any organization. Each individual is the expert on his or her own perceived reality, and work needs to focus on helping people understand their own and others' realities as well. Dealing with these different perceived realities in constructive ways is an important step to achieving cross-cultural reconciliation.

5. *People find comfort and safety in commonality.*

It is natural for people to gravitate toward others they perceive to be similar to them, whether in ethnicity, language, values, education level, or recreational activities. This natural grouping is a given. Fighting this aspect of human nature is counterproductive. Part of the job of diversity work is to help employees develop commonalities with people different from themselves so that new connections, comfort, and trust can be built.

6. *People support change that has clear benefit to them.*

   Just as organizations need to find strategic business advantage in any action they take, so do individual human beings. For employees, employers, and corporate stakeholders to support the changes involved in any diversity initiative, they need to see that these actions will be beneficial to them.

7. *Dealing with diversity involves culture change.*

   Making the best use of differences in an organization requires more than just global recruitment, an international mentoring process, pre-departure preparation, or cross-cultural awareness training. It involves an organization development approach, focusing on individual, managerial, and organizational levels that ultimately deal with local, national, and global systemic change. This view may not be shared by those from more traditional organizational and national cultures who see change as disruptive to order and a threat to the security derived from depending on the way things have always been done.

8. *All conditions exist for a reason.*

   Before embarking on a change process, it is critical to understand the dynamics of the existing situation. Identifying how current conditions serve the organization and the individuals in it is a crucial first step in delineating the formal and informal power structures that support the status quo and resist change.

Consider which of these basic tenets are part of your philosophy about dealing with diversity. Perhaps there are others that underlie your approach. Understanding your own beliefs is a critical step in dealing with others different from you in your global interactions. It is also important to understand the beliefs and tenets of colleagues, employees, and clients with whom you do business.

The four authors make no pretense at being culture-free. While we have made every attempt to be sensitive to different perspectives and orientations, we come out of a U.S.-American cultural context that has shaped our approach. With over one hundred collective years of experience consulting with global organizations in both domestic and international settings, we have worked with employees from all parts of the world and have seen the challenges organizations face in creating systems, procedures, and methods that are effective in working with a globally diverse workforce. The enormity of the topic and complexity of the issues involved in global diversity can be overwhelming. For that reason this book provides a structure in which the reader can find the pertinent information for particular needs and adapt them to a specific reality.

OVERVIEW OF CHAPTERS

The Global Diversity Desk Reference is designed to serve as a practical reference resource at the strategic and tactical levels, for senior leaders, managers, and human resource professionals engaged in directing and managing a global work-force. Each of the tools provided is accompanied by directions for its use in face-to-face, and electronic interactions where possible, with appropriate groups within the organization as a management, staff development, training, and/or organizational change intervention. In order to help you use the tools and activities, a matrix, found in the Appendix, presents a cross-reference of tools and activities showing their potential use with various groups and for various purposes. Following this matrix are a number of sample agendas demonstrating examples of the sequencing of activities and concepts for training and for stimulating strategic discussions regarding systems and policy changes.

Part One: Foundations of Global Diversity

This first section presents the platform that forms the conceptual base for global diversity. The models provided explain the what and why to help leaders and managers understand the complexities of global diversity.

Chapter 1: Beyond Diversity: What Is Culture?

Because understanding our own culture and that of others is a critical underpin-ning of our ability to leverage diversity on a global scale, this chapter presents a necessary primer on concepts of culture: what it is and how in influences behav-ior. Various models of culture are used to address the process of cross-cultural adaptation and applied to the globally diverse workplace. The Three Culture Model™ is explained, and tools for reconciling and learning from cultural differ-ence are provided. In addition, the chapter presents the business case for man-aging global diversity and the distinction between domestic and global diversity.

Chapter 2: What Is Global Diversity?

A first step in leveraging the power of a global workforce is an understanding of the multiple dimensions involved. This chapter provides models that serve as conceptual foundations for helping your organization manage and leverage global diversity. The Six Spheres of Inclusion™ (SSI) model presents a manage-able way to understand and communicate the complexities of global diversity.

Part Two: Managing a Global Workforce

The second section moves on to the "how" of global diversity management, pro-viding information and tools to engage others in increasing organizational and individual effectiveness in managing a global workforce.

Chapter 3: Communicating Effectively Across Cultures

Culture, language, time, and distance present daunting challenges to the exchange of information and development of effective interpersonal connections necessary in global organizations. This chapter provides frameworks, guidelines, methods, and tools for overcoming barriers and building relationships across lines of nationality, language, education, and field of work, among other dimensions of global diversity. It focuses on techniques and approaches for improving results when dealing with specific kinds of communication issues, such as using interpreters, making presentations, using technology, and conducting meetings in global settings.

Chapter 4: Maximizing Global Teams and Work Groups for Higher Performance

Teamwork is severely tested when virtual or global work groups confront dilemmas around lack of face time, multiple languages, cultural differences, technology, and time restrictions. This chapter presents information about the "must have" ingredients for high-performing global teams and the cultural differences influencing teamwork. It goes on to provide a number of assessments, activities, and tools for use in both face-to-face and virtual settings to build cohesion, improve communication, foster creativity, and bridge time and distance.

Chapter 5: Managing Conflict in an International Environment

The same differences that bring the potential for creativity can also result in conflict when methods, preferences, and values clash. This chapter provides a deeper understanding of the dynamics of conflict in global organizations and methods and tools to deal with it in productive ways.

Chapter 6: Problem Solving in Global Organizations

While business cultures may vary around the world, the need to solve problems remains constant. This chapter presents information about the ways culture influences the methodologies for expressing and solving problems. It goes on to provide tools and activities for maximizing the creativity and problem-solving capability of global work groups.

Part Three: Developing
Your Organization's Global Competence

The third section continues the focus on the "how" of global diversity management, providing guidelines and tools for improving systems to support global diversity management.

Chapter 7: Systems for Using People Effectively in Global Organizations

Developing human resource systems and management practices that are appropriate and effective in global organizations is the focus of this chapter on people management. Specific guidelines and tools regarding interviewing, hiring, training, development, compensation, and benefits are provided.

Chapter 8: Managing Performance in an International Workforce

International and global organizations have continuously struggled to create performance management systems ranging from a uniform "one size fits all" model to a potpourri of location-specific models that have little value outside their national borders. This chapter gives guidance in developing and implementing global performance management systems that allow for local cultural integrity, yet identify performers who bring value to the ongoing development of the company.

Chapter 9: You as a Tool: Leader as a Change Agent

Being an effective global leader means being a change agent in order to advocate for the culture transformation required to manage the complexities of global diversity. This chapter helps leaders assess and develop the flexibility and competencies necessary for effectiveness in shepherding global diversity implementation.

Part Four: Resources and Appendix

Resources for Managing Global Diversity

While this book provides a wealth of useful information and practical tools, additional resources will be required from time to time. This chapter anticipates this need and provides an extensive listing of resources that serve as a "go-to" guide for answers to specific questions, additional in-depth information, or help in developing the skills of others. Books, articles, videos, CD-ROM resources, and websites relevant to global diversity are listed.

Additional resources in the form of a cross-referenced matrix guide to using the tools and activities in the book as well as sample agendas demonstrating the sequencing of models and activities for training and strategic planning discussions are provided in this section.

As you continue your journey through the uncharted territory of global diversity, our goal is to give you concepts and tools that provide a roadmap to guide you.

Notes

1 Palich, Leslie E., and Luis R. Gomez-Mejia. "A Theory of Global Strategy and Firm Efficiencies: Considering the Effects of Cultural Diversity," *Journal of Management,* July 1999, V25, N4, p. 587.

2 *HR World,* March/April 2000, p. 9.

3 *Enterprising Nation.* Report of the Industry Task Force on Leadership and Management Skills, Commonwealth of Australia, 1995.

4 *Global Relocation Trends: 2000 Survey Report.* GMAC GRS/Windham International, NFTC and SHRM Global Forum, October 2002.

5 Maguier, Mark. "Speaking Out Has High Cost," *Los Angeles Times,* August 12, 2002, pp. A1 and A6.

6 *Global Relocation Trends: 2000 Survey Report.* GMAC GRS/Windham International, NFTC and SHRM Global Forum, October 2002.

7 Smith, Duncan. "The Business Case for Diversity," *Monash Mt. Eliza Business Review,* November 1998, pp. 72–81.

PART ONE

FOUNDATIONS
OF GLOBAL DIVERSITY

CHAPTER 1

Beyond Diversity

What Is Culture?

Takeo Fujisawa, cofounder of the Honda Motor Corporation, once said, "Japanese and American management is 95 percent the same, and differs in all important respects." It is those "important respects" that this book is designed to address and illuminate.

Fujisawa and other business leaders like him realize that in an era of rapid globalization, while there is convergence and alignment on many traditional aspects of business management and leadership, it's the divergence and dissimilarity that make all the difference.

The current pace of globalization, technical innovation, interdependence, and competition is forcing business leaders to work across political and cultural frontiers in new ways. The administrative, legal, and financial environments of different countries and regions of the world—the United States and Japan of Fujisawa's experience—are easy to grasp because they are usually tangible and codified, easily translated and communicated. To be sure, miscommunication can always occur, but the chances of that are relatively low compared to the risk of error and misunderstanding about social systems and cultural environments, since they are quite intangible and very difficult to quantify, grasp, and communicate.[1] In this environment, knowledge of what is beneath the surface—culture—is critical to success.

A recent review of cross-cultural management literature identified five areas of inquiry that are core to this book: (1) Does individual and organizational behavior vary across cultures? (2) How much of the observed difference can be attributed to cultural determinants? (3) Is the variance in organizational behavior worldwide increasing, decreasing, or remaining the same? (4) How can organizations best manage within cultures other than their own? and (5) How can organizations best manage cultural diversity, including using diversity as an organizational resource?[2]

To begin answering those questions, this chapter will address four key areas and serve as grounding for the chapters to come. These core concepts include:

- The evolution of the concept of diversity;
- The impact of globalization on business and on diversity work;
- The fundamental, grounding concept of culture itself; and
- The business case for global diversity.

In addressing the third issue, this chapter will present a basic primer on concepts of culture and begin to address how culture impacts business. Various models of culture, stages of cross-cultural adaptation, and the realities of culture in a global organization will be addressed. By introducing these concepts, we will set the stage for future chapters in the book, which will address these issues in more depth. Each subsequent chapter will address the impact of culture on organizational behavior and processes such as communication, conflict, or organizational systems themselves. For example, in Chapter 3, you'll learn more about the impact of culture on communication; in Chapter 4, cultural difference on teams will be addressed.

To help set the stage for learning, in this chapter you will also find a glossary of terms that will be useful in reading the book and will be explanatory for non-U.S. readers who may need additional background information to understand the U.S. context for diversity work, which is the context from which these co-authors begin.

DIVERSITY: AN EVOLVING CONCEPT

The concept of diversity is not a static one—or a new one. The word was first used in the twelfth century to mean "difference, oddness, wickedness, perversity." That origin may help explain the negative perception of diversity that lingers today. Some organizations now avoid the word altogether, using words like "inclusion" instead. By the late nineteenth century, "diversity" had taken on a meaning more consistent with modern political and corporate initiatives. The *Oxford English Dictionary* defines diversity as "the condition or quality of being diverse, different, or varied; variety, unlikeness." Even today we must continually reiterate that, contrary to our cousins in the twelfth century, "different" does not have a negative connotation.

In the United States, diversity is big business—and a well-established one. Our understanding and approach to diversity has evolved in several ways—moving from a legal and social justice focus on equal opportunity, affirmative action, and assimilation to a more inclusive, market-driven, and business-directed focus. It is now evolving from a purely domestic focus to a more global one, in which culture has become a key consideration.

To more fully understand diversity, it's important to understand the driving forces behind that diversity focus in the first place. According to Lawrence Baytos, author of *Designing and Implementing Successful Diversity Programs,* there have been three key drivers for diversity work in the United States—the Three "Ds"—Demographics, Disappointment, and Demands.[3]

Demographic changes in both the workforce and the marketplace have resulted in shifts in the talent pool and in markets, according to Baytos. Organizations have been *disappointed* in traditional methods of using diversity, such as affirmative action. And the *demands* from employees and for improved performance of the human assets of the organization have all been drivers for the U.S. focus on diversity, he says.

Demographics

The first of these, demographic change, has long been a major business driver for focusing on domestic diversity issues in the United States. Two-thirds of the world's immigrants still go to the United States, and the number of foreign-born U.S. residents is at the highest level in U.S. history, according to the 2000 U.S. census statistics. *Workforce 2000,* a 1987 report by the Hudson Institute, created a stir in the U.S. business community by documenting the demographic shifts in the U.S. workforce. The report noted that nearly all the growth in the workforce through the year 2000 would come from people who were not white and male. Subsequent reports by the Hudson Institute and others continue to document this ongoing, and accelerating, trend.

Demographic change is a business driver outside the United States as well: In the future, most of the growth in the workforce of the world will be in countries with non-Caucasian populations, creating more diverse human resources to choose from and manage in the global arena. In fact, reports Carlos Cortés, *all* of European growth in the past twenty-five years has come from immigration, primarily from Asia and Africa.[4] Around the world, the numbers of women in the workforce will continue to increase, especially in developing countries; the average age of the world's workforce will rise, especially in developed countries; and education levels will increase globally as the developing world produces a rapidly increasing share of the world's skilled human capital.[5]

But worldwide labor mobility is not a new phenomenon. Irish stonemasons helped build U.S. canals; Chinese laborers raced against German workers to build North America's transcontinental railroads; Turks work in large numbers in Berlin; and Algerians assemble cars in France. What is different about current labor mobility also relates to Baytos' theory of the Three Ds: the *demographics* of today's immigrants are vastly different, countries are *disappointed* by past approaches to immigration; and there are different *demands* being made by both the immigrant population and their new homelands than ever before.

While some countries are tightening their borders in response, others, like New Zealand, are opening their doors wider to immigrants they believe can bring innovation, global linkages, and social cohesion to their island nation.

The New Zealand Immigration Experience

The past decade has been marked by increasing diversity in the New Zealand population. The primary reason for this increased diversity is a more open policy that aims to build human capital and economic growth in New Zealand by targeting skilled, qualified immigrants. Four major objectives are associated with these goals:

1. Build New Zealand's human capital by increasing the skill levels in the workforce;
2. Strengthen international linkages at government, corporate, community, and individual levels;
3. Encourage enterprise and innovation by bringing in people with vision and a desire to succeed; and
4. Maintain social cohesion while increasing New Zealand's diversity and vitality.

Non-English language skills and an understanding of other cultures are two unique features that immigrants bring to New Zealand. "These attributes have received increasing attention," report Watts and Trlin, "for their potential to enhance international business opportunities."[6]

The concept that diversity leads to economic growth and adds richness to social life also underpins Australia's immigration policies. "The 'productive diversity strategy' has been adopted to capitalize on the inflow of people from a wide variety of countries."[7]

Through negotiation of differences, an organization's repertoire of skills, knowledge, and understandings is increased, creativity is released, important synergies are created, and a "diversity dividend" is gained.[8]

In the past, the United States used what has been called a "melting pot" model of assimilation in which immigrants who arrived were expected to give up their own cultural identity and become fully American. But because of modern technology, immigrants around the world no longer have to lose their individual and cultural identity in the "melting pot." The new metaphor being used is that of a "salad bowl" or "stir fry," in which the individual "ingredients" retain their particular taste and texture, but which combined create a greater taste than they would have individually. As William McNeill has noted, "In the nineteenth century and before, moving to a foreign country meant cutting close ties with the homeland for years if not forever. Modern conditions make it possible even for very humble immigrants to keep in touch with their place of origin."[9]

In such a way, it is far easier for immigrants to maintain their cultural identity in a strange land, changing the paradigm of immigration in many nations. In the case of New Zealand (above), immigration is welcomed as a source of economic growth. In Canada's case (later in this chapter), the diversity brought by new immigrants is seen as a tool for tapping new ethnocultural markets.

Pluralism is a more modern (and realistic) way of viewing ethnicity, providing an alternative to assimilation. In a society that embraces pluralism, immigrants maintain their unique cultural identity while existing in a second culture simultaneously. This requires much more cultural awareness, knowledge, options, and action than the assimilation model of the past.

Disappointment and New Demands

Equal employment and access to employment opportunity became a legislated national objective in the United States in the early 1970s. Using an affirmative action model, organizations began focusing less on opening doors to "protected classes," such as people of color, females, people with disabilities, those over age 40, and Vietnam era veterans, and began focusing more on the numbers. Those brought into the organization were expected to assimilate or adapt to the existing norms and practices of the organization, says Baytos, rather than the organization adapting to meet the needs of the individuals. In this way, the organizational response mirrored the "melting pot" model of the country itself.

While affirmative action is still being used and hotly debated in the United States, the corporate approach to diversity has evolved to a less quantitative and more qualitative approach, yet many cynics in the United States still believe that "diversity" is just another name for "affirmative action." The Affirmative Action comparison figure on the next page outlines the major differences between affirmative action and diversity management in the United States.

Effecting social change is no longer enough in the U.S. approach to diversity; companies are increasingly tying diversity goals to the bottom line. To underscore the business implications and benefits of diversity, the following initiatives are present in many diversity strategies.[10]

- Support from the CEO;
- Senior management visibility;
- Compensation tie-in;
- Stronger retention initiatives;
- More mentoring;
- Active vendor programs;
- Diversity training at all levels;

Affirmative Action	Valuing Differences	Managing Diversity
Quantitative: Emphasizes achieving equality of opportunity in the work environment through the changing of organizational demographics. Monitored by statistical reports and analysis.	*Qualitative:* Emphasizes the appreciation of differences and creating an environment in which everyone feels valued and accepted. Monitored by organizational surveys focused on attitudes and perceptions.	*Behavioral:* Emphasizes the building of specific skills and creating policies to get the best from every employee. Monitored by progress toward achieving goals and objectives.
Legally driven: Written plans and statistical goals for specific group are utilized. Reports are mandated by EEO laws and consent decrees.	*Ethically driven:* Moral and ethical imperatives drive this culture change.	*Strategically driven:* Behaviors and policies are seen as contributing to organizational goals and objectives such as profit and productivity and are tied to reward and results.
Remedial: Specific target groups benefit as past wrongs are remedied. Previously excluded groups have an advantage.	*Idealistic:* Everyone benefits. Everyone feels valued and accepted in an inclusive environment.	*Pragmatic:* The organization benefits; morale, profit, and productivity increase.
Assimilation model: Assumes that groups brought into system will adapt to existing organizational norms.	*Diversity model:* Assumes that groups will retain their own characteristics and shape the organization as well as be shaped by it, creating a common set of values.	*Synergy model:* Assumes that diverse groups will create new ways of working together effectively in a pluralistic environment.
Opens doors in the organization: Affects hiring and promotion decisions.	*Opens attitudes, minds, and the culture:* Affects attitudes of employees.	*Opens the system:* Affects managerial practices and policies.
Resistance due to perceived limits to autonomy in decision making and perceived fears of reverse discrimination.	*Resistance due to* fear of change, discomfort with differences, and desire for return to "good old days."	*Resistance due to* denial of demographic realities, the need for alternative approaches, and/or benefits associated with change, and the difficulty in learning new skills, altering existing systems, and/or finding time to work toward synergistic solutions.

Affirmative Action, Valuing Differences, and Managing Diversity Compared

Source: Adapted from Lee Gardenswartz and Anita Rowe, *Managing Diversity: A Complete Desk Reference and Planning Guide* © Lee Gardenswartz and Anita Rowe (Burr Ridge, IL: Irwin Professional Publishing, 1993).

- Global initiatives; and

- Education/special initiatives.

In other parts of the world, this evolution has taken a different form. For example, in Europe the commercial bottom line was the starting point for managing differences, not the unused potential of disadvantaged people, according to interculturalist George Simons, author of *EuroDiversity: A Business Guide to Managing Difference.*

In the Netherlands, where diversity management is gaining ground, it is primarily understood to pertain to relations between people from different ethnic and racial backgrounds in work organizations and less to issues of gender and sexual orientation.[11] Because of increasing ethnic populations in the Netherlands, diversity management is being taken seriously, embraced as the "soft" way out of the present debate about the soaring unemployment rate among ethnic minorities.

In Brazil, despite the extremely diversified cultural context in which companies operate in this land of immigrants, the issue of cultural diversity is a new one. Brazilians value their diversified origin and imagine themselves without prejudice. But it is a stratified society, where educational and labor market opportunities are often defined by one's economic and racial origin. In this environment, addressing cultural diversity is more related to the need to create competitive advantage, usually in compliance with policies established by the local subsidiary headquarters, than to the need to follow legal procedures.[12]

Governmental measures to combat employment discrimination are very recent in Brazil and often clash with the Brazilian national ideology to conceive of itself as a heterogeneous country without prejudice. The greatest majority of companies in Brazil that are addressing diversity issues are, in fact, subsidiaries of U.S. companies, and most often the concept of cultural diversity being adopted is quite restricted, dealing with gender and race only.

Understanding the genesis of the focus on diversity—and its context—is important to the success of any global diversity effort. "North American diversity started with social and government initiatives that extended into the private sector; in Europe, economic cooperation among diverse peoples was the starting point," writes Simons.[13]

These differences have a profound impact on how diversity is viewed, managed, and leveraged around the world. Before "exporting" diversity management from the United States to other locations around the globe, it is important to understand that the starting point and area of focus might be quite different, depending on the social, political, cultural, and economic context of the country in which you are doing business. Not understanding this has caused many U.S.-originated diversity efforts to fail overseas because they are perceived as an attempt to make the world over in our own image, rather than truly listen to the prevailing conditions and cultural norms in the countries in which we are doing business.

U.S. Americans have engaged in decades of national conversation about diversity. Yet the word "diversity" has rarely been mentioned in Europe until recently, according to Simons. Equivalent terms such as *kulturelle Vielfalt* (cultural diversity) and *gerer diversite* (managing diversity) have been used in Germany and France, he notes, "but almost always to discuss North American diversity."

Why has diversity not been the "hot topic" in Europe that it has been in North America? "The issues have been very important ones, but they have been conceived of and dealt with in a different form of discourse," explains Simons. For example, he notes, the North American approach to highlight and celebrate differences is fraught with danger in Europe, where accentuating differences within and between European nations has created pogroms, mass dislocations of peoples, and the Holocaust. Other differences include the phenomenon of political correctness in the United States, in which we have thwarted our ability to have open and honest conversation about difference for fear of offending others. For example, banning Christmas parties, which has been widely done in U.S. businesses, is seen as culturally destructive by Europeans who "often think that Americans fail to realize that deliberately taking offense is as destructive as deliberately giving offense."[14]

Canada's Business Case for Diversity: The Changing Mosaic

The population of Toronto's Chinese community is estimated to be more than 350,000. Over 30 percent of Chinese Canadians now live in Vancouver. By 2006, when Canada is expected to have a total population of 30.6 million, the total population of visible minorities will be 5.6 million.

Until recently, increasing ethnocultural diversity in Canada has largely been viewed by mainstream Canadian organizations from the perspective of its impact on workforce demographics and its implications for HR management. It has not been seen as a tool for tapping new markets or improving the effectiveness of international business. That is changing.

Two key drivers now underpin the business case for diversity in Canadian organizations—the globalization of world trade and the increasing ethnocultural diversity of Canadian markets.[15]

Many firms, particularly those based in the United States, begin at a point of relative employee homogeneity and try to promote greater diversity in racial and gender representation, while multinational firms begin from a point of relative heterogeneity. A key challenge for multinationals, then, is to find ways to benefit from diversity while also forging consistency, says Philip M. Rosenzweig, professor of organization and strategy at IMD.[16]

Lacking cultural knowledge and experience abroad, and armed with a healthy sense of cultural self-esteem about our leadership role in the world, U.S. diversity professionals often err on the side of arrogance and with an export mentality. We tend to forget that 95 percent of the world's population lives outside the United States. "The first challenge," says Ron Martin, "is to define what cultural diversity means in global terms, not just in Western terms."[17]

Martin, director of global employee relations at New York-based Colgate-Palmolive Company, knows first-hand the complexity of dealing with diversity issues across borders. A two-day program at Colgate helps underscore the commitment of the company to diversity, with one day focused on the themes and values of Colgate and the second day focusing on issues within a particular country, such as race, gender, age, sexual harassment in the United States, or gender bias and class discrimination in the United Kingdom. In such a way, companies are beginning to expand their domestic diversity work to include the new global realities they are facing. Use the "What Do You Need to Know?" sheet to help you look at your own diversity initiative.

Suggestions for Using "What Do You Need to Know?"

Objectives

- To understand the kinds of information necessary before undertaking global diversity initiatives
- To assess personal knowledge of the conditions for global diversity
- To prioritize information-gathering needs of the organization
- To identify internal resources for global diversity information

Intended Audience

- Managers responsible for diversity initiatives
- HR professionals with global responsibility
- Diversity council or task-force members
- Managers of international or multicultural teams

Time

- 45 to 60 minutes

Materials

- Copies of "What Do You Need to Know?"

Directions

- Discuss and define the types of information needed (Column 1).
- Ask participants to fill in their answers on the worksheet.
- Have participants share their responses in small groups of three to five people, comparing their prioritization and self-assessment or needs.
- Ask small groups to discuss the implications for the organization of their findings.

What Do You Need to Know?

Directions: When expanding your diversity initiative outside your home country, there is information you must have or acquire in order to make informed decisions about appropriate strategies. Use this worksheet to outline information you will need, the priority of importance of each, your current level of expertise, and those individuals in the company who can best serve as cultural informants for you.

Information Needed	Priority of Importance	Level of Current Knowledge (1 being lowest, 5 being highest)	From Whom in the Company Can I Obtain That Information?
National history and experience regarding equal opportunity and diversity			
Definitions of diversity used in the country, including metaphors used to talk about diversity			
Past company experience (positive and negative) with diversity			
Demographic changes, current and projected			
Legal requirements or issues surrounding employment discrimination and diversity			
Key issues of the business in that country			
Other:			

Questions for Discussion/Consideration

- How did the priorities of your group differ?
- Were there other types of information that you felt you might need in order to assess your readiness to undertake a global diversity initiative?
- How can you use this sheet as a planning tool for the organization's global diversity initiatives?
- Are the internal resources you identified currently involved in diversity initiatives? If not, how can you best involve them and tap their expertise?
- What resources will you need to gain the necessary information and expertise you need?
- Brainstorm additional internal resources that are not currently being used (such as the legal department or expatriate staff) and that could be helpful in this effort.

Cultural Considerations

- Talking about the self-assessment of knowledge openly may be uncomfortable for some team members. In such cases, have small groups create a composite of knowledge needs that can be shared with the larger group.

Caveats, Considerations, and Variations

- This sheet can be used as a planning tool for a diversity council or team charged with rolling out the diversity initiative overseas.
- Once self-knowledge needs have been identified by individuals, engage the group in a "skill exchange" where those who have knowledge in a particular area are paired with those who need to gain that knowledge.

WHAT IS DIVERSITY?

Each organization focused on diversity issues creates its own definition of what diversity means in its particular context. The American Society for Training and Development (ASTD) has defined diversity as "the mosaic of people who bring a variety of backgrounds, styles, perspectives, values, and beliefs as assets to the groups and organizations with which they interact." For the Pillsbury Company, diversity is defined simply as "all the ways in which we differ." Kraft Foods Inc. spells out its commitment to diversity in metaphors with which people can identify: "A stellar meal requires contrasting and complementing textures and tastes. A winning sports team depends of the different talents of its members. A first-class orchestra needs many varied instruments. And a successful business team requires a variety of thought, energy, and insight to attain and maintain a competitive edge."[18]

The Four Layers of Diversity, created by co-authors Lee Gardenswartz and Anita Rowe, is a widely used model of dealing with domestic diversity and broadens our perception of what diversity means beyond traditional issues of race and gender. At its center is *personality*—the innately unique aspect that gives each of us our own particular style. The next layer includes *internal dimensions* of diversity over which we have little or no control, such as gender, age, and race. The next layer, *external dimensions,* includes outside influences such as where you grew up or live now, whether you have children, and your

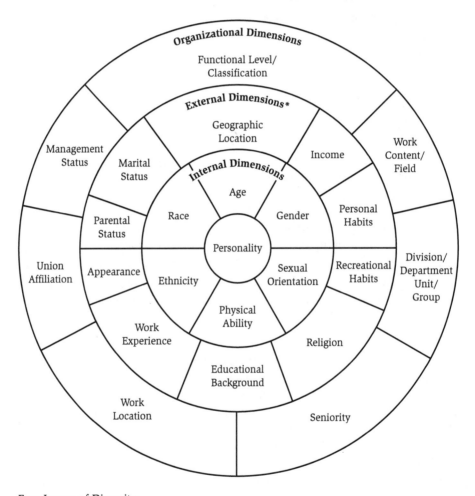

Four Layers of Diversity

*Internal and External Dimensions are adapted from Marilyn Loden and Judy Rosener, *Workforce America!* (Business One Irwin, 1991).

Source: Adapted from Lee Gardenswartz and Anita Rowe, *Diverse Teams at Work* (Burr Ridge, IL: Irwin Professional Publishing, 1994).

personal habits. The final layer, *organizational dimensions,* includes your level, department, seniority, and worksite in the organization. Using this model has helped corporations identify and understand the filters through which we all see the world and which could create barriers to accepting others. Yet, as you'll see in Chapter 2, tackling issues of global diversity requires an even newer and broader model of diversity and definitions that includes national and civilizational cultures.

Values Underpinning Diversity

According to diversity consultant Neal Grove, there are strong American values behind our nation's diversity agenda. As Grove indicates, they include our values on:

- *Egalitarianism*—our belief that people should compete on a "level playing field" to get ahead and that equal opportunity and fairness should prevail in the workplace as in all other places;
- *Achievement*—our belief that people should get ahead in life on the basis of their own accomplishments, not on the basis of their ascribed traits (such as being a native-born white male); and
- *Individualism*—our belief that people should be self-sufficient and self-expressive; businesses should give each employee an opportunity to productively use his or her best individual talents.

Other basic beliefs and assumptions underlying diversity initiatives in the United States include, but are not limited to, the following:

- Human rights should be universal;
- U.S. approaches to civil and human rights are more advanced;
- Diversity and the ability to harness different talents and strengths adds value;
- Paying attention to and allocating resources for diversity affects the bottom line;
- All people should be treated with equal dignity and respect;
- Business has the resources and responsibility to increase justice and equality and strengthen the social fabric;
- An inclusive climate/environment increases productivity and profits;
- Legal compliance is mandatory and, therefore, helps to create a compelling case; and
- Individual needs, preferences, and perspectives are of primary consideration.

While these values are core to our U.S. American approaches to diversity, they may not "translate" across cultures. For example, there are many nations in the world whose peoples believe much more deeply in the ascription model of advancement (who you are) rather than our strong focus on individual achievement (what you've done). In some cultures, concepts of "fairness" and a "level playing field" are counter to their strong systems of hierarchy. Where those kinds of differences appear around the world, exporting U.S. approaches to diversity—with their inherent, if often unspoken and sometimes unconscious value sets—will not work effectively and may cause more harm than good. Understanding those cultural differences is key to the success of our diversity efforts abroad.

There may be other philosophical underpinnings unique to your organization's culture and diversity focus—and the assumptions underlying diversity work in other nations may well be different. For each assumption you articulate, several questions must be asked:

- How might a different national culture respond to each statement?
- In what way, if any, would the religious, cultural, and social norms of another culture come into conflict with this approach?
- How might we imaginatively mediate between local cultural norms and our corporate expectations, values, and norms?
- On which assumptions is there no room for flexibility or variation?

At the core of each of these questions is a more fundamental one: What must I know about culture itself in order to answer these questions? We'll begin answering that question later in this chapter and throughout the rest of this book. You may wish to use "Diversity Values: How Well Do They Translate?" to begin answering the questions for yourself.

Suggestions for Using
"Diversity Values: How Well Do They Translate?"

Objectives

- To clarify and articulate one's own cultural values around diversity issues
- To understand differences in diversity values among workgroups and between cultures and nationalities
- To stimulate discussion of value differences and their impact on their workplace
- To learn to negotiate the differences between value sets

Intended Audience

- Members of a global multinational work team, task force, or department
- Managers of international or multicultural teams

- HR professionals responsible for global diversity initiatives
- Diversity councils or task forces

Time

- 45 to 60 minutes

Materials

- Copies of "Diversity Values: How Well Do They Translate?"

Directions

- Discuss and define the U.S. cultural values around diversity.
- Ask participants to respond to the questionnaire, following directions.
- Have small groups of participants share their work and prepare to report to the larger group their findings about values differences and potential clashes.

Questions for Discussion/Consideration

- What similarities and differences do you see among group members?
- Were there any surprises for you?
- How did you react to the list of U.S. cultural values around diversity?
- Was it easy or difficult to provide possible alternative viewpoints? Why?
- How flexible are you in adapting to others who have different views on these issues?
- How do the differences play out in work behaviors and team interactions?
- Where are there potential "hot spots" that may lead to misunderstanding or conflict?
- What are the challenges to the organization? To you?
- If you are not from the United States, what reactions do you have to the list of U.S. values around diversity?
- What implications does this have for the global diversity initiative?

Cultural Considerations

- Talking about differences openly may be uncomfortable for some team members. It may be necessary to gather worksheets anonymously and report back to the group a composite version of the answers.

Caveats, Considerations, and Variations

- To challenge the group, particularly if it is a diversity council or HR team that has been working on domestic diversity issues for a while, delete the U.S. values column and ask the group if, working together, they can create a list of values or assumptions underlying their diversity work.

Diversity Values: How Well Do They Translate?

Directions: Look at the ten values that are among those that underpin diversity work in the United States. If you are not from the United States, use the second column to indicate the values that underpin diversity work in your country. Use column three to make notes about alternative viewpoints that might exist in a country other than your own, preferably a country in which your organization already does business. In the last column, brainstorm possible clashes that might occur in the workplace if your diversity value is exported "as is" without cultural adaptation. An example is given.

U.S. cultural value around diversity	If you're not from the United States, your nation's cultural value around diversity	Possible alternative viewpoint	Possible culture clash if value is exported
Human rights should be universal		*Example:* Human rights don't extend to certain classes or groups, such as women.	*Example:* Legal boundaries might be overstepped unknowingly.
Equal opportunity and fairness should prevail in workplace			
People should get ahead based on what they've achieved, not who they are			
Belief in the "level playing field"			
Diversity adds value to the corporation and nation			

Diversity Values: How Well Do They Translate? (continued)

U.S. cultural value around diversity	If you're not from the United States, your nation's cultural value around diversity	Possible alternative viewpoint	Possible culture clash if value is exported
All people should be treated with equal dignity and respect			
One role of business is to increase justice and equality			
The needs of individuals, their preferences, and their perspectives are of primary importance			
An inclusive environment increases productivity and profits			
U.S. approaches to civil and human rights are more advanced			

GLOBAL DIVERSITY AS THE NEXT STEP

Although more than 75 percent of major American companies now focus on diversity as a strategic advantage and business leverage in the United States, there is minimal carryover internationally, even while business becomes more global in scope. These companies find themselves in the perplexing position of attempting to "roll out" overseas those diversity initiatives that were designed for a domestic workforce—in many cases without knowing why or, more importantly, how. What are the issues and questions that emerge when organizational and national cultures come into contact and when the need to capitalize on global diversity poses significant dilemmas? Four key issues arise:

1. What is the business case for global diversity and how is it different from the domestic business case for diversity?

2. How do value statements underlying domestic diversity efforts need to be altered to have meaning and relevance outside our home country?

3. How well are we applying our learning in the domestic diversity arena to our efforts globally—or are we reinventing the wheel?

4. Are we actively learning from other cultures or are we simply attempting to make them "more like us"?

Companies do not need to do business outside their home country to face global diversity issues. In the United States, for example, immigration is at its highest point in fifty years—and the face of that immigration has changed dramatically—bringing global diversity to our own backyards and providing significant challenges and opportunities to U.S.-based businesses as well.

There are two big shifts away from the past. Previously only a very small portion of people in the enterprise needed international expertise. Now, according to Nancy Adler, "Almost every manager needs at least some veneer of international, cross-cultural competencies because they're dealing with suppliers, clients, and colleagues from various countries and cultures around the world." Second, organizations used to focus on getting a small cadre of people to learn a lot about a particular place. Now, "You're on multinational task teams, on multinational projects . . . companies need global representation, people from multiple cultures who can work in multicultural teams talking about strategy, and that strategy has to be global in content."[19]

What, then, are the major issues surrounding globalization and what impact do they have on our ability to manage diversity—across borders?

GLOBALIZATION AND DIVERSITY

While domestic concepts of diversity were vital tools for economic and social change in the United States, they fall short in a new, global environment. As we've seen, the values underlying U.S. domestic diversity initiatives do not translate wholesale to other cultures, nor do they adequately reflect the importance of culture itself. Yet, as Ellis Cose, author of *The Rage of a Privileged Class*, says, "It is going to be awfully hard to forge a globally competitive workforce if the races can't learn to work together." As Cose notes, managing diversity domestically is a prerequisite for succeeding globally. Conversely, because of the increasing internationalization in home markets, addressing global diversity issues is increasingly a prerequisite for succeeding domestically.

To understand the complexities of managing diversity in a global environment, we must first understand the phenomenon of globalization itself. To do that, we'll investigate the causes and forms of globalization, discuss the threat of cultural convergence and cultural imperialism that often accompany discussions of globalization, give sample corporate responses to globalization, and provide a Three Cultures Model that helps articulate the three key cultures whose interaction must be mediated in global corporations.

Hallmarks of Globablization

The cover of a recent *Economist* magazine is simple and clear: A picture of a hurricane from space is shown with three words in large print—"Storm over Globalization."

Referencing the recent flurry of activities over World Trade Organization (WTO) and International Monetary Fund (IMF) meetings around the globe, the *Economist* article was as much about fear of loss and the erection of cultural barriers as it was about globalization and economic policies. Yet the structural approaches to globalization taken by many corporations tend to neglect culture as a key variable or treat it superficially. International HR practitioners typically address global compensation, sourcing, relocation issues, and even cultural adaptation at its simplest—but often there is a gap between domestic diversity practitioners and those dealing with the complexities of the global business. In many organizations, global diversity and cultural differences are still seen as obstacles to be overcome rather than as tools to be leveraged for business success. In fact, domestic and global diversity is often still seen as an end in itself, rather than as a means to some other business end.

It is this attention to global competitiveness that marks the next phase of the evolution of the concept of diversity. Globalization has brought with it intense international competition, not just among the major corporations of the world, but in small businesses as well. A global war for talent, domestic and cross-border mergers and acquisitions, joint ventures and alliances, changing employee expectations and demands, and pressures for greater productivity are just some of the business drivers facing executives and business leaders worldwide. Michael Marquardt has said that four "Ts"—technology, travel, trade, and television—have brought us quickly to the global age.

Fortune 100 companies aren't the only ones going global. Even small and traditionally domestic businesses are crossing new borders in response to dramatic global shifts in demographics, markets, and products. In fact, one of the five major business reasons for focusing on diversity in the United States is globalism, as reported by the New York-based Conference Board, an organization focused on research about corporate issues. Individuals in nations around the world are recognizing—and capitalizing on—the power of globalization. For example, why else would Iranian and Chinese demonstrators carry their signs in English if not expressly for American TV audiences?

"Globalization," says *New York Times* reporter Thomas Friedman, "is the next great foreign policy debate." Friedman is the author of *The Lexus and the Olive Tree*, a 1999 bestseller that helped readers understand the implications of globalization by focusing attention on the delicate balance and tension between our simultaneous dedication to modernizing, streamlining, and yearning for advancement (symbolized by the Lexus) and our ongoing yearning for our cultural heritage and identity as we fight over who owns which olive tree.

The globalization "system," as Friedman calls it, "is not static, but a dynamic ongoing process: globalization involves the inexorable integration of markets, nation-states, and technologies to a degree never witnessed before—in a way that is enabling individuals, corporations, and nation-states to reach around the world farther, faster, deeper, and cheaper than ever before, and in a way that is also producing a powerful backlash from those brutalized or left behind by this new system."[20]

Cross-border mergers such as those between Citigroup (United States) and Nikko (Japan), BP (Britain) and Amoco (United States), and Daimler (Germany) and Chrysler (United States) have become more common and also drive the need for managers to confront diversity head-on and to develop a global mindset. Cultural clashes are typically the most difficult aspect of these partnerships. Also, billed as "mergers of equals," they often are not. "How do you pronounce the company's name?" goes one joke heard often after the BP/Amoco merger. The answer? "BP: the 'Amoco' is silent."

Globalization's Impact

While many view globalization as either good or bad, Friedman understands more clearly that the tension in globalization is holding "both-and" in our minds at the same time. Globalization is neither inherently good nor evil, but, like the demographic changes that have driven U.S. diversity work, simply a current and future reality. The sooner we stop debating its merits and focus on understanding its implications and the ways in which we can benefit from it without losing our own unique identities, the better. To take it a step further, one goal of global diversity work—and by extension, this book—is to help us not only understand global diversity and its impact on business, but to help us understand how to leverage those differences for human, business, and societal gain.

Let's look at the globalization process as it relates to diversity. Facilitated by the rapid development of new information and communication technologies and resulting in greater transparency and accountability, globalization represents a challenge for maintaining cultural diversity and also creates the conditions for renewed dialogue and learning among cultures and civilizations. It also creates the conditions for renewed hostilities and fear that with globalization comes a loss of cultural identity.

Companies are increasingly going global for several reasons—to serve new markets, to gain access to lower cost or higher quality, to build economies of scale, to diversify because of lagging domestic market share, or to preempt competitors. McDonald's, for example, faces a maturing fast-food market in the United States, but the portion of operating income from abroad is expected to grow 20 percent annually.[21] McDonald's executives prefer to call their company "multilocal," rather than multinational or transnational, building local supplier chains, using local talent, and exerting little management control from their Illinois headquarters.

The term "global corporations," says professor Ronald Bosrock, "generally describes *where* the company does business, but not *how* the company does business."[22] Bosrock offers the following shorthand for understanding the different stages of global perspective:

- *Ethnocentric:* Tending to regard one's own culture as superior; tending to be home-market oriented. All controls located at home office.
- *Polycentric:* Tending to regard each culture as a separate entity; tending to be oriented toward individual foreign markets. Allowing foreign entity control for one market.
- *Regiocentric:* Tending to be oriented toward large regional markets, with regional headquarters that have separate strategic plans and separate support staff.
- *Geocentric:* Tending to view the world as one market; tending to set worldwide strategy. Interdependent markets with no regional headquarters and no regional supporting staff. Management coming from whatever country produces the best talent. Ideas accepted from whatever location produces the best results.

In Chapter 2, you will find more detailed information on corporate stages of globalization as well as the ways in which the stage of globalization of an organization can influence global diversity needs and strategy.

Regional responses to globalization often reflect the skill of various countries to manage international and global diversity. European companies have a tendency to put nationals at the head of foreign subsidiaries and a small number of nonlocals, while the Japanese like to reproduce Japanese management and their corporate culture. In general, U.S. companies have historically tried to reproduce their corporate culture by authority of the top management and through the imposition of headquarters' procedures.[23]

"Building a value system that emphasizes seeing and thinking globally is the bottom-line price of admission to today's borderless economy," writes Kenichi Ohmae in *The Borderless World.* But the world isn't borderless, as his book title suggests—instead, it is only money that transcends borders. The world remains full of borders—racial, national, linguistic, economic, organizational, functional, market, and many others. Human resources and diversity professionals must be realistic and respectful about these borders and cultures and must learn to effectively mediate among competing interests, demands, and cultures both within—and without—their organizations. Above all, we must sublimate the American urge to eliminate or blur rather than learn from those borders and cultures. "Globalism," says diversity consultant R. Roosevelt Thomas, Jr., "is unadulterated complexity." In answer to that complexity, Adler warns in *International Dimensions of Organizational Behavior,* "Today we no longer have the luxury of reducing international complexity to the simplicity of assumed universality."

Krispy Kreme, a North Carolina-based company, has only scratched the surface of the U.S. market, with a mere 226 stores nationwide, compared to competitor Dunkin' Donuts' 3,500. But that's not stopping them from going global to capture a greater market share: The first European Krispy Kremes should open in Britain and Spain in early 2003. As reported in *Time* magazine (August 12, 2002), Krispy Kreme first opened a store in Toronto, followed by the announcements of franchise agreements for thirty stores in Australia and New Zealand. They are expanding internationally because they believe there is a market for their very American deep-fried, sugary products. It is a strategy that has worked for other food and beverage product companies such as McDonald's, PepsiCo, and Starbucks. Still, Krispy Kreme must avoid the mentality of "We like it in America, so you ought to like it too," warned John Stanton, a food-industry expert at St. Joseph's University in Philadelphia.

Cultural Bereavement

Understanding this delicate balance between exporting Americana and being respectful to the local culture is a key challenge facing those U.S. companies going global. Because of the immense size of the internal market of the United

States, it is not a lesson that many American businesses have taken to heart until very recently.

When Pizza Hut entered Yemen, it created integrated dining rooms in a traditional Moslem society where meals rarely take place outside the home and, when they do, separate rooms or curtained-off areas are provided for men and women. "The forces of internationalization and traditional culture clashed: Women could no longer be separated from men unrelated to them while they ate, or eat in public without removing their veils."[24] Of concern in this and other similar examples is globalization's tendency to demolish local norms that traditional societies use to provide a common identity and purpose to individuals.

In some cases, the subjugation of local culture is not the intent. For example, for some people Microsoft's dominance in operating systems for computers is an indication that they are pursuing cultural dominance as well. When Microsoft recently decided not to support the Icelandic language in its Windows 98 product, it created an uproar in Iceland. The Icelandic Language Institute saw Microsoft's intent as destroying their cultural heritage; however, Microsoft's motive wasn't cultural, but commercial. The market for an Icelandic Windows 98 just wasn't big enough. But as Claude Smadja, managing director of the World Economic Forum, has said, "Corporations will have to find ways to reconcile their search for maximum return to shareholders with their inescapable social responsibility to the people and environments in which they operate."[25]

Corporations will increasingly be faced with a demand for their products and a concomitant cultural bereavement as consumers fight to maintain their own sense of identity. While economist Robert Reich wrote in his 1991 book, *The Work of Nations,* that "There will be no national products or technologies, no national corporations, no national industries," others believe that view is far too simplistic.

Francis Fukuyama believes that homogenization and an affirmation of distinctive cultural identities will occur simultaneously. On a macro level of large economic institutions and political institutions, Fukuyama believes, there is a greater homogenization of institutions and ideologies. On a cultural level, though, he believes it is not clear that homogenization is proceeding nearly as rapidly. Fukuyama believes that our attention to global consumer culture is superficial. "A culture," he says, "really consists of deeper moral norms that affect how people link together."[26]

Benjamin Barber's influential book, *Jihad vs. McWorld,* reminded us that, if we looked only at the business section of the newspaper, we would be convinced that the world was increasingly united, that borders were increasingly porous, and that mergers were creating a single, global market. But if we looked only at the front page of the paper, we would be convinced of just the opposite—that the world was increasingly involved in civil war and the breakup of nations. Jihad, Barber says, pursues a bloody politics of identity, while McWorld seeks a bloodless economics of profit. The tension between these two world views is a hallmark of globalization.

It's a confusing debate for many: Is globalization the source of economic growth and prosperity or is it a threat to social stability? By many measures, the world economy was more integrated at the height of the gold standard in the late nineteenth century than it is now.[27] The pros and cons of globalization have centered around issues such as competition for markets, workers' rights, loss of workers' jobs, human migration, environmental concerns, and the growing sense that the process has not yet delivered on the promise of improving the lot of a very large part of the world.[28] Some believe that the rapid pace of globalization has outstripped the ability of the corporation to evolve and adapt.

According to the *World Dictionary of Multinational Enterprises,* the economic power commanded by the world's five hundred largest corporations accounts for 80 percent of the world's direct investment and ownership. The top twenty-five global employers have a combined payroll exceeding ten million workers. Corporate headquarters for the five hundred largest industrial firms are located in thirty-two different nations.[29] With that power comes great responsibility.

One of the most controversial aspects of globalization is the worldwide spread and dominance of American culture through the dramatic growth of mass communications such as music, television, films, and the Internet, as well as through the penetration of American corporations overseas. When EuroDisney opened in 1992, Michael Eisner, CEO of the Walt Disney Company, declared it "the most wonderful project we have ever done." Jean Cau, a French critic, had another viewpoint: "A horror made of cardboard, plastic, and appalling colors; a construction of hardened chewing gum and idiotic folklore taken straight out of comic books written for obese Americans."

The biggest tourist attraction in Romania today is not one of its own national treasures. Instead, it is Southfork Ranch, a million-dollar replica of the home made famous by TV's nighttime drama, "Dallas," in the 1970s. In 2000, Jose Bove was led away in handcuffs after the French farmer was sentenced to three months in jail for assault on a McDonald's being built in his hometown in the middle of France. Bove was a national hero.

Yet this pervasive and negative image of Americans on a mission to spread their culture through globalization is not borne out in a recent survey of Europeans. In a November 2000 United States Information Agency (USIA) poll, only minorities in Italy (19 percent), Great Britain (23 percent), and Germany (31 percent) perceived U.S. popular culture as a serious or very serious threat. The French were more critical, with 38 percent agreeing that American culture poses a serious or very serious threat.[30]

When Americans themselves were asked how they felt about McDonald's opening up in cities around the world or the popularity of U.S. TV shows in other countries, only 43 percent said they had positive feelings. It appears that Americans are cognizant of the dangers of wholesale "export" of American culture abroad. And there is also awareness of the need for us to become more culturally competent as a nation. In a recent poll, a near-unanimous majority (91 percent) of U.S. citizens agreed, "The global economy makes it more important than ever for all of us to understand people who are different than ourselves."[31]

Companies are beginning to realize the truth in that statement. When Swedish furniture retailer Ikea entered the U.S. market, it replicated its Swedish concepts, such as no home delivery and beds that required sheets conforming to the Swedish rather than U.S. standard. Swedish nationals constituted virtually the entire management team of the company and fluency in Swedish was considered essential at the senior levels.[32] The company learned from its mistakes. While its model was to build a huge building with a thousand parking spaces around it, when they entered Hong Kong, they put a small IKEA in the middle of Causeway Bay with no parking spaces. That store is now second in the world for sales per square foot.

McDonald's "multilocal" approach realizes that some elements—such as lining up and self-seating—have been readily accepted by consumers for whom those practices are out of the cultural norm. But other aspects of their U.S. model have been rejected, especially those relating to time and space. In Hong Kong, Taipei, and Beijing, for example, consumers have turned their neighborhood restaurants into leisure centers and after-school clubs for students. "Fast" in that case refers to the delivery of food, not its consumption.[33] The Pillsbury Company realized, after airing its "Doughboy" ads in the U.K., that British women did not like the idea of taking cooking advice from a young boy, so their ads were changed to use a man's voice with a British accent. The reasons for all these adaptations? Cultural difference—those "all-important respects" that Takeo Fujisawa referenced in his discussion of Japanese and American management.

Kenichi Ohmae, in *The End of the Nation State* (1995), denounces the view that globalization will result in the deculturation of the world. Instead, he says, there will be partial convergence of tastes and preferences. Global brands, writes Ohmae, "overlay new tastes on an established, but largely unaffected, base of social norms and values." Where some warn of the creation of a "McWorld," Ohmae envisions strong cultural identities that enjoy what the world marketplace has to offer—on their own terms. "The contents of kitchens and closets may change," he writes, "but the core mechanisms by which cultures maintain their identity and socialize their young remain untouched." Indeed, there is convergence in economic systems around the world, not in value systems.

Strong national, regional, and civilizational cultures continue to challenge us in doing business globally. But to fully understand and address those challenges, we must first understand the issues of culture and cultural identity themselves.

What is culture? What is its impact on business practice? How can we begin to see culture less as an obstacle to be overcome and more as a business advantage to be leveraged?

Globalization Hits the Executive Suite

Jacques Nasser, born in Lebanon and raised in Australia, ran Ford in the United States. Danny Rosenkrantz, born in Kenya of Polish parents, heads Britain's BOC Group. Fernandez Pujals, born in Cuba and a U.S. citizen, leads Telepizza in Spain. Deutsche Telekom's CEO is from Israel. Andy Grove, a Hungarian immigrant, chairs the board of Intel. Charles Wang, of Taiwan, runs Computer Associates. Philip Morris has an Australian CEO. A native of Morocco, who holds a Brazilian passport, runs Alcoa. Becton Dickinson's CEO, Clateo Castellini, was born in Italy, speaks English, Italian, French, Spanish, and Portuguese, and has worked in Italy, Brazil, and the United States. A Frenchman runs Britain's Body Shop. An American is CEO of Britain's Pearson publishing empire, The Anglo-Dutch consumer giant Unilever is chaired by Niall Fitzgerald, an Irish native. A Dane runs the Anglo-American drug maker SmithKline Beecham. An Australian is the chief of Coca-Cola.

Source: From *The Global Me*, by Gregg Pascal Zachary. Copyright © G. Pascal Zachary. Reprinted by permission of PublicAffairs, a member of Perseus Books, L.L.C.

Global Diversity Strategies

In addressing the needs of globalization and in building global corporate diversity strategies, research by The Conference Board has shown that the following practices are necessary to achieve success:[34]

- Establish common values and purpose across cultures;
- Provide support and resources at international sites;
- Share best practices;
- Establish a multicultural, multinational team to develop and oversee initiatives;
- Create both centralized and decentralized structures;
- Develop global diversity councils;
- Initiate worldwide diversity conferences;
- Organize region- or country-specific task forces; and
- Design and implement global diversity education and training.

In addition, we would add the following:

- Learn *from* other cultures, not just *about* them. You can use the "Global Diversity Strategy Audit" for your company.

Global Diversity Strategy Audit

Directions: In the nine areas listed below, indicate which diversity strategy steps are being done or have been done (with specific examples from your company), what else needs to be done, and who needs to be involved from different locations in the company.

Steps	What Is Being Done	What Needs to Be Done	Who Needs to Be Involved
Management commitment			
Assessment and diagnosis			
Establish common values across cultures			
Multicultural, multi-national diversity team to oversee initiatives			
Global diversity councils and region-specific or country-specific task forces			
Global diversity education and training			
Policies and procedures review to ensure alignment with global diversity strategy			
Share best practices across cultures			
Measurement and evaluation			

Suggestions for Using the "Global Diversity Strategy Audit"

Objectives

- Assess level of an organization's stage of development in dealing with global diversity
- Increase awareness and knowledge about aspects of a global diversity strategy
- Target areas of needed development
- Provide data for strategizing regarding organization development
- Identify individuals who need to be involved in the global diversity strategy of the organization

Intended Audience

- Members or managers of diversity task forces or planning teams
- Executive staff involved in strategic planning or diversity development strategies
- Executive staff charged with organizational strategy regarding diversity

Time

- 45 to 60 minutes

Materials

- Copies of the "Global Diversity Strategy Audit"

Directions

- Discuss and define the steps of global diversity strategy outlined on the audit.
- Ask team members to individually respond to the questionnaire, following directions.
- Ask small groups of three to five to discuss their responses and be prepared to report back to the large group their suggestions for what needs to be done, based on their assessment of where the organization is on each strategic element.

Questions for Discussion/Consideration

- What are our organization's strengths and weaknesses?
- How similar or disparate are perceptions of different individuals in your group? What does this say about the communication of global diversity strategies in the organization?
- Who needs to be involved in dealing with the issues surfaced?

- What does this tell us about our organization?
- What do we need to do to improve our effectiveness?

Cultural Considerations

- Talking about organizational performance may be uncomfortable for some team members. In such cases, have participants focus on Column 2 (What Is Being Done) in order to first allow for celebration of those global diversity strategies before focusing on any problem areas.

Caveats, Considerations, and Variations

- Participants may not have enough information to answer each item. If not, ask them to focus their attention on those areas in which they do have experience.
- This can be used as a planning tool for diversity councils or teams responsible for global diversity in the organization.
- It can be reassessed quarterly to track progress.

Underlying these strategies are the need for cultural competence, the ability to understand cultural difference, and the ability to leverage it for business gain—and at a deeper level than simply global branding and global consumer preference. Globalization has forced corporations to move from their focus on domestic diversity to a broader focus in which understanding the impact of national and civilizational culture is a core competency. To fully understand the impact of this and learn to manage it, we must first understand more clearly what is meant by culture itself.

In his 1999 book, *Globalization and Culture,* John Tomlinson suggests that globalization cannot be understood simply in terms of increased mobility around the world or through the development of electronic networks, but must be set in relation to a host of cultural practices that are embedded within the "mundane" experience of everyday life. At the center of his thesis is how "the impact of globalization is felt not in travel but in staying at home."

Success in the next twenty years, for many companies, will stem from successful—and innovative—joint ventures and alliances, many of them across cultures as well as across product and service lines. But the conditions for success of such global collaborative ventures has changed. No longer simply product-driven, the survival of new global enterprises will depend as much on flexibility in managing cultural diversity as on sophistication in marketing techniques. This entails not only the successful management of a multicultural workforce in a global context, but also the ability to vary services across cultures—not simply by using marketing ploys imposed from the outside, but by an understanding of how culture drives differences from within. It's essential to grasp the deep structures—religious, social, ethnic, and ethical—which influence the way the others reason, what they expect, and *how* they listen. This requires a level of genuine understanding that goes beyond rapidly acquired skills or cultural "dos and taboos."

For while business is global, management remains culture-bound. Being culturally competent, notes Henry Lane in *International Management Behavior*, entails "a willingness to acknowledge cultural differences and to take steps to make them discussible and, thus, usable." Increasingly, the question we must ask ourselves when working across cultures—whether in our own country or across borders—is "Do we understand how they are thinking about the world?"[35] To do that, we must understand both our own culture and that of others.

DEFINITIONS OF CULTURE

In one of the first modern definitions of culture, E.B. Tylor (1877) defined it as "that complex whole which includes knowledge, belief, art, law, morals, customs, and any capabilities and habits acquired by man as a member of society."[36] A century later, anthropologist Victor Barnouw wrote in *Culture and Personality* that "A culture is a way of life of a group of people, the configuration of all of the more or less stereotyped patterns of learned behavior, which are handed down from one generation to the next through the means of language and imitation."

In cataloging more than 150 definitions of culture, A.L. Kroeber and Clyde Kluckhohn provided this comprehensive definition: "Culture consists of patterns, explicit and implicit of and for behavior acquired and transmitted by symbols, constituting the distinctive achievement of human groups, including their embodiment in artifacts; the essential core of culture consists of traditional (i.e., historically derived and selected) ideas and especially their attached values; culture systems may, on the other hand, be considered as products of action, on the other as conditioning elements of further action."[37]

Other definitions they catalogued in their work include: Culture is the ways humans solve problems of adapting to the environment or living together; culture is social heritage, or tradition, that is passed on to future generations; and culture is ideas, values, or rules for living.

"Culture," says Geert Hofstede, "is learned, not inherited." Hofstede defined culture as the "collective programming of the mind which distinguishes the members of one category of people from another."[38] His landmark research on cultural difference across nations was designed to help identify the major differences in thinking, feeling, and acting of people around the globe. Realizing that we all have what he calls "software of the mind," Hofstede sought to understand more fully the impact of that programming as we interact in the world and in organizations, and to make cultural difference discussable.

In addressing culture and cultural difference, it's important, says Hofstede, to distinguish between human nature on one side, and an individual's personality on the other. His model is shown in Three Levels of Uniqueness.

Human nature is what all human beings have in common, writes Hofstede. "It represents the universal level in one's mental software." Our human ability to feel emotions such as fear, anger, and love and the need to associate with others—these all belong to this level of mental programming. However, "What one does with these feelings, how one expresses fear, joy, observations, and so on, is modified by culture," Hofstede reminds us.

On the other hand, the *personality* of an individual is his or her unique personal set of mental programs he or she does not share with any other human being.

Between these two is *culture,* which is specific to a group and is learned, not inherited. Each of these levels of uniqueness has an impact on individuals and groups in the workplace; for our purposes, we will focus on culture—that set of assumptions and cultural traits that each of us brings to the workplace every day—many times unconsciously.

Dominant Culture

We are often unconscious of our own cultural programming. In a September 1999 Harris Interactive poll, only 29 percent of Americans thought having a

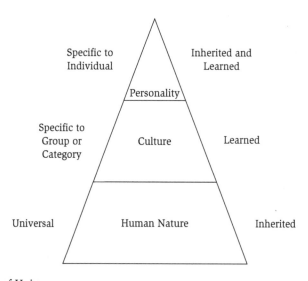

Three Levels of Uniqueness

Source: Geert Hofstede, *Cultures and Organizations: Software of the Mind* (New York: McGraw-Hill, 1997, p. 6).

"unique culture and tradition" best described the United States, while many more felt that way for countries such as China and Japan. We don't see ourselves as having a "culture"; we see others as being cultural creatures.

Members of the prevailing culture in any nation are considered part of the dominant culture, but they often do not know that. They do not think of themselves as part of a "group" because they simply perceive themselves as "normal." But according to Milton J. Bennett, co-director of the Portland, Oregon-based Intercultural Communication Institute, it's necessary to first place yourself in context in your own culture before you'll be able to see other culture clearly.

"The dominant group, whether Han Chinese in China or European-Americans in the United States, tends to neglect their own cultural context," Bennett explains. "We tend not to see our own culture because the dominant group is defined as 'standard.' We don't think we have a culture—that is just the way things are. But the failure to perceive yourself as operating in culture subtly creates the dynamic that you're operating in a standard mode and everyone else is deviant." As interculturalist Edward T. Hall so brilliantly stated it, "Culture hides much more than it reveals and, strangely enough, what it hides, it hides most effectively from its own participants."

When we're operating in a cultural context and actually see ourselves as operating in a specific culture, Bennett notes, then we can begin to see others as variation, not deviation. To understand this issue of dominant culture, we must first create a boundary so there is differentiation between "us" and "them." "We must clarify the boundaries between our culture and the other, as well as generate contrasts between the values and artifacts of our culture and the other," Bennett advises. As Hall observed, the ultimate purpose of the study of culture isn't so much the understanding of foreign cultures as the understanding of our own culture. Complete the "You as a Culturally Diverse Entity" form to get an idea of this concept.

Suggestions for Using "You as a Culturally Diverse Entity"

Objectives

- To identify the sources of one's own cultural programming
- To increase awareness about the complexity of each individual's cultural programming and cultural identities, which in turn affect behavior
- To raise awareness about the need to find out more about the backgrounds of others in the workplace
- To understand that everyone has a culture

Intended Audience

- Individuals wanting to increase their understanding and awareness about cultural influences and intercultural interactions on the job

You as a Culturally Diverse Entity

Directions: Think about what cultures you belong to (such as Southern, Israeli, women, corporate, mothers). Then think about the beliefs, values, and biases that come from these experiences. What is their impact on you in your professional life? Label each circle with a culture you identify as being part of and next to each write the most important rules, norms, and values you have as part of the group.

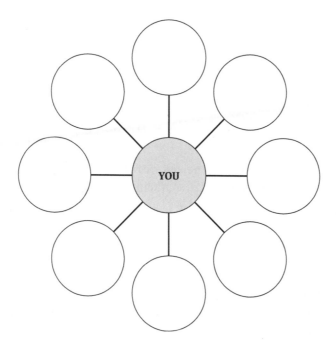

1. What reactions and/or surprises do you have to your own cultural diversity?

2. Do any of your cultural programs come in conflict with one another? If so, where?

Source: Adapted from Lee Gardenswartz and Anita Rowe, *Managing Diversity: A Complete Desk Reference and Planning Guide* © Lee Gardenswartz and Anita Rowe (Burr Ridge, IL: Irwin Professional Publishing, 1993).

- Trainees in diversity seminars
- Members of work teams wanting to understand each other better
- Managers wanting to learn more about employees
- Members of a global multinational work team, task force, or department
- Managers of international or multicultural teams

Time

- 45 to 60 minutes

Materials

- Copies of "You as a Culturally Diverse Entity"

Directions

- Ask the group to brainstorm sources of cultural programming and chart responses on an easel or board. Some responses might include family, school, the media.
- Ask the group to brainstorm the cultures they belong to. Some responses might include female, marketing, Israeli, Southern.
- Individuals write one culture they belong to in each circle on the diagram. Next to each, they write the most important rules, norms, and values they have as part of that group.
- Individuals, in small groups or pairs, share information from their circles.

Questions for Discussion/Consideration

- What reactions or surprises do you have to your own cultural diversity?
- What are some of the cultures you belong to?
- Do any of your cultural programs come in conflict with one another? If so, where?
- What similarities and differences did you find with your partners/your discussion group?
- What do you know about the programming of your colleagues, staff members, and bosses?
- What insights did you gain?
- How will knowing this information help you work better together?

Cultural Considerations

- Talking about cultural identity openly may be uncomfortable for some team members. Tell people at the beginning of the activity that they will be sharing their diagram with another person or a small group. In this way, individuals can control the degree of disclosure.

Caveats, Considerations, and Variations

- Rather than ask participants to identify cultures they belong to, ask them to identify sources of cultural programming, which may be individuals such as parents or teachers.

- Have members pair or group with those on the team they know least about.

Cultural values and norms are deeply held and almost always implicit and taken for granted, notes Pasi Raatikainen, writing in the *Singapore Management Review*.[39] Their deepest effects on behavior and interaction are usually hidden, says Raatikainen, and extremely difficult to identify and address. Cultural differences inevitably hinder smooth interaction, Raatikainen continues. But because of the nature of culture, say DiStefano and Maznevski, cultural differences also provide the greatest potential for creating value.[40] "Culture affects what we notice," they write, "how we construe it, what we decide to do about it, and how we execute our ideas."

As Clifford Geertz noted in his influential book, *The Interpretation of Culture,* "Men unmodified by the customs of particular places do not in fact exist, have never existed, and most important, could not . . . exist." Since culture has such a pervasive influence on us, it's important to understand more clearly exactly what culture is by examining its component parts.

Culture Matters

That icon of Americanism, McDonald's, sells standardized products around the world, yet "localizes" their product to suit cultural differences. For example, they sell "bulgogi" burgers in South Korea and offer teriyaki sauce in Japan and beer in Germany. In the Middle East, Pillsbury puts lamb in its toaster strudels rather than jam; in China it uses pork and dough to make them taste like dim sum.

In building and launching an e-commerce site to sell PCs to consumers in Japan, Dell Computers learned about the impact of culture the hard way—after the fact. Their e-commerce site was built with black borders around it, a sign of negativity in Japanese culture. Other firms have realized that even the icons on their sites must be reviewed for cultural "fit." Mailboxes and shopping cart icons, for example, won't make sense in Europe where people don't take their mail from boxes and don't shop in stores large enough for wheeled carts.

These "accommodations" to local cultural norms address only the tip of the iceberg in terms of cultural difference, literally.

Visible artifacts of a culture—such as food preferences, the size of shopping carts, or the meaning of colors in various countries—are simply superficial signs of the deeper values and norms of a culture. It is to that deeper level of meaning that we must go in order to fully understand cultural difference.

One model often used to describe this dichotomy between what we see on the surface of a culture and the unspoken and unconscious rules of that culture is that of an iceberg, as in the Iceberg Model of Culture.

The iceberg model is a useful way to conceive of culture because it clearly delineates the small proportion of what is visible from the vast piece of culture that is underwater or under the surface. Above the water line are those aspects of culture that are explicit, visible, or taught, such as music, art, food and drink, greetings, dress, manners, rituals, and outward behaviors. Below the water line is "hidden" culture, those things that are implicit in a culture and are often unspoken or unconscious, such as our orientations to the environment, time, action, communication, organization of space, power, individualism, esthetic values, work ethic, beliefs, competitiveness, structure, and ways of thinking.

Culture has also been described as being ordered into three layers by management theorists Fons Trompenaars and Charles Hampden-Turner, like an

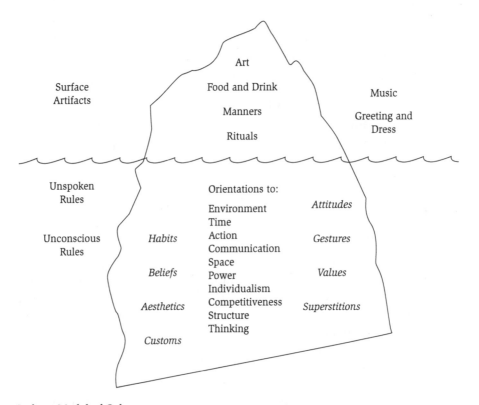

Iceberg Model of Culture

Source: Adapted from Wendell L. French and Cecil H. Bell, Jr., *Organization Development: Behavior Science Interventions for Organization Improvement* (Englewood Cliffs, NJ: Prentice Hall, 1973).

onion where one layer of peel has to be taken off to see the following layer. In this model, the three layers of culture are explained as:

- *The outer layer*—Artifacts and products such as language and food, architecture and style;
- *The second inner layer*—Norms (the mutual sense of what is right and wrong) and values (the definition of what is good and bad); and
- *The innermost layer*—Basic or core assumptions of what life is and assumptions about how to handle everyday problems.

Historian Patricia Ebrey suggests that if we really want to understand a culture, we should examine the following:

- *Values*—What people say one ought to do or not do. What is considered good and bad, for instance, the importance of honesty or chastity;
- *Laws*—What political authorities have decided people should do and what the sanctions are, for instance, laws about murder or robbery;
- *Rules*—What a society has decided its members should do and the sanctions imposed for not doing it, for instance, social rules about marriage ages, child rearing;
- *Social categories*—Ways of thinking about people as types, for instance, "kings," "friends," "criminals";
- *Tacit models*—Implicit standards and patterns of behavior that a person does not think about, for instance, knowing how to address a police officer rather than friends or knowing how to dress for a job interview as opposed to a dance;
- *Assumptions*—Implicit, not usually articulated ideas and beliefs, for instance, a belief that hard work will be repaid or the belief that things will get better; and
- *Fundamentals*—Categories and ways of thinking that people take for granted and may not be recognized even when pointed out, for instance, thinking in dualities such as good/bad, male/female, beastly/godly or seeing history as circular or as a straight line toward a definite goal.[41]

In addition, it is also necessary to look at more formal, and in some cases more visible, aspects of society such as:

- *Government*—The structure of government (monarchy, aristocracy, bureaucracy);
- *Economic life*—How wealth is owned and transferred (through family ties, money), the type of production (farming, industry, services);
- *Social structure*—The class system, gender roles;

- *Religion*—Religious organization, belief systems, clergies;
- *Literature*—Types of literature (oral, written), extent of literacy; and
- *Art*—Place of art in society, methods, purposes.

ANSWERING UNIVERSAL PROBLEMS—DIFFERENTLY

Social anthropologists Ruth Benedict and Margaret Mead, and many others since them, developed the conviction that all societies face the same basic problems; only the answers differ. As Louise Damen put it, "Culture is mankind's primary adaptive mechanism."[42]

Charles Hampden-Turner defines culture as the way in which people resolve dilemmas that emerge from universal problems. He and colleague Fons Trompenaars have built their work around this premise, outlining key areas that form the basis for cultural difference:

1. What is the relationship of the individual to others? (*relational* orientation);
2. What is the temporal focus on human life? (*time* orientation);
3. What is the modality of human activity? (*activity* orientation);
4. What is a human being's relation to nature? (*man-nature* orientation); and
5. What is the character of innate human nature? (*human-nature* orientation).[43]

Others have delineated slightly different ways of categorizing human experience. In their "values orientation culture model," Kluckhohn and Strodtbeck (1961) outline five basic cultural dimensions:

1. What is the relationship of people to nature?
2. What is the temporal focus on human life?
3. What is the character of innate human nature?
4. What is the modality of human activity? and
5. What is the modality of a person's relationships to other persons?

Among the first to study culture in this systematic way, they believed that these five questions were relevant to every cultural group and society, and that the way in which each group or society answered these questions defined its cultural values.

In the same way, Hofstede based his cultural dimensions on four fundamental problems that he perceives society faces:

1. The relationship between the individual and the group;

2. Social inequality;

3. Social implications of gender; and

4. Handling of uncertainty inherent in economic and social processes.

You will note significant overlap in their thinking and models. Common to each of them is the belief that culture arises out of our human need and ability to answer basic questions and solve basic dilemmas with which we are faced daily. To more fully understand their thinking—and its implications for your organization—we need to explore more deeply the "answers" they found in their research about *how* people resolve those dilemmas and how those resolutions vary around the world.

DIMENSIONS OF CULTURE

To master all this information about a culture in which you are doing business is prohibitive. Learning about cultural difference is a complex task because we run the risk of turning learning about cultural differences into the institutionalization of stereotypes. In fact, many do err on the side of simplicity, memorizing cultural "rules" for doing business in a particular culture. But "The culture of the other," writes Folke Glastra, "is not just a grammar to be learned, but also a catalyst of emotions and an integrative framework for interests."[44] It's important to go beneath the "water line," as it were, to understand more fully the ways in which different cultures answer those fundamental questions of human life.

As we study culture, we must also remember that much of the literature about cultural dimensions and difference has been written from a Western perspective, which itself is culturally biased or influenced. The very language with which we write about culture is, itself, a product of culture.

Because culture is so pervasive, intangible, and complex, and because it has such a strong impact on personal and organizational life, many scholars have identified those dimensions they consider more significant in helping us understand culture in general. To help understand the impact of culture on business, we must first understand the dimensions of culture.

You will also note overlap in the following dimensions of culture. Obviously, in developing your own global diversity initiative, you must determine which dimensions of culture most affect your organization. We are indebted to our colleague, interculturalist Urusa Fahim, from whose work the following synopsis of the major theories surrounding culture is derived.[45]

One culture schema is that developed by Philip Harris and Robert Moran. They use the following ten categories as a means for understanding any group of people:[46]

Sense of Self and Space.   The comfort one has with self can be expressed differently by culture. The sense of space that individuals require differs by culture as well. Western cultures focus their attention on objects and neglect the space in-between. The Japanese honor the space in-between as "ma." The distance between people, touch, and whether the culture is formal or informal are ways in which cultures can differ along this dimension.

Communication and Language.   Communication systems, verbal and nonverbal, distinguish groups from one another. In addition to differences in language, nonverbal gestures can vary widely by culture as well. Subcultures like the military have their own terminology and signals that cut across national boundaries. Whether communication is direct or indirect is another aspect of this dimension.

Dress and Appearance.   Native dress and body adornments tend to be distinctive by culture. Sarongs, headdresses, kimonos, cosmetics, jeans, piercings, and uniforms are among the ways in which dress and adornment can vary. Clothing, hair, and grooming are part of this dimension.

Food and Feeding Habits.   What foods are prepared and eaten often differs by culture. Certain foods are restricted or forbidden in some cultures and eaten extensively in others. Feeding habits also vary—from use of hands and chopsticks to knives and forks. Manners while eating are also culturally learned.

Time and Time Consciousness.   Sense of time differs by culture. Some are precise and exact, like the Germans, while many Latins are more casual about time. Cultures vary in how they conceive of time, their perspective on it, and how they experience the past, present, and future. Some cultures are monochronic, emphasizing schedules, segmentation of time, and promptness, while others are polychronic, stressing involvement with people and the completion of transactions rather than adherence to a preset schedule. Some cultures perceive time as linear (Western perception) or circular (Eastern perspective).

Relationships.   The groups that exist in various cultures are social structures that can vary widely. Family units are common expressions of relationships and can also vary from culture to culture. The identification and status of the authority figure and relationships between people (such as the young and elderly) and how they are expressed vary as well.

Values and Norms.   The needs and behaviors of different groups derive from a group's value system. Acceptable standards for group membership are often in the form of unspoken rules and are passed down from generation to generation, often without being explicitly taught. Concepts of independence, privacy, and respect are all aspects of this dimension.

Beliefs and Attitudes.   Major belief themes for different groups of people vary, from their belief in different spiritual beings to attitudes toward life itself, death, and the hereafter. Beliefs about the status of women and social order and authority also can differ widely.

Mental Process and Learning.   The way we think is influenced by culture. Reasoning is a universal, but the ways that reasoning occurs can be quite different. Some cultures are based on analytical, linear, and rational logic, while others are more holistic, associative, and affective. Some cultures have developed a highly abstract way of thinking, while others favor a more emotional and concrete mode of thinking.

Work Habits and Practices.   Attitudes toward work, work ethics, kinds of work, who does what work, and work practices are culturally determined.

These ten dimensions are a useful starting point for exploring the differences we see in different cultures. Anyone who has traveled abroad will have experienced at least the most explicit of these dimensions, such as dress and appearance and food and feeding habits. Others of these dimensions, such as beliefs and values or mental processes and learning bear more investigation before understanding can be reached.

As a result of his research comparing forty countries, Hofstede defined four key dimensions that distinguish different national cultures and affect human thinking, organizations, and institutions in predictable ways: individualism/collectivism, masculinity/femininity, uncertainty-avoidance, and power distance. They are described below.

Individualism/Collectivism

This refers to the extent to which group membership is emphasized and valued in each culture. According to Hofstede's research, the United States is the most individualist country in the world. In individualistic cultures such as the United States, Australia, or Great Britain, the individual is given more importance than the group. Collectivism refers to cultures where interdependence is the norm, such as Guatemala, Ecuador, Panama, and Colombia.

Imagine a photograph that shows a group of people in a room, with one individual standing in the front of the room. A colleague tells the story of showing that photograph to a group of Chinese and a group of Americans. When asked who the person was in front of the room, the American group responded that he was the leader. When asked the same question, the Chinese group responded that he was the outcast. Same picture, very different cultural interpretations.

Clark Johnson, CEO of Pier I Imports, tells the following story: "With our Japanese partners, we had a little flareup with one of their associates who said he was going to do all these things and didn't do them. The president of our Japanese company drew a circle and in the circle he drew a stick man and he said, 'In Japan the associate is the company and the company is the associate.' And then he drew a stick man outside the circle and he said, 'In the United States, the associate is kind of on his own.'"[47]

Masculinity/Assertiveness and Femininity/Modesty

Reward systems will also reflect national culture. Masculine cultures such as Japan, Australia, Venezuela, and Italy emphasize monetary incentives, recognition, and promotion, while feminine cultures such as Sweden, Norway, the Netherlands, and Denmark compensate employees with quality of life rewards and emphasize good working relationships, cooperation, and employment security. In feminine societies, roles are often merged or overlap for the sexes. Conflict is resolved by fighting it out in masculine societies, while feminine societies prefer compromise and negotiation.

Uncertainty Avoidance

This refers to the tolerance for ambiguity that different cultures demonstrate. Cultures high in uncertainty avoidance, such as Japan, Portugal, and Greece, work to reduce ambiguity and increase certainty by resisting change. They look for rules to follow in any and all situations. Cultures that score low on uncertainty avoidance, such as Singapore, Hong Kong, and Denmark, have a high tolerance for ambiguity and are more tolerant of deviant behavior. They take more risks.

Details of corporate life, from staffing patterns to buying patterns, can be traced to cultural dimensions. For example, consumers from countries with different levels of uncertainty avoidance might not equally appreciate and pay for extremely high-quality products.[48]

High uncertainty avoidance individuals such as the Japanese might purchase the product for its reliability, but those with a higher tolerance for uncertainty, as are Americans, might not. Management's collective level of uncertainty avoidance may also impact the length of planning horizons, levels of acceptable project risk, and desire for decentralization, according to Hofstede.

High uncertainty avoidance nations are characterized by bureaucratic rules and procedures to govern hiring and promotion, use of seniority in career advancement, and limited use of external hires past the entry level.[49] Roland Berra, head of Corporate Executive Resources of Hoffmann-La Roche, understands the impact of this aspect of culture on business: "American managers coming to Europe have the impression that the system is chaotic. Europeans going to the States find written responses and procedures on practically any issue."[50]

Power Distance

This dimension indicates the extent to which a society accepts that power in institutions and organizations is distributed unequally. High power distance cultures such as the Philippines, Venezuela, and India are authoritarian and formal, while low power distance cultures such as Denmark and Israel are less formal and have a flatter social structure and little emphasis is on making distinctions between individuals on levels of authority and hierarchy.

Other important dimensions of culture are the following, outlined by Kluckhohn and Strodtbeck and summarized in the Cultural Orientations and Their Implications for Management figure.

Relationship to the Environment. People in different cultures are subjugated to their environment, live in harmony with nature, or assume mastery over it. In many Middle Eastern countries, people see life as essentially preordained. Americans and people in some Western nations believe they can control nature. This continua ranges from "It can't be helped" to "If God is willing" to "I will do it" responses to situations.

Time Orientation. Different cultures focus on the past, present, or future. Western cultures perceive time as "money" and use it efficiently. Italians focus on past traditions and historical practices. North Americans are short-term and future-focused, whereas Japan is a much longer-term culture.

Nature of People. Some cultures view people as good, evil, or a mix of the two. For example, Americans see people as a mixture of the two, while other cultures take a rather evil view of human nature, believing people to be sinful when they are born. A more autocratic management style is likely in countries that focus on the evil aspects of people, while participation or laissez-faire styles prevail in countries that emphasize trusting values.

Activity Orientation. Some cultures such as the United States and Taiwan stress doing or action and emphasize accomplishments. Others like Mexico stress "being" and living for the moment. Still others like France focus on controlling and emphasize restraining desires. Doing and controlling cultures are likely to stress pragmatism and rationality in decision making; in cultures with "being" orientations, decisions are likely to be more emotional.

Focus of Responsibility. Cultures can also be classified according to where responsibility lies for the welfare of others. For example, Americans focus on personal achievements to define themselves; Taiwanese focus on the group. This dimension is similar to Hofstede's individualism/collectivism dimension.

Cultural Dimensions	American Cultural Orientation	Contrasting Cultural Orientation
What is the nature of people?	Mixture of good and evil. Change is possible.	Good (Evil) Change is impossible
Example:	*Emphasize training and development; give people the opportunity to learn on the job.*	*Emphasize selection and fit; select the right person for the job; don't expect employees to change once hired.*
What is a person's relationship to the external environment, including nature?	People dominant over nature and other aspects of the external environment.	Harmony (Subjugation)
Example:	*Policy decisions made to alter nature to fulfill people's needs, that is, building dams, roads.*	*Policy decisions made to protect nature while meeting people's needs.*
What is a person's relationship to other people?	Individualistic	Group (Hierarchical or Lateral)
Example:	*Personnel director reviews academic and employment records of candidates to select the best person for the job.*	*Personnel director selects the closest relative of the chief executive as the best person for the job.*
Example:	*Decisions are made by individuals.*	*Decisions are made by the group.*
What is the primary mode of activity?	Doing	Being (Controlling)
Example:	*Employees work hard to achieve goals; employees maximize their time at work.*	*Employees work only as much as needed to be able to live; employees minimize the time at work.*

Cultural Orientations and Their Implications for Management

Source: Adapted from Kluckhohn and Strodbeck, *Variations in Value Orientations* (New York: Row, Peterson, 1961), as cited in Nancy J. Adler, "Women as Androgynous Managers: A Conceptualization of the Potential for American Women in International Management" and included in Nancy J. Adler, *International Dimensions of Organizational Behavior* (3rd ed.) (Cincinnati, OH: South-Western, 1997).

Cultural Dimensions	American Cultural Orientation	Contrasting Cultural Orientation
How do people see space?	Private	Public
Example:	*Executive holds important meetings in a large office behind closed doors and has the secretary screen interruptions.*	*Executive holds important meetings in a moderate-sized office or in an open area, with open doors and many interruptions from employees and visitors.*
What is a person's temporal orientation?	Future/Present	Past (Present)
Example:	*Policy statement refers to five-year and ten-year goals while focus is kept on this year's bottom line and quarterly reports; innovation and flexibility to meet a dynamic, changing future are emphasized.*	*Policy statements this year reflect policy statements ten years ago; the company strives to use tradition to perform in the future as it has in the past.*

Cultural Orientations and Their Implications for Management (continued)

One additional model of note and useful to global diversity practitioners is that of Fons Trompenaars and Charles Hampden-Turner, based on their study of more than thirty-five thousand managers in forty countries. Several of their dimensions of culture are outlined below:

Universalism/Particularism. Universalistic cultures such as Canada operate along the lines of universal rules and standards and believe that laws are written by everyone and must be upheld by everyone at all times. These cultures tend to rely on extensive documentation of business relationships. Particularist cultures such as South Korea and Venezuela tend to ignore rules because relationships are more important than rules. They view detailed contracts as signs they aren't trusted.

Individualism/Communitarianism. Do people regard themselves primarily as individuals or primarily as part of a group?

Specific/Diffuse. Specific refers to cultures in which there are clear boundaries around relationships and relationships are contained within the boundary of that context and do not permeate into other spheres of life. Managers from specific cultures tend to focus only on behavior that takes place at work. In diffuse cultures, relationships overlap and permeate across boundaries. Managers from more diffused cultures include behavior that takes place in employees' private and professional lives.

Neutral/Affective. Should the nature of our interactions be objective and detached, or is expressing emotion acceptable? Members of neutral cultures don't express their emotions, while affective cultures are very expressive.

Achievement/Ascription. In some cultures, status is assigned as a result of some achievement, whereas in others status is the result of membership in certain groups. In an achievement culture, you'll be asked *"What* did you study," and in an ascriptive culture, the question will be *"Where* did you study?"

There are many other categorizations of the dimensions that comprise culture, not all of which are included here. For example, Edward T. Hall's important work on two basic cultural differences in communication styles (low- and high-context) has great relevance to the workplace and is covered in some depth in Chapter 3 on communication.

The Impact of Culture

In this, and particularly in subsequent chapters, we have attempted to introduce the concepts of culture in a way that helps readers begin to see how culture might have an impact in their own workplace. Knowing the theories of culture and cultural difference is not enough—it's the application of that knowledge that is most important. The "Cultural Dimensions at Work" tool will help you understand how these cultural differences have an impact at work.

Suggestions for Using "Cultural Dimensions at Work"

Objectives
- To understand the impact of cultural norms on the workplace
- To understand that there are alternative viewpoints on cultural norms
- To stimulate discussion and negotiation of differences

Intended Audience
- Members of a global multinational work team, task force, or department
- Managers of international or multicultural teams
- Trainees in diversity training session

Time
- 45 to 60 minutes

Materials
- Copies of "Cultural Dimensions at Work"
- Enlargements of "Cultural Dimensions at Work" (optional)

Directions
- Discuss the aspects of U.S. culture and provide examples of possible alternatives and management functions that might be affected by them.
- Ask participants to respond to the questionnaire, following directions.
- Have participants share their responses in small groups and discuss similarities, differences, and implications for the organization.
- If using an enlarged version of the worksheet for each group, ask the groups to complete the enlarged sheet with examples of their responses for discussion in the large group.

Questions for Discussion/Consideration
- What was difficult and what was easy about completing this exercise?
- What similarities and differences do you see among group members?
- What did you learn from brainstorming possible alternative aspects to values of U.S. culture?
- What are our challenges as an organization around these issues?
- How flexible are you in adapting to others who have different cultural orientations on these cultural values?
- What can we learn from people who have different cultural norms?
- What are the potential "costs" to the organization if these cultural nuances are not recognized and used in organizational planning?
- Where are there potential "hot spots" that may lead to misunderstanding or conflict?
- How could cultural difference be an advantage to the organization?

Cultural Considerations
- There is a potential for defensiveness regarding U.S. and other national cultural values. Discuss this possibility in giving directions for the exercise.

Caveats, Considerations, and Variations
- After the large group discussion, have the small groups reconvene to brainstorm possible adaptations or accommodations in management functions that will make them more culturally sensitive.

Cultural Dimensions at Work

Directions: In the first column are common aspects of U.S. culture. For each, determine what other cultural norms might be possible and what management functions might be affected by both.

Aspects of U.S. Culture	Alternative Aspect	Examples of Management Function Affected
The individual can influence the future.	*Example:* Life follows a preordained course and human action is determined by the will of God.	*Example:* Planning and scheduling.
We must work hard to achieve our objectives.	*Example:* Hard work is not the only prerequisite for success. Wisdom, luck, and time are also required.	*Example:* Motivation and reward systems.
Commitments should be honored.		
One should effectively use one's time.		
The best-qualified persons should be given the positions available.		
Each person is expected to have an opinion and to express it freely, even if his or her views do not agree with those of his or her colleagues.		

Cultural Dimensions at Work (continued)

Aspects of U.S. Culture	Alternative Aspect	Examples of Management Function Affected
A decision maker is expected to consult persons who can contribute useful information to the area being considered.		
Change is considered an improvement and a dynamic reality.		
Competition stimulates high performance.		
Employees will work hard to improve their position in the company.		

Source: Adapted from Philip R. Harris and Robert T. Moran, *Managing Cultural Differences* (5th ed.) (Houston, TX: Gulf, 2000, pp. 66–68).

VALUES

One key element underlying these dimensions of cultural difference is that of values, both consciously and unconsciously held. Values reflect general beliefs about what is "right" and 'wrong" in a given group. It is from our values that our cultures set norms of behavior.

Most importantly, there are two types of values: *terminal* or "end result' values and *instrumental* or "behavioral" values. When studying culture or when, more practically, managing people, it is necessary to understand that, while two people may espouse similar values, the manner in which they behave to get to those values might be vastly different. For example, in the figure Terminal and Instrumental Values to follow, two people share a strong value of "family," but the means by which they define that and operationalize it is vastly different.

In the same way, the behavior of two colleagues may be the same, but they may actually be working toward very different ends or values. As shown in the figure, we may both work hard, but the end goal of that hard work can be quite dissimilar.

There are two basic types of values: "terminal" or those that describe the end state we want to achieve (for example, peace or success) and "instrumental" or those that define how we should behave in order to consider ourselves good or moral.

As indicated below, two people can share the same terminal value ("family," for example) but get to that end state in very different ways (for example, defining and operationalizing family differently). On the other hand, two people can act the same ("work hard"), but be doing so for very different reasons (for personal gain or for the good of the group).

Terminal Values (End)	Instrumental Values (Behaviors)
Family	Nuclear, blood related; male/female parents
Family	Extended; created; gay/lesbian parents
Individualism; competition—wants the next promotion	**Work Hard**
Group; cooperation—wants the team to succeed	**Work Hard**
Leadership	Hierarchical
Leadership	Inclusive
To achieve security	**Hard Work**
To financially enable you to have more life experiences	**Hard Work**

Terminal and Instrumental Values

Source: Copyright © Executive Diversity Services, Inc. Seattle, WA, 2001.

This simple distinction can have great impact in the workplace, not only in averting misunderstandings, but also in helping us manage and motivate from the true values of the people in our organizations.

THREE CULTURES MODEL

Cultural difference is complex. To simplify the process of identifying cultural difference in the workplace, we have created the Three Cultures Model from our work with global diversity professionals. This model posits three key cultural influences that are at work in global corporations: *personal* culture, *national* culture, and the *organizational* culture itself (shown in the figure). Being in an organization with a strong corporate culture does not negate the fact that individuals come to the table with their own personal characteristics and national tendencies, neither of which are sublimated to the organization's culture.

Professor André Laurent makes the following observation based on his study of multinational organizations: "Multinational companies do not and cannot submerge the individuality of different cultures. That is, strong as a corporate culture may be, the template for behaviors isn't from the company—but from the national culture."[51] Recognizing the dramatic influence of national culture is key to operating globally.

Personal culture is the integration of an individual's traits, skills, and personality formed within the context of one's ethnic, racial, familial, and educational environments.

National culture is a shared understanding that comes from the integration of beliefs, values, attitudes, and behaviors that have formed the heritage of a nation-state.

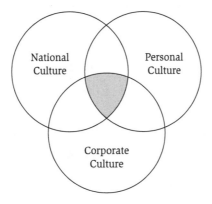

Three Cultures Model

Corporate culture represents the integration of widely shared institutional beliefs, values, and a guiding philosophy of an organization frequently espoused in its vision, mission, and values statements.

Adler asked fundamental questions about the interplay between these three cultures as early as 1986: Do organizational culture and structure determine people's behavior in organizations or does national or ethnical cultural conditioning limit the organization's influence? Does the culture that enters the organization through employees limit the influence of management-created organizational culture and structure? Apparently yes. Researchers such as André Laurent, Geert Hofstede, and Fons Trompenaars have found that national culture determines more about work-related values and behavior than position, role, age, gender, or race.

Some organizations try to downplay the possible impact of cultural difference between national, personal, and corporate cultures through careful employee selection. For example, Lotus Development Corporation appointed a team of local executives in their Japanese subsidiary with idiocentric cultural values (that is, individualists within a collectivist culture) to match the home culture more closely.[52] In doing so, they often lost the very advantage that difference could bring the organization.

The Three Cultures Model is useful in analyzing culture clash situations. While there is no ideal "balance" among the three cultures in any organizational situation, using the model to analyze which cultural dimensions are at work in a given situation provides a starting point for dialogue and reconciliation. Filling out the "Three Cultures Model at Work" sheet may be helpful for an organization.

Suggestions for Using "Three Cultures Model at Work"

Objectives

- To help assess causes of cultural clashes in the organization
- To deemotionalize cultural clashes and see them as issues to be analyzed and resolved
- To challenge participants to build their own diagnostic tool for use in diagnosing cultural clashes

Intended Audience

- Members of a global multinational work team, task force, or department
- Managers of international or multicultural teams
- Participants in diversity training programs

Time

- 45 to 60 minutes

Three Cultures Model at Work

Example: What is the national heritage of the people involved and what cultural norms might they hold about this issue as a result of that national heritage?

_____

_____

_____

_____

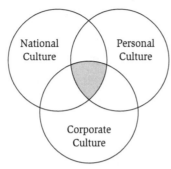

National Culture

Personal Culture

Corporate Culture

Example: What dimensions of their personal culture are we asking people to either give up or adapt to accept this new reward system?

_____

_____

_____

_____

Example: What are the elements of this reward system that might be offensive to non-headquarters locations?

_____

_____

_____

_____

Materials

- Copies of "Three Cultures Model at Work"
- Enlargements of "Three Cultures Model at Work" (optional)

Directions

- Discuss the Three Cultures Model.
- Ask participants to think of a clash that has occurred in the organization and ask them to respond to the questionnaire, following directions.
- Have small groups members share their thinking and create jointly a set of diagnostic questions for each culture.

Questions for Discussion/Consideration

- What challenges did you face in completing this worksheet?
- How could you best gather the information you have indicated as necessary in the questions you created?
- What are the benefits of gathering the type of information you have requested in your questions?
- How can you employ this tool in your work group?

Cultural Considerations

- The kind of abstract thinking required is not central to some cultures. Help those participants having difficulty with additional examples of questions that might be helpful.

Caveats, Considerations, and Variations

- Sometimes participants will have difficulty identifying a situation on which to base their responses. Have several such examples ready for the group to use if this situation occurs.

DEVELOPING INTERCULTURAL SENSITIVITY

Like most change processes, understanding culture is an ongoing and incremental process. Interculturalist Milton Bennett developed a model that helps us understand the stages that individuals—and organizations—go through in reconciling cultural difference. To explain the process, Bennett developed the Developmental Model of Intercultural Sensitivity (DMIS), articulating six Stages of Intercultural Sensitivity, shown in the model and described below.

The first three phases are *ethnocentric*. In these phases people unconsciously experience their own culture as central to reality. At the other end of the scale is *ethnorelativism*, a successful blending of more than one culture. People often move subconsciously through these stages as their international and intercultural experiences grow. As you engage in global diversity work in your organization using the tools from this book, you will observe individuals in each of these stages.

Ethnocentric Stages

1. *Denial of Difference.* In this stage, there is no recognition of cultural difference because individuals isolate themselves or intentionally sepa-

Stages of Intercultural Sensitivity

Source: Developmental Model of Intercultural Sensitivity, Milton J. Bennett, Ph.D., The Intercultural Communication Institute, Portland, OR, USA, www.intercultural.org.

rate from those who are different. The "other" is often thought to be deficient intellectually or to demonstrate culturally deviant behavior. In this stage, we tend to dehumanize outsiders.

2. *Defense Against Difference.* In this stage, we recognize cultural difference, but couple that recognition with a negative evaluation of most variations from our native culture—the greater the difference, the more negative the evaluation. We tend to view cultural development as evolutionary, with our own culture as the pinnacle of that evolutionary process. In this stage, there is also a tendency toward the social or cultural proselytizing of "underdeveloped" cultures.

3. *Reversal.* In this stage, we tend to see another culture as superior while maligning our own.

4. *Minimization of Difference.* Here we recognize and accept superficial cultural differences, such as eating customs, while maintaining that all human beings are essentially the same. The emphasis in this stage is on the similarity of people and the commonality of basic values. Our tendency is to define the basis of commonality in ethnocentric terms (that is, everyone is essentially like us).

5. *Physical Universalism.* In this stage, people tend to emphasize the commonality of human beings in terms of physiological similarity.

6. *Transcendent Universalism.* In this stage, we emphasize the commonality of human beings as subordinate to a particular supernatural being, religion, or social philosophy.

Ethnorelative Stages

1. *Acceptance of Difference.* Here we recognize and appreciate cultural difference in behavior and values. We accept cultural differences as viable alternative solutions to the organization of human existence. Cultural relativity marks this stage.

2. *Adaptation of Difference.* In this stage, we begin to develop communication skills that enable intercultural communication. Hallmarks include effective use of empathy or shifting our frame of reference to understand and be understood across cultural boundaries.

3. *Integration of Difference.* In this stage, we internalize bicultural or multicultural frames of reference. We are able to maintain a definition of identity that is "marginal" to any particular culture.[53]

Bennett's model helps us understand that even those people in our organizations who resist global diversity work are moving from the model's first stage of intercultural sensitivity—denial (failure to recognize that cultural differences exist)—into the second stage, defense (recognition of differences).

CULTURAL COSTS

Not understanding cultural difference—or remaining stuck in one of the ethnocentric stages of the DMIS model—can lead to disastrous results, and not just for corporations.

When the 2002 Miss World contest was slated to take place in the Nigerian capital of Abuja, protests from Muslim extremists and a newspaper article indicating that the prophet Muhammad would have approved of the pageant triggered four days of violence between Christians and Muslims in the Nigerian city of Kaduna, leading to the deaths of more than two hundred people, injuries to more than five hundred people, and forty-five hundred people left homeless.

When a Korean Airlines jet crashed in Guam in 1997, killing 228 people, it was widely reported that culture might have played a role in the crash. The junior officer on board hesitated to provide the senior officer with information that might have averted the crash because of cultural traditions of respecting seniority and saving face.

Corporate cultural faux pas are widely reported in management and business literature. One such incident recently involved British Cadbury-Schweppes. In India, Cadbury marketers tried to be relevant by referencing the biggest issue facing India—Kashmir, which threatens to plunge India and Pakistan into a nuclear war. Their ad, with a map highlighting the boundaries of India's Jammu-Kashmir state and the tagline: "I'm good. I'm tempting. I'm too good to share. What am I? Cadbury's Temptations or Kashmir?" The gimmick incited the ire of the local community, which accused the company of trivializing the Kashmir issue.

Each instance of cultural failure—and its related costs, both financial and in terms of reputation costs—helps shore up the business case for addressing global diversity inside our organizations.

But our business case for managing global diversity cannot be based only on the potential costs of mismanaging diversity. Instead, it must also include the potential benefits and opportunities that accrue to our organizations when we manage well the global diversity both inside and outside our companies.

BUILDING A BUSINESS CASE FOR GLOBAL DIVERSITY

With the background provided previously in this chapter—the evolution of diversity as a management concept, globalization and its impact on corporations, and an introduction to the concept of culture itself—it is time to begin framing a business case for managing global diversity. Articulating the business case is key for those readers wishing to undertake global diversity work inside their own organizations. As you read this section, think about your own corporation:

- What are the key business drivers for doing this work in your industry and in your company?
- What are the core benefits that accrue to your organization from managing global diversity?
- What would success look like for your organization?

In this section we will articulate potential business gains (and business losses) from managing, or mismanaging, global diversity.

Diversity Is the Key Predictor of Global Success

In *Global Literacies: Lessons on Business Leadership and National Cultures,* the authors reveal survey data that identify the predictors of global business success. Two factors alone predict success in the global marketplace, according to the *Global Literacies* research: (1) developing leaders at all levels of the business and (2) placing a high value on multicultural experience and competencies. The most successful companies do both, say the authors.[54]

Royal Dutch Shell, for example, requires four global expatriate assignments before it will consider a manager for promotion into senior management.[55] The British Imperial Chemical Industries (ICI) regularly bring their British and Italian managers together to reveal their different cultural approaches and identify the strengths of each.[56]

Yet, although cultural competency is a proven key to global success, leaders from the United States, Canada, and Australia ranked last in a twenty-nation survey of business leaders when asked whether multicultural experience matters.[57] In fact, only 15 percent of the top fifty executives in most American corporations have worked abroad. In a *Fortune* magazine report, a senior American executive stated that a typical American company "wants to do business in a cookie-cutter way—why not do it the same in Vietnam as in South Carolina?"[58]

That is, while culture is acknowledged as a key ingredient for global business success, executives in some parts of the world—including the United States—still do not value or leverage it for competitive gain. In many cases, it is not only *not* a competitive advantage, but a liability.

Global Diversity Readiness

The chairman of a major technology company goes to China with a slide presentation that includes the more complex writing characters used in Hong Kong and Taiwan, not those of the People's Republic of China, a serious oversight. Failure: poor preparation. *Loss: a contract worth $2.5 million.*

A negotiator from a German pharmaceutical company is approached by an American negotiator about a deal. The German mentions that his company had problems with the American firm several years before. The American replies: "I wasn't with the company then and, besides, you could make mega-marks." The German, offended by the American's unwillingness to discuss past business history and his emphasis on profits, rejects the deal. Failure: inability to understand cultural cues. *Loss: a superb market entry opportunity.*

A proposal by a U.S. mining company in Chile is held up by a vocal group of grassroots environmental activists with influence in the Chilean government. Failure: not understanding critical local environmental challenges. *Loss: a $1.3 billion proposal and the expenses of putting it together.*

Contrast those scenarios with the following one in which cultural knowledge is leveraged for business advantage.

An Egyptian company requests a training program. A training firm sends its top expert. When the Egyptians realize that the trainer is a woman, they protest that they would be uncomfortable looking at her in session for two days. Solution: She offers a slide presentation and presents the program from the back of the room. Success: creative accommodation on both sides. *Gain: contract saved, reputation earned for competence, and more than $100,000 in new business from other companies in Cairo.*

Source: Excerpted from Diane L. Simpson and Sybil Evans, "Ready or Not: Embracing the Challenge of Global Diversity." (Internal newsletter, n.d.)

New Assets of Business

"In today's business environment," writes Vladimir Pucik in *Globalizing Management,* "the traditional sources of competitive advantage cannot provide a sustainable edge." What, then, can provide that competitive edge? How can we best articulate the linkages between global diversity, business strategy, and firm performance, as measured by productivity, return on equity, and market performance?

According to the authors of *Global Literacies,* the old assets of business—*land, labor,* and *capital*—still remain necessary in our new global business environment, but their importance pales in comparison to the new assets of business—*people, relationships,* and *culture.* Traditionally seen as "soft" issues in business, the new global environment has placed these three assets front and center for companies trying to succeed and win in a fast-paced, interconnected, and multicultural business world.

It defies conventional wisdom, write the authors, but in the new, borderless economy, culture doesn't matter less; it matters more. Doug Ivester, former CEO of Coca-Cola, painfully discovered that lesson during the 1999 Coke scare in Europe. "As economic borders come down," Ivester remarked, "cultural barriers go up, presenting new challenges and opportunities in business."[59]

Leaders like Allen Freedman, the first CEO of Fortis, Inc., have begun to realize just how palpable and vital culture is to their businesses: "I find it amazing to see the difference between the Belgians and the Dutch, who speak the same language mostly and are miles apart. I find that where we get into trouble is always on a cultural point that's never spoken. It's the implicit cultural conclusion or assumption that one or the other side makes that takes you so far down the road before you've even figured it out."[60]

William Longfield, CEO of C.R. Bard, understands, too, the fact that culture is a business asset to be protected: "When you acquire a German company, for example, you acquire them because of the culture they've got. That's what you're buying and if you change it, you're not getting what you bought. So what you've got to do is figure out how you can overlay the values of your company on that culture."[61] For Longfield and others like him, the culture is the asset—to be protected and leveraged.

Denmark-based pharmaceutical giant Novo Nordisk knows that culture matters—and has institutionalized cultural learning in the corporation by sending "culture coaches" around the world to help teach and facilitate cross-cultural learning across the company and by expecting executives to come to the table having "bought" and "sold" best practices from divisions around the world to cross-pollinate their thinking at the top of the organization.[62] Compensation is tied to cultural competence in the organization.

Some organizations demonstrate cultural competence in other ways. For example, when then-Gillette CEO Alfred Zeien planned the 1993 launch of the company's Sensor Excel razor, his primary reason for introducing it first in Europe was, as he said, "Europe isn't Boston, where Gillette is headquartered. I was trying to make a point. Why should we do it in our home market first?"[63] Zeien and other like-minded CEOs are trying to do away with the very notion of a home market, erasing distinctions between domestic and international operations and allowing ideas, people, and products to move across borders in all directions. Of course, American CEOs and business executives who are global thinkers are playing catchup to Japanese and European competitors, who have been thinking and acting globally for decades because their small home markets dictated that mindset.

Just as personal values play an important part in understanding the cultural norms of individuals, so too do corporate values. Dermot Dunphy, chairman of Sealed Air, is clear about the requirement to value cultural diversity; he is just as clear about the need for those diverse individuals to adhere to the company's values: "We say, 'Look, we love you all, we're very open to views, we're very sensitive to local culture, but there are certain absolutely inviolable, fundamental principles of Sealed Air culture; if you don't like it, you've got to go.'"[64]

The Benefits of Global Diversity

Management and organizational research over the past twenty years can shed light on the key ways in which global diversity can provide competitive advantage.

A recent survey of European business leaders found that four benefits of diversity were most often mentioned there:

- Improved team effectiveness and cooperation;
- Increased productivity;
- Improved customer intimacy; and
- Broader access to labor markets.[65]

Global diversity can also have an impact on customer and market penetration. For example, in 2002, Spanish tourism chief Juan Jose Guemes outlined his plan to emphasize the country's cultural diversity to compete with cheaper European destinations, using diversity as a clear market differentiator. Americans view the mixing of cultures as synergistic. In May 1999, a Pew poll found that 71 percent of Americans agreed that cultural diversity was a "major reason" for America's success.

Other benefits of global diversity include:

Creativity and Problem Solving

Proponents of diversity maintain that different opinions provided by culturally diverse groups make for better-quality decisions.[66] As U.S.-based communications firm Bell Atlantic's CEO Ivan Seidenberg once said, "If everybody in the room is the same, you'll have a lot fewer arguments and a lot worse answers."

Zurich-based Asea Brown Boveri began the practice over a decade ago of requiring that at least three different nationalities be represented on any management team, both for the sake of increased creativity and to provide the message to the rest of the organization that they were a global organization solving global problems. More than half of Hewlett-Packard's twenty-four thousand products were developed in the last two years, according to a company website. That level of innovation demands the kind of creativity that is present when diverse groups of individuals butt heads and challenge each other.

Radha Basu, an Indian software manager, knows first-hand that creativity results from diversity. As cited in *The Global Me* by G. Pascal Zachary, he said: "The advantage is you get the whole world. From the Singaporeans you get process knowledge and discipline. From Indians you get outside thinking. From Germans you get reliability and accuracy. From the Brazilians you get snazziness. From the Japanese you get correctness; every 'i' is dotted." American psychologist Howard Gardner finds the source of creativity in what he calls "a lack of fit" or asynchrony.

Further, a laboratory study found that initially culturally homogeneous teams performed better than culturally diverse groups. However, as time passed, the between-group differences began to converge, and after a certain point the heterogeneous teams performed better than the homogeneous ones.[67]

Innovation and Alternatives

Research has shown other business gains of diversity as well: Minority views also stimulate consideration of nonobvious alternatives in work settings and are useful for making valuable judgments in novel situations.[68] "Heterogeneity in decision-making and problem-solving styles produces better decisions through the operation of a wider range of perspectives and a more thorough critical analysis of issues."[69]

Environmental Scanning and Flexibility

Still others have argued that diversity may be coupled with better environmental scanning[70] and greater flexibility to respond to environmental changes because members of diverse teams are more likely to disagree with each other and find fault with the status quo.[71]

Comprehensive Decision Making

One key variable linking employee diversity with organizational performance is the comprehensiveness of decision making.[72] That is, diversity aids teams in their attempts to be exhaustive or inclusive in considering alternative options or solutions to the task at hand. An empirical study in 1993 found that comprehensiveness makes a greater contribution to firm performance in "relatively fast changing, unpredictable environments."[73]

Social Cohesion

Paul Collier, chief development economist at the World Bank, advances a thesis that takes the impact of diversity a step further: that diversity in a country inversely correlates with peace and harmony. "In other words, the less diversity, the greater chances of violent social conflict. The more diversity, the more likely that differences will be resolved peacefully."[74] Examining conflict over the period 1960 to 1995, Collier found that "heterogeneity strengthens, not weakens, social cohesion."[75]

As Pascal Zachary reminds us in *The Global Me*, this information should provide a wake-up call to the many Americans and Europeans who believe that they can reduce the likelihood of social tensions by restricting the pool of aliens they allow into their countries. In fact, in the case of New Zealand (see box earlier in this chapter), national policy is designed to achieve greater social cohesion through increased immigration.

Economic Development

Writing in the *Singapore Management Review,* Pasi Raatikainen notes additional business drivers for global diversity, including the ongoing need for skilled labor in countries such as Thailand, where there is a shortage of skilled and unskilled workers because of rapid industrialization. "Without a multicultural and diverse workforce," says Raatikainen, "economic growth cannot continue."[76] The same is true in Singapore, where about five hundred thousand non-Singaporean and culturally diverse people are doing unskilled work, contributing heavily to the economic development of that nation.

To summarize, global diversity:

- Enhances the quality of problem solving and innovation;
- Enhances productivity;
- Enhances global customer and market penetration;
- Enhances the ability to attract and retain top talent;
- Contributes to social cohesion; and
- Contributes to economic development and growth worldwide.

Use "Building Your Own Business Case" for your organization.

Suggestions for Using "Building Your Own Business Case"

Objectives

- To assess the key reasons the organization should focus on global diversity
- To understand the dynamic nature of business drivers for diversity and how they can change over time
- To provide a basis for the creation of a cogent business case for global diversity
- To understand the different perspectives that people from different parts of the organization might have about the core issues of the business
- To stimulate discussion of what the organization needs to focus on vis-à-vis global diversity

Intended Audience

- Members of a global multinational work team, task force, or department
- Managers of international or multicultural teams
- HR or other managers of diversity teams
- Members of diversity councils or task forces
- Trainees in diversity training
- Executive staff responsible for organizational strategy

Time

- 45 to 60 minutes

Materials

- Copies of "Building Your Own Business Case"
- Enlargements of "Building Your Own Business Case" sheet (optional)

Directions

- Discuss and define the business drivers.
- Ask participants to respond to the questionnaire, following directions.
- Have participants share their responses in small groups and discuss similarities and differences in their responses and implications for the organization.
- Ask each small group to come back to the larger group with their assessment of the most critical business drivers presently and in the future.

Questions for Discussion/Consideration

- Are there other business drivers for diversity that you would add to this list?
- Which are the most critical business drivers for the organization?
- Of those considered most critical, which are being addressed presently?
- How could you use this information in building a strong business case for the organization to address global diversity issues?
- Are there "hot spots" that may be costly to the organization if not addressed quickly?

Cultural Considerations

- Some participants may not feel they have enough expertise to add value to the discussion. In such cases, preempt that reaction by explaining in giving directions for the exercise that everyone's opinion on these issues matters and that each of them is bringing a unique perspective to the discussion.

Caveats, Considerations, and Variations

- Have each team member mark his or her responses on the enlarged worksheet using a different colored marker. Ask them to use that sheet to prompt discussion of the various perspectives represented in the group.
- Have each team come to consensus about the top five business reasons, past, present, and future, and ask them to indicate that group consensus on the enlarged worksheet for discussion in the larger group.

Building Your Own Business Case

In your opinion, what are the top five business reasons that your company has been, is, or should be focusing on global diversity (1 being most important)? Make your selection in five-year intervals (past, present, future).

Driver	5 Years Ago	Today	5 Years from Now
Market Share			
Increased stake-holder diversity			
Need for market differentiation			
Market demand for innovation			
Increased supplier diversity			
Diversity in cus-tomer base			
Talent			
Need for broader access to labor markets			
Recruitment of top talent			
Retention of top talent			
Increasing work-force diversity			
Use of multicultural teams			

Building Your Own Business Case (continued)

Driver	5 Years Ago	Today	5 Years from Now
Globalization			
Global vision and values of company			
Organizational changes (such as restructuring)			
Technological advancements			
Increased inter-national market			
Cross-cultural merg-ers and acquisitions			
Environmental scanning			
Profitability			
Legal concerns			
Cost containment			
National or regional economic develop-ment			
Social responsibility agenda of company			

One in four senior executives responding to the Conference Board's benchmarking survey of the diversity management practices of over 150 Canadian companies views the increasing diversity of the workforce as "a competitive opportunity." But there's a big gap between recognizing the importance of people, relationships, and culture to our businesses and knowing how to maximize their contributions.

A colleague, David Rippey, reminds us that even oil was considered a nuisance when it was first discovered—because we didn't know what to do with it. The same is often still true of our attempts to maximize value from the people in our organizations, the relationships they can build for our companies, and the cultures represented inside and outside the workplace itself. As Stuart Hall has said, "Diversity is, increasingly, the fate of the modern world. The capacity to live with difference is . . . the coming question of the 21st Century."[77]

Recognizing the national and cultural context for diversity—and the way that context differs around the world—grappling with the unadulterated complexities and impact of globalization, understanding cultural difference itself, and building a business case are all just the beginning in truly capitalizing on global diversity. The following chapters grapple in greater detail with each of these issues, providing tools for you to use in your own workplaces as you face global diversity issues head-on, keeping in mind—as Blaise Pascal wrote in *Pensées*—that "there are truths on this side of the Pyrenees which are falsehoods on the other."

GLOSSARY OF TERMS

This listing is designed to help the reader understand the terms used in this book to discuss global diversity, as well as help non-U.S. readers understand diversity in the U.S. context. The authors wish to thank our colleague Maricel Quintana-Baker for her assistance in compiling this glossary.

Acculturation. The process of intense socialization which brings about an individual's integration into or adoption of another culture, especially that of a foreign country. In the case of a corporate merger or acquisition, the acquired company often adopts the culture of the acquiring organization.

Affirmative Action. Refers to efforts and programs designed to remedy and prevent discrimination by protecting the civil rights of certain groups, initially women and minorities in the U.S. context. Affirmative action plans were initially meant to remove the barriers that prevented these groups from full participation in American society. Later, compensatory opportunities were provided to members of these groups. Currently, this concept is being replaced or augmented by those of "managing diversity" and "inclusion."

Assimilation.   The process of absorbing or blending into another culture. Immigrants have traditionally been assimilated into the mainstream culture, thus incorporating themselves into the dominant culture while giving up their individual cultural traditions. This idea of amalgamation led to the "melting pot" theory. Lately, assimilation and the melting pot theory have come under debate, as the theory of "multiculturalism" has gained popularity, and the image of a "mosaic" or "salad bowl" in which individual components retain their uniqueness has replaced that of the melting pot.

Backlash.   Backlash refers to a reactionary movement regarding diversity and affirmative action. Backlash occurs when nonminority individuals or groups feel threatened, when diversity programs are ill-perceived and unskillfully presented, and when the majority group (white males in the United States) do not understand the importance of their full participation in the process of inclusion.

Civilizational.   This refers to large cultural entities and their influences on the people who belong to those groups, such as the Christian and Muslim world, or Western and Eastern civilizations. Without evaluative implications, that is, does not imply different levels of being civilized.

Civil Rights.   Refers to the basic rights afforded and guaranteed by the Constitution to all individuals who reside in the United States. At least one of these rights does not apply to noncitizens, who, for example, do not have the constitutional right to vote. The Civil Rights Movement began as an effort to end discrimination on the basis of race. Other segments of the U.S. population (such as the disabled, women, older Americans, gays and lesbians, and ethnic minorities) have sought protection for their civil rights through legislation and national efforts.

Corporate Culture.   The fundamental philosophy of an organization is determined by its corporate culture. The behavior and actions of individuals within a corporation illustrate the existing culture of that organization. Culture change within organizations can be difficult to implement, but diversity work is less apt to succeed within an organization without attention to the culture of the organization and whether it will support diversity.

Cross-Cultural.   Comparing or dealing with two or more different cultures.

Cultural Values.   The individual's desirable or preferred way of acting or knowing something that is sustained over a period of time and which governs actions or decisions.

Culture.   The set of distinctive spiritual, material, intellectual and emotional features of a society or a social group, encompassing art and literature, lifestyles, ways of living together, value systems, traditions, and beliefs (UNESCO Universal Declaration on Cultural Diversity, 1998).

Discrimination.   Discrimination is the denial of equal rights or equal treatment to people who are considered different from the majority norm. Discrimination in the United States can be based on race, ethnicity, religion, age, sexual orientation, gender, or disability. "Reverse discrimination," when used by members of the dominant group, reflects the blaming of affirmative action recipients for the dominant member's inability to improve his or her socioeconomic position.

Diversity Management.   The use of the term "diversity" has changed over the years. Initially, it referred to the differences inherent in peoples of different races, ethnicity, and nationalities in the United States. Lately, the term has become more inclusive, addressing differences of gender, sexual orientation, age, family status, religion, and physical abilities. Due to increased immigration and demographic changes, the composition of the U.S. population is becoming more diverse. Organizations with diverse constituencies afford themselves the benefits of many different perspectives on issues. An organization's movement toward diversity must be self-initiated, proactive, and business-driven.

Dominant Culture.   There is usually one "dominant" culture in each area that forms the basis for being able to define that culture. This is determined by power and control in cultural institutions (church, government, education, mass media, monetary systems, and economics). Often those in the dominant culture do not see the privilege that accrues to them by being dominant "norm" and do not identify themselves as being the dominant culture. Rather, they believe that their cultural norms are self-evident and that people who act differently are not just different, but are deviant.

Equality.   Although the democratic concept of equality, that is, equal treatment of all people, has remained constant in the United States since the time of statesman Thomas Jefferson, the application and implementation of that concept has undergone metamorphic changes, particularly during the last century. Because of legislative and social changes, equality now refers to the "equal treatment of all persons" in matters of housing, employment, and education.

Equal Opportunity.   Based on specific anti-discrimination legislation in the United States, equal opportunity in housing, employment, and education endeavors to provide equal access to these to all people, regardless of social position, race, national origin, gender, age, sexual orientation, or disability. The concept of equal opportunity is fundamental to diversity work in the United States and is contrary to concepts of meritocracy and elitism.

Ethnic.   Refers to any group of people who share a common culture. In the United States, the term has been used to describe people whose origins are other than the mainstream Anglo-Saxon Protestant American culture. Historically, Italians, Irish, Jews, Catholics, Poles, Hispanics, and most foreigners have been identified as "ethnic groups." Depending on the context in which it is used, the term may carry both positive and negative connotations.

Ethnocentrism.   The perception that one's own way is best when viewing the world. Our perspective is the standard by which all other perspectives are measured and held to scrutiny.

Global Diversity Management.   Managing global diversity is a proactive, strategic approach that leads to business success. This approach is best defined as the capability of an organization and the individuals within it to effectively manage or be managed, using and maximizing the total workforce potential by having the knowledge, attitude, and skills to identify and use alternative cultural styles and behaviors to achieve the business objective with respect to the national culture(s) and the multiple locations in which they operate.

Heterogeneity.   This is a common subject in business literature research about teams and the elements and characteristics of well-functioning teams. Heterogeneity in a team may refer not only to race, gender, and ethnicity, but also to the attitudes, roles, thinking styles, and personalities of the members.

Inclusion.   Increasingly in greater use, this term has come to mean "encouraging all to work in a cooperative, synergistic, and inclusive way." To practice inclusion is to maximize the resources of a diverse population, leveraging the differences among them and encouraging participation of all. This concept has replaced the "melting pot" idea of the amalgamation and absorption of different cultures into one, implicitly superior, mainstream culture.

Intercultural.   Refers to communication or interaction between people of different cultures. Efforts in intercultural training and communications aim to bridge the differences and eliminate bias among culturally diverse populations. At times, it is used synonymously with such related terms as cross-cultural and multicultural.

Intercultural Communication.   The information exchange between one person and any other source transmitting a message displaying properties of a culture different from the receiver's culture.

Internal Cultural Diversity. Where managers need to deal with foreign-owned transnational companies in their own country, such as a British manager dealing with a Korean manufacturer in the U.K.

Intranational Diversity. Involving the range of cultures within a single nation such as the United States.

Managing Diversity. In managing diversity, organizations can bring about desired change by leveraging different skills and viewpoints. Managing diversity is promoting a proactive and open environment that creates opportunities and values and leverages all differences.

Melting Pot. A 1908 play, *The Melting Pot,* originated this metaphorical term. During the first part of the twentieth century in the United States, it referred to the assimilation and amalgamation of different immigrant and ethnic cultures into one mainstream dominant culture. During the past few years, other metaphors such as "salad bowl" and "mosaic" have emerged. These new concepts deemphasize the amalgamation and stress inclusion while allowing cultural differences to remain and thrive.

Meritocracy. The theory of meritocracy presumes that those who are the best will naturally, through their merits, rise to the top. The theory works as long as all those who have equal merit also have equal opportunity and equal access to the social, educational, and economic goods. Usually, the cultural and political realities of most nations do not provide equality for people who are different from the mainstream.

Minorities/Minority Groups. The terms minority group or minorities have special connotations in today's society. Generally in the United States, the term describes someone of a race other than white, as well as someone of non-European ethnicity, regardless of race. The sociopolitical implication of the term is one of oppression, poverty, lower class, and lack of education. However, as the U.S. population continues to change, the meaning of minority will change, as those who are minorities today will become majorities in the next thirty to fifty years.

Multicultural. Refers to the consideration and respect of all cultures and their values. Progressive thinkers value multiculturalism, whereas cultural and political conservatives consider it a threat to the concept of assimilation, opining that it promotes fragmentation and divisiveness in our society. Because of increasing globalization, the respect and tolerance of other cultures inherent in multiculturalism is very valuable.

Pluralism.   A condition in which numerous distinct ethnic, religious, or cultural groups are present and tolerated within a society and the belief that such a condition is desirable or socially beneficial.

Relativism.   A willingness to consider other persons' or groups' theories and values as equally reasonable as one's own.

Notes

1   Pant, Dipak R. "Anthropology and Business: Reflections on the Business Applications of Cultural Anthropology," Liuc Papers N42, *Serie Economia e Impresa 11*, giugno 1997.

2   Adler, N., et al. "From the Atlantic to the Pacific Century: Cross-Cultural Management Reviewed," 1986 Yearly Review of Management, *Journal of Management*.

3   Lawrence Baytos. *Designing and Implementing Successful Diversity Programs* (Englewood Cliffs, NJ: Prentice Hall, 1995).

4   Cortés, Carlos E. "Beyond Affirmative Action," *Multicultural Review*, March 1996, V1, pp. 16–21.

5   William B. Johnston. "Global Work Force 2000: The New World Labor Market." In Mary C. Gentiles (Ed.), *Differences That Work* (Cambridge, MA: Harvard Business Review Press, 1994).

6   Noel Watts and Andrew Trlin. "Diversity as a Productive Resource: Employment of Immigrants from Non-English-Speaking Backgrounds in New Zealand," *Social Policy Journal of New Zealand*, December 2000, p. 87.

7   Ibid.

8   Cope, B., and M. Kalantzis. *Productive Diversity: A New Australian Model for Work and Management* (Annandale, NSW: Pluto Press, 1997).

9   McNeill, W. "Polyethnicity and National Unity in World History." In A.D. Smith and J. Hutchinson (Eds.), *Nationalism* (London: Oxford University Press, 1994, p. 304).

10   "Diversity Programs Become Valuable Tools for Increased Profitability," *Black Enterprise*, July 1998, V28, N12, p. 120.

11   Glastra, Folke, et al. "Broadening the Scope of Diversity Management: Strategic Implications in the Case of the Netherlands," *Relations Industrielles*, Quebec, Fall 2000.

12   Fleury, Maria Tereza Leme. "The Management of Cultural Diversity: Lessons from Brazilian Companies," *Industrial Management + Data Systems*, Wembley, 1999.

13   Simons, George. *EuroDiversity: A Business Guide to Managing Difference* (London: Butterworth-Heinemann, 2002).

14   Ibid.

15   Taylor, Christine. "Building a Business Case for Diversity," *Canadian Business Review*, Spring 1995, V22, N1, p. 12.

16 Rosenzweig, Philip. "Strategies for Managing Diversity," *Financial Times,* Mastering Global Business (special supplement, n.d.).

17 Solomon, Charlene Marmer. "Global Operations Demand That HR Rethink Diversity," *Personnel Journal,* July 1994, V73, N7, p. 40.

18 From www.astd.org; www.pillsubury.com; www.kraft.com

19 Adler, Nancy. *Competitive Frontiers: Women Managers in a Global Economy* (Oxford, England: Blackwell Publishing, 1994).

20 Friedman, Thomas. *The Lexus and the Olive Tree* (New York: Farrar, Straus and Giroux, 1999, p. 8–9).

21 Simpson, Diane L., and Sybil Evans. "Ready or Not: Embracing the Challenge of Global Diversity." (Internal newsletter, n.d.)

22 Bosrock, Ronald. "Going Truly Global," Business Forum, *Minneapolis Star Tribune,* February 28, 2000, p. 3D.

23 Calori, Roland. "Management European Style," *The Academy of Management Executive,* August 1, 1995, V9, p. 61.

24 Gary, Loren. "Reflections on a Pizza Hut in Yemen," *Harvard Management Update,* April 2001, V6, N4, p. 10.

25 Smadja, Claude. "Forecast 2001/Politics: Wake Up to Globalization: The Sequel Euphoria over the New Economy Is Finished and It's Time to Start Thinking About Global Governance," *Time International,* January 1, 2001, pp. 46+.

26 "Economic Globalization and Culture," Merrill Lynch, www.ml.com/woml/forum/global.htm.

27 Rodrik, Dani. *Has Globalization Gone Too Far?* (Washington, DC: Institute for International Economics, 1997).

28 Bosrock, Ronald. "Going Truly Global," Business Forum, *Minneapolis Star Tribune,* February 28, 2000, p. 3D.

29 Ibid.

30 Kull, Steven. "Culture Wars? How Americans and Europeans View Globalization," *Brookings Review,* Fall 2001, V19, N4, p. 18.

31 "Globalization of Culture," Americans and the World: Public Opinion on International Affairs, www.americans-world.org/digest/global_issues.

32 Govindarajan, Vijay, and Anil Gupta. "Success Is All in the Mindset," *Financial Times,* Mastering Global Business Series.

33 Watson, James L. "China's Big Mac Attack," *Foreign Affairs,* May/June 2000.

34 Wheeler, Michael. "Global Diversity: A Culture-Change Perspective," *Diversity Factor,* Winter 1999.

35 Williamson, O.E. *The Economic Institutions of Capitalism* (New York: Free Press, 1986).

36 Tylor, E.B. *Primitive Culture: Researches into the Development of Mythology, Philosophy, Religion, Language, Art, and Custom* (Vol. 1) (New York: Henry Holt, 1977).

37 Kroeber, A.L., and C. Kluckhohn, C. *Culture: A Critical Review of Concepts and Definitions* (Cambridge, MA: Harvard University Peabody Museum of American Archeology and Ethnology, 1952).

38 Hofstede, G. "National Cultures and Corporate Cultures." In L.A. Samovar and R.E. Porter (Eds.), *Communication Between Cultures* (Belmont, CA: Wadsworth, 1984).

39 *Singapore Management Review,* 2002, V24, N1, pp. 81–88.

40 "Creating Value with Diverse Teams in Global Management," *Organizational Dynamics,* V29, N1, pp. 45–64.

41 Ebrey, Patricia. *Chinese Civilization and Society: A Sourcebook* (New York: Free Press, 1981, pp. xxvii-xxxiii). Reprinted with the permission of The Free Press, a Division of Simon & Schuster Adult Publishing Group.

42 Damen, L. *Culture Learning: The Fifth Dimension on the Language Classroom* (Reading, MA: Addison-Wesley, 1987).

43 Trompenaars, F. *Riding the Waves of Culture: Understanding Diversity in Global Business* (Burr Ridge, IL: Irwin Professional Publishing, 1994).

44 Folke Glastra, et al. "Broadening the Scope of Diversity Management: Strategic Implications in the Case of the Netherlands," *Relations Industrielles,* Quebec, Fall 2000.

45 Fahim, Urusa. "Becoming a Culturally Sensitive Person: An Exploration into the Development of Cultural Sensitivity." Unpublished doctoral dissertation, California Institute of Integral Studies, 2002.

46 Harris, P., and R. Moran. *Managing Cultural Differences* (5th ed.) (Houston, TX: Gulf, 2000).

47 Donlon, J.P. "Values, Culture & Global Effectiveness," *Chief Executive,* April 1998, V133, p. 52(10).

48 Gomez-Mejia, Luis R., and Leslie E. Palich. "Cultural Diversity and the Performance of Multinational Firms," *Journal of International Business Studies,* Second Quarter 1997, V28, N2, pp. 309–335.

49 Gomez-Mejia, L.R., D.B. Balkin, and R. Cardy, 1998. *Human Resources: A Managerial Perspective* (Englewood Cliffs, NJ: Prentice-Hall, 1998).

50 Calori, Roland. "Management European Style," *The Academy of Management Executive,* August 1, 1995, V9, p. 61.

51 Laurent, Andre. "The Cross-Cultural Puzzle of Human Resource Management," *Human Resource Management,* Spring 1986, V25, N1, pp. 91–102.

52 Gomez-Mejia, Luis R., and Leslie E. Palich. "Cultural Diversity and the Performance of Multinational Firms," *Journal of International Business Studies,* Second Quarter 1997, V28, N2, pp. 309–335.

53 Bennett, Milton J. "Towards Ethnorelativism: A Developmental Model of Intercultural Sensitivity." In Michael Paige (Ed.), *Cross-Cultural Orientation: New Conceptualizations and Applications* (Lanham, MD: University Press, 1986).

54 Rosen, R., P. Digh, et al. (Eds.). *Global Literacies: Lessons on Business Leadership and National Cultures* (New York: Simon & Schuster, 2000).

55 Adler, Nancy J. *International Dimensions of Organizational Behavior* (3rd ed.) (Cincinnati, OH: South-Western, 1997).

56 Brake, T., et al. *Doing Business Internationally: The Guide to Cross-Cultural Success* (Burr Ridge, IL: Irwin Professional Publishing, 1995).

57 Rosen, R., and P. Digh. *Global Literacies: Lessons on Business Leadership and National Cultures* (New York: Simon & Schuster, 2000).

58 *Fortune,* April 14, 1997, cited in Diane L. Simpson and Sybil Evans, "Ready or Not: Embracing the Challenge of Global Diversity" (internal newsletter).

59 Rosen, Robert H., Patricia Digh, et al. (Eds.). *Global Literacies: Lessons on Business Leadership and National Cultures* (New York: Simon & Schuster, 2000).

60 Donlon, J.P. "Values, Culture & Global Effectiveness," *Chief Executive,* April 1998, V133, p. 52(10).

61 Ibid.

62 Rosen, Robert, Patricia Digh, et al. *Global Literacies* (New York: Simon & Schuster, 2000, p. 231).

63 "New Breed CEO Markets Locally, Worldwide," *USA Today,* February 8, 1996.

64 Donlon, J.P. "Values, Culture & Global Effectiveness," *Chief Executive,* April 1998, V133, p. 52(10).

65 Stuber, Michael. "Corporate Best Practice: What Some European Organizations Are Doing Well to Manage Culture and Diversity." In George Simons (Ed.), *EuroDiversity: A Business Guide to Managing Difference* (London: Butterworth-Heinemann, 2002).

66 Richard, Orlando C. "Racial Diversity, Business Strategy, and Firm Performance: A Resource-Based View." In T. Cox (Ed.), *Cultural Diversity in Organizations: Theory, Research, and Practice* (San Francisco: Berrett-Koehler, 1994, p. 164).

67 Watson, Warren E., Kannales Kumar, and Larry K. Michaelsen. "Cultural Diversity's Impact on Interaction Processes and Performance: Comparing Homogeneous and Diverse Task Groups," *Academy of Management Journal,* 1993, V36, N3, pp. 590–602.

68 McLeod, P.L., et al. "Ethnic Diversity and Creativity in Small Groups," *Small Group Research,* V27, pp. 246–264.

69 Jackson, S. "Consequences of Group Composition for the Interpersonal Dynamics of Strategic Issue Processing." In P. Shrivastava, A. Huff, and J. Dutton (Eds.), *Advances in Strategic Management* (Vol. 8) (Greenwich, CT: JAI Press, 1992, pp. 345-382).

70 McCann, J., and Jay R. Galbraith. "Interdepartmental Relations." In P.C. Nystrom and W.H. Starbuck (Eds.), *Handbook of Organizational Design: Remodeling Organizations and Their Environments* (Vol. 2) (London: Oxford University Press, 1981, p. 6084).

71 Glick, William H., George P. Huber, C. Chet Miller, D. Harold Doty, and Kathleen M. Sutcliffe. "Studying Changes in Organizational Design and Effectiveness: Retrospective Event Histories and Periodic Assessments," *Organization Science,* 1990, V1, N3, pp. 293–312.

72 Miller, C. Chet. "Cognitive Diversity Within Management Teams: Implications for Strategic Decision Processes and Organizational Performance." Doctoral dissertation (Austin, TX: University of Texas, Graduate School of Business, 1990).

73 Glick, William H., C. Chet Miller, and George P. Huber. "The Impact of Upper-Echelon Diversity on Organizational Performance." In G.P. Huber and W.H. Glick (Eds.), *Organizational Change and Redesign: Ideas and Insights for Improving Performance* (New York: Oxford University Press, 1993), cited in Luis R. Gomez-Mejia and Leslie E. Palich, "Cultural Diversity and the Performance of Multinational Firms," *Journal of International Business Studies,* Second Quarter 1997, V28, N2, pp. 309–335.

74 Cited in G. Pascal Zachary, *The Global Me* (New York: PublicAffairs, 2000).

75 Collier, P. "Doing Well Out of War: An Economic Perspective." In Mats R. Berdel and David M. Malone (Eds.), *Greed and Grievance: Economic Agendas in Civil Wars* (Boulder, CO: Lynne Rienner Publishers, 2000).

76 Raatikainen, P. *Singapore Management Review,* 2002, V24, N1, p. 81.

77 Cited in G. Pascal Zachary, *The Global Me* (New York: PublicAffairs, 2000, p. 222).

CHAPTER 2

What Is Global Diversity?

Over the last forty years, the word "diversity" has become part of the language and management of North American firms and increasingly of European-headquartered corporations as well. However, the rise in globalization requires us to expand our vision of what "diversity" means in the workplace.

When used to address this new business reality, the term "global diversity" does not yet have a broadly shared or universally understood meaning. For some it denotes race and gender, for others it means accepting all things "that make us different," and for others it means ethnicity and culture.

Often, those varying interpretations stem from the user's national context, political agenda, dominant culture, or minority group identity—making the term "global diversity" even more complex. For example, many people in the United States connect issues of diversity to human rights and civil liberty; Europeans may connect them to cultural heritage and language differences; many in Latin countries focus their diversity dialogues around the innate dignity of the individual; and many Asian societies interpret diversity in terms of collective accountability. This chapter will examine this dilemma and suggest a new model, the Six Spheres of Inclusion (SSI) Model. It will also provide tools to apply the model to global organizational development as well as interpersonal assessments. Last, it will provide a process to evaluate your company and its current stage of global diversity management.

EVOLVING DOMESTIC DIVERSITY MODELS

Domestic diversity models often examine exclusion and inclusion in terms of who is left out or deprived of opportunity. For example, in the early stages of diversity evolution in the United States, these included factors such as race, gender, and sexual orientation. Each nation has its own historical context—that shapes its reactions to diversity and helps determine what constitutes an injustice, a violation, or an affront. What is considered discriminatory in one nation may be labeled as a national cultural preference or style in another. How do professionals committed to diversity evaluate this range of responses?

Such segmentation often reflects the history of a specific nation. In the United States, diversity initiatives began in the military and the YWCA in the 1940s. It the 1960s, U.S. corporations, legislators, and their respective constituents addressed the fact that the "American dream" was inaccessible to some citizens—primarily African Americans, who were excluded from many aspects of social and corporate life.

At that time, affirmative action and equal employment opportunity (EEO) programs were seen as appropriate devices to address inequities faced by African Americans as well as the inherent moral imperative facing the United States regarding the civil rights of all individuals. This approach initially focused on compliance to quotas. While compliance is not the only diversity focus in corporate America today, it still exists in the United States and is gaining momentum in Europe. In London, for example, police services' hiring quotas have been established and the BBC has declared quotas to hire minorities in proportions exceeding the proportions in the United Kingdom's population.

In addition to racial issues, gender has been a consistent theme in domestic diversity efforts. In the early part of the twentieth century, women's suffrage in the United States provided a legislative response to a clear diversity injustice— the inability of women to vote—yet only recently have other gender inequities been more fully addressed. In other countries, the same is true. It is surprising that only in August 2001, after twenty-six years of debate, the Brazilian Congress approved a legal code that for the first time in the country's history makes women equal to men in the eyes of the law.

In the United States in the 1970s, women's issues and the interests of other minority groups expanded the parameters of diversity to include not only women but Latinos, Native Americans, Asians, and dimensions such as physical ability and age, among others. This broadened definition of diversity in the United States gained legislative and moral clout with the passage of Title VII of the Civil Rights Act of 1964, protecting individuals against employment discrimination on the basis of race and color as well as national origin, sex, or religion.

However, Title VII governs U.S.-headquartered companies in their domestic operations and some global subsidiaries, but does not travel well abroad. Legislation in other nations responds differently to inclusivity in the workplace as well as to whether the country in question is more intent on maintaining societal homogeneity or building the heterogeneity that the economy of the world increasingly demands.

In the 1990s and into the 2000s, rapid internationalization requires a fresh look at diversity. Rolling out a U.S.-centric diversity program designed for the needs of one nation will not address the complexity of a multicultural, global workforce. Simplistic definitions related to parity and individual rights may not apply in counties that prescribe gender definitions or hierarchical societies. A new model is necessary, one that incorporates new perspectives of civilization and nationality as tools to use global resources. The Six Spheres of Inclusion Model is an attempt to fill this void.

SIX SPHERES OF INCLUSION MODEL

The Six Spheres of Inclusion[1] (SSI) Model is a tool that helps us to understand what is at play in any global diversity encounter, either interpersonal or organizational. It allows us to break out of a domestic diversity bias that might thwart the broader development of employees and the organization itself.

This tool identifies six key areas that are core to global cross-cultural diversity interchanges—whether in a performance review, a sales call, a multicultural presentation, a team meeting, or a virtual conference call. In the SSI Model, six dimensions of global diversity will be identified: *civilizational orientation, national identification, organizational factors, societal formation, individual identification,* and *individual personality/style.*

Civilizational Orientation

The outer layer of the SSI Model shown in the figure focuses on eight civilizations that are most significant in global business today: Western (European and North American), Middle Eastern (Islamic and Judaic), Confucian or Sinic (China and Chinese-influenced subsocieties), Japanese, Latin American, Slavic/Orthodox (Eastern European and Russian), Hindu and Sub-Saharan African.

Understanding corporate global diversity begins when an employee identifying himself or herself as influenced by a core civilization or, as Samuel Huntington notes, "The 'we' of our civilization, against the largest 'them' of another civilization."[2]

Our individual civilizational heritage shapes how we understand life. It contextualizes relationships with others, especially those we perceive as different.

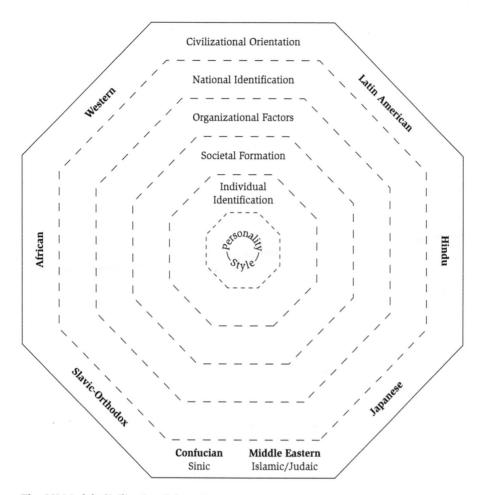

The SSI Model: Civilization Orientation

Source: Adapted from Lee Gardenswartz and Anita Rowe, *Diverse Teams at Work* (Homewood, IL: Business One Irwin, 1994); M. Loden and J. Rosen, *Workforce America* (Homewood, IL: Business One Irwin, 1991); Samuel P. Huntington, *The Clash of Civilization and the Remaking of World Order* (New York: Simon & Schuster, 1996); and F. Trompenaars and C. Hampden-Turner, *Riding the Waves of Culture* (2nd ed.) (New York: McGraw-Hill, 1998).

To be inclusive of the heritage of others requires moving beyond the artifacts of culture—art, literature, music, architecture, and food, to name a few—to accepting the diversity of thought, belief, and values in people who may advocate very different approaches to human existence.

The man who identifies himself in Asia as a "Westerner," the woman who claims her Asian heritage in Brazil, the African who affirms his tribal heritage in Europe, or the Japanese who speaks to an American and indicates that the American will never understand Japan are all people acknowledging the civilization with which they most identify while also signaling their desire to affirm interpersonal civilizational differences.

The tragic terrorist attacks of September 11, 2001, in the United States in which thousands were murdered, as well as other historical crusades, intifada, revolutions, riots, and mass genocides are committed and rationalized, at least in part, because of the inability to understand, acknowledge, or even value the deep civilizational heritage of others. These frequent eruptions and conflicts press the need for a reconciliation process that values the diversity of civilizations. It also goes beyond reconciliation to learning from others whose values and beliefs will bring positive value and enrichment. Why is it we can be enriched by experiencing another civilizations art, let us say an African Black Madonna, yet not equally be enriched by the inclusion of African civilizational values in our lives or corporations?

At the corporate level, confrontations that arise when civilizational mindsets collide—as well as our inability to leverage the strength inherent within civilizations—can result in lost income, depreciated corporate capital, and the loss of talented staff.

National Identification

While values and beliefs shape civilizations, geopolitical and natural boundaries define nations, creating sometimes artificial, but very real, barriers between people who share a common belief system, that is, civilization. Those boundaries, whether they are rivers, walls, or passport gates, signal a departure from one political, economic, and social state and entrance into another.

As citizens of a nation-state—even if we belong to a subgroup within that country—we regularly mirror to varying degrees the dominant beliefs, behaviors, and styles of the nation itself, as seen in the figure. We learn its anthem, its governmental process, the ways to confront those governmental processes, its language(s), and cultural norms. To a large degree, nations demonstrate a national mindset or way of living in the world that is unique to that territory.

The research of Fons Trompenaars and Geert Hofstede[3] has shown that national orientation affects the way we do business. Political and economic structures, wealth distribution, whether we identify primarily as an individual or as a member of a group, and social as well as functional hierarchy all have an impact on national culture and consequently on the international workplace. These national dimensions of diversity create inclusionary patterns between individuals, work units, and functions. They are legitimate areas of diversity that require reconciliation.

National identity still matters, even in a global environment. Many members of the European Union share a history and its unifying Western civilization, yet the resurgent cultural behavior of countries like France and Germany signal that nationalism is still strong and needs to be respected. In the same way, although

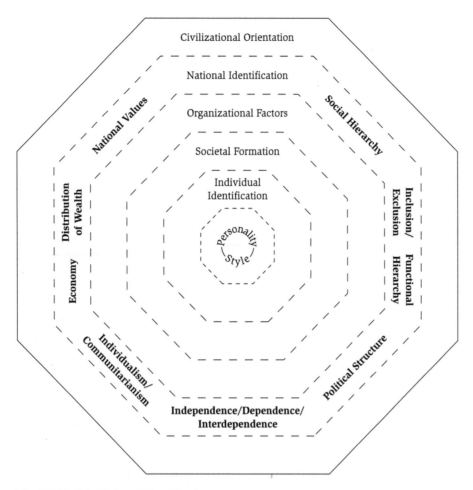

The SSI Model: National Identification

Source: Adapted from Lee Gardenswartz and Anita Rowe, *Diverse Teams at Work* (Homewood, IL: Business One Irwin, 1994); M. Loden and J. Rosen, *Workforce America* (Homewood, IL: Business One Irwin, 1991); Samuel P. Huntington, *The Clash of Civilization and the Remaking of World Order* (New York: Simon & Schuster, 1996); and F. Trompenaars and C. Hampden-Turner, *Riding the Waves of Culture* (2nd ed.) (New York: McGraw-Hill, 1998).

the Association of Southeast Asian Nations (ASEAN) nations seek stronger cross-national economic relationships, national pressure between Singapore and Malaysia continues to demonstrate that nationalism plays an important role, even among relatively young nations of similar civilizations. Mastering an understanding of national identity is important for the resolution of global diversity issues.

Multicultural nations formed voluntarily by immigration, such as Canada and New Zealand, or involuntarily because of exploitation or political upheavals, such as the United States, Australia, Singapore, Israel, India, and Pakistan, have all attempted to achieve cultural respect between diverse citizens who profess opposing social beliefs and cultural patterns. They have done so successfully at times and chaotically at other times.

To begin the international differentiation process, carefully consider how nations vary according to the following dimensions:

- The degree of independence-dependence-interdependence of their citizens and their relationships with other nations in their region of the world;

- The inclusion and exclusion processes for minorities, be they ethnic, racial, religious, or any other subset;

- The establishment or not of interpersonal and intergroup hierarchy;

- The strength of the political structure and the process of influence;

- The range of formal and informal social hierarchy among its citizens;

- The balance of individualism and collectivism among people;

- The distribution of wealth and sharing of national assets;

- The structure and purpose of the national economy; and

- Mechanisms to reinforce—and in some cases enforce—national identity, such as governmental communication, public relations campaigns, or propaganda.

Each subcategory highlights a potential national dilemma that must be addressed. For citizens within a nation, how does the inherent conflict become resolved? Externally, in examining multiple nations, how do we cross-reference international dilemmas to reconcile them? The SSI Model allows us to make those comparisons for dialogue and resolution. The global diversity dilemma of a corporate manager is the degree to which we include or exclude the contributing values and beliefs of a different nation.

Organizational Factors[4]

A core premise serves as the framework for this book's approach to global diversity. To effectively address global diversity issues, organizations must understand how having diversity in their workforce and in the way they think and approach strategic issues will bring greater value to the company and its stakeholders. In addition to civilizational orientation and national identification, organizational factors impact how diversity is used, as shown in the figure. Global diversity is the search for value drawn from the richness of the human capital of an organization's employees.

Understanding this informs our approaches to organizational dimensions of diversity such as management status, work location, union affiliation, divi-

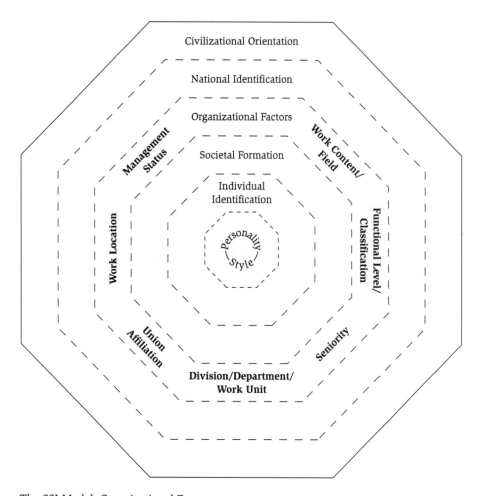

The SSI Model: Organizational Factors

Source: Adapted from Lee Gardenswartz and Anita Rowe, *Diverse Teams at Work* (Homewood, IL: Business One Irwin, 1994); M. Loden and J. Rosen, *Workforce America* (Homewood, IL: Business One Irwin, 1991); Samuel P. Huntington, *The Clash of Civilization and the Remaking of World Order* (New York: Simon & Schuster, 1996); and F. Trompenaars and C. Hampden-Turner, *Riding the Waves of Culture* (2nd ed.) (New York: McGraw-Hill, 1998).

sion/department/work unit, function/level/classification, seniority, and work content or field. Are some divisions favored in budget deliberations? Is an engineering mindset preferred over a legal one? Do the judgments of nonnational staff carry more weight than the judgments of local nationals? Is input solicited from those at lower levels in the hierarchy? Are all employees, regardless of global location, able to have equal opportunity to advance within the corporation?

Domestic diversity efforts have long identified these organizational dimensions. They are seen as areas in which exclusion or inclusion can occur to the

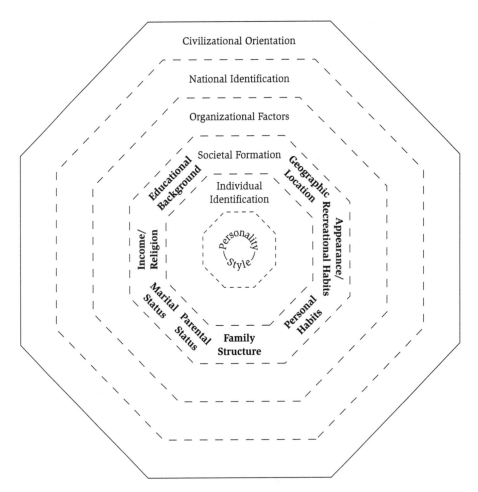

The SSI Model: Societal Formation

Source: Adapted from Lee Gardenswartz and Anita Rowe, *Diverse Teams at Work* (Homewood, IL: Business One Irwin, 1994); M. Loden and J. Rosen, *Workforce America* (Homewood, IL: Business One Irwin, 1991); Samuel P. Huntington, *The Clash of Civilization and the Remaking of World Order* (New York: Simon & Schuster, 1996); and F. Trompenaars and C. Hampden-Turner, *Riding the Waves of Culture* (2nd ed.) (New York: McGraw-Hill, 1998).

detriment of workers and the organization. In a global context, resolving these organizational dimensions provides an opportunity to create diversity programs, policies, and structures that bridge the values of the civilizations and nations.

In the SSI Model, the organization serves as mediator between the broader diversity influences (such as civilization and national identity) and those personal diversity dimensions that employees bring to the workplace. The latter are the result of their social formation and individual identification. Because of its historical development, a global company may be biased by one national style and civilizational influence to the exclusion, whether consciously or unconsciously, of other national-based and civilization-based employees' values. A global company may recognize that its corporate success is solely based on its civilizational affiliations. It can become aware that as an organization it has dismissed alternative cultural solutions because of civilizational or national bias that, if implemented, could provide competitive business advantage.

Societal Formation[5]

Many of us are socialized in comparatively mono-cultural institutions that both unconsciously and consciously shape our values, attitudes, beliefs, and behaviors about how to live in the world. These belief orientations also shape how we perceive ourselves, how we perceive and deal with others, how we believe that others perceive us, and the tolerance others have for accepting (or rejecting) our values and our beliefs.

This sphere of the SSI Model, as shown in the figure, outlines external socialization factors that make a difference in the workplace, such as economic class, caste systems, literacy levels, education standards, leisure, recreation, and personal habits, the balance between work and life, language, religion, spirituality, location, family, marital roles and responsibility, appearance, and style.

Built into our socializing processes is the reality of bias and exclusion. Often, it is only when we cross a border or work in an international team that we are acutely aware of the impact of our ethnocentric socialization legacy. Same-sex partners given an international assignment may be acceptable in one's home context, tolerated in another, such as the United Kingdom, and persecuted in a Middle Eastern environment. Attitudes toward change are equally driven by social formation. Either accepting the "will of God" or one's predetermined position in life or radically driving change in one's life are beliefs that are supported—or disavowed—by social institutions. Many of these are so deeply rooted that we cannot easily identify them and their influence on our workplace thinking. What is the appropriate role of women in the workplace? How do different religions influence work responsibilities? Our societies directly and indirectly teach these answers and many more.

Successfully addressing global diversity requires us to decipher social traditions. They are less vestiges of ethnic lineage of our country of origin and our cherished civilization and are more current and justified expressions of personal and collective identity. The SSI Model provides a catalyst for identifying difference across social norms, increasing communication across them, and allowing organizations to support the process of accepting, valuing, and reconciling difference.

Individual Identification

People throughout history have been striving for integration, although the definition of that "integration" may vary from culture to culture. For example, from the Western perspective of Abraham Maslow[6] self-actualization is viewed as the

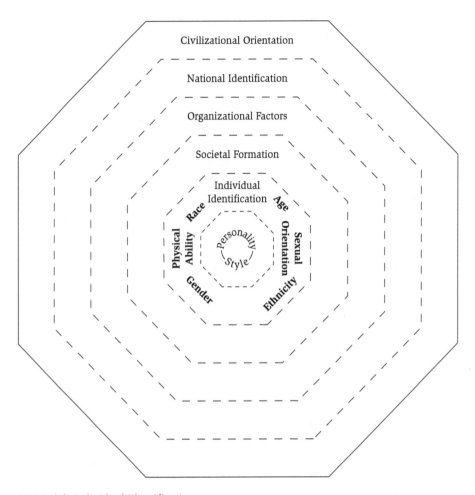

SSI Model: Individual Identification

Source: Adapted from Lee Gardenswartz and Anita Rowe, *Diverse Teams at Work* (Homewood, IL: Business One Irwin, 1994); M. Loden and J. Rosen, *Workforce America* (Homewood, IL: Business One Irwin, 1991); Samuel P. Huntington, *The Clash of Civilization and the Remaking of World Order* (New York: Simon & Schuster, 1996); and F. Trompenaars and C. Hampden-Turner, *Riding the Waves of Culture* (2nd ed.) (New York: McGraw-Hill, 1998).

pinnacle of personal integration. An Asian perspective may focus less on the "self" and more on the goal of "responsibility to others" as a means to actualization. The key to diversity integration is that it is a process by which we identify ourselves for who we are and the very "givens" that constitute our identity.

A "given" is a quality or characteristic that is an outcome of birth and the natural developmental process. Six of these "given" categories are significant in discussing global diversity: race, gender, ethnicity, sexual orientation, physical ability, and age.

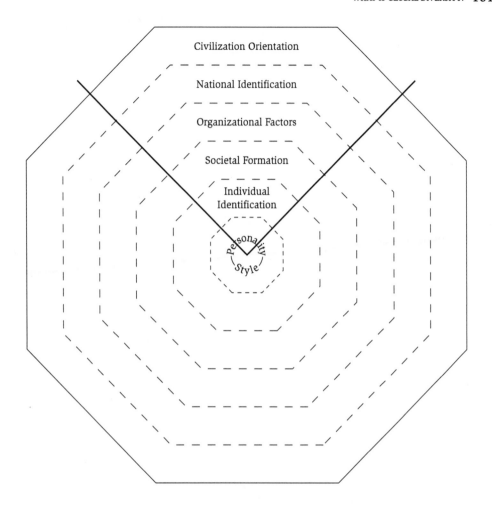

An individual SSI Profile consists of the intersection of
- The values of the civilization that surrounded you,
- The behaviors rewarded in your national culture,
- The norms and standards of your corporate culture,
- The forces of society that formed and taught you,
- The orientation and attributes of your birth, and
- The limits of your personality.

SSI Model: Individual Personality/Style Profile

Source: Adapted from Lee Gardenswartz and Anita Rowe, *Diverse Teams at Work* (Homewood, IL: Business One Irwin, 1994); M. Loden and J. Rosen, *Workforce America* (Homewood, IL: Business One Irwin, 1991); Samuel P. Huntington, *The Clash of Civilization and the Remaking of World Order* (New York: Simon & Schuster, 1996); and F. Trompenaars and C. Hampden-Turner, *Riding the Waves of Culture* (2nd ed.) (New York: McGraw-Hill, 1998).

How we react to and address these internal dimensions of diversity has a lot to do with how we have been socialized—we interpret these "givens" from our own national or civilizational perspective and the exclusiveness of our socialization processes. Core to global diversity work is the ability for individuals to affirm their own identity and core assumptions while not being threatened by the presence of another individual whose expression of the "givens" is opposite. Few employees in global companies are so gifted to "know" the contextual realities of globally diverse co-workers.

Personality/Style

The deepest and most intangible level of diversity within the SSI Model is the personal integrative dimension, as shown in the figure. It supports interpersonal relationships identified with behavioral patterns such as flexibility, adaptability, tolerance, and risk taking.

Psychic integration, identified in the West by Erik H. Erikson,[7] is an important aspect of individual identity as well as the final stage of adult development. In the case of a global diversity model, these integrated personal attributes, either inherent at birth or learned, support our ability to interact with people whom we identify as different. A person described by others as being inflexible, rigid, intolerant, and risk adverse would face serious obstacles in dealing with global diversity. This does not mean that in their personal lives people cannot have set values, beliefs, and behaviors that may be counter to those of the organization or people of other nations and civilizations. They can, but within the globally diverse corporate setting, their behavior must demonstrate openness to others and interest to dialogue for the best interests of the organization and its mission.

The SSI Model brings together six key areas for employees to consider when working in a global or international company. The roots of our global diversity success or failure are at the intersection of the values of the civilizations that surround us; the behaviors that are rewarded or punished in our national cultures; the norms and standards of our corporate culture; the forces of society that formed and taught us; the orientation and attributes of our birth; and the inherent scope of our personality.

Create your own SSI profile. Review each of the dimensions and its subsets and decide what aspects of the model capture the diversity that you bring to the workplace. That combination of diversity descriptors makes you unique and identifies the value you bring to the organization. Begin also to create SSI profiles for colleagues and use them as tools for reconciliation.

The tools that follow are designed to enable global diversity practitioners and others to move beyond diversity perspectives that used a mono-focused lens on race, gender, sexual orientation, age, and other ethnocentric approaches to organizational change. This book's tools bring the positive value of global diversity forward. This approach does not mean that the goals of other approaches have been met. Nor does it deny the reality that many people continue to face unresolved diversity expectations and discriminatory situations. They do. Managers and human resource professionals need to continue to address those issues with their national contexts as well as move toward a greater reconciliation of values, beliefs, and behaviors that reflects the new global reality.

By using the SSI Model, the multiple levels of diversity will become clearer. A major U.S.-headquartered electronics firm suspected that their corporate culture had some bearing on their female Malay Islamic employees as they observed changes in their relationships in the workplace and suggestions of changes in their homes. Can using the SSI Model help them understand this dilemma? How do professionals identify the core diversity elements that need to be reconciled? Were the managers seeing the impact of the differences in civilizations between an Islamic society and the predominately Western U.S. corporate culture? Were they looking at the reconciliation of the national preferred style of individualism of the managers in contrast with the strong Malaysian and Islamic orientation to collectivism of the employees? Was it an issue of the isolation of the women in certain roles and functions in the manufacturing process? Was the conflict based on the inability of Islamic husbands to deal with their newly empowered wives who could not leave their empowerment at the factory door? Was it a gender or family role issue that was being challenged? On the other hand, was it that when the women discovered the power of risk taking, they wished to shift it to other areas of their lives? Using the SSI Model, we can see that all these elements are simultaneously occurring and need to be processed in a thoughtful and integrated manner.

In using the exercises in this and the chapters that follow, keep the SSI Model in mind. Each exercise will focus on the chapter's theme, that is, communication, team building, performance management, and so on. The individuals or trainees who will be using the exercises will each have different SSI profiles. Those profiles affect the way they talk, how their teams are formed, and outcomes of their work.

Suggestions for Using "Global Assessment for Inclusivity"

Objectives

- To understand which dimensions of global diversity have an impact on your organization's operation
- To identify aspects of global diversity that may be most relevant to your organization in different parts of the world

Intended Audience

- Members of any employee group exploring global diversity issues
- Any manager, facilitator, internal/external consultant, HR professional, or trainer charged with the task of creating a global diversity initiative

Global Assessment for Inclusivity

Directions: Review the SSI Model with its six dimensions and each dimension's subcategories. Consider the degree to which your company needs to address that specific issue or in some cases reconcile a dilemma. Consider how each dimension and subcategory supports the inclusion of staff or creates exclusion. If there is a high degree of exclusion surrounding that category, mark that category with an "H" for high; if there is a moderate degree of exclusion occurring, mark an "M" for moderate; and if there is a low degree of exclusion, mark an "L" for low.

	Global Organi- zation	North America	Latin America	Europe	Middle East	Africa	Asia/ Pacific
Civilizational Orientation							
Latin American							
Slavic Orthodox							
Japanese							
Islamic/Judaic							
Confucian/Sinic							
Hindu							
African							
Western							
National Identification							
Interdependence/ Dependence/ Interdependence							
Inclusion/Exclusion							
Functional Hierarchy							
Political Structure							
Social Hierarchy							
Individual/Collectivism							
Distribution of Wealth							

Global Assessment for Inclusivity (continued)

	Global Organization	North America	Latin America	Europe	Middle East	Africa	Asia/ Pacific
Economy							
National Identity							
Organizational Factors							
Management Status							
Work Location							
Union Affiliation							
Division/Department							
Functional Level							
Seniority							
Work Content/Field							
Societal Formation							
Educational Background							
Marital Status							
Family Structure							
Parental Status							
Appearance							
Recreational Habits							
Personal Habits							
Religion							
Income							
Geographic Location							

Global Assessment for Inclusivity (continued)

	Global Organization	North America	Latin America	Europe	Middle East	Africa	Asia/Pacific
Individual Identification							
Gender							
Age							
Physical Ability							
Sexual Orientation							
Race							
Ethnicity							
Personality/ Style							
Flexible							
Adaptable							
Tolerant							
Risk Taking							

Source: Adapted from Lee Gardenswartz and Anita Rowe, *Diverse Teams at Work* (Homewood, IL: Business One Irwin, 1994); M. Loden and J. Rosen, *Workforce America* (Homewood, IL: Business One Irwin, 1991); Samuel P. Huntington, *The Clash of Civilization and the Remaking of World Order* (New York: Simon & Schuster, 1996); and F. Trompenaars and C. Hampden-Turner, *Riding the Waves of Culture* (2nd ed.) (New York: McGraw-Hill, 1998).

Time

- 45 minutes

Materials

- An overhead transparency and copies of "Global Assessment for Inclusivity"
- Enlargement of the handout (18"x 24" blowup)
- Chart paper and markers

Directions

- Discuss and define each of the six dimensions of the SSI Model.

- Ask participants to scan each region of the world and identify which dimensions create exclusion in the organization. Remind the participants that each subcategory is a dilemma that needs to be resolved.
- Divide members into small groups. Ask them to compare their individual profiles. Using an 18" x 24" wall chart blowup of the tool, use different colored markers to plot individual profiles. (This makes a great visual and helps people see the profile very quickly.)
- Come back to the whole group for discussion.

Questions for Discussion/Consideration

- What examples, similarities, and differences were most notable among group members?
- What surprises, if any, did you find in the responses of any members of your group?
- When you look more closely at the differences, what impact do they or might they have on the development of a global company?
- How can we make those differences work to support the company? What are the steps of reconciliation?
- Where does our organization not function effectively?
- In what areas can we do a better job in leveraging the benefits of diversity?

Cultural Considerations

- Identify the national and civilizational heritage of your examples. Are there national preferred values that enable diversity to be more successful?
- Words such as "diversity" and "empowerment" have a wide range of meaning and interpretation. Continually process respondents' understanding of these terms. Record those differences.
- Have conversations that lead to a more Eastern contemplative mode and less direct communication. One way might be discussing examples of situations where differences in various dimensions were experienced. Also try using a more pragmatic Western approach by asking participants how they will use this tool with their groups.

Suggestions for Using "Personal Assessment for Inclusivity"

Objectives

- To understand which dimensions of the SSI Model are most relevant to each participant in the workplace
- To identify aspects of global diversity that may be most relevant in creating a difference in an individual's behavior and commitment

Personal Assessment for Inclusivity

Directions: Describe a personal example of exclusion that you have experienced or observed. For example, "I have seen individuals passed over for promotion because English is not their native language. Vague comments are made about communication skills." My Incident: [Say who, what, why, when, and describe the outcome]. The worksheet is filled in as an example.

Personal Assessment for Inclusivity Worksheet

	My Perception and Values	**Others' Perception and Values**	**Areas to Reconcile**
Civilization Orientation	Western	Western	Degree to which core values are mutually shared
National Identification	Born in United Kingdom	Born in France but lived in U.K. for the past twenty years	Balancing current political/economic reality with stereo-types
Organizational Dimensions	One year's experience in company	Ten years' experience in company	Degree to which "loyalty" is rewarded versus opportunity based on competency
Societal Formation	Educated in U.K. public system (the private school system of England)	Primary and secondary school in France, University of Manchester	Balancing socializa-tion and schooling for exclusion or inclusion
Individual Identification	English heritage for generation; married into established family; protestant	Married to a Welshman; children bi-cultural—French and English spoken in home; Catholic	Balancing traditional and evolving family roles and structure
Personality/Style	Conservative	Risk taker	Tolerance toward change and ambiguity

Source: Adapted from Lee Gardenswartz and Anita Rowe, *Diverse Teams at Work* (Homewood, IL: Business One Irwin, 1994); M. Loden and J. Rosen, *Workforce America* (Homewood, IL: Business One Irwin, 1991); Samuel P. Huntington, *The Clash of Civilization and the Remaking of World Order* (New York: Simon & Schuster, 1996); and F. Trompenaars and C. Hampden-Turner, *Riding the Waves of Culture* (2nd ed.) (New York: McGraw-Hill, 1998).

- To create strategies for reconciling global diversity disconnects
- To practice using the SSI Model to coach a person in global diversity conflict resolution

Intended Audience

- Members of any employee group exploring global diversity issues
- Any manager, facilitator, internal/external consultant, HR professional, or trainer charged with the task of creating a global diversity initiative

Time

- 60 minutes

Materials

- An overhead transparency and copies of "Personal Assessment for Inclusivity"
- Chart paper and markers

Directions

- Discuss and define each of the six dimensions of the SSI Model and how they affect personal and professional behavior.
- Ask participants to reflect on their work experience and select one specific event where they experienced or observed a global diversity disconnect.
- Request that they write out the story of the event. Ask them to be specific: who was involved, what they did, why they did it, when it happened, to what extent they responded, and what the outcome was?
- Have each person find someone to talk to. Ask one member of the pair to talk about his or her global diversity incident. Have the listener use the Personal Assessment for Inclusivity worksheet to record what is being said.
- When the communicator has finished, discuss strategies that could have been used to reconcile the difference.
- When one member is finished, switch.
- Come back to the whole group for discussion of core trends and resolution strategies.

Questions for Discussion/Consideration

- What examples, similarities, and differences were most notable among group members?
- What resolution strategies were suggested?
- What surprises, if any, did you find in the responses of any of your group?

- When you look more closely at the differences, what impact do they or might they have on the development of a global company?
- How can we make those differences work in your favor? In the favor of the company?

Cultural Considerations

- Identify the national and civilizational heritage of your examples. Are there national preferred values that enable diversity to be more successful?
- This exercise works best with groups that are international because that will often result in a more open and fruitful exchange of experiences around regional and cultural differences. Mono-cultural groups may not have the scope or insight to give examples, even when their company is global or international. In such a situation, prepare ahead and use a real case from the organization for analysis.

Caveats, Considerations, and Variations

- This exercise can be used to identify diversity between co-workers in a one-on-one relationship such as manager/subordinate and in teams or work units. It is a good tool to continually monitor interpersonal diversity.

THE STAGES OF GLOBALIZATION: APPLYING A DIVERSITY MODEL

In a world in which European offices are powered by Japanese semiconductors set in American computers housed in Thai teak office furniture that rests on Iranian rugs, it is clear that the world is increasingly our corporate environments and that we cannot position ourselves in isolation from others. Even so, not all corporations are global—and not all will become global. Before evaluating or developing your global diversity program, it is important to understand the stage of globalization that currently exists in your company as well as your desired corporate diversity goal.

Managing global diversity requires an expanded paradigm and additional models. Understanding the drivers and stages of the organization's global development as well as the various diversity dimensions involved are critical beginning steps in formulating an effective global strategy as well as in identifying and addressing obstacles. In reading the following descriptions of the four stages of global organization,[8] consider where your company best fits and plot it on the Continuum of Globalization and on the Continuum of Diversity Development. This assessment will be useful when filling out the "Global Diversity Organizational Development" tool later.

Domestic	Import/Export	International	Global

Continuum of Globalization

Source: Nancy J. Adler, *International Dimensions of Organizational Behavior* (4th ed.) (Cincinnati, OH: South-Western Publishing, 2000).

Domestic Focused Organizations

Most domestic enterprises operate, produce, and sell within a home marketplace and do not have a true global focus. While a manager in this type of company might have cross-border employees, the overriding perspective is national, with primary attention on compliance to national law as far as diversity goes.

Global diversity is still important, even in domestic companies, because the corporation must understand the different patterns of social and professional behavior that can be expected from potential international customers, global peers, transnational alliance partners, or the nonnational workforce employed by the company. While primarily domestic in focus, managers in these companies also need cross-cultural knowledge to understand international threats to their markets. For example, a small craft artisan, Wild Wood of West Virginia, who employed ten people in making a unique rocking wooden horse sculpture lost market share to the Chinese Taiwanese manufacturer who entered the market with a "slightly" different sculpture and took customers away. Domestic firms need to scan globally. The Internet has helped this process.

Import/Export Enterprises

Import/export businesses focus primarily on domestic markets, but buy or sell materials from other countries. This type of corporate structure usually works with local nationals hired on a contract basis and responsible for the exchange of goods and services. These in-country corporate agents represent the hiring or home corporation, manage a small in-country office or operation, and typically follow their own country's approach to diversity issues, which may or may not align with the corporation's national perspective.

In the United States, and particularly in the apparel industry or any other industry that uses offshore manufacturing labor, this type of company is a major source of diversity confrontation due to the role of women in the workplace, work/life balance, sexual harassment, and child labor laws. Many investors in the parent U.S. corporation are critical of export contractors and subcontractors and increasingly include diversity requirements as part of the contracting and negotiating process. Since much of this business is contractual and governed by home country representatives and laws, it is difficult to create sustainable national change related to diversity to address their interest. The choice is withdrawing from that contract, as Levi Strauss did in China over issues of human rights.

International Enterprises

International enterprises generally have production and sales activities both in the home country and outside their national borders; however, they are highly influenced by the corporate culture of the home-country headquarters. While there is an interchange of staff across borders, the overall tone and definition of the organization is established from the home country with its preferred national business style, whether that center be in Stuttgart, Seoul, or Saginaw.

When headquartered in the United States, these companies demonstrate a strong bias to "roll out" their U.S.-centric domestic diversity program to their international units. There is minimal attention to redefining diversity to address the new trans-border context. Clearly, models of diversity built on the power and confrontational models forged from a history of race and gender conflict, as in the United States, have experienced difficulty moving across borders to countries that do not share that historical context nor that approach to social change. Equally true, a company forged primarily from a homogeneous national perspective, like Japan or Korea, might have difficulty in absorbing and using the diversity within their American and Western workforce. This was demonstrated when the Japanese automotive industry entered into European and American manufacturing contexts.

Global Enterprises

Truly global organizations have planning, production, and sales operations in multiple countries that are coordinated as an integrated entity. By definition, these organizations consistently use national, cultural, and personal diversity to run their businesses. Few companies begin as global entities. Many that have become global retain residual programs, patterns, and processes that maintain a cultural bias, creating the need for tools and processes to help them become globally diverse.

The following exercise, "Stages of Corporate Development and Global Diversity," is a tool to audit your company's stages of global development, its diversity issues and initiatives. Most respondents will find that generally several developmental areas are occurring simultaneously. It is important for global diversity practitioners and managers to understand the diversity issues that each stage of global development demands within their company

Suggestions for Using
"Stages of Corporate Development and Global Diversity"

Objectives

- To demonstrate that global diversity is a concern that needs to be addressed in all organizations, regardless of their current level of development

- To provide an organizational tool to assess a corporation's current level of global development
- To analyze different levels of diversity that the company needs to use to function effectively in a global environment
- To assess the appropriateness of current programs and identify alternative programs required to be more successful as a global company that excels in the use of diversity

Intended Audience

- Members of any human resource staff or management group exploring global diversity and its organizational implications
- Any manager, facilitator, internal/external consultant, HR professional, or trainer charged with the task of creating a global diversity initiative

Time

- 45 minutes

Materials

- An overhead transparency and copies of "Stages of Corporate Development and Global Diversity"
- Chart paper and markers

Directions

- Review the four stages of global development, highlighting the diversity issues in each stage.
- Divide the participants into groups of six.
- Invite the participants to identify which stage of development best describes their organization.
- Ask each group to discuss the diversity programs that exist in their company and their relationship to the current organizational stage.
- Ask participants to chart those programs or aspects of existing programs that are helping and those that are hindering in a global context.
- Then ask each group to create a list of programs that are needed in order to be successful on a global scale.

Questions for Discussion/Consideration

- Is your company global or international? How does that designation make a difference in how you deal with diversity?
- What have you discovered about the breadth and depth of your company's diversity programs, policy, and structure? What additional suggestions need to be made?

Stages of Corporate Development and Global Diversity

Directions: After reviewing the stages of development and their associated diversity issues, list in the last column all the programs, policies, and processes that your company has instituted to support global diversity.

Stage	Definition	Diversity Issues	Examples in Your Organization
Domestic Focused	Operate, produce, and sell within a home country marketplace	Different domestic ethnic markets Work style and language differences Cross-border market intelligence	HR provides language lessons in English and Spanish to facilitate communication in first language Lessons only at lunch time and not helpful
Import/Export Enterprises	Operate in and focus primarily on domestic market while buying from or selling to other countries	Cross-cultural business practices (negotiation, contracting, legal) Language differences Alignment of local practice with HQ policy and practice Public relations and image management	
International Enterprises	Production and sales activities in home country and other countries with a headquarter-centric approach	Cross-cultural values, norms, and business practices Language differences Differences in HR laws Cross-border employee exchange Workforce development	

Stages of Corporate Development and Global Diversity (continued)

Stage	Definition	Diversity Issues	Examples in Your Organization
Global Enterprises	Planning, production, and sales around the world using an integrated strategy	Cross-border systems integration (HR, legal, operations, sales, marketing, and so forth) Global leadership development, worldwide staffing, and career movement Communication (virtual and real language) Balancing the corporate culture with national and regional perspectives	

Source: Developed from the work of Nancy J. Adler, *International Dimension of Organizational Behavior* (4th ed.) (Cincinnati, OH: South-Western, 2000).

- What specific diversity issues do you believe your company will face as it moves along the stages of development to become a more fully international or global company? What are some programs, policies, or structures to address the organizational and attitudinal changes required?

- Would employees who are nationals of countries other than those in your group list these issues the same way that your group has? What might be different? What would they want to include? How would they approach creating organizational and attitudinal change?

Cultural Considerations

- When facilitating, be aware that as people describe examples of diversity, those examples will be nationally limited. Continue throughout the debriefing process to solicit worldwide examples so that the exercise is not supporting a mono-cultural perspective of diversity but a more inclusive perspective.

Caveats, Considerations, and Variations

- This exercise draws on the participants' ability to conduct a structural analysis and some background in organizational development. Some employees may not have the breadth of knowledge to respond to this exercise. Do sufficient prework to have an accurate picture as to the stage of global development the company is experiencing, as well as the scope of diversity issues experienced. If participation is limited, have information to share as a point of discussion.

Using Diverse Workforces in a Global Corporation

Like it or not, diversity is being played out in global corporations. Corporations have a rich opportunity to shape global interactions, frequently transcending the efforts of government as well as nongovernmental organizations (NGOs). Let's look at how organizations intentionally manage the diversity dynamic within its boundaries.[9]

There are four dynamics in corporate diversity initiatives, each with its own drivers, objectives, methods, and outcome measures: (1) using *legal* structures; (2) *managing* performance of diverse workforces; (3) *using* individual talents; and (4) *empowering* leadership and vision. They are shown in the Continuum of Diversity Development and described below.

Using Legal Structures

Nations—as well as some regions like the European Union—have varied histories of employment law and specific laws addressing workplace discrimination. While founded on common principles of individual worker rights and collective social responsibility, statutes governing workplace diversity may have different interpretations depending on the national culture. Even the definition of "law," as well as how infractions are defined and dealt with in national courts, are different. As a result, the legal departments of global corporations guide their firms in worldwide compliance to employment law. Do you have cause to fire employees who engage in sexual harassment, based on your own national standards or on the standards of the headquarters country? Is it legal to ask whether a candidate is married? What candidate or employee information can I put into my files and what cannot be recorded? With whom can I share that information? What are the consequences of termination for discrimination and am I required to pay termination indemnities?

Diversity approaches that are legally focused affirm the value of inclusion, but in a limited, protective, reactive, and socially compliant way. In many cases, compliance efforts focus on protecting the corporation from financial and market consequences of legal action and the subsequent loss of reputation capital or brand equity should legal action be taken.

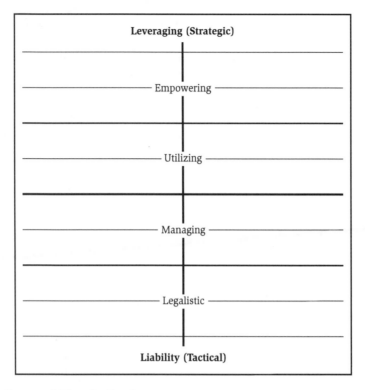

The Continuum of Diversity Development

Source: Adapted from A. Kahn and S. Gomez, *Challenging Diversity: Taking the Next Step* (available: www.culture-link.com).

Measuring results in this stage of diversity utilization often requires numerical analysis of demographic profiles of employees and customers. That data can influence the creation of staff quotas from targeted groups as defined by national legislation or social "persuasion." Another legal measure is the decrease in the number of diversity complaints related to individual worker rights, particularly around issues of hiring and promotional opportunity. Using this approach, organizations such as Operation Push in the United States continue to place considerable pressure on corporations for minority workforce and management representation. On the other side of the globe, Malaysia's bumiputra laws require that a set number of Malaysian employees be drawn from the Malay community, as distinct from Malaysian citizens of Chinese or Indian heritage. The target groups are different, but again, this legalistic approach drives change. The "Legal Drivers and Implications for Global Diversity" tool can be used to heighten knowledge and compliance to global legislation in your firm related to international employment law and is a good tool to begin the dialogue.

Legal Drivers and Implications for Global Diversity

Directions: This exercise will compare laws pertaining to International Employment Law in different parts of your global organization. Identify the law and its specific diversity intent. Note the positive and negative implications of that law within your organization. Example: In the United States you cannot ask if a job candidate is married or if he or she has children. In Indonesia there are no laws that prohibit this question.

Location	Laws	Implications
Headquarters *Example:* New York	U.S. EEOC requirements	Employment practices and policies that guarantee equity regarding gender, race, national origin, and age
Other Global Locations		
1. *Example:* Malaysia	Bumiputra laws	Hiring quotas for ethnic Malays
2.		
3.		

Suggestions for Using
"Legal Drivers and Implications for Global Diversity"

Objectives

- To understand how different national contexts have structured their employment law

- To identify the global diversity requirements related to reconciling nationally biased employment law

- To position corporate diversity efforts in the context of an emerging global diversity plan

Intended Audience

- Members of any employee or manager's group exploring global diversity

- Any manager, facilitator, internal/external consultant, HR professional, or trainer charged with the task of creating a global diversity initiative

Time

- 45 minutes

Materials

- An overhead transparency and copies of "Legal Drivers and Implications for Global Diversity"

- Chart paper and markers

Directions

- Define and discuss specific legal drivers for diversity and their impact in creating change. In the large group, solicit examples from participants.

- Ask participants to review their experience and identify one law related to diversity that best demonstrates legislative excellence in one's country of origin and at lease three other laws coming from different national contexts.

- Continue to have participants record the implications of those laws, highlighting the positive outcomes that the laws have provided as well as the inherent limitations of those legislations in their country.

- Divide members into small groups. Ask them to compare their individual responses and create a listing of significant legislation that best supports their company's commitment to global diversity.

- Conduct a whole group discussion of findings and insights for expanding legislation to support global diversity.

Questions for Discussion/Consideration

- Has legislation been an effective tool for creating inclusive workforces and supporting diversity? In your home country? In other countries where your organization works? In countries where multinational companies work?
- When discussing legal drivers for diversity, what is consistent or inconsistent across nations?
- Based on your responses, is there a need for a global legal standard to support diversity and, if so, what might it be?
- What specific aspects of diversity need to be included in legal response in the countries where your company works?
- Do you believe that legal interventions will create the required change to broaden global diversity? If so, why? If not, why not? What will work better?

Cultural Considerations

- Be aware that some participants may value religious law as much as civil law. Model a diversity perspective by allowing open conversation of the implications of religious law and its role in establishing global diversity within corporations.

Caveats, Considerations, and Variations

- Before any discussion, the facilitator should have studied different aspects of law and how they apply to global diversity. Contact your corporate legal department to find out the number of diversity-related cases legal is managing and how they differ from country to country.
- This exercise can be used in program prework and can be used as a needs assessment tool for gathering valuable corporate information.
- This exercise can be used as a research and education tool for human resource staff both at headquarters and in regional locations.

Managing Performance

While legal requirements provide one set of drivers for workforce inclusion, they do not directly address the impact of diversity on performance. Another impetus is performance management, an approach to diversity that seeks to sharpen awareness of the impact of difference in the workplace, help employees master knowledge around those differences, and sharpen their skills for dealing with employees and managers who are different. But frequently these kinds of diversity programs focus on awareness rather than skill building around how to be inclusive, how to actually reconcile differences, and how to achieve transformative organizational change by using diversity.

Corporate training and organization development's mission is to provide the tools to help diverse individuals enhance their interpersonal and intergroup skills, thus increasing their influence and effectiveness inside the corporation. In the United States, corporate universities frequently integrate a diversity component into all training programs and/or they may design specific courses to help employees value, manage, and leverage the diversity within their teams.

When implemented in international and global companies, these kinds of courses typically focus on expanding employees' understanding of and ability to work with people of different national cultures. Frequently, they focus on "dos and don'ts"—a nationally focused version of "Men are from Mars, Women are from Venus"—or specifics associated with the national culture being studied and its political, social, and economic context. These cross-cultural curricula often do not provide an in-depth understanding of the national values that have created these dissimilar approaches to life, business management, thinking, and industrial workforce interactions. They also do not deal comprehensively with issues related to traditional diversity themes, such as gender, sexual orientation, and race, and explore them relative to another national culture. They focus on questions such as "Can a woman lead a team in Brazil?" or "As an African American, can I work in Japan?"

Measuring success in this approach involves organizational audits where people of different backgrounds and nationalities assess how well workplace differences are acknowledged and managed. Other performance management tools, such as corporate 360-degree assessments, can be effective measures, particularly when those tools assess skills related to diversity. One example is a major telecommunications company that asks worldwide employees on a quarterly basis to rate their managers on their demonstration of diversity skill and cultural respect. Often, the Chartered Institute of Personnel and Development (CIPD) in London and the Society for Human Resource Management (SHRM) in the United States, through its Global Forum, will identify best-of-class companies who excel in programs and policies related to managing global diversity performance. You can use the "Global Performance Management Audit" to assess your team on these points.

Suggestions for Using "Global Performance Management Audit"

Objectives

- To identify the core diversity programs, policies, and structures in the firm
- To evaluate the effectiveness of these programs, policies, and structures in implementing and capitalizing on diversity within the global organization
- To gather insights as to what participants feel are appropriate programs, policies, and structures to enhance and leverage diversity management in their firm

Global Performance Management Audit

Directions: To manage performance, organizations need to provide programs, policies, and structures that heighten global diversity awareness, train employees in appropriate skills supportive of diversity, and create structures that integrate global diversity throughout the organization. A training program might be designed to help build skills in using Asian perspectives in negotiation; a policy might be that all senior leadership will be able to function in business meetings in a second language; a structure may be worldwide postings for all manager and senior management positions. In the space below, please identify existent programs, policies, and structures in your company. Record their intent and evaluate their positive and negative outcome.

	Name of Program	Intent of Program	Global Diversity Outcome (skills, demographics, productivity)
Programs	1. *Example:* Cross-cultural negotiation skills	Train employees in Asian perspectives in negotiations	Sets stage for inclusive implementation phase that has cross-national support
	2.		
	3.		
Policies	1. *Example:* Language acquisition	Enable all senior managers to function is business meetings in a second language	Increase respect for fellow workers supporting inclusion
	2.		
	3.		
Structures/Systems	1. *Example:* Open posting system	Create worldwide access for all manager and senior manager positions	Signals opportunity to workforce for potential of leadership positions regardless of nationality
	2.		
	3.		

Intended Audience

- Members of any employee or manager's group exploring global diversity
- Any manager, facilitator, internal/external consultant, HR professional, or trainer charged with the task of creating a global diversity initiative

Time

- 45 minutes

Materials

- An overhead transparency and copies of the "Global Performance Management Audit"
- Chart paper and markers

Directions

- Expand on the concept of performance management and how an effective diversity program functions through targeted programs, policies, and structures.
- Ask participants to fill out the form individually and encourage them to list at least two examples in each category.
- Ask the participants to form into groups of six and discuss their individual responses and the effectiveness of their company's response.
- Select a group recorder to lead the group in coming to consensus as to which example was the most creative in advancing global diversity within their company and which was the most effective in creating change.
- Have the group come to consensus as to what might have been overlooked within the corporate global diversity program.

Questions for Discussion/Consideration

- What nation or region of your company has been most effective in dealing with global diversity through their use of programs, policies, or structure? To what extent?
- In reviewing your company's response to diversity, what aspect of diversity still seems to be lacking awareness programming, policy adjustments, or organizational change? What can be done about it?
- Are these programs, policies, and structures equally implemented in all nations and regions? If not, why not? What prevents universal enforcement within the corporation? Should there be universal enforcement?
- If yes to the above question, how successful has the company been and what has been learned that will facilitate the advancement of the global diversity agenda across boundaries?

- What have been major resistances in the corporation for the institution of programs, policies, and structures to advance global diversity? Who has the authority and role to address them and what might he or she do?

Cultural Considerations

- A natural tension exists between corporate culture and national or regional culture that may be reflected in various programs, policies, and structures. Caution participants not to minimize national and regional differences by resorting to an uncritical acceptance of corporate culture.

Caveats, Considerations, and Variations

- This exercise can be used as prework for a program as well as a needs assessment tool for gathering valuable corporate information.

Using Individual Talents

At this stage in the evolution of corporate diversity initiatives, efforts focus on using individual talent. Corporations intentionally begin advancing employees into leadership positions because they believe that their diversity perspective compliments other proven professional competencies and enables the company to function better and be more competitive. This cadre of diverse leaders brings specific characteristics, qualities, and competencies that are closely aligned with their national identity and that can bring value to the global organization.

To fully use individual talent inside the corporation, executives, managers, team leaders, and all staff responsible for human resource allocation must be able to effectively identify the unique contributions of an individual employee and effectively position that talent within the organization. We must first understand and be able to measure the value that a specific diversity perspective brings to a global company—be it gender, ethnic, national, or civilizational perspective, to name a few. For example, what does being French or espousing a Cartesian mindset add to the bottom line of a global or international corporation in comparison with the analytical perspective of a Scotsman? What benefit does being a Brazilian man or Brazilian woman bring a senior management problem-solving session and how can we quantify that value to the company?

How many international people are on your corporation's board of directors? Of the senior leadership group and high-potential employees, how many managers are not nationals, by either birth or citizenship, of the country in which the corporate headquarters is located? Do all high-potential employees worldwide have access to promotions regardless of the location in which they are currently working? Of the board members and the senior leadership group, how many have a first language that is different from the "business" language of the company? While not an exhaustive list, the answers to these and similar questions can provide valuable information about how an organization uses inclusivity in its workforce, selects its senior managers, and creates global leaders.

Outcome measures at this level may include whether the company has cross-national and transnational leadership development and succession plans inclusive of all potential candidates, regardless of the location in which they work. The "Identify Global Exemplars" exercise can be useful to determine this.

Suggestions for Using "Identify Global Exemplars"

Objectives

- To increase the capability to identify global diversity exemplars (GDE)
- To acknowledge global contributors who are developing an inclusive environment in the company
- To set in motion a rudimentary competency study and begin the process of identifying the attitudes, skills, and attributes of successful global diversity leaders
- To document the qualitative and quantitative value that global diversity exemplars bring to the corporation
- To create an action plan to increase personal skills in becoming a GDE

Intended Audience

- Members of any employee or manager's group exploring global diversity
- Any manager, facilitator, internal/external consultant, HR professional, or trainer charged with the task of creating a global diversity initiative

Time

- 60 minutes

Materials

- An overhead transparency and copies of "Identify Global Exemplars"
- Chart paper and markers

Directions

- Begin by explaining the meaning of an "exemplar"—a person whose actions demonstrate a commitment to a standard of excellence, in this case, the ability to operate effectively in a corporation using diversity. Provide examples from one's organizational context as well as two other international corporations.

Identify Global Diversity Exemplars

Directions: Many corporations have employees whose professional behaviors demonstrate what it means to fully utilize diversity. Some identify these people as being aware of their cultural heritage as well as highly skilled in reconciling their cultural orientation with others. In this exercise, please identify employees who are global diversity exemplars (GDE). Identify the specific affinity group(s) that the GDE most frequently acknowledges. Describe the specific contribution, skill, or competency that the GDE most frequently demonstrates. Give details as to how those competencies add value to the company.

Global Diversity Examplar's Name	Identify the Specific Global Diversity Descriptors	Diversity Contribution— Core Competency	Benefit to Company (Financial, Reputation, Intellectual Capital, etc.)
1. Louh Lai Wah	Allows others to speak their minds without judging; speaks with authority yet not imposition	Flexibility Nonjudgmental Self-reliant Strategic thinker	Limits wasted time on conflicts; draws consensus quickly
2.			
3.			
4.			

- Ask participants to list at least two exemplars from their home country and name two or three exemplars from international settings.
- Direct participants to review their lists and identify which of all their responses best typify a global diversity exemplar for their corporation.
- Form into small groups of six and share the background related to your selected global diversity exemplar.
- Ask the group to create a generalized list of the common characteristics of their chosen exemplars that may be helpful to develop the required competencies for future global diversity change.
- Identify the five most important competencies that will advance the company's global diversity initiative.
- Ask participants to personally review the list and create one action step to increase their capability to be a GDE.

Questions for Discussion/Consideration

- What characteristics and skills demonstrate a global diversity exemplar in your own national context? In another regional context? Within the global context of the company?
- Are the exemplars a result of the programs, policies, and structures that the company established? If so, which programs, policies, and structures?
- What programs, policies, and/or structures are not helpful in creating global diversity exemplars?
- If exemplars are people with innate diversity skills, what are they and how do they function in bringing global diversity to a corporation? How can others be trained in these qualities and skills?

Cultural Considerations

- Cultures vary in their belief that exemplars are "born" or that exemplars are "developed." Explore this difference as well as the organizational structures that groom people for leadership across cultures. Attempt not to be too definitional or prescriptive because that will inhibit the participation of low-context people. Being too vague will also limit participation of high-context people, whose answers may not be sufficiently focused to bring value to the discussion. Aim at striking a balance by giving good examples that allow individuals with different learning styles to answer the questions.

Caveats, Considerations, and Variations

- Participants, depending on their core cultural heritage and its learning style, may require a specific definition of "exemplar" as well as the meaning of "competency." Explore these variables before beginning the exercise.

- If participants do not have a great deal of exposure in the company, allow them to identify global exemplars from their previous work experience or their personal knowledge of other companies.

Empowering Leadership and Vision

This final phase addresses the fuller employment of those cultural skills inside the organization. Empowerment, a term most used in United States and Western European firms, suggests the ability of a person or leader to act using his or her own judgment and potential for the betterment of the organization. This phase of diversity work focuses on the full capability of employees to leverage the multiple perspectives that exist within themselves and their workforce.

What is critical is the employees' ability to align the core values, beliefs, and styles of their own affinity groups and others in the workforce with the vision, values, and strategic and operational focus of the corporation. A European CEO of a U.S.-headquartered company may be much different in his or her thinking, perspective, and strategic approach from his or her American counterpart. That difference brings potential to the global corporation since it allows problem solving, communication, and decision making to begin from a different perspective and ultimately affects the outcome. The difference in starting point and the ability to reconcile one's starting position with other divergent views is the essence of diversity reconciliation and global inclusivity.

Outcome measures at this level are difficult to prescribe. In prior stages we count numbers. Later, we have rated and recorded how aware and sensitive we are and finally have promoted diverse candidates to more complex opportunities. Our outcome measure at this new level requires a measurement of some process measurement skill that takes the "different," whether a different idea, process, program, or group, and creatively reconciles that difference for the strategic value of the corporation. In this stage of global diversity work, we must measure and articulate the value of a consistent orientation to "difference" as a core tool for learning and leading the company.

Assessing Your Organization

Knowing where your organization is on the continuum from "domestic" to "global" and in its development from a "legal" to "empowering" organization is the foundation for applying the SSI Model as well as many of the exercises in this book. By understanding both the breadth of diversity initiatives within your company and the level of global corporate development, you can more rapidly analyze how well your diversity programs are functioning and supporting the type of organization that you aspire to become. You will also be able to assess where you may need to create new diversity approaches to operate more effectively as a global company.

For example, having a U.S.-centric legalistic diversity approach may work well at all levels within a domestic company, but that approach may not be as effective when the company becomes international in focus.

Use the "Global Diversity Corporate Assessment Tool" to assess your corporation's global diversity strategy. This integrated tool enables you to assess your corporation's diversity program and cross-reference it to the requirements of the four different levels of global corporate development.

Think of concrete examples of your corporate diversity initiative that demonstrate a program, policy, or behavior that was successful in each of the boxes of the diagram. For example, if your organization has a strong diversity training program for its domestic operations, that would fit into the lower-left quadrant. If you have an active international recruitment, relocation, and career development process, and you operate in six countries yet are still headquartered in one, that would fit in the upper-right quadrant close to the center of the diagram.

Many domestic-focused companies are able to demonstrate a relatively integrated program and policy on diversity, but few can demonstrate those kinds of integrated examples on a more international or global scale.

Suggestions for Using
"Global Diversity Corporate Assessment Tool"

Objectives

- To understand how diversity expresses itself differently within a domestic, import-export, international, or global organization
- To identify the different diversity requirements related to current levels of global organizational development
- To position national diversity efforts in the context of an emerging global diversity plan
- To highlight major domestic diversity accomplishments in relationship to global diversity requirements

Intended Audience

- Members of any employee or management group exploring global diversity
- Any manager, facilitator, internal/external consultant, HR professional, or trainer charged with the task of creating a global diversity initiative

Time

- 45 minutes

Global Diversity Corporate Assessment Tool

Directions: Think of each diversity program, policy, and process in your company and consider if its frame of reference is a national, import-export, international, or global orientation. Then consider whether it is a tactical or strategic diversity response. Consider its intent as legalistic, managerial, utilization, or empowerment. Place an X at the appropriate coordinates. Continue for as many programs, policies, and processes as possible.

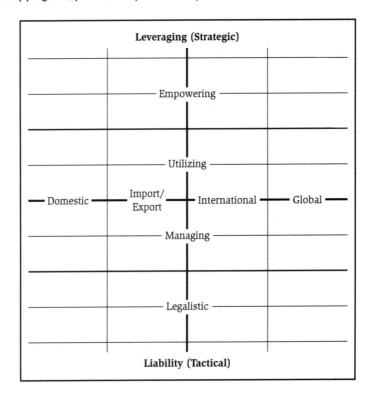

Source: Adapted from N.J. Adler, *International Dimensions of Organizational Behavior* (4th ed.) (Cincinnati, OH: South-Western, 2000) and A. Kahn and S. Gomez, *Challenging Diversity: Taking the Next Step* (available: www.culture-link.com).

Materials

- An overhead transparency and copies of the "Global Diversity Corporate Assessment Tool"
- Chart paper and markers

Directions

- Define and discuss each dimension of the profile's two axes.
- Ask participants to plot their company's programs and operations as a national, import-export, international, or global company and the current level of diversity activity.
- Ask participants to think of concrete examples that illustrate the current company structure and diversity accomplishment as they have plotted it.
- Divide members into small groups. Ask them to compare their individual profiles and create one shared profile that best reflects their company's current level of global diversity.
- Conduct a whole-group discussion of findings and insights.

Questions for Discussion/Consideration

- Where is your organization in its diversity processes?
- What examples, similarities, and differences were most notable among group members?
- What surprises, if any, did you find in the responses?
- When you look more closely at the differences, what impacts do they or might they have on the development of a global company?
- How can we make those differences work in our favor?

Cultural Considerations

- Identify the national and civilizational ideals that are contained in your examples. Are there national preferred values that enable diversity to be more successful?
- Words such as "diversity" and "empowerment" have a wide range of meanings and cultural interpretation. Process participants' understanding and use of these terms.

Caveats, Considerations, and Variations

- This exercise works best with groups that are international, providing for an open and fruitful exchange of regional and cultural differences. Mono-cultural groups may not have the scope or insight to give examples, even when their company is global or international. In this case, bring data regarding programs or have participants gather data through interviews with managers in other locations, for example.
- Respondents can also use this tool to identify current state and future state and strategize on the action steps required to create the change.

CONCLUSION

In this chapter we have provided a tool long needed for managers and practitioners interested in expanding the global diversity dialogue. The SSI Model provides a base for understanding the multiple levels that exist within any dialogue between employees in an international or global company. It suggests the move from mono-focused identifications of diversity to a more inclusive discussion for all that makes us different. It relies on good will to explore the multiple differences drawn from our civilizational and national heritages in conjunction with the identities we have forged through our socialization and individual development. It calls for the continued reconciliation of these multiple expressions of diversity for the best interest of our corporate organizations.

Notes

1 Adapted from Lee Gardenswartz and Anita Rowe, *Diverse Teams at Work* (Homewood, IL: Business One Irwin, 1994) and M. Loden and J. Rosener, *Workforce America!* (Homewood, IL: Business One Irwin, 1991).

2 Huntington, Samuel P. *The Clash of Civilization and the Remaking of World Order* (New York: Simon & Schuster, 1996).

3 Hofstede, Geert. *Cultures and Organizations: Software of the Mind* (Berkshire, UK: McGraw-Hill, 1997) and F. Trompenaars and C. Hampden-Turner, *Riding the Waves of Culture* (2nd ed.) (New York: McGraw-Hill, 1998).

4 Adapted from Lee Gardenswartz and Anita Rowe, *Diverse Teams at Work* (Homewood, IL: Business One Irwin, 1994) and M. Loden and J. Rosener, *Workforce America!* (Homewood, IL: Business One Irwin, 1991).

5 Adapted from Lee Gardenswartz and Anita Rowe, *Managing Diversity: A Complete Desk Reference and Planning Guide* (rev. ed.) (New York: McGraw-Hill, 1998).

6 Maslow, A. *Motivation and Personality* (New York: Harper & Row, 1987).

7 Erikson, E.H. *Childhood and Society* (New York: Norton, 1950).

8 Adapted from N.J. Adler, *International Dimensions of Organizational Behavior* (Boston, MA: Kent, 1997).

9 Adapted from A. Kahn and S. Gomez, *Challenging Diversity: Taking the Next Step* (available: www.culture-link.com).

PART TWO

MANAGING
A GLOBAL WORKFORCE

CHAPTER 3

Communicating Effectively Across Cultures

Sending and receiving information accurately and maintaining cooperative, productive relationships is a challenge for organizations and the human beings who work in them, even in the most homogeneous, mono-cultural settings. Struggles abound, whether bridging departments, genders, or generations. These challenges become exponentially greater when global business adds language and differences in national culture and civilization to the mix. Variations in communication styles, orientations to life, concepts about reality, social norms, economic systems, and rules of etiquette, as well as vocabulary, syntax, grammar, and nonverbal behavior frequently create barriers to understanding and sow the seeds of discord and conflict, as illustrated in the following examples.

- A U.S.-born manager in a Japanese firm is admonished by her Japanese boss for giving a "Yes!" cheer at the end of her first successful presentation. He tells her that her behavior is not professional or dignified and erodes her credibility.

- A global team member of a U.K.-based organization withers in embarrassment when effusively thanked publicly at a team meeting by her colleague from outside the U.K.

- A U.S. manager takes offense at her German colleague's e-mail messages, which to her seem aggressive and pushy to the point of rudeness.

Her German counterpart, on the other hand, feels betrayed by what she sees as a lack of responsiveness and support when her American colleague does not follow through.

- A Chinese staff member from the PRC demonstrates unusual anxiety when he finds out his performance review will be put in his personal file.

- A Dutch manager is viewed as argumentative and difficult by his U.S.-American colleagues because of his direct confrontational style in discussions at meetings.

- Phone conference and videoconference staff meetings are scheduled by headquarters-based staff for their convenience, requiring staff members in other time zones to participate in calls well after midnight.

How are relationships and information flow impacted when these kinds of cross-cultural differences play out? More importantly, what can organizations do to help staff members overcome these barriers to effectiveness and productivity?

This chapter sheds light on the cultural differences influencing communication and provides activities and tools to explore these differences and engage others in learning about them. It also offers guidelines and suggestions to bridge cultural differences, build productive relationships across dimensions of diversity, and effectively communicate with colleagues and clients throughout the world.

UNDERSTANDING THE CULTURAL UNDERPINNINGS OF GLOBAL COMMUNICATION

A critical beginning point for global organizations and staff who work in them is to understand the powerful role culture plays in communication. From how close we stand and how loudly we speak to our orientations to time and relationships, we are influenced by the cultures that have shaped us and given us what Hofstede refers to as "software of the mind." Just as computers would be useless without their operating systems and other software, all humans are dependent on cultural programming to give us the rules for interacting with others. How long to pause, when to interrupt, how to disagree, what topics are appropriate, and how to address others are parts of our "automatic pilot" system, yet we are probably unaware of that knowledge. Our software is largely invisible to us until we meet up with someone who has different programming. When we engage in intercultural contact, we see our software in contrast to that of others and we begin to be aware of the differences in the rules, norms, and orientations. Generally this first realization brings with it frustration, judgments, and exasperated comments about how difficult and frustrating it is to do business with "them."

A proactive step in dealing with these kinds of issues is to learn about cross-cultural communication. This learning needs to focus on three steps: (1) increasing awareness about the differences to be encountered and one's reaction to them, (2) gaining knowledge about the wide variations in cultural norms and practices, and (3) acquiring skills in dealing with these differences in business interactions.

Once we become aware of the potential obstacles presented by cultural differences, the instinctive response is to ask for a list of rules for each culture, a compendium of dos and don'ts, or what one executive referred to as a "playbook." The danger of this approach is that generalizations about cultural norms, while helpful in giving us clues about the meanings of behaviors, are not accurate about each individual's behavior. You may learn, for example, that smiling and laughter are signs of embarrassment and confusion for many Asians. That knowledge can prevent you from jumping to the conclusion that the Taiwanese engineers on your global team are snickering at you, as one manager thought. However, you cannot be sure until you check out your assumption by investigating further. Perhaps these engineers have spent many years in other countries, are acculturated to different norms, and are laughing at something you said or did. On the other hand, they may in fact be confused and embarrassed and do not want to cause loss of face by telling you they do not understand.

Angelika Plett, an organization development consultant in Germany, advises us to remember that "the map is not the landscape" when using culture-specific information. There are no shortcuts. It is only by spending time getting to know individuals in all their complexity that we really succeed in communicating with them. In addition, it would be humanly impossible to memorize lists of norms for all the cultures we come across, and even if we could, the generalization would not be accurate for every individual in a particular culture. A more effective approach is to give employees a framework for understanding cultural differences and methods for dealing with the specifics in each relationship or situation. One helpful way to do this is to focus on the major aspects of cultural difference that influence communication around the world.

High and Low Context

One of the most significant cultural differences is that between high and low context, as described by Edward Hall. In low-context cultures, such as Switzerland and the United States, people find the meaning in words, hence communication is specific and explicit. "Tell it like it is," "Put your cards on the table," and "Get to the point" express this direct, explicit form of communicating where little is left to interpretation by the receiver. In high-context cultures such as Japan and China, on the other hand, communication is general, indirect, and implicit, and meaning is found less in the words than in the context surrounding the communication. The relative positions and relationship of communicators, such as boss/subordinate, newcomer/oldtimer, host/guest, as well as nonverbal cues such as gestures and facial expressions, are also important in a system that relies on the listener to infer meaning from an array of contextual clues. The effective manager in such cultures would need to attend to subtle clues and infer the meaning of his or her subordinates' messages.

This difference can be the source of misunderstanding and frustration if communicators do not understand each other's orientation on this dimension. Take the case of the Japanese manager who returns his U.S.-American staff member's report with the vague direction, "I've had a chance to read your report. Perhaps you'd like to take another look at it." His staff member is perplexed. "Why do I have to look at it again? It's finished," she thinks. "How am I supposed to know what's wrong if he doesn't give me feedback?" Yet if she understood the subtle contextual clues, that her Japanese co-workers undoubtedly do, she would know that there were some problems with her report and that it was her job to figure out what they were and remedy them.

Hierarchical–Egalitarian

Another cultural difference with a powerful impact on communication is the degree of hierarchy, or as Hofstede would put it, "power distance." Differences in treatment based on one's level are expected in more hierarchical systems. Knowing one's place gives order and stability in life and predictability in relationships. Whether shown in the dropped eyes of many Asians, the use of the formal "you" by the Spanish, German, and French, or how one is standing when speaking to the senior manager in a Korean company, the respect for positional authority is a fundamental rule in such cultures. In hierarchical cultures, to disregard this rule is to give offense, show poor breeding, or to be insolent. Because those in positions of authority are expected to know more, disagreeing or questioning a boss would be unthinkable in this orientation. On the other hand, in a more egalitarian framework, such as that in the United States, there is an attempt to disregard levels and treat everyone the same, from most senior to junior, from CEO to hourly employee. In such an environment, being on a first-name basis with the boss would be expected and to give special treatment to those in power is seen as toadying, while to demand it is perceived as arrogant and condescending.

One tax department middle manager, frustrated at a division director who would not return his calls because of their differences in level, explained the consequence of a clash of cultures regarding this dimension. Irritated at the director's habit of only returning calls to those at his level or above, he exploded, "I know I could have my director call him, but right now I'm so angry I won't and he won't be able to take advantage of the million-dollar tax savings he could have through a new tax law I've just discovered."

How one communicates with others of different levels will depend in great part on one's orientation on this continuum. Do you give orders or ask, give feedback or acquiesce, ask questions or remain silent, use first names or titles? Answers will vary based on your cultural software and that of others in the interaction.

Collective–Individual

How different are the messages between the Japanese aphorism that "The nail that sticks up gets hammered down," the Australian, "Tall poppies get cut down," the Chinese, "The first bird is the one that is shot," and the U.S.-American one that "The squeaky wheel gets the grease"? These differences can be heard in the responses of bilingual Japanese women who, when asked to respond in both English and Japanese to this open-ended statement, "When my wishes conflict with my family's. . . ." When one woman responded in Japanese she said, "It is a time of great unhappiness." In English she responded, "I do what I want."[1]

Whether we see ourselves as individual players or an integral part of societal groups is a powerful influencer of our communication. Speaking out, stating an opinion, voicing disagreement, and taking credit, blame, or responsibility are all connected to this dimension. Critical communication behaviors such as giving and receiving feedback, solving problems, resolving conflicts, and giving rewards are impacted by this dimension.

Relationship–Task

While most people would agree that both focusing on the task and attending to relationships are key to getting the job done, it is in the time, emphasis, and priority placed on one or the other end of this continuum that we differ. For those on the task side, such as the Swiss and Germans, the numerous meetings, small talk, and after-work socializing are an irritating burden that hinders productivity. For those on the relationship end, such as Mexicans and Arabs, these same behaviors build trust and grease the wheels of task accomplishment. Jumping into task-related matters before spending time developing comfort and familiarity would create unnecessary barriers with them.

In more task-oriented cultures such as the United States, spending time on relationship building is often disparaged as a waste of precious time and as a less than honorable way to get ahead, as in the frequently heard, "It's not what you know but who you know" complaint. However, building connections is a respected, legitimate way to do business in parts of the world where relationships take precedence. Professionals in China rely on *guanxi* or connections, interpersonal networks that involve reciprocal obligations. Establishing and maintaining these relationships with classmates, relatives, colleagues, and friends is essential for success in business.

This difference can be seen in the disparity between the behavior of Western and Chinese employees. According to Maura Fallon, a human resources professional working in China, Western employees see themselves as responsible for the task, getting things done, while Chinese see themselves as accountable to someone, a boss or authority figure to whom they are loyal. They also view effective managers as those who maintain harmony and cooperation between employees. Without attention to relationships, a manager would not be able to be successful in accomplishing the task in such an environment.

Relationships matter in all cultures. However, it is especially important in non-Western cultures. Fallon advises the following specific ways to attend to relationships, show respect, and build trust in order to get the best from employees in China:[2]

1. Be introduced by a trusted, respected person.

2. Show interest in the unique aspects of the other person.

3. Respect the other person's agenda.

4. Start by listening rather than leading.

5. Set the other person up for success, especially in front of his or her boss.

6. Give opportunities for training, visibility, connections, and gaining information.

7. Connect the individual with others who may be able to enhance his or her opportunities and career growth.

8. Coach the individual and anticipate problems so you can prepare the individual for dealing with them.

9. Learn about and do something for his or her family members.

10. Introduce your family to the individual.

11. Have fun by socializing together.

12. Find ways to give face by increasing the individual's esteem, image, and respect.

While these guidelines are suggested specifically for doing business in China, they would also be effective in other high-context cultures of Asia such as Thailand, India, and Vietnam. Time spent finding out about the national cultures in which you are working as well as the individual cultures of your employees or co-workers is an investment critical to success.

Polychronic Time–Monochronic Time

How one views and deals with time is still another culturally influenced factor with significant consequences in work groups. Those with a more monochronic view see time as a commodity to be saved, spent, and divided into segments, all for the accomplishment of goals and tasks. On the other end of the spectrum are those with a polychronic view, seeing time as a circle within which many things can happen at once and with other priorities such as relationships and enjoyment having as much importance as task accomplishment. While the industrialized world functions with a more monochronic orientation, when organizational schedules, deadlines, and project timelines meet up with polychronic cultural norms, frustration, misunderstanding, and conflict often result.

The situation of a manager in a U.S.-headquartered manufacturing organization transferred to Puerto Rico is a case in point. As the new plant manager, he soon recognized the value of socializing with his managers in this highly relationship-oriented culture which, although a U.S. territory, had much more cultural affinity with its Caribbean and Latin American neighbors. He found his staff competent and productive, but he was perplexed by the lack of energy and productivity at his weekly staff meetings. He scheduled these meetings on Friday afternoons, a habit he'd brought from his former plant, because it seemed the most logical time to review the past week and get ready for the next. After a number of low-energy, ineffective sessions, he went out with some of his direct reports for a few beers. When he casually brought up the subject of the meetings, they explained that, in Puerto Rico, the weekend began at noon on Fridays and employees considered the rest of the day their time. Suddenly the reason for their lack of participation at the meetings became clear. He could have taken a hardnosed stance based on his own monochronic sense of time and insisted that Friday afternoons were part of the work week for which people were being paid. Instead, he recognized that he would undoubtedly get better performance and higher productivity if he adapted to their more polychronic time sense. When he changed the meetings to Thursdays, he saw an immediate upswing in energy and results.

In dealing with this difference, the manager took two important steps. First, he resisted the common response of making judgments about his staff. Because he'd seen their competence and performance, he didn't assume they were lazy or unmotivated. Second, he investigated, asking questions to understand the reasons behind their behavior. Once he understood it from their cultural perspective, he found a solution that was the most effective for meeting his goals.

Maintaining Harmony–Surfacing Differences

How we deal with conflict is yet another culturally influenced aspect of behavior. Voicing concerns, criticizing, challenging, and disagreeing are seen as productive steps toward creativity and problem solving in the United States and Western Europe. In Japan, China, and much of Asia, the disharmony, tension, and loss of face these behaviors cause creates a strong social prohibition against them. Sparring and playing devil's advocate are energizing and may be a way to refine ideas for employees from the Netherlands. On the other hand, those from cultures, such as the Philippines, that prize harmony and smooth inter-personal relationships would find this behavior offensive, off-putting, and a rea-son to withdraw from the discussion, negotiation, or the group.

Tact in giving criticism and handling conflict is important most everywhere; however, in cultures that place a priority on harmony, it is even more critical. Not only does criticism or anger disrupt harmony, but it brings with it loss of face for both parties and the ensuing loss of trust. Each side suffers when this happens because both lose face and are hindered in their ability to be effective. In addition, political and legal systems, aspects in the National Identification sphere of the SSI Model explained in Chapter 2, may also influence this dimen-sion of communication. For example, in China's state enterprises, employees' political files follow them from secondary schooling throughout their careers, anything included in this dossier may have far-reaching consequences, so employees may be particularly nervous about any written feedback.

When these kinds of differences are experienced without conscious under-standing of the cultural factors influencing them, results for the team or organiza-tion can be damaging. On the other hand, when understood, they can be dealt with effectively. Helping employees understand their own and others' conflict styles, then taking time for one-on-one negotiations between staff members with differ-ent conflict styles, setting group norms about dealing with differences, finding com-patible ways to critique projects, or using a third-party mediator, as many Asians and Arabs do, are a few ways groups can deal with differences in this dimension.

DEALING WITH CULTURAL INFLUENCES ON COMMUNICATION

When we communicate with others, we are continuously observing their behav-ior and reactions, interpreting what they mean, then acting on our interpreta-tion. In cross-cultural interactions, the chance for misinterpretation is high because, without awareness and knowledge, we interpret and act through our own cultural lenses, based on our own programming. With awareness and knowledge, we can make more accurate interpretations and choose more appro-priate and effective actions.

Helping individuals and workgroups deal with these differences is critical to productivity and teamwork. To deal effectively with these differences, we need a conscious awareness of them and how they play out. Second, we need to under-stand our own cultural programming and how it influences our behavior and inter-pretation of others' behavior. Finally, we need to understand others' programming that may be different from ours. Once we have this added awareness and knowl-edge, we have the capacity to make more appropriate choices about how to act.

The "Cultural Orientation Questionnaire" can help you and your employees gain this awareness and understanding by providing an opportunity to clarify both your and their own cultural programming, learn about others' software in a nonjudgmental way, and finally negotiate ways of working together to resolve any difficulties, misunderstandings, or conflicts these differences may cause. After completing the questionnaire, fill out the Profile form.

The profile range gives you an indication of your orientation on each of these dimensions of culture. Analyze your results with regard to your communication effectiveness. How does this profile work for you? Where does it help you and where does it hinder your communication? You might want to have a colleague or friend give you feedback to help in your analysis. Where do you need to develop your ability be more flexible and expand your range in order to increase your effectiveness in communicating across cultures?

Suggestions for Using the "Cultural Orientation Questionnaire"

Objectives

- To clarify one's own cultural programming
- To understand differences in cultural programming among co-workers
- To stimulate discussion and negotiation of differences

Intended Audience

- Members of a global multinational work team, task force, or department
- Managers of international or multicultural teams

Time

- 45 to 60 minutes

Materials

- Copies of the "Cultural Orientation Questionnaire," scoring sheet, and profile
- Enlargements of the "Cultural Orientation Profile" (optional)

Directions

- Discuss and define the dimensions on each continuum.
- Ask team members to respond to the questionnaire and score responses, following directions.
- Have members share profiles and discuss similarities, differences, and implications for the team, either by showing each other their worksheets or by putting their marks with a colored marker or stick dots on an enlarged chart of the profile sheet posted on the wall. (One for the whole team, or one chart for each group of five to six people.)

Cultural Orientation Questionnaire

Directions: In each pair of statements below, distribute 10 points between the two choices, based on how much each describes you, for example, 7 points for the a. statement, 3 points for the b. statement. If both describe your orientation equally, you would give each 5 points.

1. ____ a. I like specific directions that tell me exactly what is expected.
   ____ b. I like more general, open-ended directions that give me some leeway and autonomy.

2. ____ a. When feedback is vague, I'm confused and frustrated.
   ____ b. When feedback is direct, I'm embarrassed and upset.

3. ____ a. I'm perplexed when I don't receive specific, to-the-point information.
   ____ b. I feel limited and micromanaged when I receive very specific communication.

4. ____ c. I like to know who will take responsibility.
   ____ d. I like feeling that we all have shared responsibility.

5. ____ c. Knowing someone's in charge gives me a sense of security.
   ____ d. Titles, status, and formality create barriers for me.

6. ____ c. I work best when there's order from a chain of command.
   ____ d. I work best when I can rely on information and ideas from anywhere in the organization when levels are disregarded.

7. ____ e. It's embarrassing to me to be singled out for praise.
   ____ f. I feel best when I'm responsible only for my own work.

8. ____ e. What's best for me is what's best for the group.
   ____ f. Each individual's needs must be respected and considered.

9. ____ e. I work best in a team or group setting.
   ____ f. I work best independently on my own.

10. ____ g. I need to get to know people in order to work productively with them.
    ____ h. Spending time talking and socializing interferes with productivity.

11. ____ g. Teamwork is enhanced when there are strong interpersonal bonds.
    ____ h. Productivity is enhanced when people focus on getting the job done.

12. ____ g. I enjoy socializing with my co-workers in and out of work.
    ____ h. I keep my work life and social life separate.

13. ____ i. I rarely look at the clock or a watch.
    ____ j. I run my day by a schedule.

14. ____ i. What happens at the meeting is more important to me than when it starts.
    ____ j. I like to be on time and expect others to do the same.

15. ____ i. For me, a schedule and appointments are guidelines not rules.
    ____ j. It's frustrating for me when others are late.

16. ____ k. I become tense and upset when there is conflict at work.
    ____ l. When there is a conflict at work, I want to get to the bottom of it.

17. ____ k. Differences are best dealt with quietly, behind the scenes.
    ____ l. Differences are best dealt with when the issues are discussed openly.

18. ____ k. I try to avoid conflict wherever possible.
    ____ l. I generally confront the issue when I perceive there is conflict brewing.

Cultural Orientation Questionnaire (continued)

Scoring

Write the points for each statement, then add the total points for each letter and divide by three to find an average score for the three items with the same letter.

High Context	**Low Context**
1a. _____	1b. _____
2a. _____	2b. _____
3a. _____	3b. _____
Total _____ ÷ 3 = _____	Total _____ ÷ 3 = ____
Hierarchical	**Egalitarian**
4c. _____	4d. _____
5c. _____	5d. _____
6c. _____	6d. _____
Total _____ ÷ 3 = _____	Total _____ ÷ 3 = ____
Collective	**Individual**
7e. _____	7f. _____
8e. _____	8f. _____
9e. _____	9f. _____
Total _____ ÷ 3 = _____	Total _____ ÷ 3 = ____
Relationship	**Task**
10g. _____	10h. _____
11g. _____	11h. _____
12g. _____	12h. _____
Total _____ ÷ 3 = _____	Total _____ ÷ 3 = ____
Polychronic	**Monochronic**
13i. _____	13j. _____
14i. _____	14j. _____
15i. _____	15j. _____
Total _____ ÷ 3 = _____	Total _____ ÷ 3 = ____
Maintaining Harmony	**Surfacing Differences**
16k. _____	16l. _____
17k. _____	17l. _____
18k. _____	18l. _____
Total _____ ÷ 3 = _____	Total _____ ÷ 3 = ____

Cultural Orientation Profile

Directions: Circle the average for each letter. Draw a vertical line connecting the circled numbers on the left and another line to connect the circled numbers on the right side of the chart. The space between the two lines represents your cultural-orientation range, while the position of your profile, left, right, or center, will give you an indication of your cultural orientation on each of these dimensions.

High Context   **Low Context**

   a.   10 9 8 7 6 5 4 3 2 1   1 2 3 4 5 6 7 8 9 10   b.

Hierarchical   **Egalitarian**

   c.   10 9 8 7 6 5 4 3 2 1   1 2 3 4 5 6 7 8 9 10   d.

Collective   **Individual**

   e.   10 9 8 7 6 5 4 3 2 1   1 2 3 4 5 6 7 8 9 10   f.

Relationship   **Task**

   g.   10 9 8 7 6 5 4 3 2 1   1 2 3 4 5 6 7 8 9 10   h.

Polychronic   **Monochronic**

   i.   10 9 8 7 6 5 4 3 2 1   1 2 3 4 5 6 7 8 9 10   j.

Maintaining Harmony   **Surfacing Differences**

   k.   10 9 8 7 6 5 4 3 2 1   1 2 3 4 5 6 7 8 9 10   l.

Questions for Discussion/Consideration

- What similarities and differences do you see among group members?
- How does your profile reflect a preferred national or organizational profile?
- How does your own profile help and hinder you in communicating?
- How flexible are you in adapting to others who have different cultural orientations on these dimensions?
- How do the differences play out in work behaviors and team interactions?
- How does your combined profile help and hinder you as a team?

- Where are there potential "hot spots" that may lead to misunderstanding or conflict?

- What adaptations do you need to make to communicate more effectively with one another?

- How can you make your combined profile work in your group's favor?

Cultural Considerations

- Talking about differences openly may be uncomfortable for some team members. In such cases, have team members turn in their profiles anonymously and draw a composite group profile for the team to discuss.

Caveats, Considerations, and Variations

- Have each team member mark his or her profile on a separate transparency printed with the profile scoring sheet. Then juxtapose transparencies on an overhead to show differences and similarities in profiles.

- If there are distinct cultural groups, have each group mark profiles using a different colored marker for each group. First show collected profiles of each national or civilizational group together, discussing similarities and differences within a group. Then combine all profiles. (Variation suggested by the work of Mila Hernán Alvarez, Business Communication Consultant, Madrid, Spain.)

- Have members pair or group with those on the team they most need to communicate with to share profiles and negotiate adaptations.

DEALING WITH VERBAL AND NONVERBAL ASPECTS OF CROSS-CULTURAL COMMUNICATION

Understanding the influence of general cultural orientations is one step in increasing skill in cross-cultural communication. The next step is to recognize and deal with the specific differences in the verbal and nonverbal aspects involved. Even when we speak the same language, transmitting meaning involves more than knowing vocabulary, grammar, and syntax. The tone of one's voice, the look on one's face, or the lengths of our pauses can broadcast volumes. Credibility can be built or lost by using the proper or wrong form of address, asking an appropriate or inappropriate question, or observing or ignoring the necessary social norms before moving to the task at hand. Consider which of these you have found to be most difficult in your global interchanges.

Verbal Aspects of Cross-Cultural Communication

Degree of Directness.   Whether we get to the point because not zeroing in on the issue seems like a waste of time or we find that kind of directness rude and off-putting, we all have a preference about degree of directness. Some of us would prefer a clear, direct "no," while others would infer a negative response from "That would be very difficult" or "I'll see what I can do." The range from direct and explicit to indirect and implicit communication is closely tied to high-context and low-context cultural orientations. Those from high-context cultures, such as that of Japan, who prefer less direct communication, depend on the complex web of clues from the history and relationship between participants to nonverbal cues to give them the information they need. Meaning is implied and left to the listener to infer. Those from low-context cultures, such as the Swiss, on the other hand, rely much more on the words, hence communication needs to be specific and explicit.

Differences between these two communication styles can be the source of much frustration and misunderstanding. Europeans are often frustrated by U.S.-Americans' lack of directness, while Japanese might be put off by their lack of subtlety. Americans may be confused by the circular communication of Koreans, wondering when the point will be made, while the Chinese see the unambiguous "No" response from Americans as impolite and confrontational.

Topics.   The acceptability of topics for conversation is another area of cultural difference impacting communication. Asking about money is generally considered impolite in U.S. culture. What one earns or how much one paid for a house, for example, is considered private. In China, though, sharing information about salaries and bonuses is common and, in the Philippines, asking how much one paid for something is considered acceptable. Commenting about the weather is generally not done in Muslim countries, as the weather is given by Allah, not to be questioned or criticized by humans.

Forms of Address.   A nonprofit executive was surprised at her first meeting in Vietnam when her host immediately asked her age. It was only later she found that he needed to know if she was older or younger than he in order to use the proper form of address for her. One's status, whether from age or position, is dealt with differently depending on the adherence to a hierarchy. Using titles such as Director, Doctor, Mister, or Missus is expected in hierarchical cultures, while addressing someone older or in a position of authority by first name would be the height of disrespect. Titles and first and last names are used not only in introductions but in business communication such as signatures on letters. Communicating on a first-name basis, no matter the level or age, on the other hand, is common in more egalitarian cultures and organizations.

Task/Relationship Balance.   While communication involves both task and relationship aspects, the priority we place on one or the other is influenced by culture. Spending time on relationship-oriented communication is seen by some as an essential social lubricant and a trust builder and by others as a time-wasting obstacle that is inappropriate for business communication. Yet research on diverse virtual teams done by Dianne Hofner Saphiere[3] revealed that, on the most effective global teams, members had more frequent nonwork-related social communication with one other, in person, on the phone, and via e-mail. Whether at a quarterly meeting that team members fly in for or at a regular weekly teleconferenced staff meeting, beginning with some personal connections is important.

Nonverbal Aspects of Cross-Cultural Communication

While nonverbal aspects are not apparent in written communication, they do impact face-to-face and in some cases voice-to-voice communication.

Eye Contact.   When to make and break eye contact is a factor in communication around the world. However, norms differ. Sustained eye contact may be seen as hostility, honesty, attentiveness, or insolence, depending on one's background. Conversely dropping the eyes can be seen as respectful by Chinese and Japanese but self-effacing or deceitful by U.S.-Americans.

Proximity.   How close we get to one another when we speak is another arena of cultural programming. Nose to nose or arm's length is a preference we each bring, and differences in these norms can cause discomfort and misunderstanding by Arabs and those from the Mediterranean, who are comfortable with more physical proximity, while Northern Europeans prefer greater distance. Too far can be interpreted as aloofness, coldness, or rejection. Too close, on the other hand, can be interpreted as aggressive, intimidating, or inappropriately intimate, leading to sexual harassment complaints.

Touch.   Physical contact is yet another area of difference across cultures. A handshake, a bow, a hug, or even a kiss are all accepted greetings in business, depending on culture. A pat on the arm or shoulder may be reassuring to one person but insulting or an invasion of privacy to another. In addition, male-female physical contact may be directed by religious rules.

Pace.   The speed with which we speak is still another arena of difference. A slower pace and pauses can be viewed as the sign of a good listener who is thoughtfully considering the speaker's comments. However, for someone preferring a quicker pace and more rapid-fire response, it may be seen as the sign of a slow wit and a dull mind.

Pitch and Tone.   One Swiss banker working in the United States recently asked, "When my boss says something I've done is 'pretty good,' what does that mean?" To answer her question, even a native English-speaking American would need more information. What was the emphasis, tone, and inflection of the "pretty good" comment? "This is pretty *good*," with the emphasis on good and the voice going up at the end would indicate a positive evaluation. "This is *pretty* good," emphasizing pretty and the voice going down at the end would mean not so good at all. However, this nuance might not be apparent to someone speaking English as a second or third language.

Silence.   Language systems and individuals differ in their use of silence in conversation. For the Japanese it is respectful to pause before responding, showing that the speaker's words and ideas are being given consideration and thought. However, for those who find it acceptable to interrupt or respond immediately, silence may be disconcerting and a sign of lack of interest, enthusiasm, or intelligence. It is said that many Japanese find U.S.-Americans' habit of responding immediately rude because it indicates that the individual is not listening and giving thought to what is being said. In addition, the amount of information expressed openly varies among cultures and personalities. Some "hold their cards close to the vest," keeping thoughts to themselves, while others "wear their hearts on their sleeves," disclosing their thoughts freely. The Expressed Speech and Thought chart displays examples of this variation among national cultures; the more above the water line, the greater the degree of disclosure.

The "Cross-Cultural Communication Style Inventory" will give you an opportunity to examine your own style and compare it to the style of one of your co-workers.

Suggestions for Using the "Cross-Cultural Communication Style Inventory"

Objectives

- To increase understanding of cultural factors influencing communication
- To analyze one's own cultural "software" regarding communication
- To identify cultural differences that may present obstacles in global communicating with co-workers in a global workgroup

Intended Audience

- Managers and employees in multinational workgroups
- HR professionals coaching managers of multinational groups
- Employees working with clients or customers from other countries

Time

- 60 minutes

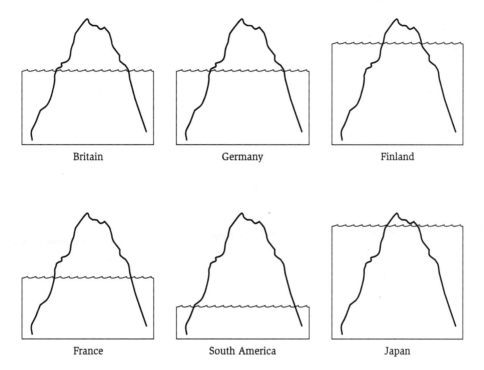

Britain   Germany   Finland

France   South America   Japan

Expressed Speech and Thought

Source: Adapted from Richard D. Lewis, *When Cultures Collide: Managing Successfully Across Cultures* (rev.) (Yarmouth, ME: Intercultural Press, 2000).

Materials

- Copies of the "Cross-Cultural Communication Style Inventory"

Directions

- Explain or discuss the differences in cultural software that influence communication.
- Ask participants to follow directions, marking their own preferences and profile, then that of a co-worker, boss, staff member, or customer/client of another cultural background.
- In pairs, staff members discuss their own and a co-worker's, boss's, staff member's, or client's profile, focusing on similarities and differences and challenges.
- Discuss insights, learning, and application.

Questions for Discussion/Consideration

- What similarities and differences are there in the two profiles on your worksheet?

Cross-Cultural Communication Style Inventory

Directions: Consider your own style of communicating at work and indicate your preferences on each of the continua by placing an X on the line. Then connect your Xs, forming a profile. Then think of an individual from a different culture with whom you work. Put a check mark on each line representing that person's style. Draw a dotted line to connect the check marks to form that person's profile. Then compare profiles to analyze the interaction of your two styles.

Verbal

Directness
Implicit, indirect .... Explicit, direct

Topics
Personal, much .... Impersonal, little
self-disclosure   self-disclosure

Formality
Formal .... Informal

Task/Relationship Balance
Task focus .... Relationship focus

Nonverbal

Gestures
Much facial and .... Little facial and
physical expression   physical expression

Eye Contact
Direct, ... Not direct
sustained   or sustained

Proximity
Close .... Distant

Touch
Much touch .... No touch

Pace
Slow .... Rapid

Pitch/Tone
High .... Low

Silence
Frequent pauses, ... Few pauses,
much silence   little silence

Source: Adapted from Lee Gardenswartz and Anita Rowe, *Managing Diversity in Health Care* (San Francisco: Jossey-Bass, 1998). This material is issued by permission of John Wiley & Sons, Inc.

- How do the two profiles reflect national preferences?
- Where does your own profile help and hinder you as a communicator?
- What are your cross-cultural "hot spots," those preferences or behaviors of others that are difficult for you to deal with in communicating with them?
- What do the two profiles tell you about your communication with each other?
- What challenges do you see?
- What style shifts can you make to reconcile differences and communicate more effectively with this person?
- What style shifts can you help the other person make in order to reconcile differences?

Cultural Considerations

- Employees from more collectivist backgrounds may find the focus on the individual awkward. In such cases, ask the group to draw the preferred organizational communication style, then discuss advantages and disadvantages of that style.

Caveats, Considerations, and Variations

- If staff members know each other and work together, they can give each other feedback about their styles.
- This can be done as a team activity with team members sharing their answers by posting them and giving each other feedback. They can also post answers without names and guess the owner of each.
- Team members can have rotating rounds, meeting in pairs to share profiles and give and receive feedback from one another about their styles.
- On a multinational team have members draw their profiles, each using a different colored marker, on an enlargement (18" x 24") of the inventory. Then conduct a discussion about team communication patterns and challenges.
- On a team that has groups of employees from different national cultures, have each culture use a specific colored marker (for example, Italians use green, Chinese use blue) and have each employee draw his or her profile on a transparency. Stack transparencies of each culture together and show on the overhead, one culture at a time. Then stack all profiles and show together. Discuss intracultural and intercultural similarities and differences. (Adaptation suggested by Mila Hernán Alvarez, business communication consultant, Madrid, Spain.)

Again, it is important to remember that cross-cultural knowledge is necessary but not sufficient in communicating effectively in a global organization. As one former global manager who currently works as an international business consultant pointed out, "What I found to be the most important thing is that people feel that they are valued and respected as individuals, their opinions and their objectives, and as organizations, and that in that sense they are treated as equal."

JUDGING THE EFFECTIVENESS
OF GLOBAL COMMUNICATION

Beyond developing cross-cultural competence at an individual level, communicating effectively in a global arena requires attention to the three Ps of organizational functioning—*practices, procedures,* and *policies* (see the model) regarding communication. *Practices* encompass the behaviors of managers in cross-cultural interactions and the national, corporate, and personal norms that govern interpersonal relations. Can managers shift styles to deal with a range of differences among multinational employees? Are staff members knowledgeable about civilizational and national differences influencing communication? Are managers and employees fluent in the languages needed to conduct business with clients/customers and colleagues around the world?

Corporate and departmental *procedures* must also contribute to effectiveness through methods and formats that facilitate communication, from meetings and presentations to written communication and conference calls. Do meeting for-

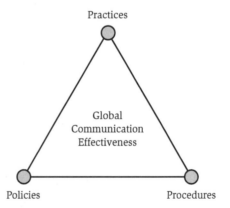

The Three Ps of Global Communication Effectiveness

mats vary to accommodate different national cultural preferences? Are conference calls scheduled taking into account the convenience of those in different national or worldwide time zones?

Finally, organizational *policies* need to support the exchange of information and the building of relationships among staff members. Are language policies clear and conducive to effective information flow? Do policies about meetings, e-mails, conferences, and telephone usage contribute to effectiveness?

The "Global Communication Effectiveness Checklist" will give you an opportunity to assess your organization in light of these three dimensions of global communication.

The more points you have in each section of the checklist, the more effective your organization is in communicating globally. First, look to see which categories have the most and least points to find overall strengths and weaknesses. Then pay particular attention to specific items that were checked "Almost Never." These may indicate issues to address and actions to take in order to increase effectiveness. Discuss these with leaders in your organization to determine the best ways to address these communication saboteurs.

Suggestions for Using the
"Global Communication Effectiveness Checklist"

Objectives

- To identify practices, policies, and procedures conducive to effective global communication
- To assess global communication practices, policies, and procedures
- To identify obstacles to be addressed in order to strengthen global communication

Intended Audience

- Leaders and policymakers in global organizations
- Managers of global teams, departments, divisions, or units
- Human resource managers in global organizations

Time

- 45 to 60 minutes

Materials

- Copies of the "Global Communication Effectiveness Checklist"
- Easel and flip chart
- Markers

Global Communication Effectiveness Checklist

Directions: Check the appropriate column for each statement with regard to your organization.

Practices	Almost Always	Sometimes	Almost Never
1. Managers are assisted in developing cross-cultural awareness, knowledge, and skills.			
2. Managers are skilled in style shifting, using different communication styles appropriately.			
3. Managers are effective in giving feedback to employees of a wide range of backgrounds.			
4. Managers are able to write clear, understandable memos, letters, and reports in the language(s) of the organization.			
5. Managers are able to use interpreters effectively to communicate across language differences.			
6. Managers are skilled in building productive relationships with colleagues and clients of a wide range of cultures.			
7. Managers are sensitive to and knowledgeable about cultural differences influencing communication.			
8. Managers are able to examine their own assumptions, interpretations, and behaviors and assess their impact on business interactions.			
9. Managers are skilled in listening, hearing both the stated and unstated messages.			
10. Managers have developed multiple methods for dealing with cross-cultural communication obstacles.			
11. Managers seek to learn about the national cultures and styles of those with whom they need to communicate.			
12. Managers and international employees are fluent in the official corporate language and at least one other language.			

Global Communication Effectiveness Checklist (continued)

Policies	Almost Always	Sometimes	Almost Never
13. The organization has a clear policy about which language(s) are to be used for official communication.			
14. Corporate/organizational language policy distinguishes between different types of communication (such as internal/external, employee/client, corporate/local).			
15. The organization encourages the sharing of information among different locations.			
16. The organization has a clear policy about the format, style, and use of written communications, including e-mails, which contributes to effectiveness.			
17. The organization encourages employees to share their cross-cultural experience and learning.			
18. The organization has a clear policy about socializing among employees outside of the office, which contributes to effectiveness.			
19. The organization subsidizes the cost of learning other languages.			
20. The organization has a clear policy about meetings and conferences, which contributes to effectiveness.			
21. The organization promotes cross-cultural learning.			
22. The organization has a clear policy about translation and interpretation, which contributes to effectiveness.			
23. The organization has a stated policy about inclusion.			
24. The language policy allows for the use of the most appropriate language for each situation.			

Global Communication Effectiveness Checklist (continued)

Procedures	Almost Always	Sometimes	Almost Never
25. Meeting formats vary in order to be appropriate for the national cultures and preferred styles of participants.			
26. Feedback is a regular aspect of meetings, conferences, and presentations.			
27. Presentation styles vary according to the audience.			
28. Interpreters are selected according to guidelines that ensure effectiveness.			
29. Professionally trained interpreters are used when needed.			
30. Conference calls are arranged taking into account different time zones and the convenience of all participants.			
31. Written communication (memos, reports, letters, e-mails) is used effectively.			
32. Face-to-face meetings are held in different locations on a rotating basis.			
33. Some time is spent on relationship building during meetings and conference calls.			
34. Inconveniences in scheduling and location caused by meetings and calls are shared among participants.			
35. Adaptations and flexibility are required only for the good of the organization, rather than for any particular individual's convenience.			
36. Different communication formats (e-mail, phone calls, meetings, videoconferences) are used appropriately.			

Global Communication Effectiveness Checklist (continued)

Scoring

Almost Always   2 points

Sometimes   1 point

Almost Never   0 points

Add the number of points in each category.

Practices: _____

Policies: _____

Procedures: _____

Total Points: _____

Directions

- Explain the Three Ps of Global Communication Effectiveness: practices, policies, and procedures, giving examples of each and soliciting examples from the group.
- Ask members to respond to the checklist, checking the appropriate column for each statement.
- Ask members to tally the number of points in each category.
- Conduct a group tally of the highest and lowest scoring categories.
- Have members focus on the items scoring zero, then in small groups share the most needed growth areas noted on their checklists, charting the group's agreed-on top three areas to target for improvement.
- Have each group report its top three global communication areas for development, charting responses.
- Lead a group discussion of areas for development, honing the total group list down to three or four.
- Assign one area needing development to each group and have members brainstorm possible ways to strengthen that aspect of global communication in the organization.
- Have groups report their most workable suggestions.
- Summarize and indicate next steps.

- Ask each member to commit to one action he or she can take to strengthen some aspect of communication that is currently presenting an obstacle in global business communication.

Questions for Discussion/Consideration

- Which areas for development most hinder effective global communication in the organization?
- What is the cost of these hindrances to the organization?
- What needs to be done to address these areas?
- Which suggestions are we willing to undertake?
- What can you do individually to improve communication in one of these areas?

Cultural Considerations

- Some members may be reluctant to surface any "bad news" for fear of disrupting harmony and causing embarrassment. Explain that improving communication is everyone's responsibility and that pointing out areas for development helps the organization improve in those areas.
- Some members may be more comfortable discussing without a checklist. In those cases, use the items as questions to stimulate discussion. Or put group members at three charts and ask each to discuss and list the helping and hindering factors in one of the three aspects, practices, policies, or procedures. Then have groups prioritize hindering factors, sharing the top three with other groups. If time permits, have groups brainstorm suggestions for improvement.

Caveats, Considerations, and Variations

- Have members fill out the checklist anonymously and turn it in. Then tally scores and present data to the group for discussion.
- Send and have members respond to the checklist electronically. Tally responses and present for discussion at a teleconferenced meeting.
- Checklist items can be changed to focus practices on "international employees" or "multinational team members" rather than "managers."
- Members can pair up with a partner from another location to discuss responses.
- Data from checklists can be separated by group (for example, by location, national culture, or language). For example, do headquarters-based staff rate the organization's communication practices, policies, and procedures differently than do staff in other countries? Do managers from some regions or national cultures rate the organization differently from

those of other regions or national cultures? Results can then be compared to see if practices, policies, and procedures are experienced differently. Such data could be presented to the team, unit, division, or organization for discussion.

All corporate practices, policies, and procedures have a cultural heritage, generally growing out of the culture of the organization's leaders and the national culture of its origin. Those practices, policies, and procedures may mesh or clash with the national cultures in which the organization operates or with individual employees' orientations. The "Global Communication Analysis" gives you an opportunity to consider the cultural orientations that may underlie some of your organization's practices, policies, and procedures. For example, having a policy that prohibits managers from socializing with their subordinates outside of work may come out of a highly task-oriented culture and may inhibit communication with Japanese employees, who expect to go out drinking with the boss in the evening and who use this time to freely express what they might never disclose in a meeting during working hours. Or a clearly stated policy about memos and e-mails requiring direct, explicit messages might come out of a low-context cultural orientation needing some high-context augmentation, such as pictures of each employee on the organization's intranet directory, bios introducing new team members, or individuals' pictures included in the tag line at the end of e-mail messages, to help employees connect to one another. Analyzing where any clashes might be hindering effectiveness, then taking steps to address them, moves the organization forward.

Consider the specific communication practices, policies, and procedures in your organization and the cultural orientation they reflect. For example, written performance evaluations would come out of a low-context orientation. Guidelines that state that meetings must be scheduled or approved by managers would emerge from a hierarchical orientation. Note your examples on the "Global Communication Analysis." Then consider individual and national orientations that may differ from the organization's.

Suggestions for Using the "Global Communication Analysis"

Objectives

- To raise awareness of the cultural orientation of the organization's practices, procedures, and policies
- To surface conflicts between organizational practices, procedures, and policies and those of employees of different civilizational and national cultures
- To stimulate discussion about cultural orientations and their influence on communication within the organization

Global Communication Analysis

Directions: In the six areas listed below, write down examples of communication practices, policies, or procedures used in the company.

Range in Cultural Orientations	Organizational Practices, Policies, and Procedures	Individual and National Differences
High/Low Context	*Example:* Written performance evaluations are required.	*Example:* Some employees would respond better to face-to-face discussion with managers, not just written analysis.
Hierarchical/Egalitarian		
Collective/Individual		
Relationship/Task		
Polychronic/Monochronic		
Surface Differences/ Maintain Harmony		

Intended Audience
- Executives in a global organization
- Managers of global or international divisions or teams
- HR professionals engaged in setting and modifying communication policies

Time
- 60 minutes

Materials
- Copies of the "Global Communication Analysis"
- Chart paper, markers, and tape

Directions
- Give, or solicit from the group, a few examples of communication practices, procedures, or policies that are followed in the company and discuss which cultural orientations they follow. For example, written performance evaluations would come out of a low-context orientation. Guidelines that state that meetings must be scheduled or approved by managers would come out of a hierarchical orientation.
- Have group members fill in the analysis by jotting down specific examples of practices, procedures, and policies that demonstrate the influence of each cultural orientation.
- Form participants into six groups, each group addressing one of the cultural orientation ranges. Each group discusses and charts examples of both organizational and individual/national orientations.
- Each group reports out examples, with other groups suggesting any additions.
- Groups then brainstorm suggestions for modifying policies to make them more effective with a wider range of employees.

Questions for Discussion/Consideration
- What are the biggest differences between organizational practices, procedures, and policies and the individual and/or national preferences of employees in the organization?
- What are the consequences of these differences?
- What challenges do they present to the organization?
- What can the organization do to modify or augment policies to address these challenges?

Cultural Considerations

- Some members may be reluctant to surface any "bad news" for fear of disrupting harmony and causing embarrassment. Explain that improving communication is everyone's responsibility and demonstrates loyalty. In addition, pointing out potential obstacles and areas for improvement helps the organization deal with them.

- Some members may be more comfortable with discussion without anything in writing. In those cases, use the categories as questions to stimulate discussion.

Caveats, Considerations, and Variations

- It may be helpful to have the group brainstorm communication practices, procedures, and policies by giving them topics such as time, meetings, feedback, e-mails, conference calls, or memos and charting responses. For example, ask them "How do we give and receive feedback?" "What are the norms and rules about schedules, deadlines, and appointments?" or "What are the unwritten rules about meetings, such as, who calls them, how are they conducted, and who talks and who does not?"

- Bring copies of existing policies for the group to examine in order to stimulate thinking about specific rules, guidelines, and requirements.

USING INTERPRETERS IN A GLOBAL ORGANIZATION

Even for multilingual employees, there will be times in global business communication when the use of interpreters is called for. A common misstep regarding interpreters is to call on a bilingual manager within the company to help in that capacity. When this happens, the manager is disempowered and relegated to a service role, possibly losing status or face by serving in that function.

Making effective use of an interpreter is a skill that needs to be developed. Check your own use of interpreters by filling in the "Use of Interpreters Checklist." The checklist items can be used as guidelines to help managers and employees in your organization select appropriate interpreters and make the best use of their assistance.

The more of these items you incorporate into your interactions, the more effective you will be in communicating with the assistance of an interpreter.

Suggestions for Using the "Use of Interpreters Checklist"

Objectives

- To increase effectiveness in using interpreters
- To assess one's effectiveness in using interpreters

Use of Interpreters Checklist

Directions: Think of times when you have used an interpreter recently. Then respond to the items on the checklist based on your behavior.

	Usually	Sometimes	Rarely
1. I use an interpreter who knows my business, field, and industry and is fluent in its concepts and terminology.			
2. I use a professional interpreter who is completely fluent in both languages.			
3. I use an interpreter hired by and loyal to my organization.			
4. I use an interpreter who is from an appropriate social-political background.			
5. I meet the interpreter ahead of time to explain the situation, my objectives in the interaction, and my expectations of him or her.			
6. I speak clearly, avoiding jargon and slang, pausing to give the interpreter time to relay the information.			
7. During the interaction, I address and face my business counterpart or audience, not the interpreter.			
8. I introduce the interpreter formally at the beginning of the conversation, session, or meeting.			
9. I meet with the interpreter ahead of time to gain more culturally effective ways of expressing concepts and information in my own language.			
10. I rely on internal corporate bilingual employees to give me feedback about the interpreter's effectiveness in capturing meaning in light of the languages spoken and the corporate culture.			
11. I debrief with the interpreter after the interaction to gather any additional information about non-verbal and cultural aspects of the interchange.			
12. I avoid asking business advice or involving the interpreter in decision making.			

Source: Adapted from Lee Gardenswartz and Anita Rowe, *Managing Diversity in Health Care* (San Francisco: Jossey-Bass, 1998). This material is issued by permission of John Wiley & Sons, Inc.

- To identify approaches for improving communication with the help of an interpreter

Intended Audience

- Global managers and employees who make use of interpreters
- Staff preparing for assignments or projects where the use of interpreters will be necessary

Time

- 45 minutes

Materials

- Copies of the "Use of Interpreters Checklist"
- Easel, flip-chart pad
- Markers

Directions

- Ask members to share some of their experiences in using interpreters, both successful and unsuccessful, and what they've learned that has worked.
- Explain that effectively using interpreters is a communication skill that most of us could improve.
- Ask staff members to respond to the checklist, reflecting on their own experiences with interpreters.
- Once members are finished, explain that the more checks in the "Usually" column, the more effective one is. However, the most important information may be in those items marked "Rarely," as these indicate potential areas of improvement.
- Lead a discussion about any suggestions that were surprising or that stimulated questions.
- Ask small groups to discuss those guidelines that are seldom followed, charting obstacles that prevent them from being followed.
- Have groups brainstorm ways to overcome obstacles listed. For example, one obstacle may be not knowing qualified interpreters in each location. Actions that might be suggested are to have each location compile a list of highly rated interpreters used by the organization, then make lists available to staff.
- Have each member make a commitment to taking one action to increase effectiveness in using interpreters.

Questions for Discussion/Consideration

- Which guidelines were surprising?
- Which do you have questions about?
- Which are most difficult to follow? Why?
- What could the organization do to help?
- What could you do to increase your effectiveness in using interpreters?

Caveats, Considerations, and Variations

- Some of the guidelines may be out of the control of individual staff members. In such cases, have the group discuss who in the organization they need to involve in order to get the help they need.
- This tool may be used to coach managers and high-potential employees whose work requires the use of interpreters.

USING TRANSLATORS EFFECTIVELY

Translation, different from interpretation, refers to written rather than oral communication. Budgeting for this service so that your organization is well-represented in its written communication is critical. The following guidelines are helpful.

1. Use the services of a professional translator. Conveying information accurately in another language is a skill that requires a significant amount of training and experience. Translators are officially certified in many countries and are well-versed in the nuances of the languages in which they work. These professionals have the ability to adjust the translation to suit different target groups.

2. Use translators who understand your industry, field, business, and the information to be conveyed, including the relevant terminology and concepts being used. Each field of work has specific vocabulary, processes, and concepts that need to be understood in order to be translated appropriately. A legal contract, engineering proposal, medical procedure, or employee stock option plan would each call for very different terminology and knowledge.

3. Use a translator who is a native speaker of the language he or she is writing. According to Monica Moreno, an experienced business translator and cross-cultural consultant, a native speaker will have the most complete grasp of a language. While trilingual herself, Monica only writes translations in Spanish, her first language.

4. When translating into a language that is spoken in different countries, have a native speaker from a different country than the translator's edit or review the document. The Spanish spoken in Argentina will undoubtedly have some differences

from that spoken in Cuba, Mexico, or Spain. English varies between Australian, South African, British, Indian, and Canadian versions. For example, a proposal in U.S. English means a bid for a project, while in the U.K. it refers to what Americans would call an agenda. The German spoken in Switzerland, Austria, and Germany may have differences that alter meanings. In some Spanish-speaking countries *descansar* is used to mean "to lay off," in others "to take a break," a critical distinction in translating an employee handbook. Other examples are *discusión*, which can mean "argument" or "discussion," and *asistencia*, which can mean "help" or "attendance," depending on the country. When dealing with such issues, having speakers from more than one country check translations is critical.

5. Provide the option of translations in a nonincriminating way, especially for in-house documents. If your organization has a language policy regarding the standard corporate language, many employees will not want to advertise the fact that they have greater comfort in their first language. Providing translations in a matter of fact way, back to back or on alternating pages, for example, will make the information accessible to those who need it without calling attention to language proficiency.

SELECTING APPROPRIATE COMMUNICATION VEHICLES

E-mail? Phone call? Memo? Videoconference?

In exchanging information across time and distance, effectiveness is increased when the vehicle for communication is chosen with up-front analysis and clear intention. Considerations in determining which mode to use in conveying information fall into a number of categories.

Cultural Factors

Knowledge of the backgrounds of those participating in the communication is key. Cultural differences regarding factors such as task/relationship and high/low context play an important role in choosing the best vehicle. How much do receivers need and value personal attention and the human touch? How much is trust a factor in getting the message across? Are receivers more focused on the task-related aspects or on the relationship aspects?

For example, when giving feedback in a low-context environment, clear and specific points in writing might be called for. In a high-context environment, a brief conversation might suffice, saving face for both boss and employee.

When one U.S.-American director tried to "clean up" a poorly run, chaotic, and inefficient operation, she approached it from her task-oriented vantage point. After careful analysis of the problems, she sent memos to all staff informing them of the changes she was instituting to streamline and systemize procedures. While the changes she made were good from a task perspective, she had not taken into account her mostly Filipino staff's priority on relationships. The lack of personal connection involved in the method she chose, which they saw as cold, inhuman, and even discriminatory, created resistance to what were objectively productive moves that could have increased effectiveness. Only in retrospect did she realize that had she spent time on the relationship aspects of the communication by having some face-to-face talks with staff, asking for input in informal conversations, and announcing the changes at small group meetings, she might have increased the chances of the changes being implemented successfully.

Another cultural difference involves interpreting e-mail messages. The use of "cc" in communication may be used in low-context cultures to protect oneself and can be interpreted as putting pressure on one's boss by copying those at higher levels. On the other hand, in high-context environments the "cc" may cause embarrassment and loss of face at the fact that now everyone knows.

Logistical Factors

Aspects such as time zone differences, distance, and cost also enter into the equation. Are participants in the same building or time zone? What are the difficulties and costs of getting people in the same place or finding a mutually acceptable time?

In addition, what are the technological capabilities required and what equipment is available to those who need to be included? Do all have access to computers? Is videoconferencing available at all locations onsite? In one case of an organization with offices in the United States and mainland China, conference calls were set up during office hours of the American staff but late in the evening for their counterparts in Asia. Since Chinese staff did not have telephone conferencing available from their homes, they had to stay at their offices until after midnight to take calls. Not wanting to cause problems or disruption by complaining, they continued to stay late to participate in calls, although feeling some resentment and irritation. It was only when one of the U.S. staff members was in China during one of these calls that the problem came to light. While the U.S. team knew about the time difference, it had never occurred to them that their Asian colleagues could not take calls at home. In another instance, an employee of a global consulting firm fell asleep during an international conference call that took place during predawn hours. He was shocked when his hotel presented him with a telephone bill of $2,000 U.S.

Cost of the method is an additional factor. E-mail is cheaper than a phone call, videoconferencing cheaper than a meeting requiring international flights. However, the short-term cost must be balanced against the objectives of the communication and the benefits of the mode. While videoconferencing is less costly than a meeting, it does not provide the team-building spinoff that a face-to-face group session can give. Relationship benefits can mushroom when staff members have offline conversations during breaks, socialize during meals, and informally connect in the exercise room.

Intrinsic Factors

The choice of mode is also influenced by corporate purpose, organizational urgency, and interpersonal sensitivity, which are aspects inherent to the communication itself. Whether to convey information, solicit input, build relationships, or entertain, all communication has a purpose. The objectives of the communication play a big role in signaling the best method. Memos or e-mails are less effective in building trust. However, these same vehicles may be very effective in distributing data in a consistent way to many people at once.

Urgency is another deciding factor. E-mail and fax are quicker than a meeting or a letter if time is an issue. They also enable the message to be sent simultaneously to all so that no one is disadvantaged by receiving information later.

Another factor relates to the sensitivity of the information. E-mail and fax do not provide the privacy and confidentiality that a phone call or letter might. Announcing a promotion decision via memo before privately talking with the candidate involved, as was done in one organization, can have personally devastating and organizationally counterproductive results.

Human Factors

Ultimately, communication is between people, and the individual aspects of those involved are critical to consider. What is the language ability of participants? While all may speak the official language of the corporation, those working in a second or third language may be at a disadvantage without advance written communication to prepare for a conference call or follow-up minutes from a meeting for reference later. Phone conversations might help avoid unintentional misunderstandings in written communication, but e-mails and faxes can help avoid difficulties with accents in oral interchanges.

At a personal level, how much tolerance for ambiguity or need for direction do receivers have? Giving detailed information can be clarifying and helpful to one individual, yet seen as micromanaging and a lack of confidence and trust by another.

The Comparison of Communication Methods chart can help to clarify some of the advantages and disadvantages of each communication mode.

COMMUNICATING IN WRITING

No matter how great the desire to reduce paperwork, all business and organizational life requires some forms of written communication, yet the norms vary across national cultures. From how to write the date to how to organize one's thoughts, differences in these practices can cause confusion at best and major problems at worst. Understanding and adapting to the preferences of the culture

Mode	Advantages	Disadvantages
Face-to-Face	Personal Relationship and trust building Two-way Nonverbal cues Immediate feedback Private	Travel expense Scheduling difficulty Time requirements Lack of paper trail/backup
Telephone	Personal Relationship building Two-way Immediate feedback Auditory nonverbal cues (for example, tone) Private	Time congruence needed Cost Limited to one-to-one Lack of paper trail/backup Lack of visual nonverbal cues
Videoconference	Two-way Group synergy and focus Nonverbal cues Immediate feedback Multiple participants	Time congruence needed Availability of technology Convenience (setup requirements) Lack of privacy
Teleconference	Immediate feedback Two-way Auditory nonverbal cues Multiple participants	Time congruence needed Lack of visual nonverbal cues Lack of privacy
E-mail	Quick, immediate Low cost Clear, direct Time convenience Paper trail/backup	Lack of privacy One-way No immediate feedback No nonverbal cues Open to misinterpretation Reliance on writing skills
Fax	Quick, immediate Time convenience Low cost No time required for input Clear, direct Paper trail/backup	One-way No immediate feedback No nonverbal cues Reliance on writing skills
Memo	Specific, clear, direct Consistent message to all Low cost Paper trail/backup	One-way No immediate feedback Requires written fluency Time-consuming Impersonal Lack of privacy
Letter	Specific, clear, direct Conveys importance Low cost Can be personal Private	One-way Formal Requires written fluency Time-consuming No immediate feedback

Comparison of Communication Methods

of the reader and eliminating confusion wherever possible are some of the fundamental guidelines in written communication in a global organization. Other guidelines are listed below:

1. Investigate the expected format for organizing information. For example, Canadians prefer recommendations at the beginning followed by supporting points, while Germans expect information in chronological order.[4] Understanding the expectations of your readers can help you write in a more acceptable and accessible style for them.

2. Avoid jargon and idiomatic expressions that are hard to understand, and sometimes meaningless, for a second-language or third-language speaker. What would such an employee make of "We have them over a barrel" "It's a slam dunk" or "Let's get our ducks in a row"? Similarly words such as "snafu" and "glitch" are not as easily understood as "problem." Since the use of such shorthand is often unconscious, it is helpful to have a second-language speaker read your written communication to check for these kinds of inadvertent slips that could cause confusion.

3. Avoid abbreviations and acronyms. Letters and reports containing acronyms such as EEOC, ASAP, CEO, OSHA, or GNP may look like alphabet soup to a reader unfamiliar with them. Similarly, abbreviations such as e.g. or etc. may be confusing.

4. Use headings and white space to make the document more reader-friendly and to help the key points of the message stand out.

5. Pay attention to details such as using correct titles and accurate spelling of names. Also recognize that dates are written in various orders in different parts of the world. 8–10–02, 10.8.02, or 2002, 08, 10 all refer to the same date. Write out the month and give the full year (2002 rather than 02) to avoid confusion. Numbers are also written differently, with decimal points and commas having different functions. $3,618.54 in the United States would be written as $3.618,54 in European languages.[5]

Organizational Language Policies

Most organizations have official policies and guidelines for communication. While in more mono-cultural environments many of the rules and norms are unconsciously shared by all, in global organizations, being clear and explicit about these expectations is even more important. Without these guidelines, many employees will flounder or avoid communicating rather than risk making mistakes.

The first aspect to consider is the language of the company. Generally in the early stages of becoming international, the language of the home country of the corporation is the accepted language. However, as organizations become more multicultural in staff and in customers, changes in this pattern are seen. Royal Dutch Shell, for example, based in the Netherlands, has two corporate languages, English and French, although the first language of many of its employees is Dutch.

Having one or two languages in which employees can communicate with one another across the globe is essential. Yet how does an organization determine to what extent this policy applies? Varner and Beamer maintain that language policy is to some extent directed by staffing patterns.[6] They differentiate among three distinct staffing patterns that would require different language policies: *ethnocentric, polycentric,* and *geocentric* staffing. *Ethnocentric* staffing refers to a pattern where all managers at headquarters, regional offices, and local sites come from the home country and speak one language. This requires that interpreters be used in regions where staff and customers do not speak the language of the corporate home country. However, it makes for easy communication among managers, both remote and at headquarters.

In *polycentric* staffing, managers at headquarters come from the home country, while those in the regions come from the local areas. These local managers can communicate easily with staff and customers in their own regions and they understand the culture and needs of that market. The difficulty arises with communication between and among regional offices and with headquarters. The use of interpreters and translation or having bilingual local management who speak the language of the company's home country is required.

In *geocentric* staffing, which tends to be the direction in which global firms are moving, placement of staff is based on the best person for the job, not on linguistic background or nationality. In such organizations the designation of an official company language is called for. However, even designating one or two languages does not eradicate all language-related communication problems. If English is the company language, some employees may speak British English, while others use American or Australian English. Chinese, Indian, Nigerian, and Italian employees, who may all be fluent in English, will undoubtedly speak with different accents and intonation patterns and may find it difficult to understand one another.

When Airbus was founded over thirty years ago as an amalgam of French, British, German, and Spanish aerospace companies, it made English its official language to facilitate communication.[7] This use of English as the corporate "language" is shared by many other global players, such as French-based LVMH Moët Hennessy Louis Vuitton, Italian appliance manufacturer Merloni Electrodomesticï, and Finnish elevator maker Kone. However necessary this "lingua franca," it remains a kind of mechanical tool for communication that lacks the nuance, warmth, and personal touch of communicating in local languages. It also tends to be limited to formal communication with local languages continuing to be used on shop floors, with customers, and even among top executives who share a common native tongue.

Finally, while this policy facilitates career mobility from local areas to head-quarters, it creates barriers to lateral career moves, which are often necessary to prepare managers for executive leadership positions. In a French-owned firm that uses both French and English as its languages, a bilingual manager may be fine in Paris and Sydney, but not be able to succeed in a position in China, Italy, or Sweden without knowing the local language as well. One Singaporean employee of a British firm explained that he could take a promotion that placed him in the United States or Great Britain, but would not be able to manage operations in Milan, as he did not speak Italian. While he could communicate with the top management team in Italy, he would be cut off from lower management and hourly employees, who were monolingual Italian speakers.

Another aspect of language policy relates to the speaking of multiple languages in a work location. Teams and staffs often polarize around this issue, with some wanting a one-language-only rule because of what they perceive as rude and exclusionary behavior and others claiming the right and efficacy of speaking their first languages. When this divisive dynamic develops, changing the paradigm from either/or to both/and is critical.

Employees need to understand the perspective of those on the other side of the language divide. One approach is to have employees explain their experience through open-ended statements such as:

- I speak my first language at work because . . .
- When someone speaks another language I don't understand in my presence, I . . .
- When someone doesn't understand what we're saying, I'd like him to . . .
- When someone sees I don't understand, I'd like her to . . .

You can also phrase these as questions:

- Why do you think people speak their first language at work?
- What do you want your co-workers to do when they see you don't understand what they are saying?

Another strategy is to ask employees to imagine how others feel.

- Think of a time when you were the only person who did not understand the language being used. How did you feel and react?
- If you lived in another country and learned its language, but worked with a colleague who spoke your first language, what language would you speak with one another?

A more high-context approach would be to use a third party, perhaps someone who is bilingual and has relationships with people in both groups, to serve as a go-between.

PLANNING AND LEADING MEETINGS

While meetings may be the bane of corporate existence, they are a staple of business life and a prime arena for communication. How they are structured and led in global settings can determine their effectiveness. The first step in planning any meeting is to determine its purpose, as that will become the foundation upon which you build. Why a meeting is called differs according to both national and corporate culture. In some places it would be a regular, expected way for a team to share information and solve problems. In other organizations and locations it would be seen as a corporate command performance where communication would be one-way and top-down. In other cases calling a meeting might signal a crisis and be seen as announcing a serious problem. Whether the meeting is a full-day team-building retreat held in an idyllic setting or a one-hour staff meeting done via videoconference, both the content and processes will be planned around the following purposes:

- *Problem solving*—Will you be analyzing and investigating a problem and designing ways to solve it?
- *Idea generation*—Do you need to use creative techniques such as brainstorming or a pre-survey to come up with multiple alternatives?
- *Decision making*—Will it be important to come to a decision about a particular course of action or to make a choice among alternatives?
- *Information sharing*—What data, facts, policies, guidelines, updates, or other information will need to be given by you or others?
- *Data generating*—What kinds of information will you need to collect from participants? Is it more effective to collect beforehand through an electronic survey, for example, or on the spot at the meeting?
- *Relationship building*—How much do you need to focus on team building and connection making to increase cohesion in the group?
- *Planning*—Will you be strategizing and planning actions to be taken?
- *Evaluation*—Are there processes, programs, or projects for which you will need to measure progress, take stock of conditions, or evaluate results?

Once you have determined the purposes of your meeting, use the guidelines that follow when designing your agendas.

Guidelines for Planning and Leading Effective Meetings

1. Send the meeting agenda to participants ahead of time to give them a chance to prepare their thoughts. Those who are more reflective and less spontaneous will appreciate the advance warning.

2. Send any written material ahead of time so that those who are working in a second language and those who are more reflective can have time to digest information before the meeting. Also provide materials in translation if needed by participants.

3. Tell people ahead of time what will be expected. If information, data, or reports are to be shared, let people know what to bring. If their input will be sought, give them advance warning so they can consider ideas and compose their thoughts.

4. Use processes that are appropriate for the cultural backgrounds of participants. If group members are from more hierarchical or collective cultures where singling oneself out or giving feedback to a superior would be awkward, avoid calling on individuals or expecting people to speak out. Instead, divide the staff into small groups for discussion and input, having them chart information. Then have a spokesperson from each subgroup report its data to the total group.

   Another variation would be to collect input anonymously from staff members ahead of time, for example, via a checklist or questionnaire e-mailed or faxed, then present the collected data at the meeting with your response.

5. Vary communication styles in meeting agendas. If direct, linear, task-oriented communication is your style, find a way to explain using a story or bring in a case study example for the group to discuss. If switching style is difficult for you, share the leadership of the meeting with a colleague or team member who has a different style and have the individual tell a story or describe a case. The Cultural Contrasts During Multicultural Meetings figure is helpful in determining appropriate styles.

6. Present information in a variety of modes. Use statistical data and case examples, provide diagrams and narrative explanations, show pictures and give written directions based on preferred national styles. Vary audiovisual media as well, making use of PowerPoint® presentations, overhead transparencies, videotaped segments, easels and flip charts, and prepared handouts as appropriate.

7. Prepare any written materials in advance so they are in front of participants during the meeting. This is especially important for teleconferences and videoconference sessions. Without the pertinent material in front of them, participants will be at a loss in following the agenda from a distance.

8. Allow people to use the language that is most effective. In multilingual settings, even when all participants are fluent in the official language

	American	Japanese	Arab
Objective	Formulate plan of action	Seek information; no conclusion	Build rapport and establish trust base
Opening	Direct to objective	Identification of seniority; period of silence for harmony	An introductory period to warm up expression of hospitality
Participation	Expected from all in attendance	Led by seniors; seek feelings of group; more listening	By seniority; specialist involved; indirect to task
Self-image	Equality; independence; competition	Part of group; modesty	Rich culture; generosity
Use of Language	Statement direct; to the point	Indirect no; yes/no	Flattering; looping
Nonverbal Communication	Informal; minimum emotional expression	Hierarchy; occasional silence	Seniority/age; dress level; emotion
Spatial Orientation	Opposite—across the table	Circle; prearranged	By status and age
Time Orientation	Always punctual; future-oriented	On time for first meeting important	Historical context
Decision Making	Fact-based; risk taking; appeal to reason	Information-based; group consensus	Intuition; religious background
Closing	Conclusion; plan of action; responsibility	Will discuss with others; no commitments	Future meeting oriented/open loop
Applied Values	Cultural directness; action-oriented; individuality; future-oriented; risk taking; achievement; accomplishment	Information-seeking; hierarchy; group harmony; listening/observing; patience	Hospitality; religious belief; age/seniority; flattering/admiration

Cultural Contrasts During Multicultural Meetings

Source: Adapted from Farid Elashmawi and Philip R. Harris, *Multicultural Management: New Skills for Global Success* (Houston, TX: Gulf, 1993).

of the organization, there may be times when having staff members use their first language in subgroup discussions is most effective. For example, presentation of data may be done for all in the official corporate language, followed by small-group tasks done in employees' first language. Then the report-back by groups would be given in the common language.

9. Consult with a cultural informant to find out the expected meeting norms. How are people seated, for example? In the Arab world, where hierarchy and status are respected, seating the most senior person in the place of honor would be expected. In some U.S.-American companies, this would also be the practice, while in others there are no assigned places and participants choose their own place on a first-come, first-served basis. Who ends the meeting? In Poland, the guest, not the host, signals when the meeting is over.

10. Recognize the limits of a meeting and find other ways to achieve your objectives. You may be able to gather more honest input through informal discussions during after-work socializing, or you may be able to generate more support for your proposal by having one-on-one talks over lunch. You may find the real issue underlying a thorny problem when you comment on your colleague's deep sigh and rolled eyes as you walk back to your office from the meeting. Real, honest communication is not structured around time schedules and meeting agendas, and much important information is exchanged outside the confines of official channels and settings.

Often presentations are called for in meetings. As with many other kinds of communication, it's not what you say but how you say it that determines effectiveness. Preferred presentation styles vary around the world and from person to person.

MAKING PRESENTATIONS

A number of factors need to be considered when making presentations in cross-cultural settings. Not only will there be language differences to consider, but also culture will influence both presenter and audience. For example, in some settings a relaxed, informal style would be preferred so as to set a comfortable tone and create a closer connection between speaker and listeners. Generating participation from the group and creating discussions and a lively give-and-take would be valued. However, in more hierarchical cultures, this style might appear unprofessional and disrespectful, thereby damaging the presenter's credibility or placing participants in an awkward position. In this case, dressing and behaving in a more formal manner would be more appropriate. Before you make a presentation, consider the organizational, cultural, and human factors that would influence your choice of format, style, material, and medium.

Many organizations have guidelines for presentations, for example, calling for PowerPoint formats and stipulating layout of slides. If this is the case, following these guidelines will make your presentation more understandable to audiences that are used to a predictable format. In addition, check into the technological capabilities and equipment availability at the location where you will be presenting. If there is no LCD projector or video playback in the room, can one be brought in or do you need to reconsider the medium you are using?

Consider the cultural factors as well. In more hierarchical settings, you might want to wear a suit and speak from a podium. In less hierarchical ones, perhaps sitting around a conference table would be more appropriate. If there is a strong relationship orientation, arriving early to chat with the group might be called for. If the group is more task-oriented, then laying out clear objectives and getting down to business immediately would be more appropriate. If the audience is more polychronic than you, check your impulse to get irritated or disconcerted by late-comers. What level of detail will be expected? For example, Germans generally want to discuss topics deeply, while U.S.-Americans are generally satisfied with getting an idea of what is meant.

Finally, find out about your listeners. Will you need an interpreter? Although all may speak your language, it may also be helpful to have your materials available in translation. It is generally a good idea to have your presentation on hard copy so audience members can make notes as you speak and have the information to reread or refer to later.

Audiences also have format and style preferences. For some groups, PowerPoint slides demonstrate professionalism and preparation. For others, they are off-putting and distance the group from the speaker. Some groups will warm to humor and a down-home, folksy approach; others will prefer a more reserved, serious presentation. In some teams statistical backup would be required for credibility or a process flow chart for clarity. Do your homework to find out about your audience so you can avoid creating unnecessary barriers that will hinder communication. The charts comparing Preferences for Corporate Presentations and listing Influencing Strategies and Presentation Expectations provide information about some differences in preferences among various cultural groups.

It is important to recognize your own preferences first so that you will be able to predict your natural style. Then investigate the styles and preferences of your audience at a specific presentation based on the national, civilizational, and corporate cultures involved. Finally, decide what adaptations might be called for to have the most effective impact on the group and achieve the objectives of your presentation. "Considerations in Planning Presentations" can assist you as you work.

Concept	U.S.-American	European	Asian	Latin American
Objective	Presents facts Present status	Reach agreement Seek information Open discussion	Examine premises	Present big picture with rationale
Opening	Very short Direct to task	Identify credentials and authority Establish goals	Identify expertise	Identify self and connection
Process	Objectives Justification Sense of needs Conclusion Action	Reactive Cognitively challenging	Formalized participation	Top-down Authoritarian
Self-image	Self-reliant	Qualified	Group belonging Modest	Group belonging Status
Use of language	Very direct	Subtle Nuanced Appropriate to class/status Conservative	Non-confrontational	Indirect Diplomatic
Media	Use of multimedia for persuasion	More verbal Research valued	Visual presentation valued Aesthetics important	Visual presentation valued Aesthetics important
Closing	Seek agreement Set up action plan	Verify learning Consequences are taken elsewhere	Express the harmony of the group	Express group effort Emphasize affiliation and individual responsibility to group
Applied cultural values	Logical Factual Directness Equality	Research-based Appropriateness Maintains order	Group-oriented Information exchange	Group-oriented Authority and responsibility

Preferences for Corporate Presentations

Source: Adapted from Farid Elashmawi and Philip R. Harris, *Multicultural Management: New Skills for Global Success* (Houston, TX: Gulf, 1993).

United States	United Kingdom	Germany
Humor	Humor	Solidity of company
Joking	A story	Solidity of product
Modernity	"Nice" product	Technical info
Gimmicks	Reasonable price	Context
Slogans	Quality	Beginning—middle—end
Catch phrases	Traditional rather than	Lots of print
Hard sell	modern	No jokes
		Good price
		Equality
		Delivery date
Attention Span: 30 minutes	Attention Span: 30 to 45 minutes	Attention Span: 1 hour

France	Japan	Sweden
Formality	Good price	Modernity
Innovative product	Synergy with company image	Quality
"Sexy" appeal	Harmony	Design
Imagination	Politeness	Technical information
Logical presentation	Respect for their company	Delivery dates
Reference to France	Good name of your company	
Style, appearance	Quiet presentation	
Personal touch	Well-dressed presenter	
May interrupt	Formality	
	Diagrams	
Attention Span: 30 minutes	Attention Span: 1 hour	Attention Span: 45 minutes

Med/Arab	Finland	Australia
Personal touch	Modernity	"Mate-ly" opening
Rhetoric	Quality	Informality throughout
Eloquence	Technical information	Humor
Liveliness	Modest presentation	Persuasive style
Loudness	Design	No padding
May interrupt		Little contexting
Want "extra" talk afterward		Innovative product
		Essential technical info
		Personal touch
		May interrupt
		Imaginative conclusion
Attention Span: Short	Attention Span: 45 minutes	Attention Span: 30 minutes

Influencing Strategies and Presentation Expectations

Source: Based on Richard D. Lewis, *When Cultures Collide: Managing Successfully Across Cultures* (rev.) (Yarmouth, ME: Intercultural Press, 2000).

Considerations in Planning Presentations

Directions: When planning an upcoming presentation, use this analysis to help you suit your style to audience preferences by filling out each of the boxes below and adapting where necessary.

	Your Style/ Preference	Style/Preference of Your Audience Members	Suggested Adaptations
Dress			
Format			
Materials			
Media			
Communication Style			

Suggestions for Using
"Considerations in Planning Presentations"

Objectives

- To plan appropriate presentations for diverse audiences
- To assess the preferences of global audience members
- To increase flexibility and adaptability in making presentations in multinational and cross-cultural situations

Intended Audience

- Managers and employees who make presentations to multinational audiences
- Managers and employees working with clients/customers or staff members from a variety of cultures
- Employees engaged in cross-cultural business communications

Time

- 45 to 60 minutes

Materials

- Copies of "Considerations in Planning Presentations" (If used electronically, e-mail the exercise to group members.)

Directions

- Discuss the five aspects to be considered in planning presentations. Give examples of differences in each and/or solicit examples from the group.
- Ask group members to think of a cross-cultural/multinational audience to which they will be making a presentation and, with that audience in mind, to fill in the chart. (If sent via e-mail, ask members to fill in the chart and be prepared to discuss via teleconference.)
- Have group members review their SSI profile and pair up with someone from a different background (nationality, field of work, department in the organization, work location, and so forth) and share information on the worksheet, making additional suggestions for their partner's sheet. (If done via teleconference, lead a discussion of information about differences in preferences and suggestions for upcoming presentations.)
- Lead a total-group discussion of suggestions and learnings.

Questions for Discussion/Consideration

- What did you find out about your own style and preferences?
- How much do you know about the style and preferences of your audience members?

- What people and resources can help you find out more?
- What adaptations will you make to increase the effectiveness of your presentation?
- How will you obtain useful feedback about your presentation?

Cultural Considerations

- If staff members have worked in mono-cultural environments, they may find it difficult to describe their own and others' styles or preferences without any basis of comparison. In such cases, have them review the information in the comparison figures presented earlier or bring in a speaker or case studies highlighting different preferences.

Caveats, Considerations, and Variations

- Managers and employees may work on their own with this chart, first filling out as much as they can. They can then interview colleagues from other cultures or co-workers who have had more international experience to gain more knowledge and insight.
- In the second column, group members can describe the organization's style preferences, describe those of a wide range of employees in the third column, and make suggestions for adaptations in the last column. They can discuss these differences in small groups with each subgroup focusing on one aspect, then report out to the total group.
- The group or team can focus on a specific upcoming presentation and use this information in planning.

At this point you may be ready to throw up your hands in defeat. How can one know about all of the communication style differences and cultural preferences that you will encounter? Even more fundamentally, because we don't know what we don't know, how does someone even know what to ask?

Two critically important strategies are suggested by a veteran of international training for the Peace Corps and Boeing. After having worked in Eastern and Western Europe and Asia with Russian, Dutch, French, Belgian, German, Chinese, Korean, Australian, Japanese, and U.S.-American employees, George Monagan has found the following two steps crucial to professional survival when working in a global arena:

1. Make Use of Cultural Informants

First, develop a strong network of cultural informants. This means taking time to talk with people who know the environment and culture in which you are going to work. Building trust and genuine relationship with staff is an investment of time and energy that pays big dividends. For example, he says, department secretaries, generally from the local area and used to "dumb" questions from foreigners, are a wonderful source of helpful information. Spending unofficial time with people, such as at smoking breaks and after work, socializing, chatting, building rapport and comfort, creates trust that enables you to get honest information and real clues about the norms, expectations, and behavior of the group.

One non-Asian manager expressed exasperation at her Southeast Asian staff because of their balking at her rearrangement of the office cubicles. Unbeknown to her, she had chosen to move furniture and partitions on the first day of the lunar new year. In frustration she asked, "How was I supposed to know about this holiday and its meaning?" Had she developed connections with at least a few of her staff, they could have served as her cultural informants, explaining to her the potential repercussions of her decision. As she painfully found out, there is no substitute for relationship building when working internationally.

In addition, the organization also has a responsibility to explain how serving as a cultural informant is of value to the company. One way that can be done is by intentionally recycling the learning. An employee working internationally can become a cultural informant for others and within twelve months be able to relay information to the next newcomer. Often this knowledge is not capitalized on, the knowledge is lost to the organization, and each newcomer has to reinvent the wheel.

In one case a consultant was preparing a group of employees to go abroad for their next global assignment. At the break he ran into another consultant who was conducting a session in another room. He was surprised to find out his colleague was debriefing a group of employees who had just returned from working in the country that was the destination for the group he was preparing. The organization had missed a prime opportunity to recycle the learning and have first-hand knowledge gained by returnees shared with those who needed it most.

2. Create a Hybrid Workplace Culture

The second strategy suggested by Monagan involves creating a "third culture," neither the local national culture nor that of the organization's or visitor's home country, but a third culture. This is the culture of the company's operation in a specific place, for example, the Boeing-China culture. One aspect of common ground in this culture consists of the shared goals and emphasis on the success of the organization. Norms can be created in this hybrid culture that are different from the cultures of origin, such as a value on having everyone serve as a cultural informant. This validates behaviors such as giving honest answers, asking questions to elicit information, and sharing negative feedback when these are important to the success of the project. Once this kind of behavior becomes the norm, people can tell one another why a presentation was unsuccessful or what changes are needed in a training agenda or how to seat people at a meeting to achieve the best results.

Business communication in global organizations requires knowledge and skills in cross-cultural encounters and the ability to apply that in specific business settings. Managing multinational work groups and interacting effectively with co-workers, customers, clients, and suppliers involves an awareness of cultural differences across all the levels of the SSI Model that impact interactions. It also necessitates the ability to learn about the needs, preferences, and norms of others and the skills to use that knowledge to send and receive accurate information and develop productive relationships.

Notes

1 Farb, Peter. "Man at the Mercy of Language." In Jaime S. Wurzel (Ed.), *Toward Multiculturalism: A Reader in Multi-Cultural Education* (Yarmouth, ME: Intercultural Press, 1988, p. 194).

2 Fallon, Maura. "Human Resources Operations in China." In Tina Fron (Ed.), *China Practical Staff Employment Manual* (Hong Kong: Pearson, 1997).

3 Saphiere, Dianne M. Hofner. "Productive Behaviors on Global Business Teams," *International Journal of Intercultural Relations,* Fall 1996.

4 Gardenswartz, Lee, and Anita Rowe. *Managing Diversity in Health Care* (San Francisco: Jossey-Bass, 1998) and Varner, Iris, and Linda Beamer, *Intercultural Communication in the Global Workplace* (Boston, MA: Irwin/McGraw-Hill, 1995, pp. 44–47).

5 Op cit., p. 50.

6 Op cit., p. 39.

7 Tagliabue, John. "In Europe, Going Global Means Alas English," *New York Times,* May 19, 2002.

CHAPTER 4

Maximizing Global Teams and Work Groups for Higher Performance

W hen Smith first joined the organization, he took everyone to dinner, from directors to drivers. At work Smith talks with his subordinates daily, setting expectations for their performance. In giving feedback he figures out how he can help them "do it right." With people outside the team, Smith makes things his subordinates "do right" visible and protects subordinates when they do something wrong. In his role as general manager he walks through the plant daily, briefly acknowledging everyone, including shop floor workers, security guards, and canteen staff.[1]

Effective team functioning may be defined differently in various parts of the world, but on one thing most organizations and cultures agree. To be considered effective, teams have to accomplish the work of the organization. It appears this is best done by exhibiting some constant values—respect, loyalty, support, and caring—something Smith knew how to do in the preceding example. These values can be demonstrated by different behaviors across cultures but, in whatever form they take, they are critical to successful management. This chapter shows how these values and behaviors are demonstrated and played out in a team environment by focusing on the task, relationships, process, and content functions worldwide.

This chapter focuses on both the limits and the possibilities of the new global reality. It provides practical tools to help managers maximize team and work-group cohesion to create a competitive advantage. Managers and group members will learn how to capitalize on the creative potential inherent in diverse

groups, despite the challenges of dispersion and differences such as nationality, language, position, gender, and other dimensions reflected in the SSI Model.

Before we introduce a model for building effective global teams, it is important to define what kind of teams we are talking about and what characterizes
a global or multinational team. In this chapter, we are looking at three different
kinds of teams. The first is a *functional work unit* that exists as part of the operational structure of an organization on a day-in and day-out basis; the next is a
project team whose members come together for the purpose of accomplishing
a specific goal. The duration of its existence may vary and it disbands when the
objective has been accomplished. Finally, the third team structure is a *task force.*
Its timelines are usually clear, and it frequently investigates dilemmas around
a given issue. The end point is a set of recommendations to a strategic body that
has the power to make decisions. Because these three team structures are being
discussed in the context of a global environment, they may all be geographically dispersed. These characteristics are compared in Three Types of Global
Teams.

The opportunity to leverage the productivity on global teams is both exhilarating and challenging. In order for a manager to meet goals and objectives,
three distinct areas require focus and attention. They are (1) understanding the
nature and impact of national culture on a team; (2) building awareness and
understanding for managing across these national cultural differences; and (3)
creating a framework for developing high-performance teams, shown in the figure and described below.

AWARENESS: UNDERSTANDING THE NATURE AND IMPACT OF NATIONAL CULTURE ON THE TEAM

In the business world of the United States and Great Britain, team building has
frequently been thought of as a Western and linear intervention designed to
refine and improve a functioning work group or team. The process is an accurate reflection of the business culture. In Southeast Asia however, team building was traditionally not an issue since the team was directed to meet the
expectations of the leader. The question for managers of global teams is what
other preferred national business styles impact not only the concept or definition of team building, but also the practice of it. How do methods and processes
need to be expanded and adapted to help a global team function in a positive,
constructive way? How can cultural norms from various continents and countries be learned from, operationalized, and integrated worldwide to ensure high
performance? Part of the answer requires first understanding and then paying
attention to the potential impact of national culture on team dynamics.

Kind of Team	Purpose	Duration	Accountability
Functional Team The New Zealand Dairy Board structures global teams for product development and placement	Part of business operations; responsible on a daily basis for adding value to organization	Ongoing part of organization's operation and structure	Joint accountability is ongoing and constant
Project Team When Disney begins their new Hong Kong project they will bring people from France, Japan, Hong Kong, and the United States for all sorts of projects	Comes together to work on an identified project; not intended to be indefinite; has the objective of implementing a specific change	Depends on resources, the complexity of the project, and commitment to its charter	Joint accountability is around achieving particular goal for which it is formed
Task Force When Infineum began to look at global diversity, they had task forces in Singapore, the United States, and the U.K.	To accomplish a specific short-term goal; make recommendations about a specific issue or problem	Depends on the issue, but six months to a year is a common length of time	Joint accountability involves coming up with a set of recommendations to be presented to a particular body

Three Types of Global Teams

THE IMPACT OF CULTURE ON TEAM PERFORMANCE

Considering the cultural values discussed in Chapter 2 and their impact in a multinational team, context is a necessary first step for the global manager balancing high performance with team spirit and effectiveness. While the values are presented as opposite ends of a continuum, preferred business styles of different nations and organizations span an entire spectrum. Examining this spectrum is essential because the values that are present deeply impact behaviors, beliefs, and perceptions around all facets of a team's operations. Think about the following seven values in relationship to your team, considering the variety of nationalities your work group is exposed to and the impact of this variety on team function.

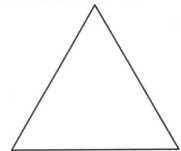

Implementation
(Creating a framework for
developing high-performance global teams)

Awareness	**Skill Building**
(Understanding the nature and impact of national culture on the team)	(Building awareness and understanding for managing cross-cultural differences)

Maximizing Performance on Global Teams

Source: Adapted from Malcolm Higgs, *Team Performance Management*, 1996, *1*, 36–42, MCB UP Ltd.

1. Value on Harmony vs. . . . . Value on Surfacing and Resolving Differences

One important measure of any high-performing team is how differences are addressed. Many Western, and certainly U.S., team-building techniques identify the differences among team members and then attempt to find a solution to deal with them. On the other hand, there are places in the world such as Southeast Asia where the value placed on harmony is so strong that to openly confront differences and upset the balance on the team would not be a way to achieve goals, show support, or build cohesion. Rather, it would disrupt any positive dynamics that exist on a team. Cultures that place a high value on harmony frequently use informal means to address differences, relying on behind-the-scenes negotiation and third-party intervention, not direct confrontation.

2. Emphasis on the Group vs. . . . . Emphasis on the Individual

It may seem like an oxymoron to talk about functioning on teams or work groups while emphasizing the importance of the individual in the same breath. But a preferred orientation, either toward the group or the individual, impacts numerous team functions, such as the reward system, work distribution, and expectations around accountability. In the collectivist cultures of Asia, emphasis on the group is natural and comfortable. Both pats on the back and discipline are given to the team as a whole so as not to single out or embarrass one person. Individual rewards are uncomfortable and not given. But in Western Europe, Canada, and the United States, individualism is strong. Even in team efforts, there is an expectation that individual contributions and talent will be acknowledged or that accommodations will be made to take individual preferences into account. Not to make accommodations is to get less than the best from a large number of people who want their uniqueness accounted for as the group does its work.

Reconciling these two different orientations is essential if a team is to function effectively. When an international petrochemical company featured pictures of high-performing team members in the company newsletter, the responses varied widely. The German awardees were appalled at being praised at all, let alone publicly, for something they considered an expected job duty. The Americans didn't mind the praise but wanted it done privately with a note in their personnel files. The Latin American team members, on the other hand, enjoyed the public recognition of their accomplishment.

3. External Locus of Control vs. Internal Locus of Control

Whether one sees herself as responsible for and in charge of her own success and achievement in this world or as a person at the mercy of the fates makes a great difference in participation and orientation to the group work. Those who feel that outcomes in their lives are in large part determined by forces outside of their influence have an *external locus of control.* For example, one Indian-based project team will not start their work without a prayerful ritual. What shapes them, they believe, is more outside their sphere of influence than inside. This can impact demonstrations of initiative on a team and even what people define as possible or desirable to achieve. On the other hand, those who feel that they are masters of their own destiny have an *internal locus of control.* They feel they shape their own world. Imagine those two world views interacting on a global team. Those who have an external locus of control may contemplate plans and goals, but, for example, in the Muslim world end commitments with *Inshallah,* meaning "God willing" or "if it is meant to be, it will be." For example, when encouraged to apply for a promotion, a very talented woman from the Middle East living in Britain felt that if she was meant to have the promotion she would get it without being her own advocate. Meticulous planning may be irrelevant to people who have an external locus of control. On the other hand, if a person believes strongly that his actions shape the outcome of a team, he will be championing a proactive, interventionist role. While neither of these views is right or wrong, the different viewpoints certainly pose challenges for managers of global teams.

4. Status Based on Family or Affiliations vs. . . . .
. . . . Status Based on Merit or Achievement

Connections, or who you know, matter in some way in every culture in the world. But how much status, entré, or access one gets because of belonging to a particular tribe, clan, family, or alumni group, as compared to how much status one gets based on job performance, definitely varies by culture. What is described as nepotism in Western culture in some parts of the world is considered doing your duty to your family, being loyal, and showing responsibility toward those you care about. What is described or seen as self-serving from an Asian cultural perspective in some parts of the world is considered self-actualization and career building.

On global teams where merit can collide with connection, who is given the opportunities and why is an area ripe for possible conflict. The key idea to remember when this issue surfaces is that, even in cultures that claim to value merit and accomplishment and tend to be more critical of employing family members, relationships and connections matter. There is no escaping the reality that who you know and what your name is have often opened doors.

5. Hierarchical Structure vs. . . . .
. . . . Egalitarian Structure

Whether a national cultural preference is hierarchical, where titles, positions, and rank matter, or whether it is egalitarian, which suggests a more informal and flat structure, the impact of these differences on teams matters. In a hierarchical structure the tone is formal and there is a high degree of respect for positional authority. The implication is that the boss knows what he is doing and has the best ideas and suggestions. In an egalitarian structure, such as in the United Kingdom or Canada, what counts in terms of team influence is the knowledge and expertise one has. If you have marketing expertise and that's what is needed, you may shine. If technology is most critical on a given project, the IT expert may be a dominant influence. The "leader" changes with need. Formal position matters less than expertise required in a given situation. The structural differences pose great challenge on a global team. How comfortable will the Chinese employee be giving feedback to his British team leader? How might the U.S. petroleum engineer feel when his Venezuelan boss gives the team orders without asking for input?

6. Indirect Communication vs. . . . .
. . . . Direct Communication

In countries with an Anglo-Saxon heritage, there is a directness and a specificity to communication. For people from parts of the world where communication is more indirect, such as in Hispanic or Confucian heritage countries, such pointedness can also be seen as crass and rude and more subtle, circuitous communication is valued. Consider the potential clash of these two communication styles taken to extreme on a global team. U.S.-American, German, and other direct communicators may be frustrated with those who go out of their way to be subtle instead of getting to the point, and Japanese, Korean, and others who value less direct communication could be regularly offended by those who insist on upsetting the harmony by telling it like it is. Without an understanding of how culture shapes communication, conflict or disgruntlement will be inevitable.

7. Elastic Time Consciousness vs. . . . .
. . . . Strict Time Consciousness

The U.S. mantra that "time is money" helps explain the strict time-conscious mentality shared by many businesses in the United States and increasingly in Western Europe. Meeting deadlines is usually essential, and promptness matters. Of course, every organization has its own norms around time as well. Contrast a norm and value placed on promptness against the preference for being elastic with deadlines. In cultures that are less exact about time, not every interaction has to relate to getting the task done. There is intrinsic merit in just spending time together, enjoying one another's company. In order to function well on a multinational team or task force, discussions about when meeting a deadline is critical versus when the group can be more flexible are essential. It is also important to realize that within national boundaries there will also be a variety of views about time. In Madrid, where work groups are quite relaxed about their meeting times and "nineish" is the norm, there may be times that "nine sharp" is demanded. In Sao Paulo, where time is more flexible, in the financial center, deadlines are met on time without question. Any team should have conversations and dialogue about these norms. When might it be important or helpful to be flexible? When is there absolutely no flexibility on deadlines? Expectations around time do impact relationships, so if one does not know the norms and honor them, the differences can be a significant source of conflict on any team.

The "Impact of Culture on Global Team Performance" tool can help a work group surface the cultural ranges just discussed in a positive, value-added way. It is designed to elicit insight and foster discussion that can lead to understanding and reconciliation. It can help team members effectively identify, understand, and use both their similarities and their differences.

Suggestions for Using the "Impact of Culture on Global Team Performance"

Objectives

- To understand how different national preferred values impact global workgroup cohesion
- To determine how much one's comfort zone resembles perceived national preference

The Impact of Culture on Global Team Performance

Directions: Consider the seven areas of culture in this tool and first determine which point on each continuum represents your own national preference by marking a check mark. Connect the dots and draw your perception of the national profile. Then with an X, go back and place a mark where you personally feel most comfortable. Once you have put an X at the appropriate number, draw your profile by connecting the Xs.

		1	2	3	4	5	
1.	Value on Harmony						Value on Surfacing and Resolving Differences
2.	Emphasis on the Group						Emphasis on the Individual
3.	External Locus of Control						Internal Locus of Control
4.	Status Based on Family or Connections						Status Based on Merit or Achievement
5.	Hierarchical Structure						Egalitarian Structure
6.	Indirect Communication						Direct Communication
7.	Elastic Time Consciousness						Strict Time Consciousness

Source: Adapted from Lee Gardenswartz and Anita Rowe, *Managing Diversity: A Complete Desk Reference and Planning Guide* (rev. ed.) (New York: McGraw-Hill, 1998, p. 139).

- To identify cultural differences that influence global team functioning
- To stimulate discussion to find ways to reconcile conflicting norms
- To identify national strengths that support the outcomes of the team and determine when different national strengths should take priority

Intended Audience

- Members of any global work team
- Any manager, facilitator, internal/external consultant, HR professional, or trainer charged with the task of creating a cohesive global team

Time

- 45 minutes

Materials

- The "Impact of Culture on Global Team Performance" handout and 18" x 24" blowup of activity
- Chart paper, markers, and masking tape

Directions

- Discuss and define each of the values on the continuum. Ask members to provide some of their own examples.
- Ask team members to first place a check mark at what they perceive to be national cultural norms. Then ask them to mark an X where they see their own values. Have them connect all the checks and the Xs to make two profiles.
- Divide members into small groups. Ask them to compare their individual profiles (Xs) by plotting profiles on 18" x 24" charts taped to a wall and discussing the group's composite profile.
- After small group discussions, have members return to the whole group for discussion.

Questions for Discussion/Consideration

- How does your individual profile compare to your preferred national style?
- What values, similarities, and differences were most notable among group members?
- What surprises, if any, did you find in the responses of any of your team members?
- Which national cultural differences are most difficult for you to deal with? Which are most difficult for the team as a whole?

- When you look more closely at the values differences, what impact do they, or might they, have on the team?
- How can these differences be used to work in our favor?
- Under what operational circumstances might one cultural norm take precedence over another?
- How would you suggest that a team reconcile the differences in perceptions of various team members?
- What might a team leader do that would create that reconciliation?

Cultural Considerations

- It may be difficult for people from collectivist cultures such as Japan to assess their own individual preferences. In such cases group members may compare profiles of the national culture with that of the corporate culture.

Caveats, Considerations, and Variations

- This tool can be used one-on-one by a manager to negotiate with individuals when there is difficulty with a particular team member, with the goal of highlighting this person's contribution and enabling him or her to receive feedback about performance as a team member.
- This could be an introductory activity for a team norm-setting intervention. It introduces important concepts that can be the source of rich and important discussion about how to operate in order to avoid clashes or deal with them when they occur.

CHALLENGES SURROUNDING NATIONAL CULTURE

Once one has a clear understanding of the impact of national culture on team behavior, the next step is to see how to be more adaptive and accommodate a wider range of cultural preferences, seeing that other ways of behaving also have validity. Malcolm Higgs,[2] in an article designed to help teams overcome lack of performance or cohesion due to cultural differences, refers to the importance of building and managing cross-cultural awareness. The Difficulties with and Tips for Taking Advantage of Cultural Preferences chart beginning on page 198 presents opposite ends of each spectrum. Many national preferences are not as absolute as indicated in the chart. People can be asked to choose where they primarily see themselves on each dimension and to check out the information in the box that shows various difficulties one might encounter and gives tips on how to reconcile and capitalize on differences.

Consider your own preferences. Read the appropriate items to gain awareness of what behaviors may be difficult for you on a multinational team and note the tips that are offered.

Possessing different national cultural norms can have an extremely positive effect on a team's productivity and interpersonal relationships, but the team process must be managed and harnessed. Managers need to remind team members that national cultural differences are real, then build awareness of how these differences impact team members personally and how differences can be bridged.

BENEFITS OF MANAGING CROSS-CULTURAL DIFFERENCES

The question of how much return on investment an organization gets from expanding resources in team development is one that almost always comes up. The costs of team development are higher when team members have been brought together from various locations around the world. It is a legitimate question to ask for the benefits and ROI. The following examples point to some gains organizations witnessed once they helped global entities understand and capitalize on a variety of cultural norms. Among the benefits are the following:[3]

- Products launched ahead of schedule;
- Cost of launches reduced;
- Creative, nontraditional ways to reach target markets;
- Market share is maintained or enhanced;
- Company image enhanced;
- International awareness among managers is increased;
- A value-added dimension to problem solving and decision making shows itself; and
- Rapid market response increases through team structure.

Factors That Enhance Global Teams

To gain these positive results, teams must be intentionally built, managed, and structured. The many national and cultural differences can work well when employees are brought together with purpose and structure. The following tips are presented to help team members build awareness and understanding so they can achieve their objectives more easily.

1. Be Aware of Different Preferred Styles and Cultural Norms

"Employees saw the general manager as the 'family head.' In return for the respect and loyalty of subordinates, superiors are expected to 'take care of' staff as a matter of obligation. For Smith this meant watching out for their career advancement and protecting them from blame when they made mistakes."[4]

Egalitarian	Hierarchical
Difficulties:	**Difficulties:**
_____ Respecting authority and structure	_____ Seeing that loyalty and performance may mean listening to and seeking input from team members, not just the boss
_____ Learning to use authority and structure to advance progress without being totally dismissive	_____ Understanding that making suggestions or giving feedback might be the best way to honor that boss or project manager and help the team
_____ Finding value in deferring to boss or person in power position	**Tips:**
_____ Finding oneself in a reciprocal relationship of respect with a superior	Recognize that seeking expertise from others does not diminish one's value or contribution; only people who are truly comfortable with their own selves and skills can do so. You can also do it if you have great confidence in the collective wisdom of the group
Tips:	View involvement of others as a way to help team and honor the boss
Reframe the way positional power is interpreted	
Enjoy the comfort of structure	

Emphasis on Individual	Emphasis on Group
Difficulties:	**Difficulties:**
_____ Viewing performance primarily in the context of the workgroup, team, or task force, with little emphasis on individuals	_____ Leaving space for individuals to follow their passion within the context of group or team goals and accountability
_____ Carving out a stimulating and comfortable niche within the group context	_____ Cultivating individual talents and gifts
_____ Being pleased that praise and blame are collective and given to the group as a whole without singling people out	_____ Identifying individual accomplishments and behaviors
_____ Using one's individual gifts for the good of all	**Tips:**
Tips:	Focus on getting to know individuals
Value behavior as a builder of esprit d' corps	Acknowledge that individual strengths contribute to group performance
Make esprit d' corps a high priority	Utilize individual talents for maximizing output
Concentrate on gaining skills while still being part of the group	
Learn about self and growing in a group context	

Difficulties with and Tips for Taking Advantage of Cultural Preferences

Direct Communication	Indirect Communication
Difficulties:	**Difficulties:**
_____ Expanding style of communication in an attempt to help one another	_____ Not interpreting straightforward communication as brash and hard to deal with
_____ Learning to be more subtle, diplomatic, or gentle in giving feedback	_____ Learning to adapt by practicing how to say something with varying degrees of directness
Tips:	_____ Trying to give feedback directly for those who desire it
Practice giving feedback in passive voice	**Tips:**
Try out different ways of saying things, using two or three different styles	Learn techniques of assertive communication, asking specifically for what one wants and needs in certain situations

Task Focus	Relationship Focus
Difficulties:	**Difficulties:**
_____ Investing in relationship building due to absence of face times	_____ Focusing more on task and putting relationships secondary at times
_____ Making sure that relationships are developed and nurtured, especially on remote teams, since the task focus will almost always be a higher priority	_____ Having work be or feel impersonal and soulless
Tips:	**Tips:**
Use team exercises in this chapter that foster interpersonal knowledge	Expedite personal contact so task can be primary
Use one team-building tool a month from the book to help team members know one another better	Utilize quick points of contact, almost like shorthand, and remember uniquenesses about team members

Difficulties with and Tips for Taking Advantage of Cultural Preferences (continued)

Facing Conflict Head On	Preference for Maintaining Harmony
Difficulties:	**Difficulties:**
_____ Accepting a preference for harmony as valuable and not seeing harmony as denial	_____ Bringing differences out into the open or even acknowledging that they exist
_____ Feeling that issues will become worse if unattended to	_____ Working in an environment that seems assertive and direct
	_____ Viewing open discussion of differences as helpful rather than harmful
Tips:	
Develop subtlety, tact, and diplomacy	**Tips:**
Go "in the back door" rather than the front in trying to settle differences	Talk to people in an outside-of-work or online context, one-on-one, rather than in a meeting environment
Surface differences more obliquely	
Use a third party go-between to resolve conflicts	Conduct behind-the-scenes fact finding, dialogue, and negotiation

Change Oriented	Tradition Oriented
Difficulties:	**Difficulties:**
_____ Adapting to slow the process some members need before they are on-board	_____ Nudging forward and bringing along people who are uncomfortable with change
_____ Managing frustration when perceiving that nothing is or will be happening	_____ Changing practices, policies, and procedures
_____ Finding value in traditions, old methods, and established practices	_____ Letting go of traditional, comfortable methods
	_____ Finding value in new ideas and processes
Tips:	
Practice patience	**Tips:**
Hold onto the idea of detachment to a particular outcome; believe that the process is happening the way it should	Keep some of most revered traditions or practices
Build a strong case of what's in it for people to change	Help calm fears and nudge yourself and others forward
Invest time talking to people trying to understand resistance and minimize their fears	Do an analysis of gains and losses from changes
Maintain enough stability that people get on-board and participate in creating change	

Difficulties with and Tips for Taking Advantage of Cultural Preferences (continued)

Strict Time Consciousness	Elastic Time Consciousness
Difficulties:	**Difficulties:**
____ Working with people whose attitudes toward time are elastic	____ Stress from working with people whose sense of time is always precise and can seem unyielding
____ Dealing with different world views toward time that result in missed deadlines not being seen as a problem	____ Acknowledging critical places where being on time is sacred and then meeting the deadlines
Tips:	
Negotiate expectations regarding time with team members up-front	**Tips:**
Determine as a group when being on time really matters and when it does not	Negotiate expectations with team members up-front
Set norms and clear expectations around time	Agree on when deadlines must be observed and when there is flexibility
Rotate meeting times so at some point all are inconvenienced	Set norms and clear expectations around time with consequences for violating agreements

Difficulties with and Tips for Taking Advantage of Cultural Preferences (continued)

This example would be less effective in the U.K., which shows just how important it is to reconcile a wide array of norms, practices, and world views so that a manager can respond appropriately around the world. One's attitude about the possibility of solving problems rather than leaving the outcome to fate or how one openly participates in meetings rather than being deferential influences the dynamics on a global team. In order to avoid misinterpreting behavior, and in order to take full advantage of all the differences available to a team, an understanding of the role of culture in shaping behavior is imperative. It allows team members to recognize that our programming is deep and formed early. Culture is subtle yet powerful. It becomes less subtle when very clear national cultural differences exist on a team, such as those between high-context Japanese and low-context Americans. The differences can be more subtle when people share a common language and culture, like the U.K. and the United States. Wide cultural differences can create a strident environment. All participants can adapt and develop a wider repertoire of behaviors once they understand that culture is a critical underpinning of their individual behavior and collective success. Having this knowledge opens team members to both the idea and reality that multicultural teams offer distinct advantages if they capitalize on their differences.

2. See Preferences as a Two-Sided Coin

The ideas (1) that all norms cut two ways and (2) that no cultural norm is intrinsically good or bad are helpful in creating an appreciation of differences. Each cultural norm we experience offers advantages in some ways and can be harmful in others. Take the issue of time-consciousness. If a team decides that deadlines are set and nonnegotiable, the advantage of a fixed time frame is that deadlines will most likely be met. On the other hand, an immovable time line compromises the amount of incubation and exploration on complex problems and can compromise the quality of the solutions suggested. Results will not necessarily be effective just because the timeline is met. Trying to determine when deadlines need to be exact and when there is room for flexibility requires good judgment, leadership, feedback, and communication. As in the example with time, other norms also cut two ways.

3. Use Skills in Conflict Resolution and Group Dynamics

Knowledge about group dynamics and conflict resolution is often underrated. They are invisible but make a huge difference in the development of group trust and achievement of honest, productive communication. There are numerous models that characterize the stages of group development, but Bruce Tuckman's classic model[5] of forming, storming, norming, and performing is among the most frequently cited. According to Tuckman, any effective team is a dynamic entity that has life cycle stages. The leader's knowledge of group dynamics makes an enormous difference in whether or not a group matures into increasing effectiveness as a unit. A few tips that help minimize conflict and enhance positive group dynamics follow:

- Pay attention to nonverbal cues;
- Build good relationships across cultures where appreciation, empathy, and sensitivity are demonstrated;
- Be patient and willing to not always have things go your way;
- Show interest in other people; ask appropriate questions that indicate a sense of knowing and caring who and how a person is;
- Monitor how decisions are made and how people participate;
- Keep a record of who is participating in the meeting, either in person, e-mail, or phone; and
- Use technology to reinforce relationships.

The use of effective structured processes online or in person can also minimize conflict as a group works to solve problems together. The kind of structured processes presented in this chapter will be very helpful.

4. Have a Shared Vision and Clarity About the Parameters of the Team

Global teams exist within the context of their global organization and they exist to get a job done. In the case of functional teams, they may produce goods or deliver services. A project team, however, may refine processes for functional teams. A task force may be set up to offer recommendations for ways in which functional teams can improve in defined areas, or they may be brought together for a short time to do fact finding and data collection. Whether a team is an ongoing part of an organization's operations or whether it exists as a short-term task force, in order to be effective it has to know its charge. Why does it exist? For what and to whom is it going to be held accountable? Is the vision one around which there is not only agreement, but also positive energy?

Any ambiguity about boundaries can spell trouble and disruption of task accomplishment. This ambiguity can be more noticeable on dispersed teams, where the usual nonverbal cues are in short supply. The distance and lack of personal contact make communication and verbal feedback about the group's purpose even more critical. However, remote team members do learn to interpret pauses and silence in conversation on the phone and patterns and phrases in written communication. Clarity helps generate energy and move the group forward. Confusion and ambiguity dissipate purpose and direction.

5. Use a Feedback Mechanism to Assess and Improve Both Product and Process

The expectation of give-and-take, particularly valued in the West, involves dialogue about how team members work together. This exchange is very helpful in creating high trust that also meets work objectives. Give-and-take is not an expectation in Asia. Clearly, paying attention to cultural norms across borders is imperative. What is viewed as a critically important question in one culture may be seen as a challenge and an attack in another. If all team members agree that communication and feedback matter, they can decide how feedback is handled to take different norms into account. For example, on one global team, a member from Cameroon made a statement about the availability of necessary supplies. He was asked a question by a team member from the United States, who wanted clarification regarding the availability of materials needed. However, some team members from Brazil and Japan took offense at the question, which they saw as a challenge, not a way to verify information. Without conversation about these different reactions, a rift might have developed that hindered effective group functioning.

6. Work Consistently and Intentionally on Developing Trust

Western psychology teaches us that trust builds through self-disclosure and feedback. We also know that trust builds more quickly or slowly in various cultures and that self-disclosure is not universally appreciated. In highly relational cultures (Latin, Asian, and Middle Eastern), a relationship between two people starts the trust-building process and it deepens with reciprocal fidelity. This book offers countless examples of how self-disclosure, communication, and feedback are culturally influenced. In the United States, people presume a much quicker trust-building process than do those in Singapore or Vietnam, for example. As the only non-Vietnamese person in her organization, one U.S.-American thought relationship building outside of work would accelerate trust and cohesion. To this end, she invited her Vietnamese co-workers to her house for dinner Sunday night. They all either said "Yes" verbally or nodded their heads affirmatively. She cooked all day Saturday. Sunday came and went, but no guests arrived. At first, the hostess assumed she had the wrong date. Further exploration into the issue showed that her fellow employees would never be rude enough to verbally turn down an invitation to her home, but their history with her was so short that it would have been inappropriate for them to go. What she learned in hindsight was that trust in Vietnam builds more slowly than she was used to. They didn't have enough history and trust to go to her home, nor did they have enough history and trust to tell her why they could not go.

There must be education and development of awareness across a whole continuum of norms, trust building being one. If understanding exists, when trust builds more slowly, team members won't be branded as standoffish, and where trust is desired or presumed more quickly, team members will not be labeled as shallow or insensitive.

7. Invest Time in Building Team Relationships and Interpersonal Knowledge

Many Westerners struggle to lead Chinese teams because of differences in team-building practices. The confusion comes about because, for most Chinese, team membership means a group has strong interpersonal bonds focused on respect for the leader, usually older and more experienced. Westerners tend to be less hierarchical and more egalitarian. The Western focus is also more on tasks, with groups brought together to collaborate on specific objectives. This often necessitates giving direct feedback and using conflict-resolution techniques. Note the differences in Chinese and U.S.-American emphasis on relationships. In the example that follows, General Manager Smith is savvy about the importance of relationships in China and he uses this knowledge to build cohesion:

> When one group of employees banded together to ask for a refrigerator for their lunchboxes, he let the line manager take care of it and play off the indigenous group behavior as the core of team building. The focus on teamwork was reinforced by having group pictures marking important events, such as the conclusion of training initiatives, visits by important guests, and extracurricular

gatherings. Group competition against groups, rather than individual competition, is encouraged, ensuring each group wins something (for example, meeting quality production targets or safety goals). After work Smith sometimes takes the group to karaoke or to a bowling alley.[6]

Is this how team building would be done in your organization? If not, what are the differences? How would this approach work in your organization?

Most teams can develop into productive, cohesive entities if they are given the time and a process to have individuals get to know one another and learn about the strengths and idiosyncrasies of each team member. One of the key determinants to this happening is time. Organizations are often reluctant to spend the resources to bring people together, even though it is critical to do so with dispersed multinational groups. The initial face-to-face contact where a relationship is born and bonds are formed is a high payoff venture essential to high performance. According to George Simons, an international diversity consultant and author whose expertise lies in building virtual teams, not only do all teams need this initial investment, but highly effective teams are brought together every three months to nurture and maintain the connections. Doing so requires investment of both time and money, but it is also well worth the expenditure. Allocating the resources speaks volumes about commitment from the organization, and in a practical sense it becomes the glue that holds a group together.

In one Chinese-Finnish venture, the more individualistic Finns balked at spending one of their vacation weeks going to a beach resort, which was seen as a perk for their Chinese colleagues. Only when the week was repositioned as a team-building experience and not billed as vacation time were the Finns willing to participate. In much of the world, relationship building does not only happen in the office or plant. In Japan, it happens after hours socializing with co-workers over drinks. In China, families take vacations as a work team, and in the United States bonding on the golf course is common. Finding inclusive ways to nurture the interpersonal connections is key.

8. Share Knowledge, Skills, and Information

Knowledge provides opportunities for team influence and power. On teams where there is more competition than collaboration and where there is more jealousy than support, it is common for people to hold onto their power and information as a way to gain influence and dominance. Many Chinese management books talk about holding back information as a bargaining chip to gain something else. On healthy teams, there is an expectation that information, knowledge, and skills are appropriately shared as a matter of course. It becomes standard operating procedure. In collectivist cultures, it is a way to ensure team success. For example, U.S.-American employees were upset when they found that the Japanese engineers on their project were regularly taking plans off their drafting tables and faxing them to Japan without asking permission. When confronted, the Japanese engineers were surprised at the Americans' reactions. They responded that the project belonged to the whole team and that all work was shared by the team members, giving each other access to others' work designs and plans. All companies have norms and parameters around sharing. It helps to clarify and understand the national and situational norms so that a trusting environment is built.

9. Have a Leader Who Is Adept and Flexible at Crossing Cultures

On multinational teams, as with any team, leadership sets the standard and reinforces expectations. If an organization has team members from different regions and nations as part of its operations, members will take clues from their leadership about valuing different norms, respecting various perspectives and being adaptive themselves. The quote by Ralph Waldo Emerson which states, "I can't hear what you're saying because who you are rings so loudly in my ears," shows us the importance of looking to people's behavior for the truth rather than listening to their words. Modeling respect for differences and adaptability is essential on high-performing teams in order to leverage the strength of diversity.

10. Develop and Use Both Formal and Informal Communication Processes

There is no leaving communication to chance or happenstance on effective teams. When teams initially set norms, they must discuss ways, means, and frequency of communicating. Some people may like phone calls, while some prefer e-mail. Across multiple time zones, e-mail is a must. Is communication always initiated by one person who starts the feedback and check-in process, or can it begin with anyone at any time? There are no right answers regarding communication, but having a process in place that is talked about, discussed, reviewed, agreed to, and refined is essential. Without it, confusion and bad feelings cause dysfunction. Within what time frame is one expected to respond to e-mail or phone messages? Is it twenty-four hours? Does the sender indicate the promptness of the response desired, which may vary depending on urgency, and does twenty-four hours mean the sender's twenty-four hours and not the receiver's twenty-four hours? What is the expectation around who should be included in e-mail? Is it just those directly involved in implementing a policy? Is it those who will be impacted by a new policy? Discussions around these precise kinds of issues will pay dividends in lessening opportunities for conflict.

Each of these ten factors plays a strong role in creating an effective team. Managers will help teams grow and develop if they take meeting time to have a discussion about how the group is doing in all areas. Just having the assessment and the dialogue will help team members realize they can shape team functions in positive ways. Strengths will surface as well as areas that need to be developed. Sharing and reconciling different perspectives will help the team grow. Use the following tool, "Factors That Enhance Effective Global Teams," to consider each of these ten factors on your team and note collective areas of strength as well as opportunities for team development. It is best used when a team has at least some history to draw on and can be reused at intervals to check progress.

The more "Almost Always" checks that exist, the more effective the team is. The value in this tool is to begin conversation around the factors that can intentionally and strategically enhance team performance. This is by no means an exhaustive list. Rather, it is the beginning point of dialogue. Team members may add factors that they think are important. For any of the items that have a strong "Almost Never" response, the first step is to discuss the consequences of this behavior on the team's productivity and dynamics. Have the group determine some changes they will commit to and agree to a follow-up discussion in three months to check the team's progress.

Suggestions for Using "Factors That Enhance Effective Global Teams"

Objectives

- To gain knowledge and awareness of factors that make cross-border teams effective
- To assess teams in these areas to determine effectiveness and areas for development
- To share perceptions with other team members

Intended Audience

- Intact global workgroups, teams, or task forces that are just forming. This then becomes a prescriptive tool. It is also useful as a diagnostic tool for teams that have been functioning for a while.
- Managers, leaders, internal/external consultants, or facilitators of global teams

Time

- 45 minutes

Materials

- Assessment tool distributed online, via fax, or face-to-face in a team session
- If face-to-face, chart paper, tape, easels, and markers are needed; if online, appropriate technology is required for all

Factors That Enhance Effective Global Teams

Directions: Identify a team you are currently part of or have been a part of at one time. Read each of the ten factors and put a check in the column that most accurately reflects your perception of this team as a unit.

Factor	Almost Always	Sometimes	Almost Never
1. Has awareness of different national preferred styles and cultural norms			
2. Values and reconciles a wide array of different cultural norms with the group			
3. Uses group dynamics skills to build esprit d' corps and help resolve conflict			
4. Has a shared vision and clarity about parameters of the team			
5. Utilizes feedback mechanisms to assess and improve both the product and process of the team			
6. Works consistently and intentionally on developing trust and group spirit			
7. Invests formal and informal time in building team relationships and interpersonal knowledge			
8. Shares knowledge, skills, and information appropriately			
9. Has a leader who is adept and flexible at crossing cultures			
10. Develops and utilizes formal and informal communication processes			

Directions

- Distribute the questionnaire and ask all team members to fill it out. If online, explain you want to collate data and will feed it back to the group by a particular date. If in a team session, explain that this assessment is important to gain a sense of how the team is working for people. Different perceptions matter because each person's perception is his or her reality.

- Once data is collected, conduct small group discussion onsite or discussion with technological support online.
- After participants complete the questionnaire, explain that the "Almost Never" responses are areas for development. People can also explore the "Sometimes" areas.
- Have team members discuss ways to develop areas that are lower scoring, coming up with specific actions to take.

Questions for Discussion/Consideration

- Which of these ten items jumped out at you? Why?
- What were your reactions to any of the items?
- What surprised you?
- Which factors seem to be team strengths?
- Where do we see the team similarly? Differently?
- Which ones present the most difficulty to team functioning and productivity?
- What areas seem most ripe for development?
- What can we do to develop those areas?

Cultural Considerations

- For those from collective cultures and cultures where saving face is critical, discussing in a small group provides anonymity. This allows and encourages rich discussion, which can ultimately come to the full group.

Caveats, Considerations, and Variations

- Team members can e-mail suggestions for change to a central person who will compile a list and send to all for review.

CREATING A FRAMEWORK FOR DEVELOPING HIGH-PERFORMANCE TEAMS

Ultimately, global teams need to perform. Performance can be measured in a number of ways. Markers of success can depend on the business of the large organization or on the expected outcomes of a functional team. But regardless of where a team is in its goal accomplishment, paying attention to four factors is critical for teams' reaching their objectives. The four areas are *task, relationship, content,* and *process,* as shown.

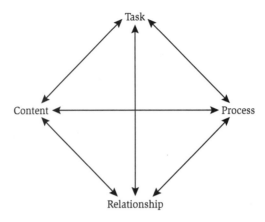

The Four Factors for Reaching Team Objectives

Task

Whatever mission a group has, whatever its reason for being, it will be held accountable for specific outcomes. The work it does should produce a product or a service that matters to other departments, consumers, shareholders, or some part of the stakeholder community. A definition of what the primary task is, or what the top priorities are within a given task, can be the basis of some important differences and conversation. Coming to clear agreement on definitions, deadlines, and other logistics can be contentious. These differences can be managed by asking and answering a number of questions ahead of time.

Task-Related Questions

- What is the primary operating language or languages of the group?
- What circumstances determine what language will be used at any given time?
- How will accountability be measured and by whom?
- For what reason is this group in existence?
- What are its current goals and objectives?
- Who in the organization is sponsoring this group? What clout does this person have?
- How important is this priority? What clues indicate its relative importance or lack thereof?
- What are the hoped-for gains from this experience for the organization and for individual participants?
- What tools will be the best communication vehicles? What communication options exist? How frequently and under what circumstances will different ones be used?

- What are the group's technological preferences?
- What individual and collective strengths does the team bring to this effort?

If you are managing a global team, you need to either provide answers to or have the group determine the answers to the questions. The questions about languages used and technological preferences impact everyone. Even in hierarchical cultures, giving input on these operational issues could be seen as a sign of respect for the leader and make a positive difference. If information is missing, how or from whom can you obtain it?

One question that frequently comes up on global teams is what work needs to be done together, face-to-face, and what work can be managed long distance. The following "to do" list offers suggestions for together and apart time. But one thing is clear from global teams we have seen. Initial contact and relationship building are essential. Once people have a sense of each other and trust exists, it is easier to have work done at remote sites. Use the following list as a starting point and a guide. Each team is unique, so there are few universal edicts.

To Do's: Together Time[7]

- Establish objectives, goals, and interim targets;
- Develop relationships;
- Set up mechanism for resolving differences;
- Develop a code of conduct in meetings, a shared behavior style that balances national preferred styles and corporate styles;
- Determine decision-making process;
- Establish procedures for evaluating and reviewing progress and making necessary changes in values, policies, or procedures; and
- At the first team meeting, balance in-session meeting time for norm setting and relationship building with appropriate out-of-session time for informal relationship building with activities such as golf games, meals, drinks.

To Do's: Long Distance[8]

- Set up a system of communication that is disciplined and consistent;
- Gather and share information;
- Clarify goals;
- Implement actions;
- Keep others posted on progress; and
- Distribute any necessary meeting material in advance.

Relationship

The relationship dimension is the neon sign of the four very important components. In the example of General Manager Smith, we saw a person demonstrate an extreme sensitivity and knowledge of cultural differences and use his interpersonal skill to build strong relationships on his team. He knew to operate in a paternalistic, "I'll take care of you" way that worked for his group. He built trust, comfort, and safety through his attention to the people he managed. His style was appropriate in the context of his group. Beyond his knowledge about cultural norms, Smith cared about people's personal preferences and priorities. He also understood some of the prime values that shaped Chinese work group responses, and he honored and respected those values.

Smith's ability to relate to his team made a critical difference, as just bringing talented people to work together on a common project does not guarantee productive outcomes. Building trust, negotiating differences, holding one another accountable, and meeting objectives is more likely to happen when relationships are good. Building these good relationships is more challenging on dispersed teams that are required to function across time and space. As we stated earlier, it helps to bring people together initially. Face-to-face meetings are a necessity at the beginning of a project, with subsequent and intermittent follow-ups built in to reinforce and maintain good contacts and high trust. Although these meetings may be resisted by management due to cost, the price of not having them is frequently failure to get the job done. In the end, the lack of results is always more expensive than the work up-front. Once relationships are started, they can be maintained by using the tools throughout this chapter, which are designed mostly to foster awareness, dialogue, and conversations about different and similar perceptions of a common team experience. A focus on relationships requires a manager to consider numerous facets of how people will work together. Think about some of the following questions.

Relationship-Oriented Questions

- How frequently will the group meet face-to-face?
- What does each person expect to get from and contribute to this experience? What is the best way for the manager or leader to find out this information? For those from collectivist cultures, the best question might be, What do we expect to contribute as a group and gain as members of the group?
- How will decisions be made as a group? If the leader or manager is from a hierarchical culture, how will the team's expertise be used?
- Under what circumstances will the decision be delegated to one person?
- Under what circumstances will the group make the decision?

- How will the group define and manage disagreement?
- What do team members and the group leadership have a right to expect from one another?

These questions are best answered face-to-face in order to get the group off to a good start. Once some of these questions have been answered and operational decisions have been made, team members will have a good sense of each other. Then much of the work can be done apart.

The following tools will help teams assess not only the strength of their relationships but how they can make them stronger and increase commitment to one another and to getting the job done. To see how your team is doing in the first two areas, task and relationship, use the "Achieving Task and Relationship Balance on a Global Team" tool.

Suggestions for Using "Achieving Task and Relationship Balance on a Global Team"

Objectives

- To assess the degree of balance between task and relationship on the team
- To identify areas of strength and those that need development regarding task and relationship
- To determine what needs to change for the team to be more effective in creating balance between these two functions

Intended Audience

- Virtual global work group, team, or task force members mutually accountable for an outcome
- Manager or facilitator of a global team

Time

- 45 to 60 minutes

Materials

- Copies of "Achieving Task and Relationship Balance on a Global Team"
- If done face-to-face, easels and flip charts
- If done virtually, the group's preferred interactive technology

Directions

- Distribute the assessment tool electronically, if in different locations, or hand it out if meeting face-to-face.
- Discuss the importance of both the task and relationship functions on a team and why each is necessary to goal accomplishment.

Achieving Task and Relationship Balance on a Global Team

Directions: The balance between doing the team's work and focusing on the human infrastructure is a delicate one. To see how your team balances task and relationship, use the following assessment tool. Consider each of the factors below and check the appropriate box. Assess the balance as it currently exists and then determine what changes, if any, need to be made to achieve more balance.

Areas for Consideration	Satisfactory (Likes As Is)	Unsatisfactory (Needs Work or Adjustment)	Suggestion for Change
Task			
1. Having clearly defined goals			
2. Managing time differences			
3. Using technology to share information			
4. Handling logistics			
5. Scheduling project meetings to foster interpersonal contact and task accomplishment			
6. Determining schedules and timelines			
Relationships			
7. Utilizing communication methods to maintain contact			
8. Scheduling time to meet in person			
9. Developing cross-cultural awareness			
10. Acknowledging the need to be cross-culturally adaptive			

Achieving Task and Relationship Balance on a Global Team (continued)

Areas for Consideration	Satisfactory (Likes As Is)	Unsatisfactory (Needs Work or Adjustment)	Suggestion for Change
11. Having team establish its own norms			
12. Using tools and techniques that foster team membership			

- Give directions and ask each group member to fill out the worksheet.

- If done electronically at a videoconference meeting, ask participants to share areas of development. (This can be done ahead of time and data can be collected at a central location or it can be done live. The latter will be more costly. One way to expedite a live discussion is to have a tool with numbers 1 through 12 visible to all and put a check for each item where there is dissatisfaction. Where there are the greatest numbers of checks would be the place to begin the discussion.)

- Lead the group in a discussion of suggested changes. If some strong answers and responses come up, some decisions can be made right away. It is also possible to engage in discussion, crystallize a few questions for people to think about, and determine when you will talk again as a group to make decisions.

- One option that always works is to close the discussion by asking individuals to write down something they will do that they believe will make a positive difference. At a future date, the group will agree on one area where they will collectively do some work.

Questions for Discussion/Consideration

- What in our group functioning seems to be working well?
- What in our group functioning can be enhanced?
- What in our operation is getting in the way or hindering our outcome?
- Can you remember a time when the group worked better for you? If so, what was different then? What should we start doing again? What should we stop doing?
- What could make things better now?

- Where would you like team members to adapt and reconcile differences?
- Where are you willing to be more adaptable?
- What will be the outcome of our group dynamics if we do nothing differently?

Cultural Considerations

- These questions are somewhat direct. In many cultures, a less direct approach might work better. Try using small groups and asking people to come up with factors that help them get the job done and also build good relationships.

Caveats, Considerations, and Variations

- If done at a single location, people can discuss first in small groups and then engage in a whole group discussion with a focus on common points.
- If this discussion is put in the context of better functioning for loyalty to one another and the boss, it may be less abrasive in collectivist cultures. The group can determine jointly an area or two that they think might make a positive difference.

ENHANCING TASK AND RELATIONSHIP FUNCTIONS THROUGH TECHNOLOGY

Technology can facilitate communication across distance. There is much good news about the use of technology. When people in organizations complain about it, it is usually because it functions almost as an end in itself and results in depersonalizing connections among employees. On dispersed teams, when infrequent face-to-face meetings exist, technology can provide some of the glue that holds a group together.

A number of factors influence the appropriate use of technology. It is important to find the correct method for the needs of a group. Before deciding which form of technology best serves your needs, consider the Enhancing Task and Relationship Functions with the Proper Technology chart (page 218), which lists various technical means and both task and relationship functions they can enhance.

Netiquette[9]

Including "netiquette" in your ground rules for electronic communication is a good way to begin. Here are a few to note in U.S.-American culture. Before starting any new electronic communication within your group, find out what other rules of netiquette would be relevant in the various parts of the world where your organization operates.

E-Mail

- Be courteous. Remember to say please and thank you.
- Reply promptly—within twenty-four hours.
- Be brief.
- Use lowercase characters. Capitals indicate SHOUTING!
- Be sure to check spelling and grammar.
- Use attachments sparingly.

Newsgroups

- Again, don't use capital letters.
- Stick to the topic of the newsgroup.
- Don't be rude or sarcastic.
- Don't include the entire message you are replying to in your response. Only quote relevant sections of the original message.
- Do a thorough review of your message before you post. Be sure to check your spelling and grammar.
- Keep it short.
- Don't send anything if you are just agreeing ("Thanks," "Right on," "I agree").

For those who want to start their own newsgroup, one source for information on procedures is Susan Sweeney's *101 Ways to Promote Your Web Site,* www.maxpress.com.

Finally, one other reality. We make the assumption that, with increased knowledge about and exposure to one another, relationships will build, grow more cohesive, and be trusting. This is not always the case. On some teams, there are personal animosities that create intense dislike, even hatred. In other circumstances, just being from a particular country, observing a particular religion, or speaking a certain language creates distance and dislike because of national and geopolitical histories that frequently have nothing to do with the particular people involved. Stereotypes and animosities of a larger world encroach on team reality. How does a manager deal with this hatred or lack of understanding? Our colleague, Dr. Jorge Cherbosque, has found some steps that work in this situation. They are outlined below.

1. Establish Core Beliefs. Always start by looking at a set of core beliefs or principles and establishing those first. An example of a core belief might be that different points of view add value and are essential to your business success.

Technology	Task	Relationship
Electronic meeting systems	Allows group to work together on any number of tasks. The strength and weakness is that participants have free flow of input and data and, if desired, comments can be anonymous. Suggestions or ideas can be added at will.	In some nations and economies, technology has been used in face-to-face settings for a while. It is now being used in disbursed teams to enable collaboration with people in different locations.
Teleconference	This can be helpful in bringing people together to exchange viewpoints, give or receive feedback, share ideas, and think through different approaches.	When people have already had face-to-face contact and some trust exists, people say what they really think and feel, enabling a group to reach agreement.
Videoconference	This is a commonly used tool, but the effectiveness of it depends on the quality of the video transmissions. Often time zone differences, uneven technology, and poor quality limit usefulness.	It is a good tool for discussing opinions, as participants can see one another and get nonverbal information in real time.
E-mail	This is certainly the most-used computer-mediated technology for people working together over distances. It is readily available, easy to use, and can be both relational and task-focused. It is quick and efficient, but still allows people time to reflect and get back to one another. Attachments can be sent, and it is an easy, cost-effective way to communicate.	Ground rules on the what and how of e-mail are helpful for a team. Communication styles differ and from written communication one can infer national styles and generational styles. People reared on technology are more staccato in style, while those fifty and older who have written letters in the past have more need for solutions and formal closures. If there is enough privacy in e-mail, team members can be real and truthful with their ideas, thereby resolving differences.

Enhancing Task and Relationship Functions with the Proper Technology

Technology	Task	Relationship
Company's intranet	If a company has its own intranet, a new division/section/area could be added for teams working on a specific project. There could even be separate areas for each team. Communication is enhanced with worldwide accessibility, posting of questions/answers and questionnaires. Similar to e-mail, but can be shared (not required) by all.	As in use of e-mail, ground rules are important, as is the role of the webmaster in being responsive to the needs of the various teams.
Internet newsgroups	When a company does not have an intranet, the members of teams can form a newsgroup where all can share the contributions of team members. Not as flexible, especially in the use of questionnaires, nor as private as an intranet location; nevertheless it can be a useful tool. Most newsgroups are shared by others from all over the world, which can be a plus for those reaching out and looking for similar experiences and possible outcomes.	Same as e-mail and company's intranet.

Enhancing Task and Relationship Functions with the Proper Technology (continued)

2. Be Crystal Clear About Missions. We mentioned this before but it's worth saying again in the context of people who may not get along. A team is in business to accomplish some purpose. What is it? Once that is defined, around that narrow parameter, help people find the common ground. They do not have to love one another, but around their common objective they need to find ways to work together.

3. Build the Business Case. How do the different skills, background, attitudes, and viewpoints build a better product? There are many examples unique to products, field of work, and industry that demonstrate the value of different backgrounds and perspectives. Amid different points of view, group thinking patterns are broken, creativity thrives, and new discoveries are more possible. We are all formed by our own background and experience. Show those involved the value added from working together.

4. Do Your Homework and Help Others Do Theirs.   Know as much as possible about the participants on the global team or task force. When it becomes clear that some differences could be prickly, help everyone know who the players are, what to expect from the session, what talents and strengths others bring, and what the expectations are for individuals working together on a common goal. Setting aside time to create norms and identify acceptable ways of dealing with conflict is also helpful.

5. Structure Interactions That Foster Common Ground.   It is easier to dislike a broad group of people, but much more difficult to dislike someone when you have seen the whites of his or her eyes. Create relaxed, out-of-session social experiences where people can interact and show their humanness. Also, use the tools in this book to foster dialogue in a work context. This, too, will create common ground.

6. Hold People Accountable for Living the Articulated Core Values.   Once principles and beliefs are visible, once the mission is clear, and the business case has been made, make working together part of expected individual and group performance. No manager or leader can legislate feelings, and we've not met any who even want to. But collecting an organization's paycheck means doing the work. Provide as many humanizing experiences as possible and be clear about the work. Ultimately, being employed means agreeing and getting beyond negative feelings.

Content

Related to the task is the nature of the work, the content on which the company, department, and team focus. Task is doing the job, but content is the "what," the nature of the job or the work a team performs. If a team's work is inventory control for Boeing, it may be responsible for inventorying the nuts and bolts. If a team works for a fast-food chain, it may manage the inventory of coffee stir sticks and artificial sweeteners. Different company, different products, but essentially the same function. Being cost-effective, minimizing waste, and having inventory readily accessible is critical. Whether the function is performed in Dublin, Auckland, or Mexico City, comparable factors are assessed and evaluated, always with an eye toward greater efficiencies and profits.

In a petroleum company, for example, depending on the department and function, the content could be

- Drilling for oil;
- Doing research to find new oil reserves;
- Understanding the environmental concerns so that drilling in sensitive places will do minimal disruption to the natural habitat;
- Engaging in legal knowledge across borders to understand or increase companies' options;
- Lobbying for licenses to drill in untapped areas; and/or
- Marketing to consumers.

If the company is in aerospace, the content could be

- Looking at ways to ergonomically improve design on commercial airplanes;
- Increasing sales of airlines all over the globe;
- Rearranging the financing of a fleet of planes in a recessionary environment for a valued client;
- Designing military aircraft to be more stealth-like; and/or
- Using technology for design feedback to test and track vulnerabilities on either commercial or military planes.

Each unit, department, or entity needs to acknowledge the relevance of content and be clear about the nature of its work so it can maximize results.

Process

This dimension of team building defines how a team carries out its functions. How does it conduct its business? Is it transparent? Does it transmit important information to employees and other stakeholders along the way? How does one unit or department communicate to the larger organization? What tools and techniques does the team use to do its work? What part does technology play in getting the job done? What part does it play in helping team members develop and maintain relationships? What processes exist for giving and receiving information? As a team explores the task of gaining market share or segmenting marketing by language, culture, ethnicity, and geography, the process may require figuring out the best way to obtain reliable data from different groups around the world. Being culturally literate may help a team realize that focus groups work in some places while paper-and-pencil questionnaires will work in others.

Once the data is in, what processes exist for discussing perceptions about what the data implies? How much of this sharing needs to be done face-to-face? How much can be done via videoconference or audioconference? How does the team view voting and consensus as decision-making processes? In the United States, voting creates the feeling of winners and losers. How do other cultures see voting and when is voting considered a legitimate team process? What issues warrant taking the time needed for consensus? No organization that has designs on being successful and effective wants to disenfranchise its team members. What processes exist both for validating people's contributions to the team and for helping them feel a sense of belonging? And under what circumstances, in hierarchical cultures where decisions are made by authority figures, is a feeling of belonging less relevant? On dispersed teams, the processes for making decisions together and building relationships take even more careful consideration.

The process, or "how" question, looks at ways a team shares information, makes decisions, negotiates differences, gives and receives feedback, builds trust, or does any other function that helps get the task done in a way that leaves team members feeling respected. The tools used throughout this chapter are designed to facilitate an effective process. To structure discussion and help develop appreciation for points of view different from one's own, take the "Expanding Views on a Global Team" instrument. This group process tool could build trust, increase the amount of information available about one another through feedback, and increase interpersonal support and understanding. It is best taken in pairs or small groups.

Suggestions for Using "Expanding Views on a Global Team"

Objectives

- To realize the many ways to view or interpret behaviors of members on a team
- To get a sense of how different team members view team behaviors
- To learn how culture influences team preferences regarding the development of tolerance and appreciation for a wider repertoire of behavior
- To become more knowledgeable about and comfortable with a wide repertoire of behaviors and viewpoints

Intended Audience

- Members of global work groups, teams, or task forces
- Managers or facilitators trying to help global virtual team members understand their own cultural programming and the need to expand their comfort with other behaviors

Time

- 45 minutes

Materials

- Copies of "Expanding Views on a Global Team" either physically or electronically
- Markers, easel, flip chart, and masking tape

Directions

- First determine whether this is a better face-to-face or online tool for your dispersed team. It will work and add value either way.
- Once the decision is made, distribute the tool and tell team members that the purpose is to hear collective perceptions and shed light on how culture influences how we interpret behaviors. It is also intended to help each person acknowledge different realities and expand one's comfort with them.
- If done online, provide the technological support to distribute online and quantify data; follow up by bringing people together using their preferred technological mode to share and discuss.
- In person, distribute "Expanding Views on a Global Team," have people answer and pair up with someone they feel comfortable with or prefer to work with. It is also helpful and valid to pair people up with others they do not know well as a way to build a relationship. If the environment is low trust, the former suggestion works better.
- If done online, have all data sent to a central location, synthesized, analyzed, and ready for discussion, then determine how the compilation will be distributed and processed. Be sure that participants know upfront how the information will be used and who will have access to it.

Questions for Discussion/Consideration

- What other views or interpretations can you assign to any of the behaviors mentioned?
- Which behaviors seem to foster productivity? Harmony?
- On your team, which seem to create the most distance and frustration?
- Which behaviors seem most difficult for you personally?
- Which seem hard for others on the team?
- Which behaviors pose difficulty for you in coming up with alternative cultural views?
- What interpretations can you provide for those behaviors so that you do gain a broader perspective?
- What must the team do collectively to improve its functioning?

Cultural Considerations

- In collectivist cultures, it would be more desirable to pair with someone known and trusted or divide into small discussion groups.

Expanding Views on a Global Team

Directions: Global teams have a variety of world views among team members. The objective in this tool is to see behaviors in a different perspective, an alternate view, in order to make reconciliation of differences on a team possible. Read the fifteen behaviors in the column entitled "Group Norms." For each one, list at least one other way to view this norm. See the example provided for the first norm.

Group Norms	Alternative Cultural View or Norm
1. The environment is easy, safe, and comfortable, which permits discussion of complicated issues.	Discussing complex issues is uncomfortable and could disrupt the harmony of the group. People won't initiate such discussions.
2. Participation by all members, especially at meetings, gives valuable input for decision making.	
3. Carrying out ideas the boss has feels right and produces good results.	
4. Harmony among team members is an expected norm.	
5. When ideas are presented, none are dismissed.	
6. People appropriately share their ideas under certain circumstances.	
7. It is no secret where everyone stands on the issues that come up; people state their positions.	
8. There is respect for the principles of others, even in the face of disagreement.	
9. Clarifying and sometimes challenging questions are asked in non-hostile tones.	
10. Positions change as a result of discussions on the issues.	
11. Feedback is given specifically and constructively.	
12. Pertinent information is shared on a need-to-know basis.	

Expanding Views on a Global Team (continued)

Group Norms	Alternative Cultural View or Norm
13. Group members build on the ideas of others and collaborate willingly.	
14. There is confidence in the group's ability to do the job.	
15. Individual and collective accountability is a high priority.	

Source: Adapted from Lee Gardenswartz and Anita Rowe, *Managing Diversity in Health Care* (San Francisco: Jossey-Bass, 1999). This material is used by permission of John Wiley & Sons, Inc.

Caveats, Considerations, and Variations

- Depending on the size of the group, processing this in pairs or small groups first is more beneficial than starting with a whole group discussion.

Any team that accomplishes its work effectively and efficiently has somehow paid attention to task, relationship, content, and process. The teams that work those four areas consciously and intentionally will see their effectiveness increase.

To enhance the team's chance of health and productivity and to maximize its output in all four areas, spend some time as a group on the next tool, "Framework for Developing a High-Performance Global Team."

Suggestions for Using the "Framework for Developing a High-Performance Global Team"

Objectives

- To identify factors critical to functioning effectively as a team in the four areas of task, relationship, content, and process
- To use a structured tool for team members to safely give one another feedback about the team
- To improve team functioning

Intended Audience

- Members of global work groups, teams, or task forces
- Managers or facilitators assisting global teams in improving their functioning

Framework for Developing
a High-Performance Global Team

Directions: This tool offers a way to obtain feedback and a perception check early in the life of a team. Respond to each of the items in the four areas of team functioning.

Areas of Team Function	What Would Help Our Team Continue to Develop in This Area?
Task	
Clearly identified outcomes by which group and individuals in the group will be measured	
Timelines by when goals must be met	
A "Who's Doing What" list with names by every item	
Clearly understood and implemented procedures that identify sequence and processes of task accomplishment	
Readily identifiable and accessible leadership	
Relationship	
Planning strategic sessions that include formal and informal time to develop relationships; bringing people together to increase trust, comfort, and safety	
Utilizing group input to design tools that help foster long distance communications	
Creating a respectful climate where different preferences are acknowledged as reality and then integrated into team function	
Avoiding back stabbing and blaming; encouraging team members to manage their own relationships across the borders of the virtual team	
Acknowledging the importance of time for fun together as well as task accomplishment	

Framework for Developing a High-Performance Global Team (continued)

Areas of Team Function	What Would Help Our Team Continue to Develop in This Area?
Content	
Clear understanding of the work our team does	
Have expertise among all team members to perform tasks	
Clear and timely information disseminated to foster task completion	
Sufficient resources (technological and financial) to take care of business, bridge distances	
Project manager or point person selected who facilitates work being accomplished	
Processes	
An ongoing evaluation of the "how" of working together and utilizing the strengths of each person for the good of the team	
Utilizing a variety of processes that recognize and leverage different national preferred styles and cross-cultural norms	
Helping every team member become more adaptable and comfortable expanding his or her roles on a team to complete a task	
Designing feedback mechanisms that help team members suggest improvements	
Utilizing previously agreed-on processes and success stories that will help a team get "unstuck" when it cannot seem to move forward	

Time

- 45 minutes

Materials

- Copies of the "Framework for Developing a High-Performance Global Team"
- Markers, easel, flip chart, and masking tape

Directions

- The facilitator or manager distributes the assessment tool with the introductory comments that indicate this is a good time to assess how effective the global team is in accomplishing its goals and working well together.
- Ask each person to take the time to read each of the five items in all four areas and have them make notes about how the team could improve in each of the areas.
- Depending on the size of the group, ask participants to pair up or get into small groups to discuss their data. In the small groups, make one or two recommendations in each of the four areas for improvement and write them on flip-chart paper taped to the walls.
- Collect the data from each group before conducting a whole group discussion.
- Ask the group to commit to making at least one change in each of the four areas.
- During the group discussion, clearly delineate measures that will indicate to the group that it is moving forward.

Questions for Discussion/Consideration

- Which items were hard to answer? For what reason?
- Where was your perspective broadened by a different viewpoint?
- What are the areas where you have been having the greatest success as a group?
- What were the areas of greatest agreement about the need for improvement?
- What areas presented the greatest difference in range of viewpoint?
- Are you satisfied with the suggested changes? Explain. If not, why not?
- What challenges and opportunities do these suggestions present to you regarding your own skills and preferences?
- Is there any part of the process you'd like to do differently next time? Think of this as an ongoing evaluation tool.

Cultural Considerations

- In collectivist cultures or cultures with clear hierarchy, having the group discuss and make suggestions instead of having individuals make them will be helpful. Asking people to get into small groups with people they trust should work well.

- Any time you can provide anonymity and group feedback instead of a person clearly expressing feedback that might feel like disapproval will also be helpful.

Caveats, Considerations, and Variations

- While this is a tool that could be done online, we suggest it be used at the second face-to-face meeting, once a team has already started functioning together, or at critical times in the group's development. A suggested time interval would be three or four months after the first face-to-face meeting. At that point, there is enough team experience together to give feedback that is useful.

- Another option is to divide the whole group into four small groups. Assign each group one area on which to focus and make recommendations about ways they want the team to work, as well as what to avoid in each of the four areas. Do so only after each person has filled out items in all four areas.

- As an alternative, have team members fill out the Framework for Achieving High Performance on a Global Team four-quadrant box on the next page and then discuss their responses.

DEFINING TEAM LEADERSHIP AT ALL LEVELS OF AN ORGANIZATION

In the final analysis, the global team experience has a great deal to do with the leadership that guides its work. For those who say leadership can or should change depending on skills and needs required at a given moment, leadership is viewed as a fluid concept. For others, positional power equates to leadership and it is a more fixed concept. On one point most people who function in global organizations agree. Effective leadership of teams enables them to fulfill their purpose of doing the work. Whether it is furthering social and corporate sustainability or increasing profits and shareholder value, groups respond to leadership in some form. Consider the ten "Leadership Behaviors" below that foster successful teams. Do they reside in those who hold formal leadership positions in your organization? Where do they exist on your team? From your experience,

Task	Relationship
Achieve: _____ _____ _____ _____ Avoid: _____	Achieve: _____ _____ _____ _____ Avoid: _____
Content	**Process**
Achieve: _____ _____ _____ _____ Avoid: _____	Achieve: _____ _____ _____ _____ Avoid: _____

Framework for Achieving High Performance on a Global Team

what qualities are you missing collectively? If you have a formal positional leader, how does this person stack up in these ten areas? Fill out the form to find out and then think about your answers as you read further.

 ## Leadership Behaviors on a Global Team

Directions: If you are leading or managing a team, place a check mark by any behaviors you regularly engage in. If you are a team member, place a check mark beside any behaviors you regularly see. After you have finished, read the explanatory text for each numbered item.

_____ 1. *Demonstrate respect for all team members in ways that matter to each person.*

It is part of being human to want and need validation for making a contribution. On work groups, being treated respectfully is a sign of such validation and encourages more commitment and connection between team members, less defensiveness, and an increased ability to work through predictable differences. The caveat here, across borders, is that respectful treatment is defined differently by civilization, nation, country, organization, and individual. An effective team leader knows this and avoids having a one-size-fits-all definition of respect. It is suited to each individual.

_____ 2. *Be willing to change, grow, and develop new skills.*

An effective team leader models effective change management and helps others adapt as well. In today's lightning-fast world, not being willing or able to adapt is the equivalent of consigning oneself to insignificance or irrelevance. Creating a norm where team members are fluid and not attached to a particular outcome is very helpful. Is lack of attachment and willingness to be flexible easier for those reared in a Buddhist culture, where detachment is a path to personal wholeness? Is it possible to make this norm work more easily on teams from more collectivist rather than individualist cultures because there might be a better sense of the whole? Whatever the predispositions or attitudes towards change might be, creating a feeling of ease and expectation around change is essential.

_____ 3. *Build relationships outside of work boundaries.*

Effective team leaders structure time together in informal surroundings. This reality on virtual teams is exceedingly difficult. In many parts of the world, people who work together like to socialize in off-work hours. Virtual teams are frequently brought together several times a year. At times like this, it is important to maximize the socialization after work, whether it means going out to dinner, a play, or taking in the local nightlife. The relationships built informally pay big dividends at work when each person is back at his or her own location. The one caveat here is that, in some locales, employees consider time after hours their own time. But when you bring people to a central location from many places, there is an expectation of hanging out together in the evenings. That is often a very successful strategy.

_____ 4. *Have clear responsibilities and accountability.*

A team leader who helps people understand their respective roles and tells them what they will be accountable for goes a long way toward setting individuals up to be successful and setting teams up to be productive. There is no substitute for clear expectations and parameters. On some teams those expectations may be arrived at autocratically, and on others the team itself may set up the roles and the measurements based on group objectives. How a team arrives at that clarity is part of its process, but an effective team leader does not miss the chance to set clear expectations.

_____ 5. *Demonstrate respect and appreciation for different cultural norms.*

On global teams, having knowledge of cross-cultural norms and being able to switch style is essential. An effective team leader models this understanding and behavior. It also means helping team members see the advantage and disadvantage to different ways of doing things. Utilizing the variety of norms that will undoubtedly exist on a global team can go a long way toward helping everyone be more adaptive and find value in behaviors that previously might have seemed uncomfortable, strange, or just plain wrong.

_____ 6. *Set up clear communication and feedback systems.*

Communication and feedback are usually difficult at various times on any team. Even in the closest relationships, communication faux pas or miscues are a part of life. A team leader can make a big difference by working with a group to agree on a process of how and when feedback will be given and set up systems for effective communication. On dispersed teams, having this structure in place is even more crucial. Clear communication systems can enhance the accomplishments of a team and the relationships within the team itself. Being the person who either facilitates the feedback and communication structures or actually provides a structure as a starting point for the team is an important leadership role.

_____ 7. *Do the prework.*

A global team leader has complex logistics to deal with. Making sure resources such as technology, a budget to bring people together during the year, and communicating all the particulars of who, what, where, when, and why are especially important across language differences, time zones, national preferred styles, and geographic boundaries. The team leader in this situation must be so clear and precise with information, logistics, and operational concerns that these questions become a non-issue and offer no distraction. That way, team members can concentrate on the work at hand. Think of the team leader as an obstacle remover.

_____ 8. *Set a tone of warmth, affiliation, and productivity.*

Any team leader, effective or ineffective, puts an imprint on the group. The team members will be a reflection of that leader. Feelings of comfort, security, risk taking, and collaboration, or feelings of competition, jealousy, confrontation, and rivalry are all influenced by the team leader. By paying attention to each team member's unique skills, by utilizing those skills for the good of the group, by demonstrating interest in and appreciation for people individually and collectively, and by really listening to different ideas, a leaders sets a productive tone. Very little good teamwork gets done in a hostile, low-trust environment.

_____ 9. *Teach the team self-maintenance.*

One goal of an effective team leader could be to legitimately take a background role and allow the individuals to demonstrate greater leadership. In individualistic cultures, this is done by grooming strong individuals. The challenge is different where some members may prefer a more hierarchical structure with a strong boss. Education has to accompany this type of shift and members must be sold on the advantages for the team effort. The idea is to create a team that functions like a self-cleaning oven, taking care of its own obstacles as they crop up. The leader can have a primary role in making this happen.

_____ 10. *Balance long-term and short-term goals, both the strategic and the operational.*

Depending on the team's level, mission, goals, and reason for being, one group may be limited to strategic issues while another concerns itself with operations. Regardless, it is critical to manage the tug of war between long-term and short-term goals. Focusing on distant outcomes is essential to stay competitive. On the other hand, paying attention to long-term strategic issues to the exclusion of short-term operational goals and issues can be harmful in a world where change is constant. The leader needs to see both forest and trees.

The reality is that most team members inherit their leaders. Usually few options exist for changing the leader, and in some parts of the world, it would be arrogant and unthinkable to evaluate the leader. But many corporations now use 360-degree feedback tools. With that process in mind, think about what leadership excellence would look like by responding to the ten questions in the "Leadership on a Global Team" tool.

Suggestions for Using "Leadership on a Global Team"

Objectives

- To generate discussion among team members about what ideal team leadership looks and feels like
- To assess the sense of how close present leaders currently comes to that ideal
- To determine what the team can do to help leaders get closer to the desired state

Intended Audience

- Members on a global team, work group, or task force
- Facilitators, managers, or consultants who lead global teams
- A manager trying to build cohesion on a global team

Time

- 30 to 45 minutes

Materials

- Copies of "Leadership on a Global Team," either online or as handouts

Directions

- Have participants discuss the answers to these questions in pairs and then conduct a whole group discussion.
- If done online, have each person read everyone else's data and then focus in on the few points of data that require more discussion, either because answers were so different or because certain questions generated the most energy.
- Get feedback from the group and determine what items bear more discussion.
- If done in a face-to-face session, have each team member fill out the form on a big piece of chart paper and tape it on the wall so each person can read everyone else's responses. (You can reproduce the chart in an 18" x 24" poster.) Distribute markers, tape the posters to the wall, and have everyone read each other's answers and then discuss.

Leadership on a Global Team

Directions: Think about what ideal team leader behavior would look as you read the following ten items. Rate, on a scale of 1 to 5, how important this factor is to you, with 5 as highly important. Then write your own idea of what the ideal relationship with a boss or manager would look like for each of the areas. For example, for the first item, relationship with boss or project manager, a team member might write, "It is one of mutual respect where I always feel valued and my talents are utilized." For the second item, time spent in social activities outside of work, one could say, "Getting together two or three times a year is great, especially if family is allowed to come at least once."

_____ 1. Relationship with boss or project manager

  Ideal:

_____ 2. Time spent in social activities outside of work

  Ideal:

_____ 3. Desired leadership skills of boss or project manager

  Ideal:

_____ 4. Ways in which I am treated by my boss

  Ideal (be specific in terms of how respect is shown; what it means to be listened to; or any other qualities that matter):

_____ 5. Utilize the strengths of team members

  Ideal:

_____ 6. Relationships with team members

  Ideal:

_____ 7. Holds team accountable and expects us to come through

  Ideal:

_____ 8. Involvement in decision making

  Ideal:

_____ 9. Guides group growth through feedback

  Ideal:

_____ 10. Creates an environment of high trust

  Ideal:

Questions for Discussion/Consideration

- What stood out for you among all the data you read? Why?
- What was the most unique or unusual content you read?
- In what ways are you both similar to and different from other team members?
- In order to get closer to the ideal as a group, what has to change?
- What will you personally commit to doing so that you move closer to the ideal?
- What are the important points for the team to focus on?
- Where are the team's biggest opportunities for growth?
- What is the team willing to commit to doing?

Caveats, Considerations, and Variations

- This can be done face-to-face as a warm-up activity. In Asian or hierarchical societies, this would not be a good warm-up because it implies a subtle suggestion that the team can set the definitions of what excellent leadership should and can be. On the other hand, this tool would work well in a leadership training seminar in companies. Each person can answer individually at first, even before the meeting itself, in order to save time.

- The form can also be completed electronically and is especially effective for a newly formed team so that participants can find out each other's preferences. This provides a good opportunity to see how people are alike and focus on the similarities.

- Team members can also write on one other's forms, initialing comments as they read posted charts.

For all their complexity, global teams still must do the work, meet goals and objectives, set clear measures, and add value for the many stakeholders invested in an outcome. Doing all of this in a global environment takes tact, diplomacy, cross-cultural knowledge, sensitivity, and the ability and willingness to walk in another person's shoes. It may not be easy, but it is definitely doable. More than that, it can be incredibly rich and rewarding to both the organization and to those members fortunate enough to be on an effectively run team.

Notes

1 Fallon, Maura. "Human Resources Operations in China." In Tina Farrow (Ed.), *China Practical Staff Employment Manual* (Hong Kong: Pearson Professional Publishing, 1997).

2 Higgs, Malcolm. "Overcoming the Problem of Cultural Differences to Establish Success for International Management Teams," *Team Performance Management*, 1996, V2, N1, pp. 36–43.

3   McDermott, Lynda, Bill Waite, and Nolan Brawly. "Putting Together a World-Class Team," *Training & Development,* January 1999, V53, N1, pp. 46–51; Lattimer, Robert L. "The Case for Diversity in Global Business and the Impact of Diversity on Team Performance," *Competitiveness Review,* 1998, V8, N2, pp. 3–17.

4   Fallon, Maura. "Human Resources Operations in China." In Tina Farrow (Ed.), *China Practical Staff Employment Manual* (Hong Kong: Pearson Professional Publishing, 1997).

5   Tuckman, B.W. "Developmental Sequence in Small Groups," *Psychological Bulletin,* 1965.

6   Fallon, Maura. "Human Resources Operations in China." In Tina Farrow (Ed.), *China Practical Staff Employment Manual* (Hong Kong: Pearson Professional Publishing, 1997).

7   Davidson, Sue Canney. "Creating a High Performance International Team," *Journal of Management Development,* 1994, V13, N2, pp. 81–90.

8   Ibid.

9   Sweeney, Susan. *101 Ways to Promote Your Web Site* (Gulf Breeze, FL: Maximum Press, 2001; www.maxpress.com).

CHAPTER 5

Managing Conflict
in an International Environment

In *The Nature of Prejudice,* Gordon W. Allport stated, "Conflict is like a note on an organ. It sets all prejudices that are attuned to it into simultaneous vibration. The listener can scarcely distinguish the pure note from the surrounding jangle."[1] Understanding conflict in an international business environment requires that we simultaneously understand the "pure note" and not contribute to the surrounding "jangle" of which Allport spoke.

All conflicts are ultimately intercultural. As business becomes more global, intercultural contact in the workplace has increased and has been associated with conflict, negative intergroup competition, and absenteeism.[2] Conflict is costly in the workplace, resulting in low morale, high employee turnover, and loss of productivity. But the costs can be much greater, too.

Failure to understand the cultural logic of the "other" can also be deadly. For example, during the Egyptian-Israeli conflict during the 1960s, Israeli officials believed they could deter aggressive behavior by making it very costly, responding to acts of Egyptian violence with disproportionate force. The Egyptians believed the Israeli attacks were unconscionable efforts to attack their honor, which had to be met. Incorrect interpretations of each other's behavior led to tragic consequences for both.[3]

Just as conflict is ultimately intercultural, so too are responses to it: Americans view conflict as natural and typically take an aggressive "winner-take-all" attitude toward it. Mexicans know conflict is inevitable, but deal with it indirectly and try to avoid it as much as possible. The Japanese value *Wa* (harmony) and avoid open conflict, as do Scandinavians. For Germans, conflict is viewed as dysfunctional. For Navajo Indians, if a dispute ends by having a winner and a loser, one conflict has ended, but another is sure to begin. In South Korea, the concept of *hwa jengor* or "escaping extremes," espoused by seventh century monk Won Yo, marks their approach to conflict.

Knowing how culture influences conflict is vital not only in preventing or resolving it, but also in ensuring that conflict plays a positive role in the organization rather than a detrimental or costly one. The key is to develop management practices that will prevent or minimize the impact of cross-cultural clashes, as well as unleash the creative potential inherent in such conflicts. The challenge for management is how best to exploit the opportunities arising from a mix of cultures—such as enhanced group performance, organizational learning, and quality decision making—while minimizing the negative consequences—such as lower group productivity and organizational performance.[4]

Samuel Huntington, in *The Clash of Civilizations and the Remaking of the World Order,* writes that "the fundamental source of conflict in this new world will not be primarily ideological or primarily economic [but] cultural." While Huntington's assessment of the deep-rooted nature and importance of culture as a source of conflict is correct, Professor Michelle LeBaron suggests a more positive approach:

> Culture also operates as a positive organizing force that lends coherence, meaning, and richness to life. It is a medium for relationship both within groups and among groups. Culture offers a system of symbols translated into behaviors that can operate as a bridge for outsiders, even if sometimes it may feel like a drawbridge. In reality, culture is neither a formidable fortress nor a dispensable platform; it is an integral part of human existence that has the potential to serve as an important resource in transforming intercultural conflict.[5]

While Huntington sees culture as the major source of conflict in the years to come, LeBaron sees it as a resource to transform conflict.

Understanding the cultural values underlying conflict will not in itself prevent conflict from occurring, but might help us avoid its escalation and begin the process of resolution. This chapter discusses some of the ways that culture has an impact on conflict, sources and kinds of conflict that we face in the global workplace, cross-cultural approaches to conflict, and methods of resolution. Several tools are included to help the readers understand the dynamics of conflict and conflict resolution in cross-cultural contexts, as well as their own personal conflict "style."

WHAT IS CONFLICT?

Conflict is a real or perceived incompatibility of goals, values, norms, expectations, process, or outcomes between two or more interdependent individuals or groups over content, identity, relational, or procedural issues. Conflict occurs at multiple levels, sometimes simultaneously—interpersonal, social, functional, organizational, national, and international.

While some intercultural conflict is rooted in deep-seated and centuries-old hatred, such as the ongoing Israeli-Palestinian conflict, most can be traced to cultural miscommunication or ignorance. The Three Culture Model discussed in Chapter 1 provides one visual representation of the kinds of cultures that are embedded in global corporations—personal, national, and corporate. Using that model to diagnose which cultural elements are at play in a given conflict situation can be helpful.

The term "conflict" is translated in some cultures into euphemisms such as "problems," "differences of opinion," or "challenges," as is often used in the United States. Key concepts of conflict include:[6]

- A *conflict* is a serious disagreement and argument about something perceived to be important by at least one of the parties involved.

- A *confrontation* is a direct challenge by A against B when A perceives B as the source of his or her conflict.

- *Conflict avoidance* is refusing both overt recognition of a conflict and engagement in any active action toward its resolution.

- *Conflict management* is a reaction to a conflict situation without necessarily entailing a resolution.

At its most basic, there are only three real options for conflict resolution: (1) we can prevent conflict; (2) we can resolve it, or (3) we can manage or contain it, as shown in the figure titled Options for Conflict Management. To do any of those, we must understand the potential sources of conflict, realize the impact of cultural norms on conflict itself, and develop options for managing conflict like any other business issue.

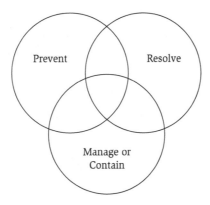

Options for Conflict Management

Source: Reprinted from Myra Warren Isenhart and Michael Spangle, *Collaborative Approaches to Resolving Conflict* (Thousand Oaks, CA: Sage, 2000, p. 163).

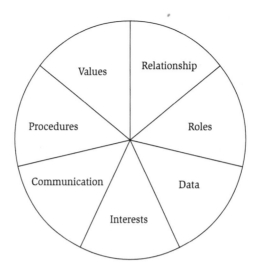

Seven Sources of Conflict

Source: Reprinted from Myra Warren Isenhart and Michael Spangle, *Collaborative Approaches to Resolving Conflict* (Thousand Oaks, CA: Sage, 2000, p. 163).

Sources of Conflict

There are seven primary sources of conflict, as shown in "Seven Sources of Conflict":[7]

1. *Data*—Differences of opinion about the best source, reliability, or interpretation of data.

2. *Interests*—Disagreements over specific, tangible wants or perceived needs are the most common type.

3. *Procedures*—Disagreements about how to solve a problem, make a decision, or solve a conflict. For example, whether to use English as the language of business is one potential hotspot in global business.

4. *Values*—Differences of opinion about the importance or priority of interests or options. These conflicts begin with a value statement about the way things should be and are frequently the hardest to resolve.

5. *Relationships*—Conflict can result if people don't trust others, don't feel respected by others, don't believe the other person is honest, or don't feel listened to.

6. *Roles*—Professional, community, or family roles can create conflict because of expectations for the role or power imbalances created by the role.

7. *Communication*—Conflict frequently results from how something is said or from misinterpretation of verbal or nonverbal messages.

To determine the sources of conflict on your team, use "What's the Source of the Conflict?"

Suggestions for Using
"What's the Source of the Conflict?"

Objectives

- To understand what kind of conflict is occurring
- To classify the conflict as either task-focused or relationship-focused
- To surface differing opinions on the causes of the conflict

Intended Audience

- Individuals or teams in conflict

Time

- 45 to 60 minutes

Materials

- Copies of "What's the Source of the Conflict?"

Directions

- Discuss and define the types of conflicts outlined on the handout, providing examples.
- Ask participants to fill in their answers.
- Have participants share their responses in pairs or small groups of three to five people.
- Ask small groups to discuss the implications for the organization of their findings.

Questions for Discussion/Consideration

- Was there agreement on the sources of the conflict?
- Were there more checkmarks in the "task" or "relationship" categories of conflict?
- Were there other types of information that you felt you might need in order to assess the source of the conflict?
- Were there other sources for the conflict that are not indicated? If so, what are those sources?
- What implications does this information have for addressing the conflict?

Cultural Considerations

- Some cultural groups prefer to deal with conflict indirectly. In such cases, ask people to submit their sheets anonymously and provide a composite profile back to the group.

Caveats, Considerations, and Variations

- This activity can be used as a planning tool for a team charged with resolving a particular conflict.

What's the Source of the Conflict?

Directions: Think of a recent or current cross-cultural conflict in which you were or are involved. To assess the source of the conflict, indicate below which statements are true of the conflict by placing a check mark in the appropriate box(es).

TASK CONFLICT

Data

☐ There is disagreement about the sources or quality of information with which we are working.

☐ The different ways in which we interpret data in our project are causing conflict.

☐ Other:

Interests

☐ Our goals are not specific and are unclear.

☐ Some of us are motivated by a personal desire to be successful and others are driven by the need for the organization or group to succeed.

☐ Other:

Procedures

☐ There is a disconnect between those who want to do things quickly and others who want time for ideas to incubate.

☐ We do not have clear procedures for decision making.

☐ Other:

RELATIONSHIP CONFLICT

Values

☐ We have limited knowledge about cross-cultural norms and how they shape our work together.

☐ Members surface negative judgments about values, attitudes, and beliefs different from their own.

☐ Other:

Relationships

☐ We are placing all our emphasis on task, to the detriment of the relationships involved.

☐ Conflict has eroded our trust in one another.

☐ Other:

What's the Source of the Conflict? (continued)

RELATIONSHIP CONFLICT

Roles

☐ In our team, we are not sure who the leader is.

☐ Roles and responsibilities are unclear.

☐ Other:

Communication

☐ We often misunderstand what another is saying or what another means.

☐ We have difficulty reading the nonverbal signals sent by others.

☐ Other:

How people respond to conflict depends on the type of the conflict and the cultural orientations of those involved and is critical to the success of any long-term business relationship.[8]

Task vs. Relationship Conflict

It's important to understand whether a conflict is task-focused (such as conflicts over data, interests, or procedures, as defined above) or relationship-focused (such as values, relationships, roles, and communication conflicts), because these two kinds of conflict can have very different results in the workplace. When people are task-oriented, they focus their efforts toward accomplishing task-related goals and monitoring progress against goals. When people are guided by a relationship orientation, their attention focuses on the interpersonal climate of the situation, and they strive to maintain social harmony. In cultural terms, many Asians are relationship-oriented, while many Westerns are more task-focused.

Examples of relationship conflict include conflicts about personal taste, political preferences, values, and interpersonal style. Task conflicts, by contrast, are conflicts about the distribution of resources, about policies and procedures, and about judgments and interpretation of facts.[9] Regardless of culture, person-related conflicts result in more negative outcomes and are less satisfying than task-related conflicts.[10]

Whether a conflict is task-focused or relationship-focused can greatly influence whether the conflict can help or hinder the organization. While conflicts focused on personal difference are often dysfunctional and counterproductive, conflicts focused on ideas and issues (task conflict) are often very productive.[11]

The challenge is to find ways to create task conflict without generating relationship conflict.[12] The "Dimensions of Conflict" can help team members compare their views about conflict.

Suggestions for Using the "Dimensions of Conflict"

Objectives

- To raise awareness about the dynamics of conflict management for individuals and groups
- To gain insight about which global diversity dimensions are involved in a given conflict
- To identify ways in which conflict helps and hinders the team or organization
- To learn about others' perceptions of the group's conflict-solving dynamics
- To stimulate discussion about effective conflict management

Intended Audience

- A functional global work team, task force, or problem-solving group
- A consultant or manager trying to teach a group to function better to resolve conflict

Time

- 20 minutes

Materials

- Copies of the "Dimensions of Conflict" and the SSI Model from Chapter 2

Directions

- Ask participants to pair up and answer the questions in random order.
- After ten minutes, conduct a whole group discussion on a select number of items.

Questions for Discussion/Consideration

- Which questions were easiest/most difficult for you to answer?
- Which were most interesting?
- What does the range of responses indicate about your group's conflict-management capability?
- What themes emerged?
- What does this data suggest the group needs to do differently?
- What can you do differently to enhance your conflict-management style?
- In what ways does conflict help and in what ways does conflict hurt the organization?

Dimensions of Conflict

This series of open-ended statements is intended to help individuals and their team members determine which dimensions of global diversity are at the core of the conflict. This exercise will be most effective if accompanied by a copy of the SSI Model (as shown in Chapter 2).

- Take turns initiating the discussion. Complete statements orally.
- Items may be responded to in random order.

1. The conflict appears to be about . . .

2. The dimensions of personal culture that appear to be involved include . . .

3. The national cultures involved are . . .

4. The civilizational cultures involved are . . .

5. The organizational dimensions involved are . . .

6. This conflict is [task-focused or relationship-focused] . . .

7. The most important consideration in solving this conflict is . . .

8. In order to resolve this conflict, we need more information about . . .

9. We can get that information from . . .

10. The greatest obstacle in resolving this conflict is . . .

11. This conflict hinders our organization by . . .

12. This conflict helps our organization by . . .

13. In my culture, we resolve conflict by . . .

14. As a work group, we resolve conflict by . . .

15. Effective conflict resolution in this organization requires . . .

16. The most difficult conflicts to solve in our organization are . . .

Caveats, Considerations, and Variations

- Depending on the size of the group, small groups can be used instead of pairs.

- The time can be lengthened and each person can select one item on which to focus for improvement. All participants still need to respond to each question and the facilitator still needs to lead an overall discussion.

THE IMPACT OF CULTURE ON CONFLICT

Reports of cultural clashes and conflict within cross-border partnerships such as that of Daimler and Chrysler are common. Even much earlier, the merger of Metal Box with Carnaud was marked by conflicts between the autocratic management style of the French and the more participative orientation of the British; the GEC and Siemens partnership featured contrasts between the British firm's decentralized and short-term approach and the centralized longer-term style of the German partner.[13] At its most basic, culture determines how we engage in conversation, dialogue, or negotiation with one another—even our conversational patterns reveal deeper cultural norms, as shown in the figure on the next page, which illustrates conversational patterns in the United States, Japan, and Brazil.

Conflict and culture go hand in hand. Different national and civilizational cultures have embedded in them different conflict styles, assumptions about conflict, conflict rhythms, and conflict norms. In the United States, for example, the very language that we use in conflict situations provides a clear picture of our direct, aggressive approach: "Lay your cards on the table," "Don't beat around the bush," and "Put it all on the line" are a few examples.

Some cultures believe that conflict provides opportunity. Western cultural groups share four primary assumptions about conflict:

1. That conflict is normal and useful;

2. That all issues are subject to change through negotiation;

3. That direct confrontation and conciliation are valued; and

4. That conflict is a necessary renegotiation of contract, a release of tensions, and a renewal of relationships.[14]

For people who see conflict as opportunity, the benefits of working through conflicts include gaining new information about other people or groups, being cognizant of and defusing more serious conflicts, and increasing overall cohesiveness. In fact, research has shown that conflict leads to stimulation, adaptation, and innovation, which are considered to be psychologically and sociologically healthy. This

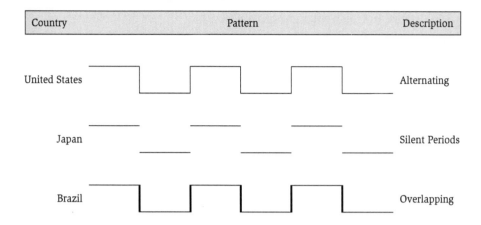

Country	Pattern	Description

Negotiators in some cultures interrupt one another; in other cultures they do not. A two-person negotiation is diagrammed for each of the three countries above. A line indicates that negotiator one or two is speaking. Blanks indicate that both negotiators are silent. Overlaps indicate that both negotiators are speaking at the same time.

Conversational Overlaps: Who Interrupts Whom

Source: Based on John Graham, "The Influence of Culture on Business Negotiations," *Journal of International Studies,* Spring 1985, V16, N1, pp. 81–96.

is an attitude prevalent in Anglo-Saxon cultures such as the United States, the U.K., and Ireland.[15]

But some cultures view conflict as unproductive and even destructive for relationships. Sometimes spiritual or cultural values dictate that conflict is dangerous or wrong. There are four assumptions underlying this approach to conflict:

1. Conflict is a destructive disturbance of the peace;
2. The social system should not be adjusted to the needs of its members, but rather, its members need to adapt to the established values;
3. Confrontations are destructive and ineffective; and
4. Disputants should be disciplined.[16]

Professor Stella Ting-Toomey suggests that these two opposed orientations are based on different cultural orientations to identity and face-saving. The conflict-as-opportunity orientation stems from a concern for saving individual dignity, while the conflict-as-destructive orientation stems from a higher value attributed to maintaining harmony in interpersonal relationships and saving the dignity of others.

In the preceding chapters, and particularly in Chapter 1, the work of Geert Hofstede was used to provide a framework for understanding cultural dimensions of nation states. Hofstede's dimensions are useful in discussing the impact of culture on conflict. To review:

- *Individualism* refers to the extent to which members of a culture view themselves as distinct persons rather than as part of a collective. Individualistic cultures include countries such as Canada, the United States, France, Germany, Switzerland, Australia, and Great Britain. Collectivist cultures include Japan, South Korea, Vietnam, Hong Kong, Greece, Italy, Brazil, Mexico, Iran, and Singapore. Because of this difference, competition is a counterproductive resolution method in Japan, but productive in the West. Some cultures have both individualist and collectivist tendencies, such as Turkey, which embodies strong individualistic elements alongside a collectivist outlook.

- *Power distance* is the extent to which inequality of power and influence is seen as normal in the culture. Low power distance cultures such as Canada, the United States, Australia, and New Zealand subscribe to equal power distribution, while high power distance cultures like the Philippines, Malaysia, Japan, South Korea, Hong Kong, Guatemala, Panama, Mexico, and many Arab countries adhere to hierarchical structures. Understanding the balance of power is vital in any conflict. There are several variables that affect this balance:[17]

Time	Which party is under the most time pressure?
Money	What are the financial stakes?
Knowledge and Skill	Which side is more experienced and knowledgeable?
Information	Who has access to what information?
Authority	Who has the authority to make decisions?
Legitimacy	Who has morality and/or law on his or her side?
Network	Which side brings the most powerful connections to the table?

- *Uncertainty avoidance* measures a culture's lack of tolerance for ambiguity and the extent to which members of the culture prefer structured to unstructured situations. Cultures that rank low in uncertainty avoidance such as the United States and Canada like to take risks, take individual initiative, and enjoy conflict, while cultures high in uncertainty avoidance like Japan and South Korea do not like conflict, but pursue group harmony. They need clear rules, procedures, and clearly defined job responsibilities.

- *Masculinity* measures the extent to which "masculine" values such as assertiveness and success prevail. Japan ranks high on masculine dimensions; males there expect an "in-charge" role. Countries like Norway and Sweden have a stronger feminine dimension and roles are more fluid there between males and females. When harmony and consensus are highly valued, as in the Netherlands, conflict is likely to have a stronger and more negative impact.

- *Long-term orientation* is the extent to which values are oriented to the future, rather than to the present and past. This can influence whether individuals take a short-term or long-term approach to conflict resolution.

Edward Hall's concepts of low-context and high-context communication (discussed in more depth in Chapter 3) are also important to our understanding of intercultural conflict. Low-context communication emphasizes expression of intention or meaning though explicit verbal messages, while high-context communication focuses on meaning being expressed through the context (such as social roles and positions) and nonverbal channels (such as pauses, silence, and tone of voice). In high-context cultures, the listener is expected to read between the lines to decode meaning. Whether a culture is low-context or high-context can affect whether direct or indirect communication is used to defuse conflict.

Of all these, the continuum of individualist and collectivist cultures may have the most impact on how people react to conflict situations.

I OR THOU?

Much of the research around cultural difference centers on the difference between how individualist and collectivist cultures define and respond to conflict. The hallmarks of these two approaches are outlined below:

Individualist Cultures	Collectivist Cultures
Conflict is outcome-focused	Conflict is process-focused
Conflict is dealt with openly and honestly	Face work management done before substantive issue discussion
Success comes with tangible outcomes or action plans	Success comes with mutual face saving and face giving
Goals of individuals addressed	Interpreted in terms of group
Achievement is important	Harmony is important
Communication is direct	Communication is indirect

As indicated above, resolving intercultural conflict is made more difficult by the fact that individualists and collectivists hold different ideas of what constitutes effective and appropriate practices in conflict resolution.

In individualistic cultures, people tend to be more verbally direct and open. Self-disclosure, clarity, and being straightforward are all part of this cultural norm. Indirect communication is preferred in collectivist cultures because the image of group harmony is vital. Western cultures value talking as a means of solving issues; in Eastern cultures there is a higher value placed on observing and reflecting. American managers often make the mistake of interpreting silence on the part of Asian counterparts as consent, while Asian managers err in reading a U.S. colleague's direct adversarial arguments as indicating unreasonableness and lack of respect.[18]

Members of collectivist cultures perceive and manage conflict differently than do those in individualistic cultures, adopting different strategies to resolve conflict, holding different expectations about possible outcomes, and being motivated by different causes.[19] For example, the Chinese culture is collective and "high context," emphasizing group harmony and interdependence, while North American culture is individualistic and "low context," emphasizing individual rights and independence. The very concept of person in Chinese culture and language, "Ren," is not of an individual person, but the person's interactions or transactions with fellow human beings. Chinese tend to see behavior resulting from social pressures, while Americans see behavior as a result of individual volition.

In individualist cultures, conflict is likely to occur when individuals' expectations of appropriate behavior are violated, while conflict occurs in collectivist cultures when the group's normative expectations for behavior are violated.[20]

Ting-Toomey notes that collective societies tend to avoid open conflict and resolve conflict in inner circles before it becomes public or serious. Chinese, for example, often use delaying techniques[21] and more obliging and avoiding conflict-resolution styles than do Americans. Research has shown that Japanese use an avoiding strategy 48 percent of the time, compared to Americans, who use avoiding as a conflict-management strategy only 22 percent of the time.[22]

Executives from individualist cultures are typically more receptive to differences in behavior, believing that deviation from group norms contributes to a diversity of opinion and, ultimately, better achievement of group goals.[23]

In a study of Chinese and Canadian executives, researchers found that executives from the PRC focused on concern for social relationships more than Canadians in their decisions, while the Canadians showed more concern for goal achievement. Chinese executives also were more inclined to classify the world into extremes—black or white, good or evil—and more likely to consult their superiors in conflict situations.

PRC executives react more negatively to conflicts than do their Canadian counterparts; their inclination is to discontinue negotiation or threaten to withdraw, particularly in relationship-related conflicts. PRC executives also show a greater inclination to be motivated by their sense of "self-esteem." "Self" in group-focused Chinese culture is defined in relationship to the other "selves" in groups to which one has long-term affiliation.[24]

Members of individualist cultures like the United States tend to separate the issue on which they are having conflict from the person with whom they have the conflict, while members of collectivist cultures generally do not make the same distinction. For example, Japanese managers consider criticism of their ideas to be personal attacks, while most American managers do not.

Ting-Toomey's research has also revealed that members of individualistic cultures are more likely to possess a confrontational, direct attitude toward conflicts than are members of collectivist cultures. Some differences are outlined below.

Individualist Cultures	Collectivist Cultures
Short-term	Long-term
Confrontational, direct attitude	Nonconfrontational, indirect attitude
Concern for self	Concern for others
Concern with immediate situation	Focus on long-term relationship with other
Little use of mediators or, if used, formal mediation	Use of informal mediators

The concept of trust is an important one in conflict situations; it too is culturally influenced. "Trust in a business context depends on the ability to interpret culturally coded signs."[25]

The word "trust" is also culturally coded—trust means to rely on the consistency of another's credibility, words, and behaviors, but how trust is exhibited varies by culture. For instance, in low power distance cultures, trust is often based on charismatic personality traits, personal credibility, and persuasive words. In high power distance cultures, it is usually based on credible roles and dependable networks.

Culture influences the ways in which the arguments of counterparts are countered—whether by objective facts (North Americans), subjective feelings (Arabs), or asserted ideals (Russians). The length of the perceived relationship also differs, from short-term (North American) to long-term (Arabs), and no continuing relationship (Russians).

THE CONCEPT OF FACE

Face saving, face giving, and face losing are all important concepts in dealing with intercultural conflict. To deal effectively with conflict, we must first understand "face" as it applies to various cultures. Ting-Toomey sees face as symbolic and as a claimed sense of self-respect in a relational situation. Face is universal because everyone would like to be respected and needs a sense of self-respect, but how we achieve, maintain, save, or honor one's face differs across cultures.

Face Saving.   The meaning of face differs. In individualistic cultures, the concept of face is equated with saving one's own face (pride, reputation, credibility, and self-respect), while in collectivist cultures, it is more related to honor and the family or organization—face in relation to others. In collectivist cultures, everyone is interlocked in an interdependent group orientation. In the Chinese term "guanxi," the interlocking relationship patterns emerge as "who knows whom" and "who is in charge of whom." Also in collectivist cultures, there is a strong link between the concept of power and the concept of face. To have a greater face in Asian cultures is to be more powerful in the organization or know more people in the system. Most Asians, reports Ting-Toomey, understand how much face they have. The Face Negotiation Theory model is based on Ting-Toomey's distinctions.

Face Giving.　This is not a common concept in most individualistic countries. To collectivist cultures in Asia, face giving means allowing room for the other person to recover his or her face—room to negotiate—so both can gain face in the end. "For Westerners, face seems to be a dichotomous concept: we either lose face or save face. For Easterners, face is considered to be a mutual, interdependent concept, and is a relational and group phenomena."[26]

Face Losing.　In individualistic cultures losing face means personal failure, loss of self-esteem, or loss of individual self-pride. For Japanese, Korean, and other collectivist cultures, face losing has ramifications for disrupting group harmony and bringing shame to their family, classmates, or company.

Recovery.　Recovery from face loss also differs. Humor is a common strategy used to recover from face loss in individualistic cultures; if humor doesn't work, defense and attack strategies may be used, causing win/lose situations. Asian cultures focus more on maintaining the image of a win/win process and involve more intermediaries to preserve face than do individualistic cultures.

Conflict.　This is also face-related, since face appears to be a predictor of what conflict strategy will be used, according to Ting-Toomey. In conflict situations,

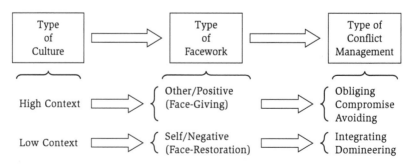

Face Negotiation Theory

Source: Based on the work of Stella Ting-Toomey, "International Conflict Styles." In Y. Kim and W. Gudykunst (Eds.), *Theories in Intercultural Communication* (Thousand Oaks, CA: Sage, 1988, pp. 213–235).

individualistic cultures tend to adopt self-preservation strategies, focus on self-face issues, use confrontation and control-focused conflict strategies, and display win/lose orientations. Asian subjects tend to use face-smoothing strategies, mutual face-preservation strategies, and conflict avoidance strategies.

Another way to characterize cultures in relation to conflict management is that developed by anthropologist Ruth Benedict and later amplified by psychologist Abraham Maslow. They discovered that some cultures are more synergistic and inclined toward cooperation, while others are predisposed toward competition and conflict. Some of the differences between high-synergy societies and low-synergy societies are shown below.

High-Synergy Societies	*Low-Synergy Societies*
Emphasis on cooperation	Competitive, uncooperative
Nonaggressive social order	Antagonistic behavior toward one another
Idealizes win/win	Win/lose approach
Belief system emphasizes good	Belief system is frightening and punishing
Encourages development of potential of all	Permits exploitation of poor and minorities

Check out your group's conflict style by using "What's Your Conflict Style?"

Suggestions for Using "What's Your Conflict Style?"

Objectives

- To clarify one's own cultural programming around conflict issues
- To understand differences in cultural programming among co-workers
- To stimulate discussion and negotiation of differences

Intended Audience

- Members of a multinational work team, task force, or department
- Managers of international or multicultural teams
- Participants in diversity training sessions

Time

- 45 to 60 minutes

Materials

- Copies of "What's Your Conflict Style?"
- Enlargements of "What's Your Conflict Style?" (optional)

What's Your Conflict Style?

Directions: In each pair of statements below, distribute ten points between the two choices, based on how much each describes you when faced with a conflict situation. For example, seven points for the a. statement, three points for the b. statement. If both describe your orientation equally, you would give each five points.

1. _____ a. I like to face conflicts head-on and get the issues out in the open.

   _____ b. I try to avoid conflict wherever possible.

2. _____ a. I prefer to deal with conflict myself.

   _____ b. I think it's more effective to use informal mediators or third parties to help resolve conflicts.

3. _____ a. When a conflict arises, I can easily separate the issues from the people involved.

   _____ b. I consider criticism of my ideas to be personal attacks.

4. _____ c. When faced with a conflict, I like to win.

   _____ d. I prefer finding creative ways to achieve win/win solutions that combine the best thinking of all the cultures involved.

5. _____ c. The belief systems in my culture emphasize a kind and caring superior being.

   _____ d. My culture's belief systems are more focused on punishing than rewarding.

6. _____ c. I like competition.

   _____ d. I'm more comfortable working in a cooperative environment where collaboration is the norm.

7. _____ e. I believe that conflict is normal and useful.

   _____ f. Conflict is disruptive and hurtful in work situations.

8. _____ e. Going through a conflict together can help a team be more cohesive and work better together.

   _____ f. Teams are negatively impacted by conflict.

9. _____ e. Conflict often drives innovation and creativity in my team.

   _____ f. Confrontations are destructive and dangerous to team effectiveness.

Scoring

Write the points for each statement, then add the total points for each letter and divide by three to find an average score for the three items with the same letter.

Individualist	Collectivist
1a. ____	1b. ____
2a. ____	2b. ____
3a. ____	3b. ____
Total ____ ÷ 3 = ____	Total ____ ÷ 3 = ____
Synergistic	**Nonsynergistic**
4c. ____	4d. ____
5c. ____	5d. ____
6c. ____	6d. ____
Total ____ ÷ 3 = ____	Total ____ ÷ 3 = ____
Conflict as Constructive	**Conflict as Destructive**
7e. ____	7f. ____
8e. ____	8f. ____
9e. ____	9f. ____
Total ____ ÷ 3 = ____	Total ____ ÷ 3 = ____

Directions

- Discuss and define the dimensions on each continuum.
- Ask team members to respond to the questionnaire and score responses, following directions.
- Have members share profiles and discuss similarities, differences, and implications for the team, either by showing each other their answers or by putting their marks with a colored marker or stick-on dots on an enlarged version of the profile sheet posted on the wall. (One for the whole team or one chart for each group of five to six people.)

Questions for Discussion/Consideration

- What similarities and differences do you see among group members?
- How does your profile reflect a preferred national or organizational profile?

- How does your own profile help and hinder you in managing conflict?
- How flexible are you in adapting to others who have different cultural orientations on these dimensions?
- How do the differences play out in work behaviors and team interactions?
- How does your combined profile help and/or hinder you as a team?
- Where are there potential "hot spots" that may lead to misunderstanding?
- How can you make your combined profile work in your group's favor?

Cultural Considerations

- Talking about differences openly may be uncomfortable for some team members. In such cases, have team members turn in their profiles anonymously and draw a composite group profile for the team to discuss.

Caveats, Considerations, and Variations

- Have each team member mark his or her profile on a separate transparency printed with the profile scoring. Then juxtapose transparencies on the overhead to show differences and similarities in profiles.
- If there are distinct cultural groups, have each group mark profiles using a different colored marker. First show collected profiles of each national or civilizational group together, discussing similarities and differences within a group. Then combine all profiles. (Variation suggested by the work of Mila Hernán Alvarez, Business Communication Consultant, Madrid, Spain.)
- Have members pair or group with those on the team they most need to communicate with to share profiles and negotiate adaptations.

CULTURALLY APPROPRIATE STRATEGIES FOR RESOLVING CONFLICT

Research has shown that there are twelve variables in every international conflict or negotiation:[27]

- *Basic conception of conflict*—What conflict is, whether it brings crisis or opportunity;
- *Mediator or negotiator selection criteria*—Whether a mediator is used and, if so, what skills he or she must display;
- *Significance of type of issue*—Whether the conflict is task-based or relationship-based and how that affects outcome;
- *Concern with protocol*—Whether protocol rules are formal or informal;

- *Complexity of language*—The degree of reliance on nonverbal cues to convey information and whether the culture is high-context or low-context, as described in Chapter 3;
- *Nature of persuasive arguments*—Whether attempts to influence the other are done through emotion or logic;
- *Role of individual's aspirations*—Whether the focus is on the achievement of the individual or of the group;
- *Bases of trust*—Whether trust is based on written laws or on friendship and mutual respect;
- *Risk-taking propensity*—Whether the cultures involved are low or high risk takers;
- *Value of time*—Whether the cultures are monochronic or polychronic in their approach to time;
- *Decision-making system*—Whether decision-making systems are "authoritative" or "consensual"; and
- *Form of satisfactory agreement*—Whether the form of agreement is a written contract or a broad oral agreement that depends on the quality of the relationship.[28]

Members from different cultures hold distinct preferences for how conflict should be resolved. All cultures tend to define what happens in their own culture as "natural" and "right" and what happens in other cultures as "unnatural" and "incorrect."[29]

Researcher Catherine Tinsley of Georgetown University has identified three culturally determined strategies for resolving conflict. First, people who disagree can defer to status or power, looking to high-ranking individuals for advice. Tinsley's study revealed that Japanese managers preferred this style. Second, conflicting individuals can turn to rules as the way to settle conflict, focusing on identifying the rule or regulation that applies. Germans favored this approach. Third, conflict participants may seek a solution that satisfies the underlying concerns of those involved by integrating their various self-interests, using strategies such as sharing information, making concessions, or brainstorming, which may lead to innovative solutions that incorporate diverse interests. American managers preferred this strategy.[30]

At its deepest level, conflict is intimately connected with meaning-making activities, according to Michelle LeBaron, and she says that in order for interventions to be successful, they must address the level where meaning is made.[31]

Yet, as outsiders to another culture, we do not really have access to how meaning is made. "Concepts of what constitutes a conflict and who is a party, what level of confrontation is appropriate, how issues should be identified and addressed, and what would be seen as resolution or transformation are intricately connected to the intervener's own cultural experiences and perceptions," LeBaron notes.[32]

A key to managing conflict constructively is to understand and address the basic human needs of those involved. Psychologist Abraham Maslow identified a hierarchy of human needs—from physiological to safety/security, social, esteem, and self-actualization. While the United States places "self-actualization" at the pinnacle of that hierarchy, different cultures rearrange its order. For instance, many Asian countries consider social needs as more important than self-actualization. Understanding the basic assumptions about needs is vital in addressing conflict situations.

To manage conflict in South Korea, for example, it is necessary to understand the Korean context of a rich protest tradition that focuses on heightening, not defusing, conflicts. Challenging a series of dictatorships, opposing U.S. military presence, and battling company unions have all required the demonstration of popular power.[33] It is also important to understand Korean aversion to language familiar to those involved in conflict resolution, such as the term "mediation." This term has been somewhat corrupted because the Korean government previously put itself forward as a "mediator" in worker disputes, but sided with the workers and did not act as a neutral party. It is also vital to know the social structures of South Korea, including the strong vertical hierarchy that marks their culture. To help you in gathering information about conflict on your team, use the "Conflict Information-Gathering Checklist."

Suggestions for Using the "Conflict Information-Gathering Checklist"

Objectives

- To understand the kinds of information necessary before undertaking conflict-resolution strategies
- To assess personal knowledge of the conditions for conflict management
- To prioritize information-gathering needs of the organization
- To identify internal resources for conflict-management information

Intended Audience

- Managers responsible for diversity initiatives
- HR professionals with global responsibility
- Diversity council or task force members
- Managers of international or multicultural teams

Time

- 45 to 60 minutes

Materials

- Copies of the "Conflict Information-Gathering Checklist"

Directions

- Discuss and define the types of information needed (Column 1).
- Ask participants to fill in their answers on the checklist.
- Have participants share their responses in small groups of three to five people, comparing their prioritization and self-assessment or needs.
- Ask small groups to discuss the implications for the organization of their findings.

Questions for Discussion/Consideration

- How did the priorities of your group differ?
- Were there other types of information that you felt you might need in order to assess your readiness to address conflict situations?
- How can you use this checklist as a planning tool for handling cross-cultural conflict?
- What resources will you need to tap the necessary information and expertise you need?

Cultural Considerations

- Talking about the self-assessment of knowledge openly may be uncomfortable for some team members. In such cases, have small groups create a composite of knowledge needs that can be shared with the larger group.

Caveats, Considerations, and Variations

- This checklist can be used as a planning tool for a team charged with rolling out a conflict-resolution strategy.
- Once self-knowledge needs have been identified by individuals, engage the group in a "skill exchange" where those who have knowledge in a particular area are paired with those who need to gain that knowledge.

Cultures resolve conflict in different ways. For example, among the Tiv tribe, the fourth largest in Nigeria, a traditional form of mediation was commonly used for interpersonal (family, community, and organizational) disputes.[34] A communitarian rather than individualistic society, they believed that "I am because you are," demonstrating the focus and emphasis on the community, not on the individual.

Conflict in this culture followed this process: First report by disgruntled party, first hearing by immediate family elder, second hearing by eldest in family, invocation of ancestral spirits, didactic on community values, "Swem" or taking an

Conflict Information-Gathering Checklist

Directions: When addressing conflict situations, there is information you must have or acquire in order to make informed decisions about appropriate strategies. Use this worksheet to outline information you will need, the priority of importance of each, your current level of expertise, and those individuals in the company who can best serve as cultural informants for you.

Information Needed	Priority of Importance	Level of Current Knowledge (1 being lowest, 5 being highest)	From Whom in the Company Can I Get That Information?
National history and experience regarding conflict and conflict mediation			
Definitions of conflict used in the countries involved, including metaphors used to talk about conflict			
Past company experience (positive and negative) with this type of conflict			
Whether the conflict is task-focused or relationship-focused			
Whether the cultures involved are individualist or collectivist, and the impact that orientation will have on the conflict			
Legal requirements or issues surrounding the conflict			

Conflict Information-Gathering Checklist (continued)

Information Needed	Priority of Importance	Level of Current Knowledge (1 being lowest, 5 being highest)	From Whom in the Company Can I Get That Information?
The cultural backgrounds of the individuals involved			
The levels of authority and decision-making power of each party			
The primary needs and wants of each party			
The description of the conflict from each party's perspective			
The organizational issues at play (time or financial pressures, and so on)			
The nature of cultural change and conflict in the countries involved			
Other • • •			

oath to maintain group harmony, and celebration of unity with traditional food at which the parties eat from the same plate and drink from one dish. Unfortunately, the persistence of Western trends of thought and conduct has gradually eroded this effective system.

The Maori society in New Zealand provides another perspective on cultural norms in conflict management. The Maori have meeting houses in which people gather and talk through conflict. The first unwritten rule of the gathering is that the issue is not addressed immediately. Speakers follow one another, building the community's conversation, circling around the issue. They must relate themselves to everyone in the room, talking about relationships, events when you or other people in the room (or their ancestors) were together, when there was a relationship and when things were good. The process of "Mihili Mihili" is one in which each individual stands up, in turn, and tells who he or she is and how he or she is connected with everyone else. Through this approach eventually comes resolution.

Some approaches to conflict reflect several cultural influences at once. Researchers have argued that Indian managerial conflict-resolution tendencies reflect Hindu norms of seeking a solution that pleases everyone, as well as British norms of active, mutual problem solving.[35] The result is a style less inclined toward competing than that in the United States, but one that does not take the form of conflict avoidance that it takes in Chinese contexts.

Overall, according to Rahim,[36] there are five basic types of conflict-resolution strategies: *obliging, compromising, avoiding, integrating,* and *domineering.* These five styles are related to the degree of concern for self and concern for others, as indicated in Five Types of Conflict-Resolution Strategies and explained below:

1. *Domineering* (win-lose)—Reflects high concern for self and low concern for others; uses forcing behaviors to win;

2. *Integrating*—High concern for both self and others, reflected in an open and direct exchange of information aimed at reaching a solution acceptable to both parties; seen as most effective for most conflicts, but requires the most time and energy;

3. *Compromising*—Reflects moderate degree of concern for self and others; involves sharing and exchanging information; valuing a kind of "fairness" whereby both parties give up something to find a mutually acceptable decision;

4. *Obliging*—One party plays down the differences that separate the two parties while emphasizing the commonalities; and

5. *Avoiding*—Reflects low concern for self and others in U.S. cultural contexts, but in some other contexts this is viewed as an appropriate style that enhances harmony of relationships.

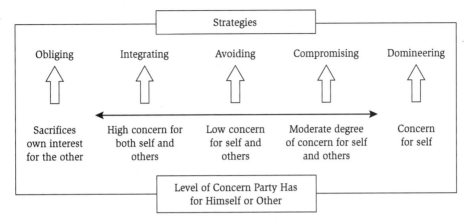

Five Types of Conflict-Resolution Strategies

Source: Based on the work of A. Rahim, "A Measure of Styles of Handling Interpersonal Conflict," *Academy of Management Journal,* V26, pp. 368–376, and D. Tjosvold, *The Conflict Positive Organization* (Reading, MA: Addison-Wesley, 1991).

There are cross-cultural differences in negotiation styles; that is, people of different cultures use significantly different negotiation approaches, including how they communicate, how they try to persuade others, and what protocols they follow. The Japanese, North American, and Latin American styles are compared in the Negotiation Styles from a Cross-Cultural Perspective figure.

One model for resolving cross-cultural conflict is the Seven-Step Conflict Resolution Model created by Clifford Clarke and Doug Lipp.[37] The steps are:

1. *Problem identification*—State problem and background briefly. Agree on what the problem is, even if it is viewed differently. Describe the situation, identify difficulties, develop explanations of the situation from both sides.

2. *Problem clarification*—Compare intentions. The gap between intention and impact can often be the source of the problem.

3. *Cultural exploration*—Examine each culture's values and how they play out in light of people's contrasting expectations and assumptions. Examine how values affect each group's intentions and perceptions, looking deeper at the origins and assumptions of culturally determined behaviors.

4. *Organizational exploration*—Look at organizational issues that affect the conflict under discussion. What is the organizational context and what are the pressures, the industry-specific or labor-directed standards?

5. *Current status*—How is the conflict affecting operations, customers, employees? Setting goals for resolution.

Japanese	North American	Latin American
Emotional sensitivity highly valued	Emotional sensitivity not highly valued	Emotional sensitivity valued
Hiding emotions	Dealing straightforwardly or impersonally	Emotionally passionate
Subtle power plays; conciliation	Litigation; not as much conciliation	Great power plays; use of weakness
Loyalty to employer; employer takes care of employees	Lack of commitment to employer; breaking ties by either if necessary	Loyalty to employer (who is often family)
Group decision making by consensus	Team provides input to a decision maker	Decisions come down from one individual
Face-saving crucial; decisions often made to save someone from embarrassment	Decisions based on cost-benefit analysis; face-saving not generally important	Face-saving crucial in decision making to preserve honor, dignity
Decision makers openly influenced by special interests	Decision makers influenced by special interests, but often not considered ethical	Inclusion of special interests of decision maker expected and condoned
Not argumentative; quiet when right	Argumentative when right or wrong, but impersonal	Argumentative when right or wrong; passionate
What is down in writing must be accurate, valid	Great importance given to documentation as evidential proof	Impatient with documentation; seen as obstacle to understanding general principles
Step-by-step approach to decision making	Methodically organized decision making	Impulsive, spontaneous decision making
Good of group is the ultimate aim	Profit motive or good of individual ultimate aim	What is good for group is good for the individual
Cultivate a good emotional social setting for decision making; get to know decision makers	Decision making impersonal; avoid involvement, conflict of interest	Personalism necessary for good decision making

Negotiation Styles from a Cross-Cultural Perspective

Source: Adapted from Pierre Casse, *Training for the Multicultural Manager: A Practical and Cross-Cultural Approach to the Management of People,* cited in Nancy Adler, *International Dimensions of Organizational Behavior* (Mason, OH: South-Western, 1997, p. 192).

6. *Impact assessment*—Determining measures or key indicators that the goal has been achieved and the conflict resolved.

7. *Organizational integration*—Integrating individual success stories into corporate learning systems, recording the results, celebrating the success, and institutionalizing the benefits.

In addition to this linear approach to conflict resolution, since cultural values operate on the symbolic level, symbolic tools are needed for effective analysis and intervention. LeBaron suggests that we also use symbolic tools such as stories, myths, metaphors, and rituals to help understand and build relationship with the "other."

The competencies needed by effective interveners in intercultural conflicts include leadership, creativity, authenticity, empathy, and cultural sensitivity, according to LeBaron. Achieving meaningful collaboration, cultivating an ongoing curiosity about the issues, and having a high level of self-awareness are key. As seen in the U.S. Negotiator's Global Report Card on the following page, U.S. negotiators do not score high on the kinds of competencies needed in intercultural conflict resolution.

Look at your own ability to handle conflict by using "Assessing Your Conflict Competencies."

Suggestions for Using "Assessing Your Conflict Competencies"

Objectives
- To identify individual practices and skills conducive to effective conflict management
- To identify obstacles to be addressed in order to strengthen personal skills

Intended Audience
- Executives in global organizations
- Managers or members of global teams, departments, divisions, or units
- Human resource managers in global organizations
- Participants in diversity training sessions

Time
- 45 to 60 minutes

Materials
- Copies of "Assessing Your Conflict Competencies"
- A flip chart and markers

Directions

- Explain the primary conflict competencies, giving examples of each and soliciting examples from the group.

- Ask members to respond to the checklist, checking the appropriate column for each statement.

- Have members focus on the items in the "almost never" column, sharing their most needed growth areas in small groups and charting the group's agreed-on top three areas to target for improvement.

- Have each group report its top three areas for development, charting responses.

- Lead a group discussion of areas for development, honing the total group list down to three or four.

- Have members brainstorm possible ways to strengthen that aspect of global communication in the organization.

- Have groups report their most workable suggestions.

- Summarize and indicate next steps.

- Ask each member to commit to one action he or she can take to strengthen some aspect of conflict management that is currently presenting an obstacle.

Questions for Discussion/Consideration

- Which areas for development most hinder effective conflict management in the organization?

- What is the cost of these hindrances to the organization?

- What needs to be done to address these areas?

- Which suggestions are we willing to undertake?

- What can you do individually to improve in one of these areas?

Cultural Considerations

- Some members may be reluctant to surface any "bad news" for fear of disrupting harmony and causing embarrassment.

- Some members may be more comfortable discussing without a worksheet. In those cases, use the items as questions to stimulate discussion.

Caveats, Considerations, and Variations

- Have members fill out the checklist anonymously and turn it in. Then present data to the group for discussion.

- Send and have members respond to the questionnaire electronically. Tally responses and present for discussion at a teleconferenced meeting.

	Competency	Grade
✓	Preparation	B–
✓	Synergistic Approach (win-win)	D
✓	Cultural I.Q.	D
✓	Adapting style to host country environment	D
✓	Patience	D
✓	Listening	D
✓	Linguistic abilities	F
✓	Using language that is simple and accessible	C
✓	High aspirations	B+
✓	Personal integrity	A
✓	Building solid relationships	D

U.S. Negotiator's Global Report Card

Source: Adapted from Frank Acuff, as reprinted from Philip R. Harris and Robert T. Moran, *Managing Cultural Difference* (Houston, TX: Gulf, 2000, p. 59).

Because of the marked differences in conflict style between individualist and collectivist cultures, Ting-Toomey suggests the following as helpful in mediating conflict between them:[38]

Individualists May Want to

- Practice patience and verbal restraint in articulating their personal interests;
- Listen more attentively;
- Be open to expressions of stories, proverbs, metaphors, and understatements;
- Use self-effacing questions to encourage the others to coach them;
- Address conflict problems to team members rather than singling out one person;
- Accept longer turn-taking pauses and reflective silences;
- Use appropriate head nods to indicate affirmation; and
- Listen to the identity and relational meanings underneath the conflict content messages.

Assessing Your Conflict Competencies

Directions: Check the appropriate column for each statement with regard to your competency in managing conflict.

Practices	Almost Always	Sometimes	Almost Never
1. I am continually developing my cross-cultural awareness, knowledge, and skills.			
2. I understand the primary ways in which cultural differences can influence responses to conflict.			
3. When faced with a conflict situation, I prepare by researching the cultural context of each party involved before moving forward.			
4. I seek to resolve conflict situations with a win/win or synergistic approach.			
5. I use language that is simple and accessible.			
6. I start by stating the problem and the background of the problem from both sides.			
7. I am sensitive to and knowledgeable about cultural differences influencing communication.			
8. I am able to examine my own assumptions, interpretations, and behaviors and assess their impact on business interactions.			
9. I am a skilled listener, hearing both the stated and unstated messages.			
10. I look at the organizational issues that affect the conflict, such as standards, policies, procedures, or pressures.			
11. I assess how the conflict is affecting operations, customers, and employees.			
12. I am fluent in the official corporate language and at least one other language.			
13. I integrate success stories about conflict resolution into corporate learning systems, celebrate the success, and institutionalize the benefits.			

Assessing Your Conflict Competencies (continued)

Practices	Almost Always	Sometimes	Almost Never
14. I show creativity in the ways I approach conflict situations.			
15. I use symbolic tools such as stories, myths, metaphors, and rituals to help understand people who are different from me.			
16. I am an authentic leader.			
17. I encourage other employees to share their cross-cultural experience and learning.			

Pay particular attention to specific items that were checked "Almost Never." These may indicate issues to address and actions to take in order to increase your effectiveness.

Collectivists May Want to

- Practice verbal assertiveness in articulating personal interests and goals;
- Use direct verbal responses to indicate agreement or disagreement;
- Articulate reasons behind the disagreement;
- Use direct, specific questions to check facts, interests, and unclear goals;
- Target questions to a specific individual;
- Learn to engage in overlap talks and faster turn-taking verbal behavior;
- Use verbal paraphrasing to summarize what they have heard; and
- Use perception-checking questions to clarify whether they have correctly interpreted nonverbal messages.

Adler's model of cultural synergy is also helpful in resolving conflict. She suggests three steps to culturally responsible conflict resolution:[39] (1) define the problem from both points of view—gaining a clear understanding of the perceptions of each; (2) uncover the cultural interpretations—reveal the historic and cultural assumptions that exist and interpret the logic of the other culture; and, most importantly, (3) create cultural synergy—investigate and search out many alternatives until the resolution transcends the behavior and patterns of each culture involved.

Suggestions for Managers[40]

1. *Use the indirect approach.* Use a go-between who can help avoid direct confrontation and allow both parties to save face by never having to confront the issue face-to-face.
2. *Emphasize harmony.* Talk about the cooperative spirit and harmony that will result when the disagreement is settled.
3. *Clarify the cultural influences operating.* Help each party understand the cultural programming of the other.
4. *Work with informal leaders.* Get help from the most respected member of each party's culture or group.
5. *Be specific.* Ask each side to describe its conflicts with the other in clear, behavioral terms. Have people focus on the actual behavior, not their interpretation of the behavior.
6. *Be honest with yourself.* Recognize your own reactions and preferences.
7. *Find out how conflicts are resolved in the culture of the other party.* Seek help from a cultural informant, someone familiar with the practices and norms in the other culture.
8. *Keep out of corners.* Avoid cornering someone in a losing position because he or she may feel threatened and strike back in unpredictable ways.
9. *Capitalize on the relationship.* Use your relationship with the individual to help work toward a solution.
10. *Respect, respect, respect.* Deal with the other party privately and as discreetly as possible, own your part in the issue, listen and do not discount what the person says, and be willing to give as well as take.

CONFLICT AS A SOURCE OF INNOVATION

Some research shows that conflict can be destructive and that it decreases group performance, but other findings point to conflict as being beneficial and conducive to higher group performance—if those involved know how to promote its beneficial aspects while minimizing its detrimental aspects.

Additionally, research shows that conflict resolution methods can have a positive effect on new product success. In other words, with conflict can come significant innovation.[41]

Research has shown that task-related conflicts can have positive effects on interpersonal relations, group performance, and customer satisfaction when team members perceive cooperative rather than competitive goals and that teams benefit from conflict when they cultivate environments tolerant of diverse viewpoints.[42]

As Jerry Harvey points out in *The Abilene Paradox*, "The inability to manage *agreement* may be the major source of organization dysfunction." That is, "group think" or the absence of diverse opinions and risk aversion may be more detrimental to our organizations than conflict. Some have advocated creating a "culture neutral" environment to diffuse conflict, but this is difficult and does not allow for the kinds of creativity and innovation that can arise out of cross-cultural conflict.

In fact, research by Adler and others shows that the possibilities for inventing mutually beneficial options in multicultural environments exceed those in single-culture situations because of the inherent differences between the parties—the difference and conflict itself provides competitive advantage.

Notes

1 Allport, Gordon W. *The Nature of Prejudice* (Reading, MA: Addison-Wesley, 1954).

2 Garza, R.T., and S.J. Santos. "Ingroup/Outgroup Balance and Interdependent Interethnic Behavior," *Journal of Experimental Social Psychology*, 1991, V27, pp. 124–137.

3 Avruch, K. *Culture and Conflict Resolution* (Washington, DC: United States Institute of Peace Press, 1998).

4 Schoenberg, R., et al. "National Conflict Within European Alliances," *European Business Journal*, 1995, p. 13.

5 LeBaron, Michelle. "Transforming Cultural Conflict in an Age of Complexity," *Berghof Handbook for Conflict Transformation* (Berlin: Berghof Research Center for Constructive Conflict Management, 2001).

6 Schramm-Nielsen, Jette. "Conflict Management in Scandinavia" (Copenhagen Business School Department of Intercultural Communication and Management, May 2002).

7 Isenhart, M.W., and M. Spangle. *Collaborative Approaches to Resolving Conflict* (Thousand Oaks, CA: Sage, 2000, pp. 14–15).

8 Tse, David K., and June Francis. "Cultural Differences in Conducting Intra- and Inter-Cultural Negotiations: A Sino-Canadian Comparison," *Journal of International Business Studies*, 1994, V25, I3, p. 537.

9 De Dreu, C.K.W., and L. Weingart. *Task Versus Relationship Conflict: A Meta-Analysis.* Paper submitted to the Conflict Management Division, 2002 Academy of Management Meeting.

10 Tse, David K., and June Francis. "Cultural Differences in Conducting Intra- and Inter-Cultural Negotiations: A Sino-Canadian Comparison," *Journal of International Business Studies*, 1994, V25, I3, p. 537.

11 Jehn, K.A. "A Multimethod Examination of the Benefits and Detriments of Intragroup Conflict," *Administrative Science Quarterly*, 1995, V40, pp. 256–282.

12 Simons, T.L., and R.S. Peterson. "Task Conflict and Relationship Conflict in Top Management Teams: The Pivotal Role of Intragroup Trust," *Journal of Applied Psychology,* 2000, V85, pp. 102–111.

13 Schoenberg, R., et al. "National Conflict Within European Alliances," *European Business Journal,* 1995, p. 8.

14 Augsburger, David. *Conflict Mediation Across Cultures* (Louisville, KY: Westminster/John Knox Press, 1992).

15 Schramm-Nielsen, Jette. "Conflict Management in Scandinavia" (Copenhagen Business School Department of Intercultural Communication and Management, May 2002).

16 Augsburger, David. *Conflict Mediation Across Cultures* (Louisville, KY: Westminster/John Knox Press, 1992).

17 Brake, T., et al. *Doing Business Internationally: The Guide to Cross-Cultural Success* (Burr Ridge, IL: Irwin Professional Publishing, 1995, p. 189).

18 Morris, Michael. "Conflict Management Style: Accounting for Cross-National Differences," *Journal of International Business Studies,* Fourth Quarter 1998, V29, I4, pp. 729–748.

19 Ting-Toomey, Stella. "Intercultural Conflict Styles: A Face-Negotiation Theory." In Y. Kim and W. Gudykunst (Eds.), *Theories in Intercultural Communication* (Thousand Oaks, CA: Sage, 1988, pp. 213–235).

20 Gudykunst, William B. *Bridging Differences: Effective Intergroup Communication* (Thousand Oaks, CA: Sage, 1998, p. 249).

21 Hendryx, Steven R. "The China Trade: Making the Deal Work," *Harvard Business Review,* July/August 1986, V64, pp. 75–84.

22 Ohbuchi, K.Y., and Y. Takahashi. "Cultural Styles of Conflict Management in Japanese and Americans: Passivity, Covertness, and Effectiveness of Strategies," *Journal of Applied Social Psychology,* 1994, V24, pp. 1345–1366.

23 Tse, David K., and June Francis. "Cultural Differences in Conducting Intra- and Inter-Cultural Negotiations: A Sino-Canadian Comparison," *Journal of International Business Studies,* 1994, V25, I3, p. 537.

24 Ibid.

25 Perks, Helen, and Michael Sanderson. "An International Case Study of Cultural Diversity and the Role of Stakeholders in the Establishing of a European/Indonesian Joint Venture in the Aerospace Industry," *The Journal of Business and Industrial Marketing,* 2000, V14, I4.

26 Ting-Toomey, S. "Cross-Cultural Face-Negotiation: An Analytical Overview," A presentation at Simon Fraser University at Harbour Center, April 15, 1992.

27 Weiss, S., and W. Stripp. *Negotiation with Foreign Business Persons: An Introduction for Americans with Propositions on Six Cultures* (New York University/Faculty of Business Administration, February 1985).

28 Harris, Philip R., and Robert T. Moran. *Managing Cultural Differences* (Houston, TX: Gulf, 2000, p. 60).

29 Triandis, H. "Theoretical Concepts That Are Applicable to the Analysis and Ethnocentrism." In R. Brislin (Ed.), *Applied Cross-Cultural Psychology: Cross-Cultural Research and Methodology* Series (Vol. 14) (Thousand Oaks, CA: Sage, 2000, pp. 34–55).

30 Adams, Susan M. "Settling Cross-Cultural Disagreements Begins with 'Where' Not 'How,'" *Academy of Management Executive,* February 1999, V13, I1, p. 109.

31 LeBaron, M. "Transforming Cultural Conflict in an Age of Complexity," *Berghof Handbook for Conflict Transformation* (Berlin: Berghof Research Center for Constructive Conflict Management, 2001).

32 Ibid.

33 Feffer, J. "Conflict Resolution in Korea," *Conflict Resolution Notes,* January 2001, V18, I3.

34 Alia, H. "Non-Traditional Form of Dispute Resolution Processes Among the Tiv People of Nigeria," *Conflict Resolution Notes,* September 2002, V20, I2.

35 Moran, Robert T., and William G. Stripp. *Dynamics of Successful International Business Negotiations* (Houston, TX: Gulf, 1991), as cited in Michael W. Morris, et al., "Conflict Management Style: Accounting for Cross-National Differences," *Journal of International Business Studies,* Fourth Quarter 1998, V29, I4, pp. 729–748.

36 Rahim, A. "A Measure of Styles of Handling Interpersonal Conflict," *Academy of Management Journal,* 1983, V26, pp. 368–376.

37 Clarke, Clifford C., and Douglas G. Lipp. "Conflict Resolution for Contrasting Cultures," *Training & Development,* February 1998, V52, I2, p. 20.

38 Ting-Toomey, S. "Intercultural Conflict Management: A Mindful Approach," excerpted from "Constructive Intercultural Conflict Management." In S. Ting-Toomey, *Communicating Across Cultures* (New York: The Guilford Press, 1999).

39 Adler, Nancy. *International Dimensions of Organizational Behavior* (3rd ed.) (Cincinnati, OH: South-Western, 1997).

40 Gardenswartz, Lee, and Anita Rowe. *Managing Diversity: A Complete Desk Reference and Planning Guide* (Burr Ridge, IL: Irwin Professional Publishing, 1993, p. 95).

41 Xie, Jinhong, and X. Michael Song. "Interfunctional Conflict, Conflict Resolution Styles, and New Product Success: A Four-Culture Comparison," *Management Science,* December 1998, V44, I12, p. S192.

42 Alper, S., D. Tjosvold, and K.S. Law. "Conflict Management, Efficacy, and Performance in Organizational Teams," *Personnel Psychology,* 2000, V53, pp. 625–642.

CHAPTER 6

Problem Solving in Global Organizations

B eing a profitable, successful global corporation is in part determined by an organization's ability to solve problems and reconcile both conflicting priorities and limited resources that are a part of organizational life. This chapter defines what constitutes a problem and provides tools and information around national culture that impacts the ability to solve problems or improve products and services on global teams. It also provides a three-step problem-solving process that will help members of global teams reconcile their differences and accomplish work together.

THE IMPACT OF CULTURE: DEFINING WHAT A PROBLEM IS

In Western culture a problem is defined as a question, dilemma, or situation that requires conversation, investigation, additional information, and ultimately, a solution and agreement regarding a particular course of action. In other cultures the concept of what a "problem" is can be quite different. For example, as was mentioned previously, the Chinese character for problem combines crisis as well as opportunity. Depending on one's point of view, it can also be seen as creating possibilities for positive change. In parts of the world where harmony is a prized value, such as in Southeast Asia, the mere mention of a problem situation can be an affront that causes loss of face, although the Southeast Asian group will work just as hard as any other civilization's group to resolve the difficulty. For some, the changes brought about by solutions are seen as steps toward progress; for others, they bring disruption to the traditional order that has provided security. In any organization, solving problems often has consequences that go beyond the issue itself. The dynamics and the outcomes can impact morale, relationships, commitment, trust, and productivity. The stakes are high. While culture has been discussed in Chapter 1 and communication related to culture has been covered in Chapter 3, it is important to understand culture specifically as it relates to problem solving and dealing with different points of view. The Influence of Culture on Problem Solving chart shows the impact of culture specifically on problem solving.

Bringing people together for problem solving is even more complicated when national, civilizational, and organizational cultural differences are factored in. Problem solving in a global context requires not only knowledge about a variety of cultural norms, but also the ability to be adaptable oneself. Theoretically, the more adaptable you are, the more you can contribute to helping a group from a variety of cultures solve problems together. The "Cultural Adaptability Assessment" provides an opportunity for you to assess your ability to adapt to different cultural norms and preferences.

Suggestions for Using the "Cultural Adaptability Assessment"

Objectives

- To understand cross-cultural norms that can impact problem-solving dynamics
- To identify one's own cultural preferences
- To become more knowledgeable about other cultural norms and learn to be a more adaptive problem-solving team member

Intended Audience

- Members of global problem-solving and decision-making teams or groups
- Facilitators, managers, consultants, or team leaders who are leading problem-solving processes in multinational settings

Time

- 30 to 40 minutes

Materials

- Copies of the "Culture Adaptability Assessment," preferably as a paper-and-pencil questionnaire in a face-to-face setting
- Easel, flip chart, markers, masking tape

Dimensions of Culture		Consequences for Problem Solving
Individualism Expects to influence the group outcome; takes strong initiative in solving problems; can be seen as competitive and overly assertive	**Collectivism** Puts group interests before individual concerns; accepts role and influence of a formal leader; can be perceived by individuals as not taking initiative or valuing individual contribution	Can cause perception problems about motivations. Collectivist may see individualists as only looking out for themselves and being self-serving but not team players. Individualists may see collectivists as lacking commitment, determination, or initiative. Questions about one another's motivation can impact trust.
Internal Locus of Control Believe in ability to influence outcome of problem solving; strong sense of self or group determinism; has faith in problem solving to improve conditions	**External Locus of Control** Feels that one's life is determined by the forces in one's environment and may not be changeable; feels less influence in outcomes; sees value in acceptance of situations and conditions rather than change	Different perceptions can cause internal locus of control members to see externals as weak, not committed, and doing little to make things happen. The externals can see internals as arrogant, too aggressive, and not team players.
Deal Openly with Differences Communicates thoughts and feelings; values acknowledgment and open discussion of problems; believes they can only be fixed if acknowledged	**Value Harmony** Feels that the harmony of the group takes precedence over direct confrontation of differences; even behaviors of others that are bothersome may be unacknowledged openly but dealt with privately	These two different views make it very difficult to solve problems rapidly. The process of how to put problems on the table will require sensitivity and agreement about what process to use. It is important to be mindful of creating a balanced environment that will not diminish anyone.

Influence of Culture on Problem Solving

Dimensions of Culture		Consequences for Problem Solving
Horizontal Flat structure allows leadership to be fluid depending on expertise, talent, and skill required at a given time; the functional leadership role can change at any given time depending on group need	**Vertical** Leadership and guidance in a vertical structure is given by position, title, status, or power; the weight of that position is the strongest influence on the group	The dilemma in different leadership designs has to do with influence and how decisions are made; deference is always paid, but in a horizontal structure it goes to the expertise and knowledge in a fluid environment, while in a vertical structure, problems are solved or decisions made by the person who assumes the formal leadership role.
Task/Content Orientation The highest priority is solving the problem; scant attention is paid to the relationships or the process of how the group solves its problem; the work itself, completing the job, is the goal	**Relationship/Process** How you do the work and how you treat the people matters as much as the task itself; the "how" and the "people" are factored in as much as completing the task; believes that the goodwill and support of all the individuals is as important as the process completion	The reconciliation here is in balancing the priorities of both task and relationship, and at different times, in different contexts, each could be a higher priority. Too much emphasis on process frequently jeopardizes getting the job done. Too little means the group is not maintaining itself and it is only a matter of time until people or process problems become a factor in the outcomes.
Explicit Communication Communicates directly; tells it like it is; communication is mainly in the words	**Implicit Communication** Attends to nonverbals and symbolism; everything around the words matters more than the words themselves	Miscommunication based on assumptions, lack of knowledge, or misunderstandings is possible and has the capacity to result in negative assumptions about teammates from other cultures, thus impacting team dynamics. Paying attention to voice tone, speed of speech, silence, taking turns, and language with which ideas are expressed is important.

Influence of Culture on Problem Solving (continued)

Cultural Adaptability Assessment

Directions: In the six areas below, first circle the orientation that best describes you. Then rate your ability to be adaptive along this continuum. For example, in the first box, a strong individualist may circle Individualism and then circle 2.

	1. Not adaptable at all (Unable or unwilling to change)	2. Adaptable under duress (If forced to change for a particular situation, will do so but not happily)	3. Adaptable on occasion (Depending on reason and importance, one may change)	4. Can shift if it makes sense to (Show this person a reason and adaptations will be made)	5. No problem to adapt (This person is bicultural or multicultural in the ability to style switch easily)
1. Individualism/ Collectivism	1	2	3	4	5
2. Internal Locus of Control/External Locus of Control	1	2	3	4	5
3. Deals Openly with Differences/Values Harmony	1	2	3	4	5
4. Horizontal/Vertical	1	2	3	4	5
5. Task/Content Orientation— Relationship/ Process	1	2	3	4	5
6. Explicit Communication/ Implicit Communication	1	2	3	4	5

Directions

- Distribute the "Cultural Adaptability Assessment" after making introductory comments that, when problem solving in a global setting, members will experience and need to work with a wide array of norms. Also mention that the culture of the organization and its norms play a part in how problems are solved.

- Give a brief statement about each of the six dimensions of culture assessed here.

- Ask participants to then assess their own behaviors and respond to the adaptability range from 1 (not adaptable) to 5 (highly adaptable).

- Depending on the size of the group, have participants either pair up or form small groups and discuss their responses and how their own adaptability helps and hinders their ability to serve as problem solvers on a global team/task force or in a global organization.

- Spend time discussing where organizational culture and national cultures are compatible and where they might conflict with individuals' orientations.

- Spend time as a whole group talking about which of these areas has the most implications for the group itself as it solves problems and works together.

- In a large group, have participants discuss the consequences of why they have and have not been able to culture shift in particular circumstances.

- Have participants make verbal commitments in areas in which each will work to develop his or her ability to be more adaptive.

Questions for Discussion/Consideration

- How are the different cultural norms reflected in the identified team a strength for solving problems together?

- What different cultural norms seem to cause the most difficulty for solving problems in the identified group?

- What have been the consequences for group dynamics of these similar or conflicting norms?

- Where are you most adaptable? Look at items for which you have checked the 4 or 5 box.

- Where are you least adaptable, that is, checked the 1 and 2 boxes?

- What is the consequence to problem solving if there is little adaptation?

Caveats, Considerations, and Variations

- In collectivist cultures, this tool can be positioned as something that will help the group learn enough about one another to improve problem-solving performance.

- Large (18" x 24") wall charts can be used and participants, each with a different color marker, can check the appropriate boxes. Then dialogue can take place about the group's adaptability profile, what obstacles the data may suggest, and what to do so that cultural differences do not impede progress. Close with a group commitment to taking action that will increase effectiveness.

ACKNOWLEDGING MYTHS AND REALITIES OF PROBLEM SOLVING

Once problem solvers have acknowledged their own and others' cultural values, it is important to understand some of the subtle beliefs that may influence the problem-solving process. Among them may be myths, a set of generally held but misleading beliefs that people hold. If these are not acknowledged, they can distort the legitimate expectations of people who come together to investigate questions and create change. See which myths and realities are most relevant for your own group from the listing below.

Myth: All problems can be solved at least to some degree.

Reality: Solutions lie in the eye of the beholder. A resolution in the eyes of some may be just a different problem to others. Often, human beings either tacitly or actively resign themselves to living with or accepting situations that appear to have no good answer, particularly if doing this suits a majority of the stakeholders. Solutions look different depending on one's world view, civilization, or nationality, and they breed their own consequences, which often spawn a whole new set of problems to deal with.

Myth: People who come together for problem solving are interested in solutions.

Reality: More often than not, some individuals, groups, functional units, or divisions get their power, status, influence, and security from maintaining a problem. When problems are solved, a person or group's importance can recede. Not solving problems can be a tremendous source of power. It is critical to recognize that, just because a person says he or she wants a solution, it does not mean he or she really does. Often an employee or group gains a great deal from the pretense at desiring a solution, all the while working hard to see that problems, hence status and influence, are maintained.

Myth: The stated problem or overt agenda is the real problem.

Reality: Rarely is the stated problem the real problem. Sometimes people or groups are actually unaware of what the real problem is. They state a problem with the best understanding they have at the time. But a good facilitator or leader will ask the right questions that probe more deeply and peel the onion. One example stands out. It involved a three-day leadership training and team-building session. The executive staff was interviewed for the purpose of identifying pertinent issues. On the surface, the issue was *communication*. Deeper probing revealed that the management structure had just changed. What had been one CEO with thirteen equal vice presidents became a CEO, one gatekeeper to the CEO, and twelve vice presidents who no longer had direct access to the CEO. The real issue was feelings of displacement, rejection, dislike of the new structure, and questions such as, "If you were going to pick someone, why not me?" Only when the onion is peeled will real issues surface.

Myth: If we can solve this problem, we can achieve stability and move on.

Reality: Stability can be achieved . . . momentarily. But in today's fast-paced world, expect fluidity and constant change, not equilibrium. Expect instead an emphasis on continuous improvement as corporations become more global. A mindset that says we are always fine-tuning, solving problems, and tinkering to make things better can help employees look at problems as an ongoing part of the landscape rather than as something particularly stressful and difficult. Even framing circumstances as less of an issue or problem is wise on cross-cultural teams where harmony is prized and difficulties or faux pas can cause loss of face.

Myth: Experience creates better problem solvers.

Reality: Experience certainly can make for better problem solving. It can also limit creative solutions when groups resort to the traditional way of solving problems. There is a tight balance between learning and using what experience has taught us and not automatically being bound by past history. On global teams, the reliance on learnings from the past will be an easy sell in cultures like Japan that have a strong emphasis on tradition and valuing the past. In cultures that emphasize innovation and change, such as the United States, there is an openness to new alternatives that can be very important to product improvement, refining internal systems, or any other kind of change that improves an organization's or a team's objectives.

As you look over these myths and realities, make a few notes in the box below about the myth that has the most implications for your own problem-solving group.

The most relevant myth in our group is:

Our reality seems to be:

The reality affects our group's work together in the following ways:

While you may see a particular myth/reality dilemma in your global problem-solving group, how might others you work with see the myths? Even if they identify the same ones, how differently might they see the impact? Communicating with others on the team is a good way to avoid speculation. Feedback can lead to a rich discussion, a sharing of perspectives, and better team performance.

One structured, deliberate way to have group or team members give each other feedback and improve performance is to use the "Problem-Solving Response Sheet." This tool is a way to deliberately assess what problem-solving participants on global teams need in order to function efficiently and well. It is very beneficial when used at the beginning of the life of a task force, but it is equally helpful when used with ongoing functional teams that can undoubtedly benefit from a little dialogue.

Suggestions for Using the "Problem-Solving Response Sheet"

Objectives

- To raise awareness about the dynamics of effective problem solving for individuals and groups
- To gain insight about what individuals want and need in order to be better participants on a problem-solving team
- To identify behaviors that will be more efficient and productive, as a group
- To learn about others' perceptions of the group's problem-solving dynamics
- To stimulate discussion about effective problem-solving dynamics and desired behaviors for group members to engage in

Intended Audience

- A functional global work team, task force, or problem-solving group
- A consultant or manager trying to teach a group to function as better problem solvers

Time

- 20 minutes

Materials

- Copies of the "Problem-Solving Response Sheet"
- Technological support if done online

Directions

- Distribute the sheet in person or online.
- Ask participants to pair up and answer the questions in random order.

Problem-Solving Response Sheet

This series of open-ended statements is intended to help individuals and their team members discover one another's reactions to and opinions about parts of the problem-solving process. The emphasis can be on general problem solving with a team or the sheet can be used in the context of a particular problem-solving situation. In either case, learnings should be applied to the larger solution processes of the group. Individuals will get more out of this exercise if it is shared either with a partner or members of a team. If high trust already exists, groups can be larger. Pairs work best in low-trust situations.

- Take turns initiating the discussion. Complete statements orally.
- Items may be responded to in random order.

1. Problem solving is . . .

2. A group is most effective in problem solving when . . .

3. The most difficult problems for work groups to solve are . . .

4. We have a good solution when . . .

5. When we are stumped and need to solve a problem, we . . .

6. The most important consideration in solving a problem is . . .

7. The greatest obstacle I've observed in problem solving with people who are different from me is . . .

8. Global work groups tend to limit options by . . .

9. It is easy to avoid facing problems when . . .

10. My greatest strength in problem solving is . . .

11. Our group's greatest strength in problem solving is . . .

12. One thing that inhibits our creative problem solving is . . .

13. In my culture, we solve problems by . . .

14. As a work group, we solve problems by . . .

15. We are most supportive of our boss's solutions when . . .

16. We contribute most in problem solving when . . .

17. Solutions tend not to be implemented when . . .

18. Effective problem solving in this organization requires . . .

19. In this organization, the most common method of solving problems is . . .

20. The most difficult problems to solve in our organization are . . .

Source: Adapted from Lee Gardenswartz and Anita Rowe, *Managing Diversity in Health Care Manual* (San Francisco: Jossey-Bass, 1999, p. 175). This material is used by permission of John Wiley & Sons, Inc.

- Follow the directions on the "Problem-Solving Response Sheet."
- Once ten minutes are up, conduct a whole group discussion on a select number of items.

Questions for Discussion/Consideration

- Which questions were easiest/most difficult for you to answer?
- Which were most interesting?
- What does the range of responses indicate about your group's problem-solving capability?
- What themes emerged?
- What surprises were there?
- What does this data suggest the group needs to do differently?
- What can you do differently as a group member and problem solver to enhance your contributions?
- What team agreements about ways to work together would benefit the group?

Caveats, Considerations, and Variations

- Depending on the size of the group, small groups can be used instead of pairs.
- The time can be lengthened if the exercise is done as a group, and each person can select one item on which to focus for improvement. All participants still need to respond to each item and the facilitator still needs to lead an overall discussion.

IDENTIFYING INFLUENCES ON PROBLEM SOLVING ACROSS BORDERS

Once problem-solving group members acknowledge and dispel myths and have a realistic sense about the problem-solving process, the next step is to look at the particular realities a group faces as it works to solve problems in organizations that span the globe. Consider each of the following factors and what their influence is on your problem-solving process.

National and Organizational History

Each organization, national culture, and functional unit has its own history. When global participants gather to solve problems together, a part of their interaction may be unconsciously impacted by their own national histories of painful conflict. The consequences of colonization, wars, and ethnic conflicts may leave a residue of feelings that participants bring to the problem-solving process. It would not be surprising, for example, if Koreans or Chinese reacted cautiously to Japanese, or Muslim and Christians in some parts of the world had a history that could impact current relationships. Another factor that generates strong reactions and long memories are mergers and acquisitions. If the organization has been merged or acquired, regardless of the success of the cultural integration, raw feelings usually remain, particularly on the side of those who feel least powerful. How might those feelings impact working together? Paying attention to national and organizational history is not a luxury. It is a necessity and requires knowledge, skill, sensitivity, and understanding about events larger and often further back than what one is currently working on in an organization.

Those Involved

James K. Sebenius, in his article "The Hidden Challenges of Cross-Border Negotiations,"[1] suggests that it is critical to know the players. While Sebenius's article focuses on cross-border negotiations, his message can be applied to cross-border problem solving and decision making. A number of pertinent questions need answers, such as, "Who is sponsoring the process?" and "How much authority does this sponsor have?" In hierarchical organizations or on teams where hierarchy is a strong cultural influence, just having a person responsible who has a title can be enough. To whom is this sponsor or manager responsible? Are there different national legal issues to deal with by country? If so, what is the impact and how will these differences be handled? Legal requirements or any regulatory body must also be factored in.

The Purpose and Boundaries for the Problem-Solving Group

What is your charge? If you are part of a global task force, where does decision-making power reside in the group? Are you more a recommending body? If "yes" to the latter question, who really makes the decisions? What kind of power do boards of directors have? Unions? Other stakeholders?

External or Informal Influences

The larger context of issues, as well as who supports them and knows what the public relations issues and political ramifications are, is critical in all parts of the globe. Every organization has written policies and procedures; it also has rules of behavior and norms that are modeled by senior members of the organization but are not written down. Until all participants know what these informal norms are, the problem-solving process will be more difficult than it needs to be. Understanding the informal rules is like having an insider's guide to the organization. The best way to make progress and go beyond the real obstacles is to be savvy about the informal structure. It is always a powerful influence.

Michelle LeBaron, in her article "Mediation and Multicultural Reality,"[2] offers some very interesting questions that challenge our basic assumptions in trying to resolve conflicts between locations in different parts of the world. While the situation in global problem solving is not entirely the same, there are some applications that can be made.

Questions for Your Global Problem-Solving Group

- In your problem-solving process, would a third-party intervener be helpful?
- If one is used, is objectivity desired? By all parties? If not, by whom?
- How would an intervener effect the dynamics of the group?
- Given the range of cultural norms represented in the group, and given the national culture of the headquarters in this organization, what processes seem workable?
- How formal should the sessions be?
- What ground rules will work?
- What processes would be helpful in involving all participants?
- Who are the people and groups that have a stake in the resulting solution?
- Considering organizational culture, what processes will be effective for identifying the issues and clarifying the benefits or desired outcomes that might appeal to each stakeholder?

THE IMPORTANCE OF ORGANIZATIONAL CULTURE IN THE PROBLEM-SOLVING PROCESS

National influences around the problem-solving and decision-making process vary greatly and can actually be compelling or conflicting influences. For that reason, knowing one's organizational culture regarding the problem-solving process is absolutely critical. Equally important is understanding the degree to which the regional and national expressions of that corporate culture actually follow the "preferred corporate" process. An example of conflicting national styles in the problem-solving process is demonstrated in the methodical, well-thought-out suggestions in Asia and most Pacific Rim countries, which are in stark contrast to the impulsive, speedy technique of brainstorming so popular in the United States. Another national difference can be seen in the very high importance given to relationships in Latin America, Central and Eastern Europe, and in the Middle East. National style in Pacific Rim countries leads to high use of consensus with people at middle and lower levels. This is not the case in the Middle East and Africa.

When one sees that the Pacific Rim countries and the United States rely heavily on consensus, while most of the world uses top-down decision making, it shows the complexity and difficulty of trying to come up with a problem-solving process or method that may work equally well within all locations. We reiterate the importance of taking cues for an effective process from the organization itself.

Once people recognize these different approaches, there is an opportunity to minimize their negative impact. They have less power to inhibit team members. Look at the "Blocks to Problem Solving" checklist and see which ones hinder your group's productivity.

Blocks to Problem Solving

Directions: In the three areas below, indicate which blocks operate in your problem-solving group by placing a check mark in the appropriate box(es).

Psychological

☐ Desire to control the environment (want things to go as planned with no surprises)

☐ Preference for the predictable and orderly (processes and procedures should unfold as designed)

☐ Unwillingness to tolerate ambiguity (does not like a climate where uncertainty and lack of clarity exist)

☐ High achievement motivation (driven by a desire to be successful)

☐ Quick success orientation (impatient with processes that take a long time; desire is to see things change quickly)

☐ Inability to allow ideas to incubate (want answers and ideas now instead of letting ideas percolate)

☐ Valuing sensory perceptions over intuition (trust what one can touch or see rather than trust hunches)

☐ Fear of failure (afraid to risk for fear of failing)

☐ Fear of success (afraid of high expectations based on past successes)

☐ Assumptions and stereotypes about other departments, locations, levels in the organization (locking people or departments into a certain set of expectations instead of being open to what they actually bring)

Blocks to Problem Solving (continued)

Cultural

☐ Limited knowledge about cross-cultural norms (inadequate information about how cultural norms shape working together in a group)

☐ Negative judgments about values, attitudes, and beliefs different from one's own (the belief that one's way is the right way to see the world or behave; therefore those different from self are viewed negatively)

☐ Value placed on reason, numbers, logic (trust and value what is provable)

☐ Limited emphasis on feelings and intuition (hunches and feelings are less valued than numbers)

☐ Viewing problem solving as humorless and serious (seeing the process of problem solving without humor and fun)

☐ Having a certain set of expectations that make it difficult to see other realities (preconceived ideas about problem definition and solutions limit options)

Environmental

☐ People threatened by new ideas (change threatens existing reality)

☐ Failure to reward innovative thinking (where good ideas are not rewarded or people are blamed for making mistakes, innovation dries up)

☐ Work environments where employees do not engage in supportive behaviors (where support is lacking, people take less risk and play it safe)

☐ Workplace that is too hot or too cold (distracted by the physical environment)

☐ Ringing phones, beeping pagers, mobile phones, conversations that intrude on your quiet (more distractions in the physical environment)

☐ Distracting noises

☐ Interruptions

☐ Selective perceptions (seeing only what one wants to see)

Source: Adapted from Lee Gardenswartz and Anita Rowe, *Diverse Teams at Work* (Alexandria, VA: Society for Human Resource Management, 2003, p. 170).

Suggestions for Using "Blocks to Problem Solving"

Objectives

- To identify obstacles that limit solutions
- To compare perceptions of barriers that hinder problem solving
- To improve group problem solving functioning by removing some of the blocks

Intended Audience

- Members of any global problem-solving group or task force
- Managers, consultants, or facilitators guiding the problem-solving process

Time

- 30 minutes

Materials

- Copies of "Blocks to Problem Solving," either online or paper-and-pencil
- If online, use preferred technology and if paper-and-pencil, also have easel, flip chart, and markers

Directions

- This exercise is most effective when the group is midway through the process and stuck. Members need enough experience together to be able to respond to the blocks each has observed.
- Distribute copies of "Blocks to Problem Solving" either online or in person.
- If online, give people a deadline by when it must be completed so there is time to synthesize the data and feed it back to the group in whatever way works best in your organization. Then conduct a conversation during which data is analyzed and acted on.
- If done onsite, blow the tool up to 18" x 24" size and post it in several locations around the room. Then divide the whole group into small groups and have members indicate by using different color markers the items each has checked.
- Then lead a discussion that focuses on areas given most weight from the data.
- Select a spokesperson from each group to report out.

Questions for Discussion/Consideration

- What does the group's data suggest? How have these blocks hindered us?
- Were there any surprises?

- What are the most obvious blocks?
- What are the consequences of not doing something to minimize this in our group?
- What suggestions might make this block less of a hindrance?
- What will we commit to do as a whole group?

Caveats, Considerations, and Variations

- This exercise can be done in pairs and then processed as a whole group. If there is low trust, pairs might provide more safety.

Identifying the blocks frees problem solvers to be more creative, no matter what process they use to achieve their solutions. Regardless of how decisions are made, good implementation requires support and buy-in.

If an employee from a hierarchical culture such as Mexico is on a problem-solving team for Sony, a strongly Japanese company, there is a good chance that consensus will be the decision-making style of choice. Employees will not only need to be taught the rules of consensus but also should be given a simulation to learn it and practice it. Consensus is a decision-making method worth learning for any circumstances in which employee involvement and input are desired. It is a tool that stimulates creativity and generates commitment and support, but it can also be frustrating because it is time-consuming. For example, in Japan, decision making is spread throughout the whole organization, and this slows down an already lengthy process. Senior people in Japan take seriously the idea of involvement, so they will wait till the consensus process runs its course and a decision is made by the group. If U.S. executives understand this, they will be less likely to think Japanese decision makers are playing games with them as the process unfolds.

The following rules should be explained before a group engages in a consensus activity. An ideal size group is seven to nine people.

Guidelines and Rules of Consensus

- Technique for shared decision making that creates a decision all can live with;
- Uses diverse opinions for creative problem solving;
- Best used when a decision requires acceptance, ownership, and support;
- Avoids creating winners and losers;
- Only used when there are more than two alternatives but no "right answer";
- Time-consuming process;
- Most effective with small groups, where only those involved with the decision are included;

- No voting!;
- Avoid arguing for your own point of view, but do present ideas and be open to discussion;
- Focus on points of agreement;
- Do not change your mind simply to avoid conflict;
- Avoid bargaining and coin flips;
- Expect disagreements and use them to spur the search for alternatives; and
- When deadlocked, divide into subgroups.

Consensus can be a valuable problem-solving tool, but it is a stretch in different ways for many national cultures. Using diverse opinions, in fact cultivating them, is not a valued part of the decision-making process in hierarchical cultures. The fact that consensus seekers use disagreements to produce a positive outcome is difficult to grasp in cultures that place a strong emphasis on harmony. Using these different viewpoints is comfortable for those in Japan and the United States. Using consensus can be seen as compatible with collectivist cultures because it shows respect for the group's ability to come to a good decision. Use the "Essential Characteristics of an Effective Member on a Global Problem-Solving Team" exercise to practice reaching consensus.

Suggestions for Using "Essential Characteristics of an Effective Member on a Global Problem-Solving Team"

Objectives

- To define and discuss the relative importance of behaviors on global problem-solving teams
- To gain awareness of behaviors that managers or facilitators can teach in global problem-solving situations
- To have conversations about what individuals and teams need to do better to solve problems effectively
- To use a consensus activity as a simulation to become better problem solvers

Intended Audience

- Team members of global problem-solving teams or task forces
- Managers or facilitators who work with global teams

Time

- 60 minutes

Essential Characteristics of an Effective Member on a Global Problem-Solving Team

Directions: In the column labeled "Your Rank," prioritize the following eight characteristics of an effective member on a problem-solving team, with 1 being the characteristic that is most important to you and 8 being the least. Then, with fellow team members, reach consensus on the ranking.

Your Rank		Team Rank
	Gathers data and pertinent information before offering solutions	
	Can adapt and style switch to work effectively with colleagues of different backgrounds	
	Has opinions but remains open to being influenced by others	
	Listens to and genuinely tries to understand the viewpoints of others	
	Has skills to help group communicate and effectively accomplish a positive outcome	
	Is able to bring a group in conflict and frustration to a point of mutual respect and decision	
	Has no personal hidden agenda	
	Puts the welfare and health of group ahead of own views and goals	

Source: Adapted from Lee Gardenswartz and Anita Rowe, *Managing Diversity in Health Care Manual* (San Francisco: Jossey-Bass, 1999, p. 179). This material is used by permission of John Wiley & Sons, Inc.

Materials

- Copies of "Essential Characteristics of an Effective Member on a Global Problem-Solving Team" for each participant
- Easel, flip chart, pencils, pens, felt-tip markers

Directions

- Have each person read all eight leader behaviors and determine the order of importance from his or her own viewpoint, with 1 being most important. Record all answers in the "Your Rank" column.

- Then ask the group members (in a classroom setting several groups of approximately seven people each may be doing this simultaneously) to discuss the ranking among themselves and reach consensus on the order of items from 1 to 8, recording answers in the column marked "Team Rank."

- At this point, give a few rules for achieving consensus before the group(s) begin the process:

  - Consensus is defined as "something we can live with for at least some period of time."

  - Each person is responsible for contributing ideas that will lead to a good decision.

  - No voting because voting creates winners and losers. Losers sabotage winners. Consensus needs the support of all.

  - Keep focusing on common ground and working toward agreement.

- Then give groups approximately thirty minutes to discuss items and reach consensus.

- Draw a grid on the board or flip chart to record all rankings of each group in order to compare responses, like the following grid.

Items	A	B	C	D

- Lead a total-group discussion of insights and learnings about consensus and the group's process.

Questions for Discussion/Consideration

- What is your reaction to having just participated in this exercise?

- Look at the different responses from each group. What do you make of them, both when group responses are similar and when they are different?

- What cultural norms or values guided your choices? Share some of the discussion points that influenced the ranking.

- What do these different rankings say about the ability to solve problems well on a global team?

- What does it suggest are the "must have" skills on a multinational and multicultural problem-solving group?

Caveats, Considerations, and Variations

- This exercise can be used for teaching consensus. The discussion question, however, would focus on the group's interaction—how easy or difficult it was to achieve consensus and what behaviors helped or hindered the group in doing so. Once they discuss this last question, apply the process to their ongoing work as part of a problem-solving team.

- Solving problems always implies dealing with different views and perspectives. In a global environment, it is more complex because, in addition to different views and perspectives about work issues, there are different cultural norms that complicate the process. This exercise gives each individual the chance to state what matters most to him or her when working together. Then the group members as a whole will have the opportunity to practice consensus by discussing and reconciling their differences as they rank them in order of importance. The discussion and understanding gained about how different participants view behaviors is as important as reaching consensus itself.

Beyond learning the technique of engaging in consensus, it is important to teach problem solvers how to present their various opinions so they will be heard. Getting people's attention and speaking in values and symbols that others will relate to will at least help one's ideas be heard. (*Note:* In Chapter 3, one of the figures compares Influencing Strategies and Presentation Expectations across nine countries.) Practice the positioning technique by using the tool entitled "Influencing Others: Unimundo Case Study." A case study is given first, followed by a worksheet.

Influencing Others: Unimundo Case Study

Directions: In order to successfully influence the thinking of others, it is helpful to first understand your own thought process. Once you've done that, pay attention to the values and desired outcomes of others, focusing specifically on the language that can influence them. Start by reading the Unimundo Case Study below and answering the questions that follow.

Unimundo Case Study

All Call Cellular, a leading U.S. telecommunications firm, recently announced a merger with Telespaña, Spain's largest telecommunications equipment and service provider. While the creation of the new organization, Unimundo, has been presented to the world as a merger, Telespaña is in fact the object of a nonhostile takeover. The unification of these two organizations is a farsighted business move because Unimundo now has operations in Europe and the Americas. Furthermore, its offices and plants in eleven countries with three primary languages (Spanish, English, and Portuguese) solidify the firm's employee and customer base on three continents. The recent joint venture with the government of Singapore has provided an increasing access to the Pacific Rim markets. With a saturated U.S. market, the strong projected growth in southern Europe and South and Central America reinforces vital business interests for the current merger and potential joint ventures. However, these benefits come with some significant challenges.

Putting a good face on this emerging organization has been difficult. Many problems have already surfaced during the past year in a recently completed joint venture between the two organizations. The cultures of these two organizations, both successful but very different, demonstrate a classic case of culture clash. Here's why.

All Call Cellular (ACC) is a young, dynamic, aggressive company whose success is attributed to rapid innovation, scrupulous attention to marketplace needs, and the heroic efforts of staff, who often work seventy to ninety hours a week. ACC's meteoric accomplishments have made them the envy and surprise of telecom companies around the world. In this competitive market, the employees at All Call are proud of their willingness to do whatever it takes to maintain their lead in the field, even though they are tired, overworked, and readily admit that a balanced life, while longed for, is not in their future any time soon.

Telespaña, on the other hand, is a revered institution in Spain and is seen as a reliable, stable, consistent company and one that has nurtured relationships with leaders in Central and South America. They realize that their widening operations and developing consumer markets in these areas are long-term investments. It has a strong foothold in these potentially lucrative markets and pays close attention to producing products and services to meet the needs of its different consumers. While the pace is less aggressive and hard-charging than at All Call, its results do show in its bottom line, with profits that beat Wall Street projections by 6 percent.

Critical issues that affect operations can be seen at all levels. At the executive level, the top management team is comprised of five individuals, four of whom are U.S.-born All Call executives and only one of whom is a Basque from Telespaña. Executive meetings and teleconferences are conducted exclusively in English. Furthermore, the meetings are conducted in a straightforward, task-focused manner with little time and attention paid to relationships. U.S. leaders generally fly in overnight for meetings and fly out afterward. To date they have not stayed beyond the perfunctory operations tour, nor have they met local employees.

One of the executive staff's first tasks is to reorganize the management team for the new organization, and they are beginning to have conflicts over what qualities are needed for these roles and what compensation should be doled out. Differences over preferred leadership styles and compensation inequities between expatriates and in-country staff have flared into heated disagreements.

At the management level, employees are worried about how to succeed. Do they have to change their work/life balance and adopt the more frenetic, unrelenting American pace? How will they be held accountable and by what standards? What corporate values and practices will change—from basic principles about treatment of employees to issues about language? They are most concerned about a feared emphasis on English in everyday communication as well as what part accents will play in presenting obstacles to promotability. The anxieties or concerns go both ways, however. American staff are worried, both about their ability to be successful in a European cultural environment as well as their own language deficiencies. They are sensitive to the perceptions about their "taking over," as they do not want to come across as the "Ugly American." Their attempts at being less formal and more collaborative by soliciting feedback and input have confused many of their European employees, who are used to working in a more hierarchical system.

At the employee level, nervousness about change exists on both sides of the Atlantic. Unimundo orientation sessions about new organizational policies, procedures, and plans have been conducted by U.S. staff in English using interpreters when appropriate. Project managers are finding it difficult to arrange conference calls because of time zone differences. Leaders of geographically dispersed virtual teams are perplexed as to how to create a cohesive work team with groups who, due to cost containment, do not have any in-person contact. In a few cases, female managers are becoming concerned about a tone of voice or attitude demonstrated in e-mails and voice mails with their male subordinates. Finally, many employees have wondered out loud whether their future career mobility depends on moving to another country—either the United States, Spain, or one of the Latin American countries—in order to move up in the organization, due to the highly broadcast global growth objectives of All Call Cellular's CEO. If the current "map" were not confusing enough, employees are also concerned about the rumored acquisition in Wuhan, China, and expectations placed on them in the Pacific Rim due to their joint venture with the government of Singapore.

Telespaña managers making the case for fully bilingual meetings and company literature	ACC's executives making the case for a more aggressive company (long work hours) while also having a less formal culture
ALL Call Cellular's existing underlying values 1. _____ 2. _____ 3. _____ 4. _____ 5. _____	Telespaña's existing underlying values 1. _____ 2. _____ 3. _____ 4. _____ 5. _____
Potential gains for ACC's increased bilingualism 1. _____ 2. _____ 3. _____ 4. _____ 5. _____	Potential gains for Telespaña employees from being more aggressive and having a more informal culture 1. _____ 2. _____ 3. _____ 4. _____ 5. _____

1. Telespaña's most potent case for bilingualism:

2. ACC's most potent case for a more aggressive stance and informal culture:

Suggestions for Using
"Influencing Others: Unimundo Case Study"

Objectives

- To help all members of a problem-solving group understand other viewpoints

- To recognize the validity and underlying values of other points of view

- To learn to influence the thinking of others by presenting ideas in values and words others can identify with and respond to

Intended Audience

- People throughout a global organization who need to solve problems together

- Managers, facilitators, and internal and external consultants who have to help employees in global organizations clarify thinking, solve problems, and make decisions together

Time

- 45 to 60 minutes

Materials

- Copies of the "Unimundo Case Study" with the fill-in sheet, either online or hard copy

Directions

- Whether online or in person, ask everyone to read the case study, identify an issue to work with, and then fill out all the data on the positioning tool.

- Have participants fill out the tool from the viewpoints of Telespaña and ACC by remembering what they have read about each one's values and considering what might influence the merging partner to buy in to the different behaviors.

- Pair people with managers or consultants to discuss what they have written and how it pertains to their actual work situation. In this case, ask the employee to select a situation and tell the manager where he or she is frustrated in not being able to influence others in a behavioral change and to identify his or her own desired values and outcomes.

- Have a whole group discussion to see what values were used in exerting influence and what was in it for each side to shift behavior.

Questions for Discussion/Consideration

- Where were participants convincing?

- Where did their arguments fall short?

- When arguments did fall short, what was missing, or what was needed, in order to be more convincing?
- What were the values of others you were trying to influence?
- What became apparent to you as you went through this process?
- In order to help others move closer to your viewpoint, how should you position your ideas?
- What language, values, and ideas could successfully sell your point of view to someone else?
- What changes do you need to make in how you talk about your ideas?
- Where are the overlaps and reconciliations?

Caveats, Considerations, and Variations

- This is also a good one-on-one coaching tool so that a manager can identify a person who needs to see other points of view more easily and openly. The manager can ask the employee to think of a real work situation where it will be helpful to understand other viewpoints and how to help others understand,
- This can be a useful group tool, but it is also a productive learning tool between any two people trying to understand different viewpoints better, not just manager and employee but any co-workers. It would be especially helpful when people are fixed in a position and want others to understand their perspectives. That understanding has to go two ways, and this exercise can help participants expand their viewpoints and see ideas from different vantage points.

In the final analysis, regardless of what kind of problem-solving process a group uses, global work groups have to be sensitive and careful to consider organizational norms, national and civilizational cultural influences, and the individuals one is working with. The "Group Experience Rating Form" shows group members that there are behaviors that enable groups to work better together.

The more answers the group has on the "Group Experience Rating Form" that are closer to 5, the better the group works together. An overall score is less important than an item analysis that helps a problem-solving group focus on its weak points. A group should spend its time looking at items where people agree that scores are low. Conversation can then follow that suggests what to do to improve group performance. It will also be worthwhile to spend time looking at any items that have a wide range of responses. Where people experience the group very differently, that also bears discussion. The goal is to have the problem-solving group work consistently well for all its members and to have group members share a common and positive experience as they work together.

Group Experience Rating Form

Directions: Rate the problem-solving performance of your group members collectively by responding to the questions below. Indicate for each question the rating (1 through 5) that most nearly describes your observation of the group experience. Simply circle the appropriate number. The scale is as follows:

1	2	3	4	5
Seldom				Always

Members in This Group					
1. Take time to find out if the presenting problem is the problem or if there are other problems involved.	1	2	3	4	5
2. Listen and try to understand the viewpoints of all group members.	1	2	3	4	5
3. Understand the different reactions and feelings of those involved in this process.	1	2	3	4	5
4. Help each other clarify our thinking.	1	2	3	4	5
5. Help people functioning in a second or third language to effectively communicate their thoughts.	1	2	3	4	5
6. Ask clarifying questions that help explore the issue more deeply.	1	2	3	4	5
7. Share their thoughts about the group's strengths and maximize these strengths or liabilities.	1	2	3	4	5
8. Support and encourage one another, both within the group meeting and outside during social time.	1	2	3	4	5
9. Give all participants a chance to talk and encourage contributions from everyone, but also accept the styles of quieter participants.	1	2	3	4	5
10. Work with quieter participants both within the group process and outside to gain and utilize their contributions.	1	2	3	4	5
11. Help each other explore alternatives without pushing one's own solution.	1	2	3	4	5
12. Find the greatest amount of information and facts related to the focus of the meeting prior to participating.	1	2	3	4	5

Group Experience Rating Form (continued)

	1	2	3	4	5
	Seldom				Always

Members in This Group					
13. Structure initial meeting time to set group goals and objectives.	1	2	3	4	5
14. At regular intervals, evaluate how the group is valuing individual contributions and collectively accomplishing the goal.	1	2	3	4	5
15. Measure the group's outcome.	1	2	3	4	5
16. Are willing to ask for advice and information from others for the good of accomplishing the goal of the whole group.	1	2	3	4	5
17. Provide different functions to the team at different times (for example, leader, clarifier, summarizer).	1	2	3	4	5
18. Include discussions about what group members want from others in order to accomplish the task.	1	2	3	4	5
19. Develop a process for reconciling differences in opinion by seeking to understand the diversity of thought.	1	2	3	4	5
20. Demonstrate respect for ourselves and all members of the group in professional and social contexts.	1	2	3	4	5
21. Demonstrate a commitment to accomplish the group's goal in professional and social contexts.	1	2	3	4	5
22. Give helpful, nonjudgmental feedback that focuses on specific behaviors in culturally appropriate ways.	1	2	3	4	5
23. Are willing to receive helpful, nonjudgmental feedback that focuses on specific behaviors in culturally appropriate ways.	1	2	3	4	5

Source: Copyright © 1999 Cendant Intercultural, The Bennett Group; Gardenswartz and Rowe; RealWork. Adapted from Lee Gardenswartz and Anita Rowe, *Managing Diversity: A Complete Desk Reference and Planning Guide* (rev. ed.) (New York: McGraw-Hill, 1998, p. 173).

Suggestions for Using "Group Experience Rating Form"

Objectives

- To identify and assess behaviors that foster effective problem solving
- To help a group develop skills that enhance productivity
- To compare perceptions to determine how a group's problem-solving process is experienced by different members

Intended Audience

- Any global team or work group engaged in problem solving
- Managers or consultants who facilitate problem-solving sessions for global groups

Time

- 45 to 60 minutes

Materials

- Copies of the rating form, either online or as a handout

Directions

- If done online, choose a technology tool of choice, tabulate data, and then find a time to have the group engage in online chat and talk about perceptions. If done face-to-face, distribute the rating form.
- Introduce the exercise by stating that the assessment will enable all participants to share perceptions of how the team works for them and, ultimately, this will result in a better team for everyone and better results for the organization.
- Give the directions and ask each individual to fill out the rating form.
- Depending on the size of the group, have participants pair up or form small groups and discuss their responses.
- Lead a discussion that not only looks at perceptions of the team but suggests areas for improvement according to the data.

Questions for Discussion/Consideration

- Where were your answers most similar to those of other team members?
- What items provided the widest range of responses?
- What does the data suggest are the team's strong points?
- Where do the opportunities for improvement exist?
- If nothing is done to strengthen performance, what might the consequences be?

- What could get in the way of our efforts at improvement?
- What are we all willing to do to make certain our collective efforts are realized?
- What is one commitment you will make toward change that improves the group?

Caveats, Considerations, and Variations

- The items are looked at from both individual and collective viewpoints to accommodate cultural differences. Some words still may need to be adapted to be culturally appropriate.
- Selected items from the list can be used as a stimulus for discussion after the group has engaged in problem solving. The actual working together could offer opportunities for ongoing discussion and refinement of the processes used.

There are many necessary steps in helping problem solvers build awareness of cultural differences and then be able to switch style. One has to first identify his or her own cultural norms, habits, and preferences. Understanding that other ways of behaving also exist and have validity is the second step. A worthy goal in any global problem-solving group is to help all participants develop a wide repertoire of behaviors so they can be comfortable responding in various ways. Overlaying the national cultural norms of members is the organizational culture. Each global entity has its own set of expectations that may coincide or conflict with national culture. Reconciling culture on personal, national, and organizational levels takes time and commitment. The "Cross-Cultural Adaptations on Global Teams" tool can help people acknowledge cultural differences and realize that adaptations will be required all around. It is designed to help participants gain an understanding of where individual adaptations can be made.

Suggestions for Using
"Cross-Cultural Adaptations on Global Teams"

Objectives

- To understand one's own cultural norms and the need to expand behaviors on a global team
- To understand and negotiate these behaviors with other group members
- To collectively seek alternatives that take into account and validate the legitimacy of all cultural norms while also realizing that, to be productive and high-performing in global settings, adaptations by all are in order at various times

Cross-Cultural Adaptations on Global Teams

Directions: Working with international employees creates an expectation that problem-solving participants need to switch style in order to achieve the best results. The following five culturally based behaviors allow each person to think about what comes easily or naturally for him or her and about where each can learn to adapt more comfortably. Read the five statements below and select the answer that suits you best by circling either a or b. Then write a statement about where you need to be more culturally flexible and expand your behavioral options.

---

1. Regarding time, it is preferable for me to . . .

    a. not have precise deadlines.

    b. have clear deadlines.

    One thing I will do to be more adaptive is

---

2. In resolving disagreements/different opinions, I am more comfortable . . .

    a. stating the issue and trying to solve the problem.

    b. keeping my thoughts and feelings to myself and settling differences outside the group.

    I can style switch more effectively by

---

3. Regarding communication, I . . .

    a. can handle any reality if people communicate clearly and directly.

    b. appreciate subtle, more implied communication, as it is more helpful for me.

    My communication skills will be enhanced if I

---

4. In this day and age, . . .

    a. we already have too much change. Let the future come from natural evolution.

    b. we live in a fast-changing world. We should be leading the charge. We either change or die.

    Regarding change, I am willing to

---

5. I am most satisfied working where the emphasis on assignments is . . .

    a. given to the individual.

    b. given to the group as a whole.

    I can reframe my preference by

Intended Audience

- Global team or work group members
- Managers or project managers of a short-term global task force charged with work groups
- Facilitators or trainers trying to create understanding and awareness on globally dispersed teams

Time

- 45 minutes

Materials

- Copies of the "Cross-Cultural Adaptations on Global Teams" assessment tool
- Easel or flip chart, markers

Directions

- Distribute the assessment and ask each person to fill it out.
- Have group members pair up and discuss their own responses.
- Conduct a large group discussion after pairs are finished.

Questions for Discussion/Consideration

- In which of these five areas is it most difficult for you to be flexible? What is the reason?
- Under what circumstances would you be unwilling to bend?
- What is your reaction when others are unyielding? Give an example.
- When there is resistance to moving, how will you resolve the dilemmas?
- Where are you willing to be flexible?
- What does the team need to do to help you out?
- What do you envision the consequences might be for team productivity if team members do not increase flexibility?
- What commitment are you making to yourself and the team about developing flexibility for the good of everyone?

Caveats, Considerations, and Variations

- This exercise would be a good follow-up to a lecturette or discussion of cross-national and cross-cultural differences and the implications of national culture on the work environment. It would be used best when bringing a team together for norm setting and interpersonal understanding.
- Trust and comfort are increased if done in pairs. Once the group has established trust, depending on the size of the team, this exercise can be conducted with all participants as a whole group. However, seven par-

ticipants would be the maximum size for one large group discussion.

- This exercise can be done online, but it requires dialogue. If people fill out the form online, schedule a teleconference or online chat room when you can talk about it.
- Give people the questions to think about before a teleconference to make better use of time and to allow for different thinking styles.

THE THREE-STEP PROBLEM-SOLVING PROCESS[3]

This chapter has focused heavily on the utilization of practical problem-solving tools for use by global teams. Tools are helpful, but a process is essential as a framework to move a team or organization forward. The Three-Step Problem-Solving Process is particularly useful on global teams, where cultural differences may create conflicts or frustration. This model is designed to help co-workers see different realities and vantage points as a prelude to finding common ground. It presumes that there are advantages to creating and exploring multiple options.

Step One: Identify the Problem from the Various Vantage Points

To begin, the problem or issues need to be identified from the various vantage points represented in the group. For example, one common issue on global teams involves identifying a language(s) in which business will be conducted. If all literature is printed in or all meetings are conducted in one language in a global organization where four or five primary languages are spoken, that can present a serious problem. Many employees may not understand all the norms, expectations, safety rules, or information needed to do the job. Poor job performance can create problems, not just of performance but also of morale and commitment. Seen in one way, a single language for conducting business may indicate efficiency and cohesion. Seen from the vantage point of people who do not speak that language, conducting business in one language may be seen as dismissive, insensitive, inefficient, and conflict inducing.

Step Two: Find Common Ground

In order to find out what the conflicting parties have in common, it is necessary to see how events are being interpreted. Assumptions need to be challenged. While it is inadequate to conduct all official business in one language when an organization has multiple languages spoken, it is important to check the assumptions one is making about why the language usage is narrow. One assumption might be that leadership in the organization is ethnocentric and uncaring. Another might be that leaders are out of touch, under-skilled, and underdeveloped for their roles in a global organization. It might also be that they are attributing linguistic competence to employees in their organization and no one has ever complained or brought up the fact that some people feel disadvantaged. Perhaps leadership also assumes that, if people need help with translation, linguistically competent co-workers at each respective location are translating everything and bridging the gap. Without data, it is hard to know what all the assumptions might be or what the reality is. But Step Two asks participants to look for the common ground. If there is no overlap, if there is nothing that all participants have in common, it will be difficult to solve the problem. In most cases, employees and executives want a prosperous, productive workforce that communicates well. Accomplishing this leads to less conflict and more efficiency and productivity. Having that or some goal in common allows the group to move to Step Three.

Step Three: Create Options That Work for Everyone

The idea in Step Three is to create as many options as possible. Depending on the problem at hand and one's viewpoint, some ideas will work better than others. But if many alternatives are created and viewed through the lens of cultural sensitivity, the chance of solving problems increases. For example, in the scenario just discussed, perhaps official translators can be hired or language lines can be used. Maybe everything written in the organization can be published in the five main languages, and software systems can be bought to foster usage of multiple language skills. Furthermore, employees may take language classes in the language that has currently been the dominant language. The point to Step Three is to create options built on the common ground. That process creates an investment in solving the problem, with solutions that demonstrate sensitivity to multiple viewpoints.

To see how the Three-Step Problem-Solving Process works, revisit the Unimundo Case Study and answer the following questions:

Step One: Identifying the Problem from Various Vantage Points

- From Telespaña's point of view, what are the key concerns and issues in the merger with All Call Cellular?

- Despite the incredible business opportunities for Unimundo in this global environment, what are All Call Cellular's primary concerns and obstacles?

- What challenges are anticipated in working in Singapore and perhaps China?

- What leadership moves by top executives are causing fear and concern with Telespaña employees?

- From a cross-cultural perspective, where are the most critical clashes?

Step Two: Finding Common Ground

- What areas of common ground exist between these two companies?

- What assumptions might Telespaña be making about ACC's leadership group? Corporate values?

- What assumptions might Unimundo's executives be making about language differences? Corporate values?

- What assumptions might be made by Telespaña or ACC employees regarding lack of face time due to cost containment?

- What assumptions or common ground exist around expansion to Asia Pacific?

- What assumptions exist about promotability and career opportunity?

Step Three: Creating Options That Work for Everyone

- List the top three concerns for Telespaña and ACC with suggestions for bridging the differences.

Telespaña	ACC
1.	1.
2.	2.
3.	3.

- What options exist for building cohesion and good relationships?

- What kind of process might be a starting point to foster cultural integration?

- What options exist for giving and receiving feedback in a culturally sensitive way?

There are no right answers to these questions, just lots of alternatives and considerations that have been suggested throughout this book. As you go through these steps, answers to the questions can be found partly in the information and tools used in this chapter. You have been given information about culture as it relates to problem solving and numerous tools that can help employees bridge differences. Information from other chapters will help as well. Chapter 1 gives clues on culture, while Chapter 3 helps with ways to effectively communicate. Certainly any of the tools mentioned in Chapter 4 on global team building can also be a big help in building relationships online. The most important learnings from the case study are these:

1. Seeing another person's reality or viewpoint and being sensitive to it is essential in working well together and moving an organization or group forward;
2. Finding common ground enables any problem to be solved. Without that there is little hope; and
3. The more options created, the better the solutions will be and the greater the chance to find some "win" for everyone.

Our goal in this chapter has been to provide a process and tools to help those involved on global problem-solving teams to overcome the differences of time, space, and culture as they try to work well together.

Problem solving in global organizations is a dynamic and complex process. It is challenging and potentially full of great value, as it reaps the benefits received from considering different viewpoints. Understanding how culture influences the resolution process is central to achieving the desired outcomes. In hierarchical civilizations where decisions are made in a top-down structure, there is less input and involvement desired and therefore it may seem less relevant to focus on group dynamics. But nowhere in the world are outcomes made better if people feel discounted or disrespected. The human condition suggests that people want to matter and to count. For any organization intent on using the talent, knowledge, skill, and expertise of its employees to solve problems effectively, the tools and process in this chapter can be used to facilitate that goal.

Notes

1 Sebenius, James K. "The Hidden Challenges of Cross-Border Negotiations," *Harvard Business Review,* March 2002, pp. 1–12.

2 LeBaron, Michelle. "Mediation and Multicultural Reality," *Peace and Conflict Studies,* 1998, V5, N1, pp. 41–56.

3 Adapted from Nancy J. Adler, "Cultural Synergy: Managing the Impact of Cultural Diversity." In J.W. Pfeiffer (Ed.), *The 1986 Annual: Developing Human Resources* (San Francisco: Jossey-Bass/Pfeiffer, 1986).

CHAPTER 7

Systems for Using People Effectively in Global Organizations

This chapter focuses on selected human resource systems and management practices that are pertinent to global diversity. We will examine in detail implications for interviewing, hiring, training, and development, as well as issues related to compensation, benefits systems, and staff mobility. Performance management, perhaps the system that is most relevant to global diversity, will be examined in depth in Chapter 8. While much has been written on global and international management systems, few authors have approached the subject from a global diversity perspective.

POLITICAL, SOCIAL, AND ECONOMIC VARIABLES

The following section will explore six specific variables that influence a corporation's approach to interviewing, hiring, training, development, compensation, and staff mobility in international and global companies.

1. Economic Development

Managers and human resource professionals should understand the influences that the national economic context has on employees, their self-perception, and how other nationals perceive them. Different values, assumptions, and workplace expectations underlie the capitalistic system of the United States and Hong Kong, the social democratic system of Germany, the post-communist system of

Russia and the Czech Republic, the transitioning systems of the People's Republic of China, and the evolving communist heritages of North Korea, Vietnam, and Cuba. Each of these systems influences what a human resource professional, a manager, and a prospective employee bring to questions related to interviewing, hiring, training, and development, as well as corporate compensation and benefits. What is fair in one economic context may not be understood or seen as fair in another. Years ago national economies were labeled as first-, second-, and third-world countries. Currently, this has transitioned to "have and have not" nations or, as described by author Thomas Friedman,[1] the people "who drive Lexus's and those who fight to protect their olive trees." Other economic distinctions are also relevant. Senior and junior managers in global companies participating in the affluent worlds of Hong Kong, London, Bombay, Sydney, and São Paulo have seemingly similar hopes and aspirations as well as expectations about compensation . . . the economic nationals of the commercially gifted. People who work in the mills, run the lathes, and assemble products in Shenzen, Madras, Gioannia, and Selma also have a common perspective . . . the nationals of the goods production. The issue is not that there are different coexisting systems, but that those systems affect employee expectations and behaviors. This dilemma frequently surfaces in hiring interviews. Is the candidate a representative of the mainstream economy of his or her country? If so, how does that affect a prospective hire working in a different economic context? Does the candidate have the flexibility to work in a less-compatible environment? Can the candidate transition from high performance in a less-developed economy to a more developed economy and vice versa? Does a manager schooled solely in a developed nation have the capacity to manage the educational, economic, and business heritage of a junior manager from a less-developed nation? Does that national economic heritage present a value to the organization, or does it present an irreconcilable disadvantage—and in whose eyes? Managing these economic dilemmas is necessary for a global company that wants to gain needed resources and not exclude valuable candidates due to limited knowledge and economic bias of hiring managers and staff. Interviewers must be trained to understand the workplace implications of diverse economic backgrounds.

2. Minority, Immigrant, Transmigrant, and Foreign Knowledge Workers

The demographic shift in the developed nations during the late 1990s and the exuberance of the market required an infusion of workers into homelands that were traditionally mono-cultural. Workforces became multicultural not because of a commitment to global inclusiveness but rather due to the commercial necessity for lower paid workers who had the knowledge to do the job—be it with a design computer, a lathe, or a vacuum cleaner. Indian IT experts in the opening years of the 2000s maintained Germany's national growth; Palestinian workers supported the manufacturing sectors of Israel; and Guatemalan, Mexican, and Pakistani workers maintained homes and infrastructure services for the national workforces of Wall Street and the City of London. This reality alone created a new level of global diversity in companies as internationals knowingly and unknowingly infused their cultural patterns, behaviors, values, and beliefs into their new workforces and communities. For some companies these workers created new solutions; for other companies they created new occasions of discrimination, polarization, and protectionism.

New members of the workforce challenge long-held diversity concepts. In the United States immigrants and transnational workers who might once have been labeled as "black" identify themselves as citizens of Ghana, Jamaica, Senegal, Nigeria, and varied West Indian nations.[2] Their presence, as well as their cultural norms and behaviors, challenged the U.S. African Americans' descriptions of "blackness" and "whiteness" and its frequently articulated "oppression/victimization" model. West Indian members of the American workforce now represent 48 percent of Miami's black population, while 33 percent of New York City's black population was born in nations other than the United States. Similar patterns are occurring in Europe, especially in the United Kingdom. Blacks, along with other persons of color, will represent one in four workers within London's workforce in 2008. These European workers' personal identities also bear less relevance to "class," "race," or "color" and more to nationality. Immigrant and foreign knowledge workers provide corporations with opportunities for a broader ethnic and national diversity and workplace dialogue.

A new type of worker, the transmigrated worker,[3] will also have an impact on global diversity. A transmigrated worker is an employee who primarily works over a sustained number of years in a nation-state other than his or her home. These workers maintain a strong political and social connection with their country of origin by travel, sending of funds, maintenance of language, and children's education. Working in another country no longer requires nationals to become socially or culturally assimilated into the dominant host country's culture. Organizations in Mexico, the Dominican Republic, Portugal, and Japan recruit and repatriate these potential emigrants, since they become effective cross-national employees. Organizations value the transmigrated workers' ability to move across international borders and utilize cross-nationals' commercial, intellectual, and emotional intelligence.

Employees are hired not only to do a specific job but also to join a diverse workforce where they can exercise their national and economic heritage. This provides a key corporate asset. In global companies, many employees have different backgrounds related to nationality and national economic status that are not known. If known, they cannot be easily accessed due to privacy limitations or the limits of technology. Use the following exercise, "Using Social and Professional National Competencies," to explore the national heritage of your current workforce, based on each employee's national diversity profile.

Using Social and Professional National Competencies

Directions: Record the names of current employees and consider the national and ethnic assets they bring your organizations due to being immigrants, second-generation nationals, transmigrant workers, and naturalized citizens or workers. Record all specific contributions that each member has or may bring to the corporation. Some examples are given.

Name	Immigrant	Second Generation	Transmigrant	National	Social Capital Implications and Contribution
Richard Chamberlain		X			Parents born in Ireland, maintains strong Irish identity and is eligible for EU passport
Arusa Garadagi			X		Potential support for acquisition opportunities in Pakistan due to distant relative in Ministry
Pang Naap Dak	X		X		Cantonese heritage, left Vietnam when 15; relatives outside Ho Chi Mihn City near proposed greenfield site

Review your responses with the following questions:

- Based on national identity, what are the diversity strengths that each employee brings to the organization? Your function? Your unit?
- How will or do these assets support current operations?
- Does the company have any future plans when this individual will support the company's strategy or enhance its operations?
- Who in the company may need to know of this current or potential asset?
- How can these candidates support the training, educational, and globalization processes of the company?
- What type of training and development might be required to support their potential career or future opportunity?

Many companies have discovered valuable employee assets after the fact, but with forethought, these assets can be more readily identified and strategically employed. Review your staff on a periodic basis and track the profiles of employees who are immigrants, transmigrants, and foreign knowledge workers. U.S. law would prohibit direct questioning about these factors. The information, however, is vital. A work environment that encourages personal disclosure would facilitate the sharing of this type of information.

3. Employer/Employee Social Contract

The social contracts between managers and workers reflect the values of their national business culture, their surrounding civilizations, and ultimately the vision and mission of companies. Founders of companies that are today global, such as Ford in the United States, India's Tatas, and Hong Kong's Wus, forged their initial cultures and their employer/employee contracts on the business values and organizational styles of their home nations. Global companies cross national boundaries and comply with the legal requirements of sending and receiving locations. Whether they comply with national preferred styles and organizational values, customs, and structures of those locations is debatable. Globally diverse employees may not always respond favorably to the cultural and social contracts required in the hiring culture of global corporations. Frequently, advocates of "the corporate culture," with their scripted interpretations of how employer and employee should interact, are the greatest abusers of the spirit of global diversity. Intentionally or unintentionally, they impose a universal corporate standard. Global diversity requires that national contexts be recognized and reconciled with those of the organization. The residual effects of Europe's feudal system continue to influence today's hierarchical system of French management. The strong hierarchical focus of the Confucian culture in China, Korea, and Japan infuses the structure of Asian family-held businesses and local public companies with a sense of reciprocity, mutual respect, and collective reliance between manager and subordinate. A global company cannot sweep such differences away, but needs to understand, access, and focus on this level of diversity. Companies, especially when undertaking a cross-border merger, acquisition, or alliance, should conduct corporate culture compatibility studies that include the compatibility of employer/employee social work contracts. Many companies that created joint ventures in China misjudged the importance of this aspect.

4. Role and Level of Women

There is probably no more visible diversity issue than the role of women in the global workplace. Gender parity has been driven by U.S. diversity initiatives, clear United Nations mandates, European Union commitments, and many multinational companies whose programs, policies, and practices support the advancement of women. The developed, democratic, and individualistic economic systems of the United States and Western and Northern Europe are staunch advocates of women's rights. In contrast, many developing nations define gender roles in a more hierarchical fashion, such as the Confucian-influenced nations of North, East, and South Asia. While Hong Kong, Singapore, and other Asian commercial centers have legislated for women's advancement, these same societies maintain well-established social patterns that seem at variance with legislative intent.

Corporations need to monitor the inbuilt gender biases within national and civilizational social patterns that intrude and create gender exclusion in the workplace. Pay equity and succession opportunities are needed, especially given the contribution of women in the global manufacturing sectors of Central and Latin America, Southeast Asia, and South Asia. However, corporate success does not always mean social success. A female junior manager in Gwongzhou, China, commented that in the office she was empowered to independently use her talents, but at home, her husband, a manager for a state-run factory, perceived her family role from a more traditional, male-dominant Chinese perspective. Corporations cannot just conduct gender headcount, but must also monitor the impact corporate culture has on gender roles, both within the company and in the external lives of employees. It is important to identify both positive and negative influences. Corporate research on the role of women in the global workforce would add much to the discussion.

5. Universal Standards and Qualifications

The globalization of education and e-learning technology has enabled the real-time exchange of professional and technical knowledge. The same MBA or engineering theories are simultaneously published in languages such as Japanese, English, Arabic, and German. Secondary and college curricula demonstrate a convergence in their syllabi by using compatible if not similar texts.

How does an employer select a global workforce if worldwide qualifications or training standards do not exist? Will the company choose international candidates who are educated in domestic schools in their headquartered country or should they choose educationally diverse candidates from foreign institutions? Is the claim that the person is "not educated" or "not professional" correct, or is that claim an example of professional narrow-mindedness that is used to discriminate against a potential or current employee—frequently presented at the service of "protecting" a fellow national's job. Should companies hire individuals who are educated at "proper" institutions only, or should they choose candidates who learned by standing by and doing what the "master engineer" did? Is there equal opportunity between persons—a person who has a certificate and a person who says he has the skills and aptitude to do the job and has a letter of recommendation to corroborate it? This dilemma is an individual concern at the managerial and interviewee level as well as a systemic issue affecting ethics, policy, and global structure.

International managers in post-Apartheid South Africa faced this challenge as they sought to evaluate talented black South African staff who had been deprived of formal education during Apartheid. White candidates and a very limited number of black South Africans had access to higher education and had earned degrees to "confirm" their claims of competency. Most black candidates in line to assume middle management positions did not have the same formal education as whites. However, they had the skills required for the positions, because they had spent years working with experts in apprentice systems. How does one compare qualifications in such a system? This dilemma is continuously debated in economically developing nations as corporate managers, whose hiring policies are based on Westernized educational standards, meet talented people who have been trained in local, less-recognized institutions. The tension between "formal" education and "on-the-job learning" has long been part of the workplaces of the United States and the United Kingdom. Global corporations must reconcile that tension. If they do not, effective succession planning will not occur. Interviewers should be aware that nations such as Germany, Switzerland, and the United Kingdom have a strong orientation toward curriculum-based education. Augmenting these educational systems are equally demanding professional systems such as the Chartered Institute of Personnel and Development in the United Kingdom and the Society for Human Resource Management in the United States. Without credentialing from the CIPD, a corporate trainer cannot function professionally in the United Kingdom. Countries that rely on such academic programs and professional certificates conduct more structured interviews in order to verify candidates' academic accomplishments. Candidates from the United Kingdom, Germany, Austria, Spain, Norway, and Sweden can anticipate questions related to their specific credentials.

In distinction, high-context cultures, such as China, Indonesia, and Japan, begin interviews by exploring a candidate's networks and associations, including membership in alumni groups or affiliation with professional institutions that have proven to be reliable sources in the past. In these cultures, relationship is a prerequisite to employment, because the company's interpersonal orientation requires that the employee "fit in" with other employees and their client base. Interviews later move to discussions that are more detailed, with a focus on competency levels and education.

6. Work/Life Balance

Work/life balance is influenced by the local culture. Norms and national social patterns fluctuate between "living to work" and "working to live" or, in cultural terms, "doing" societies versus "being" societies. The "living to work" perspective is favored in individualistic, highly competitive societies such as the United States, where work and nonwork/leisure time or family relationships— are separated. Nonwork activities generally take second place. "Work hard, play hard!" is the catch phrase, but little play is involved. There is a clear bias toward performance and accomplishment over such traits as reflection, introspection, and interpersonal development.

Other societies ascribe to the "working to live" perspective. Individual accomplishment is valued but exercised in relationship to goals that focus on personal affiliation within family and kinship networks. Motivating Mexican retail workers in Mexico City or Monterrey to work on Sunday is difficult because it means forgoing their traditional family meal. Often, they choose the meal. A human resource professional stated that staff turnover in one internationally owned Mexican retail chain was around 50 percent due to the inability of employees to balance family commitments and their work schedules. The extended lunch hours of the French signal an orientation that work is contained in the process of relationships, especially when developed over good food and wine.

The Western workplace is fueled by excessive self-induced or organizationally endorsed commitments to productivity. Pride is taken in working 24/7 and not taking one's vacation. Anyone with an international reporting function knows that there is no time free from the intrusion of an e-mail, fax, or telephone call. Within global operations, some office is always open; someone is always working and needing to be "in touch." Cell phones have made it impossible to walk the mountain trails of Montana or Mont Blanc without intrusion. It is a frightening extension of the former colonial expression that "the sun never sets on the British Empire." CEOs Bill Gates, Stan Shih, and Lars Ramqvist could probably say the same about the Microsoft, Acer Group, and Ericsson empires of today.

Cross-national differences in work/life balance should be reconciled during a hiring interview. If not, the candidate's professionalism and motivation may be improperly judged. A candidate formed by a "work to live" culture may be labeled unproductive and not motivated; a candidate from a "live to work" culture may be labeled as antisocial, overachieving, and egotistical. In global companies, employees should have the capability to embrace both approaches based on the needs and requirements of the job, their home environment, the predominant work culture, and the ability to switch to nationally appropriate styles. Interviewers cannot create inclusive workforces if they cannot differentiate this important difference.

These six variables influence how global corporations structure themselves. While corporations may have used one or two of them in their traditional domestic diversity audits, it is helpful to reevaluate company performance in light of these more comprehensive global diversity variables. As we continue in the chapter, we will present information related to some of the more important corporate systems that affect global inclusiveness: interviewing, training, development, global employee mobility, and compensation. The "Global Diversity Trend Assessment" will assist you in identifying areas of significant concern in your organization.

Suggestions for Using the "Global Diversity Trend Assessment"

Objectives

- To recognize global diversity trends that have the greatest impact on workforce inclusiveness

- To detect corporate examples that require individual and organizational attention

- To analyze current global diversity disconnects, identifying systems, policies, or local/regional standards

- To identify action steps to reconcile national and civilizational trends within a corporation's hiring, training, development, and compensation systems

Intended Audience

- Corporate supervisors, managers, trainers, human resource professionals, and executives exploring global diversity issues in interviewing, training, development, employee mobility, and compensation

- Any manager, facilitator, internal/external consultant, HR professional, or trainer charged with the task of creating an interviewing, training, development, and mobility initiative or adjusting compensation policies and practices

Time

- 60 minutes

Materials

- Overhead transparencies and handouts of the "Global Diversity Trend Assessment" and the SSI Model

- Easel, flip-chart paper, and markers

Directions

- Introduce the six variables and discuss how each can be used to evaluate a company's process, a specific corporate policy, or a local program.

- Review the SSI Model and make applications to the six variables.

- Ask participants to use each variable to analyze their company. In the first column have them provide two examples that reflect global diversity disconnects that negatively influence corporate or personal inclusiveness.

- In the next column, they should record the underlying dilemma contained in that disconnect.

Global Diversity Trend Assessment

Directions: The following global diversity variables will influence interviewing, training and development, and compensation systems in organizations. Use them to evaluate your company's structure and systems and their degree of global inclusiveness. Write down in the first column ways that your company is operating. In the second column, identify the global diversity dilemma that is contained in your findings and that requires reconciliation. In the last column, list several action steps that will facilitate diversity reconciliation.

Global Diversity Trend	Corporation's National, Regional, and Global Reality	Areas to Reconcile Regarding Interviewing, Training, and Compensation	Interviewing, Training, and Compensation Action Steps
Economic Development Context	*Example:* Headquarters' national culture is aggressively tied to Wall Street quarterly analysis demanding 30 percent return on investment; unclear worldwide return of profit	*Example:* Tension between North American cost-cutting and right-sizing and China-based joint venture requirements to maintain over-staffed factory workers on company books for benefits	*Example:* Review and understand joint venture requirement; identify alternative jobs in joint venture
Minority, Immigrant, Transmigrant, and Foreign Knowledge Workers			
Employee-Employee Social Contract			

Global Diversity Trend Assessment (continued)

Global Diversity Trend	Corporation's National, Regional, and Global Reality	Areas to Reconcile Regarding Interviewing, Training, and Compensation	Interviewing, Training, and Compensation Action Steps
Role of/level of Women	*Example:* Women in the United States hold VP and higher levels. None in Asia or South Africa; majority of factory workers are women with male managers	*Example:* Gender attitudes within and outside of company do not support the company's corporate vision and values of diversity	*Example:* Review current criteria for candidate selection and identify statistics for gender distribution
Universal Standards and Qualifications			
Work/Life Balance			

- Last, ask them to create an action step that leads to greater inclusion.
- Have them form into six small groups and share responses, each group focusing on one of the six trends.
- Have a group member create a summary sheet and identify key learnings to be shared with the larger group.

Questions for Discussion/Consideration

- Which are the most common global diversity disconnects within corporate systems in your company? What are the financial or morale implications of these disconnects?
- Which global diversity trend surfaced the greatest number of disconnects or appears to have the greatest impact on the company?
- Why do you think that trend was so significant for your company?
- What are some possible action steps to reconcile the identified differences?
- What has been the loss to the company for not having addressed this global diversity disconnect? What would the company gain if one of the selected actions were carried out?
- What obstacles may hinder taking a suggested action?

Cultural Considerations

- In high-risk-averse and high-context cultures, participants may not be comfortable in raising corporate dilemmas if they may think they are criticizing the company. If this is the case, have participants generate issues that they "know about" from other industries or organizations.

Caveats, Considerations, and Variations

- Some employees may not have the global perspective to complete this exercise. Instead of conducting this as an individual exercise where each individual completes his or her form, use the exercise as a group activity. Encourage the participants to spend time understanding each variable before they begin their collective corporate analysis.
- Facilitators should do prework to identify the core issues that are present in the company. The worksheet could be redesigned by listing those findings in the first column and by then asking the participants to discuss the issues or dilemmas that need to be reconciled. Follow up by setting action steps.
- Individuals and teams can use this sheet to report corporate achievements. Begin by listing specific diversity success in the second column, the variables that were resolved in the third column, and the actions taken in the fourth column. This approach is effective in groups and

cultures that find value in discussing positive dynamics first rather than deficits.

- Many participants lack knowledge of global diversity. Participants can use their national diversity experience, taking care to avoid drifting into domestic diversity debates and projecting them into the global arena. Facilitators need to do prework and prepare for this eventuality. Identify any local diversity issues that can be rightly transitioned into a global application. For example, if issues are raised concerning the glass ceiling for women in the United States, raise issues related to the limitations on woman in other cultures, such as the bamboo ceiling for many Asian women.

- If there is existing data from surveys, focus groups, or other sources, that data can be presented or printed onto the chart in the appropriate box, for example "45 percent of management staff are female in North America, while only 10 percent are female in Asia" in the second column related to the gender variable.

THE GLOBAL DIVERSITY CAPABILITY CYCLE

An effective global diversity initiative requires a structure or tool that facilitates the flow of information and personal expertise. It necessitates a reciprocal exchange of intellectual capital between the global organization and the local communities. Global companies have recognized this need by including the concept of "diversity of thought" in their list of diversity descriptors, but generally they focus on individuals. Few mechanisms permit the actual transfer of diversity of thought on a macro or global level. In its absence, corporate scorecards continue to validate success by communicating statistics and programs primarily related to the internal and external dimensions of diversity, specifically in terms of race and gender. Pictures of diverse-looking people hugging globes grace brochures, implying that a company is communicating and exchanging expertise and opportunity. Affinity groups are established—over 150 different groups in one global semiconductor company. Training departments suitcase programs on women around the world, and recruitment departments troll business schools to bring black and Hispanic MBA candidates into their European workforces. Managers earn bonuses by meeting their headquarters' gender targets. These activities help empower people who are labeled as diverse and address first-order change or the change that makes the "required" adjustments in the organization. It is numbers-oriented change and nontransformational in nature. Second-order diversity change occurs when a company begins to see things in a new way. It is irreversible and requires new corporate learning. This is the change generated by institutionalizing the sharing of intellectual, organizational, and social capital drawn from a globally diverse workforce, regardless of where and how it is initiated.

The assumption underlying the Global Diversity Capability Cycle (shown in the model) is that all employees have an obligation to communicate and exercise their diversity of thought. The question is "How do we access it or anticipate it in interviewing?"

The Global Diversity Capability Cycle is an integrated management model that allows corporations to identify, select, train, develop, and reward employees for their distinctive diversity contributions. When a company broadcasts that it is global, then all workers should be able to identify how they contribute to globalization to the same degree as they communicate their contribution to localization. This is accomplished by respecting and rewarding the diversity of contribution companywide.

Participating in Global Diversity of Thought and Contribution

The following material describes four ways that employees can participate in the Global Diversity Capability Cycle. Regardless of his or her geographical location or level, each employee brings a specific contribution that supports corporate performance diversity. We are not speaking of job analysis or performance guides, but are addressing a more qualitative perspective. The following descriptions can

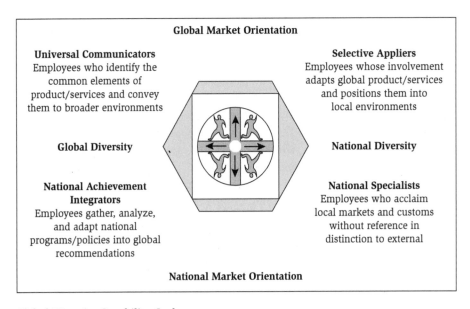

Global Market Orientation

Universal Communicators
Employees who identify the common elements of product/services and convey them to broader environments

Selective Appliers
Employees whose involvement adapts global product/services and positions them into local environments

Global Diversity

National Diversity

National Achievement Integrators
Employees gather, analyze, and adapt national programs/policies into global recommendations

National Specialists
Employees who acclaim local markets and customs without reference in distinction to external

National Market Orientation

Global Diversity Capability Cycle

help managers identify specific behaviors. Each part of the cycle contains specific competencies that can be identified at hiring, developed through training, and rewarded upon completion.

Universal Communicators

These employees have the capacity to identify and communicate essential elements of corporate policy, lead strategic programs, and impart detailed operational procedures that are core for global success, regardless of location in the world. Strong-minded nationals may consider this utilization an extension of corporate colonialism, but universal communicators are invaluable when it comes to affirming the vision of the global corporation. For example, design and manufacturing directors can communicate universal product and service standards and global training directors can teach commitments to diversity and human rights. Universal communicators have a proven awareness of their home culture, the corporate culture, and the cultures of other nations.

Selective Appliers

These employees manage the core programs, policies, and procedures in a specific cultural context. They have the capacity to blend the requirements of the global company with those of a national market. Some of these changes are cosmetic expressions of diversity, such as translating a service brochure from American English to British English or holding "ethnic food days" in the cafeteria. Others are more profound. Selective appliers implement universal standards, policies, and practices cross-culturally. They integrate the national culture with the local business style. They are skilled at identifying the difference between the universal corporate position and the local position. Key issues may be ethical, such as bribery, kickbacks, and succession strategies for woman.

Trainers, either corporate consultants or external vendor organizations, will not "suitcase" any programs, especially not classic diversity programs. Selective appliers adjust all training exercises and concepts to be inclusive both of the headquartered perspective and the local environment's learning style and values. Country managers, all managers who report up to them, and national directors of human resources need to demonstrate this competency. These employees are usually bilingual or multilingual. Monolingual leadership at this level cannot be as effective, since a monolingual employee cannot understand the nuances required for effective communication, value identification, and reconciliation.

National Specialists

These employees are able to focus on local markets, customs, and business styles. They are able to communicate detailed national intelligence to the broader global marketplace. They are rarely interested in physically moving beyond the borders of their homeland. From their national organization can come promising programs, innovative processes, and new policies that can bring vigor to other national units and ultimately to the global company. National champions support diversity of thought and performance by sponsoring the dissemination of best-of-class methodology. They also model the receptive application of other nations' best practices. Programs in global diversity competency support national specialists in maintaining their national identity.

National specialists are practical in identifying no-nonsense and verifiable programs and processes. When these employees are isolated, organizational splits occur and create "us/them" thinking, headquarters/subsidiary backbiting, and intranational corporate clashes—a true sign of the failure of the Global Diversity Capability Cycle. A global knowledge management system is vital for capturing local specialists' contributions and creating the cross-national, interregional, and global exchange of best practices. Chapter 8 provides more details on introducing this element into the performance management process.

National Achievement Integrators

These employees have the ability to take national programs, policies, and practices and transition the best of the national class back into global operations. While many companies gather this information, national achievement integrators analyze it, making the concept, programs, and policies transferable to another nation or region. Without capable individuals and systems dedicated to this analysis, the company cannot be considered diverse, since it is not reintroducing best of national class practices to the broader company. For example, Danish pharmaceutical giant Novo Nordisk sends two employees around the world yearly to identity learnings that can be universally shared and integrated. Use of IT is essential in this phase for accessing and communicating best-of-class examples.

None of the employee profiles associated with establishing a global diversity competency cycle are mutually exclusive. Employees and managers are generally drawn to one of the above profiles as a preferred personal, professional, or positional style. An interview, either at the time of hiring, during a performance review, or when doing succession planning, can be used to identify a candidate's primary diversity orientation. Most corporations have *universal communicators,* but they may have acted in ways that triggered defensiveness from receiving national units. Most employees on cross-border and cross-civilizational assignments should be *selective appliers.* Unfortunately, international assignees are still selected for technical competency and are not tested for the diversity competency of a *selective applier.* Local nationals then perceive the international assignee as the headquarters' voice and not as a person who aligns global expectations and local requirements. Global companies' largest employee base is *local specialists* who, when not charged with a commitment to global diversity and international knowledge exchange, resist the introduction of new ideas and fail to identify ways of sharing "local best practices" with others. Currently, training and development departments are introducing "Global Awareness Programs" to this group, hoping to expand their "awareness" of others. These programs are extremely limited since they do not offer practical ways of sharing knowledge, nor do they provide systemic linkages for communication. The competency area most consistently overlooked is the category of *national achievement integrators.* They actively collect and analyze best practices and stimulate organizational and global corporate cultural change. Their contribution in turn is applied and communicated by *universal communicators.* All roles in the Global Diversity Capability Cycle are needed.

The Global Diversity Capability Cycle and its inherent competencies can be used in many corporate systems to enhance global diversity. Use the "Global Diversity Capability Cycle Appraisal System" to identify specific employee competency during an interview or a management/subordinate dialogue. Before using the tool, review the job description or job posting for the primary competencies required in a specific position. For those who will staff the corporate headquarters, skills and competencies of universal communicators and national achievement integrators are very valuable. For people in HR networks and expatriate assignees, both long-term and short-term, having the knowledge, skills, and aptitudes of a selective applier are necessary. For positions where managers and employees work within their own national boundaries, the skills and aptitudes of national specialists are primary. The exercise should help facilitate an interview.

Suggestions for Using the "Global Diversity Capability Cycle Appraisal System"

Objectives

- To identify candidates who bring competencies that enable globally diverse intellectual capital to be shared companywide
- To introduce the expectations of active participation in global diversity and cross-border knowledge exchange
- To identify developmental areas for employees to participate in greater diversity exchange

Intended Audience

- Any manager, facilitator, internal/external consultant, HR professional, or trainer charged with the task of interviewing, creating a training initiative, or adjusting compensation policies and practices

Time

- 45 minutes

Global Diversity Capability Cycle Appraisal System

Directions: Current or perspective employees in a global company can demonstrate behaviors that reflect one or more of the global diversity capability competencies. Use exploratory questions to evaluate your interviewee's potential from each of the four orientations. Identify which orientation suits the candidate and his or her current or future position. Be sure to review the person's job description before conducting this appraisal. Record in the performance column your strongest findings. Evaluate the candidate's specific competencies and experience and align it with the position, indicating high alignment, moderate alignment, and low alignment.

Global Diversity Capability	Exploratory Questions	Performance
Universal Communicators: Identity and communicate the key points of corporate policy, programs, and operational procedures core for worldwide global success	Can you give me an example of when you worked with a multicultural group or team and from that experience developed a worldwide program, policy, or product? What did you do? How did you work with others? How did you come to consensus?	Findings: Alignment with position: ____ High ____ Moderate ____ Low
Selective Appliers: Introduce core programs, policies, and procedures into a specific national or regional context and align them to meet the needs of the global company and the exigencies of a specific national or regional economy	Please give me an example of when you may have introduced a corporate program, policy, or practice into a different country or culture. What was it? What part of the program, policy, or practice did you adjust to maintain the core character of the company but also make it special in that community?	Findings: Alignment with position: ____ High ____ Moderate ____ Low

Global Diversity Capability Cycle Appraisal System (continued)

Global Diversity Capability	Exploratory Questions	Performance
Local Specialists: Focus on local markets, their customs, and preferred business styles	Can you identify a program, policy, or plan that has been highly successful in your work unit, region, or country? What was it? How did you participate in it? How did you communicate your experience to another part of the company?	Findings: Alignment with position: ____ High ____ Moderate ____ Low
National Achievement Integrators Unique national offerings that can be forwarded into the company worldwide	Can you give an example when you worked with other cultural or national groups where you brought together best-of-class information and integrated it into a global policy? What was it? What did you do?	Findings: Alignment with position: ____ High ____ Moderate ____ Low

Materials
- A "Global Diversity Capability Cycle Appraisal System" form for each employee or prospective candidate
- Candidate's job description or position profile

Directions
- Before beginning a behavioral interview, review the Global Diversity Capability Cycle with the current or prospective employee, evenly highlighting the four types of competencies required.
- Position the exercise as a discussion of the organizational dimensions of the SSI Model. Be aware of the candidate's SSI profile and its implications.

- Provide concrete examples for each of the four areas, such as, "In your capacity as marketing manager for the Southern United States, you will discover aspects that Pang Nap Dak from our Hong Kong office would find valuable. Last year Pang introduced Process Electra to the company and it has helped increase market share on the West Coast by 15 percent during the third quarter."

- Use behavior-based questions to identify which aspect of the Global Diversity Capability Cycle is the preferred mode for the employee or prospective candidate.

- Based on the interviewee's data, appraise his or her suitability in the current job, identify potential positions for which the person may be better suited, or suggest training that may support the employee's current or future position.

Cultural Considerations

- This appraisal system is based on the use of behavioral interviewing techniques, a process that is not always culturally suitable in Asia since it forces the candidates to discuss their specific behaviors and call attention to their accomplishments. Interviewers may need time to establish a personal rapport with the interviewee before using behavioral interviewing techniques.

Caveats, Considerations, and Variations

- The model can become a basis for diversity training and development programs as well as specialized training modules in specific aspects of diversity exchange. Employees who by location and preference are national specialists may require more training to help them identify specific contributions that they can make to other parts of the world.

Global Diversity and the Interview Process

Whether from the perspective of new-hire selection or advancing internal candidates, the interview process is key to the utilization of diversity. How do we acknowledge the diversity of our employees when we may be too influenced by our own experience or preferred national style? Do we have the proper tools to sense the diversity potential of candidates? Next, we will examine how a global diversity perspective directs the way we gather and use data in the interview process, how we select the tools to engage the candidate, and how common guidelines will increase inclusion.

Securing Information Required for Inclusive Hiring

An effective global diversity interview brings together three types of data: hard, soft, and contextual. Each contributes to good decisions.

Hard data is quantifiable, factual information drawn from actual performance that indicates what the employee did, that is, number of units produced, rate of work, sales increases, profitability increases, projects led, or goals accomplished. It also includes background information related to educational accomplishment and institutional achievements.

Soft data, long understood to be necessary in interviewing and performance management processes, records the relationship patterns and personal traits that affect performance and interpersonal work relationships. Flexibility, the ability to see multiple perspectives, and adaptability are standard "soft" data points. Any employee who takes on cross-national and cross-cultural accountability and who wants to excel in global diversity should be assessed on these values. Referrals and letters of recommendations combine elements of both hard and soft data and differ across cultures. Interviewers should identify the soft data of the referrer and referree relationship by carefully examining letters of recommendation for subtle hints. In the United States, referral letters tend to be very functional, because a writer can only communicate the conditions of employment, namely time, dates, and function. They may even be written by a human resource functionary. In higher context cultures, things are different. The content of the letter is broader. Expansive personal comments are customary. In addition, the identity of the writer is important. The writer is usually connected to the candidate. Interviewers and recruiters should check the depth of relationship and implied networks within a high-context letter. These networks are corporate assets when working in a high-context culture.

Contextual data sums up the cultural, political, social, and economic realities in which the employee worked. In global companies, managers and human resource professionals cannot rely solely on hard and soft data in their analyses in the way that they might in domestic selection, where they share an understanding of the contextual environment. International and national contexts vary widely.

Before any interview, managers and human resource professionals need to understand the political, social, and economic context of a specific worksite so that they can thoughtfully appraise the candidate. A valuable source for this information is the Internet, especially the websites for international newspapers such as the *International Herald Tribune* (www.iht.com); the *Wall Street Journal* for the Americas, Europe, and Asia (www.wsj.com); and the *Financial Times* (www.ft.com). By scanning reports on national and regional events, as well as editorial and special features on business management, interviewers will equip themselves to identify cultural contexts that may affect performance. The "Interview Preparations and Analysis" sheet has been designed to help prepare interviewers for the role. It is intended to be used individually.

Interview Preparations and Analysis

Directions: Before your interview, consider the data that is required to fully utilize a global diversity perspective during the interview. Use the following form to check your preparation and identify specific questions you might need to ask to gain greater insight into the candidate's suitability.

Hard Data	
___ Reviewed the candidate's resume and the corporation's database for facts to elaborate on during the interview ___ Conducted background checks on all international schools and companies to understanding their global rating and ranking within appropriate social/economic/political contexts ___ Aligned the candidate's confirmed intellectual and professional capital with the job requirements	• I have noticed that you attend the University of Barcelona. Can you please tell me how that university compares with Hong Kong University, where you studied for one semester? • Please describe a project you personally worked on where you were very successful in achieving your goals and how your education allowed you to be successful.
Soft Data	
___ Expanded on the data to identify the social relationships and networks inherent in them ___ Identified the key social capital that the candidate brings to professional relationships	• Can you please tell me what some of the social responsibilities that occur in your workplace are and how you supported others? What was the end effect of those efforts? • Can you think of a situation in which there was conflict on your multinational or multicultural team? How did you deal with it? What was the result for the company?
Contextual Data	
___ Connected the candidate's social, intellectual, and professional competency with the job context ___ Identified where specific national and civilization influences affect the behaviors and outcomes of the job	• Were there any political or economic happenings in your country that affected the way you had to conduct your job and that were out of your control? What were they? What did you do? What was the outcome for your company? • What was the impact on your job of your former employer's merger with X organization? Can you give me an example of when you faced a challenge in merging the different cultures and what happened?

Suggestions for Using
"Interview Preparations and Analysis"

Objectives

- To assist interviewers in gathering the pertinent soft, hard, and contextual information required in a global diversity interview
- To create questions that allow interviewers to thoughtfully use the assembled soft, hard, and contextual information as well as identify additional exploratory and clarifying questions

Time

- 45 minutes

Materials

- Copies of "Interview Preparations and Analysis"

Directions

- Gather as much information as possible from files, letters of reference, recommendations, and external sources.
- Review and classify the information reflecting hard, soft, or contextual data and record it in the appropriate boxes in the first column.
- Review the job description for the competencies, knowledge, and skills required of the candidate.
- Review the data in the first column to see if you have the data and consider what questions you need to ask to gain greater insight concerning the candidate.
- In the second column record the questions that you will use in the interview to confirm the hard data and to explore the depths of the soft and contextual information.

Cultural Considerations

- If you do not have experience in the contextual background of the interviewee, you will have difficulty gaining full insight. Consider taking the "Interview Preparations and Analysis" form and consulting with a colleague or coach who comes from a similar political, social, cultural, and business context and who can suggest additional questions.

Caveats, Considerations, and Variations

- This exercise can be combined with a case study such as "Nordic New Co Petroleum Goes Global" (Chapter 8) to train employees in the range of information they would need to consider in conducting interviews in a global company. Participants could be asked to consider what hard, soft, and contextual data they would need to know if they were going to advance either Richard Chamberlain or Gunnar Halvorsen to a directorship in Nordic New Co.

- Conduct an SSI assessment of the potential candidate and return to the form to see what additional questions may need to be asked or explored.

Tools and Cultural Fit in the Global Interview Process

During an interview, tools should be sequenced to complement the preferred cultural styles of the interviewee and interviewer. It would be inconsistent with a commitment to global diversity to insist that the interviewee act only according to the behavioral standards of the corporate culture or interviewer. A middle ground needs to be found that respects local culture and the interviewee's style while acknowledging the company's culture and the interviewer's style. What dynamics might be anticipated? Cultures with a strong Anglo-Saxon tradition, such as those of Germany, Austria, Anglo-Canada, and the United States, prefer information that is direct, detailed, and specific. Any process that seeks to verify hard data is quickly understood and accepted by interviewer and interviewee. An interviewer can begin with a specific discussion of a candidate's academic and performance history. Later, the use of role plays, in-box activities, and technical demonstrations helps identify soft data about how the individual approaches the workplace, interpersonal work relationships, and diversity.

On the other hand, Asian and Latin contexts function in a more diffuse manner. Here the interviewer may wish to begin with more interactive, indirect, and interpersonal approaches. These will generate soft data that can later be confirmed or linked with hard data. Situational interviews encourage the candidates to generate stories about their past work performance that will confirm a required behavior or attribute. Managers using these diffuse tools can gather contextual information that the candidates themselves would like the interviewer to know.

Specific knowledge of the candidate's national and civilizational background is essential when evaluating contextual data, especially when assessing personal characteristics, national cultural alignment, motivation, and corporate cultural synergy. One U.S. company evaluating candidates for international assignment used "initiative" as a success criterion. When People's Republic of China nationals took the inventory, they scored below the norm of "successful" candidates. Given their cultural context of collectivism, this should not have been a surprise. The Chinese adage that "the first bird is the bird that gets shot" demonstrates the low value Chinese culture places on initiative. If the data from the inventory were used to fail the Chinese candidates, there could be grounds for a discrimination case.

Attempt to identify the cultural bias of all instruments and tools when using them in an interview. There are no culturally neutral instruments of examination. All show cultural bias, beginning with the fact that they rely on literacy rather than orality.

The Interview Tools diagram provides a view of widely used interview techniques. Note that some tools will generate hard data and are very specific in nature. Others are more interactive; others are focused on soft data. Use the diagram as you consider the appropriate tools to support the diversity orientation of your interviewee. As you proceed up the diagonal on the figure, there is a movement toward greater interaction between interviewer and interviewee.

Know the cultural compatibility of your selected interview technique with its preferred national or regional points of reference. Monitor the interviewee's responses for suitability, and switch techniques to gain the information needed to meet your goals. Interviewers have many choices to consider. Allowing a diversity of technique will support a diversity of response. Use the "Interviewing Techniques Chart" to consider the cultural compatibility and complexity between the national preferences of interviewer and interviewee and how they may play out in an interview.

Suggestions for Using the "Interviewing Techniques Chart"

Objectives

- To identify which tools are best with a candidate whose preferred national and cultural style is vastly different from the preferred corporate style of the company or the interviewer

- To communicate the range of intervention tools that can assist an interviewer in gaining the needed information

Intended Audience

- Corporate supervisors, managers, and HR professionals conducting employee interviews

Time

- 45 minutes

Materials

- An "Interviewing Techniques Chart"
- SSI profiles for both interviewee and interviewer

Directions

- Create SSI profile for the interviewee and interviewer.

- Carefully estimate the difference between interviewer and interviewee in communication styles, the degree of directness and indirectness

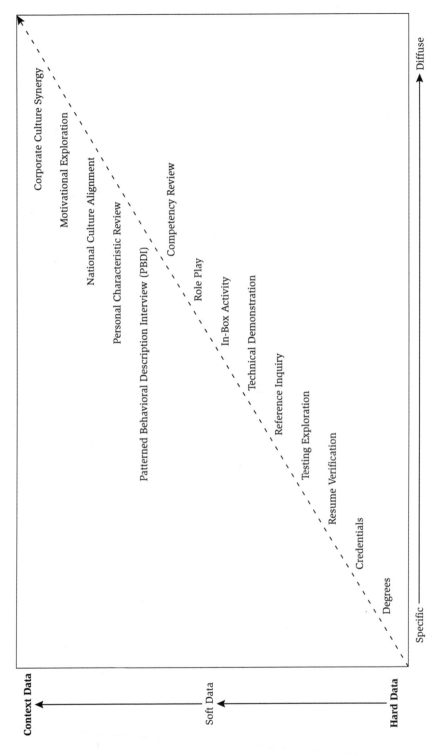

Context Data

Soft Data

Hard Data

Corporate Culture Synergy

Motivational Exploration

National Culture Alignment

Personal Characteristic Review

Patterned Behavioral Description Interview (PBDI)

Competency Review

Role Play

In-Box Activity

Technical Demonstration

Reference Inquiry

Testing Exploration

Resume Verification

Credentials

Degrees

Specific

Diffuse

Interview Tools

required, their orientations to high-context and low-context information flow, and the amount of specific and diffuse communications anticipated.

- Review the interview techniques for global diversity in column one for their style of communication, their degree of directness and indirectness, their orientation to high and low context, their manner of information flow, and the amount of specific and diffuse communication.

- Cross-reference your understanding of the SSI profiles and the interview techniques. In column three, rate how effective a specific tool may be in your upcoming interview. Rate them in terms of L = low, M = moderate, and H = high.

- In column four, list the action that you might take with this technique, which might include the order of your questions and interventions, whether you will use it or not, or how you will modify it.

Questions for Discussion/Consideration

- What are the best techniques to use in this specific interview?
- Knowing my preferences (interviewer SSI profile), what should I be most aware of during this interview?
- Knowing my interviewee's style (interviewee SSI profile) of what should I be aware?
- Do corporate requirements mandate a style that is inconsistent with the interviewer's preferred national style? What is the impact in the interview of that mandate?
- Do any areas need to be reconciled?

Cultural Considerations

- Both national preferred styles as well as level of national economic development will determine whether some or all of the interview techniques are functional in a national context. Consult local human resource and training professionals to determine whether activities such as an in-box activity or a role play are acceptable.

Caveats, Considerations, and Variations

- The case study in Chapter 8 entitled "Nordic New Co Petroleum Goes Global" can be used to apply this tool. Using the two major protagonists, Richard Chamberlain and Gunnar Halvorsen, as interviewer and interviewee, consider which techniques would be best in a new hiring interview.

Interviewing Techniques Chart

Directions: Create an SSI profile for interviewer and interviewee. Based on that data, review the following interview techniques for appropriateness. In the first column, identify the assumed cultural compatibility of a specific tool with a candidate's profile, recognizing the preferred communication styles of the interviewer and interviewee. In the next column, rate the appropriateness of that technique, providing an L for Low, M for Moderate and H for High. In the last column, record the action strategy you will bring to your upcoming interview, which may include using it as is, modifying it, or not using it at all.

Interview Techniques for Global Diversity	Cultural Compatibility	Appropriateness (L = Low, M = Moderate, H = High)	Action (Sequence, Use/Not Use, Modify)
Application Review: Review			
Degree: Clarify institutions and value of degree			
Credentials Exploration: Cross-reference all credentialing associations			
Resume Verification: Confirm data, especially if not in familiar context			
Testing Exploration: Review results and cross-reference to other contexts			
Reference Inquiry: Exploration of soft data focusing on inter-personal relationship and network			
Technical Demonstration: Observable exercises to evaluate mastered competencies			
In-Box Activity: Solving spontaneous, structured, observable activities or events related to position			
Role Play: "Play-like" roles simulating a business/work situation in diverse contexts			

Interviewing Techniques Chart (continued)

Interview Techniques for Global Diversity	Cultural Compatibility	Appropriateness (L = Low, M = Moderate, H = High)	Action (Sequence, Use/Not Use, Modify)
Competency Review: Interviewer or team ratings of candidate's observed competencies			
Situational Interview: Candidates are able to offer their own stories to support their possession of required contextual or soft competencies			
Personal Characteristic Review: Candidate discussion communicating core values			
National Culture Alignment: Demonstrate style-switching abilities across national preferred styles			
Motivational Exploration: Ability to respond to goals and lead others toward mission and vision			
Corporate Culture Synergy: Values in synergy with corporate values, with variable behavioral indicators			
Other:			
Other:			

GLOBAL DIVERSITY INTERVIEWING GUIDELINES

The interview process mirrors the corporate culture and can demonstrate the organization's tolerance for diversity of thought and style. During a cross-national or civilizational interview, both interviewer and applicants should monitor how they project themselves and check verbal and nonverbal communication that may signal inclusion or exclusion. What did the interviewer do or say that made the interviewee wonder whether the company was a good fit for him or her? What did the interviewee do that made the interviewer believe he or she would not be comfortable or a "good fit" in the company?

In the early 1990s, as Western companies established joint ventures in the People's Republic of China, human resource personnel faced this challenge. Chinese candidates wrote introduction letters and conducted interviews in the style of their customary socialistic and collectivist state-run companies. In some regions, they continue to do so. Prospective employees would not direct attention to their individual accomplishments. It was difficult to identify what the candidates "did," since the cultural norm was to present all accomplishments humbly, submerged in the collective efforts of a work unit. The "I" was buried in the "we," a reality rarely found in New York, London, or Frankfurt. Today, candidates in the urban centers of China have learned that to be successful at Western companies they need to identify their individual contributions. They read the signs to be clear about saying what "I" can do and the extent of "my" contribution.

Consider the following guidelines.

Master a Global Diversity Perspective

Interviewers and managers should use models that guide their diversity analysis, such as the SSI Model and the Global Diversity Capability Cycle. Global diversity training for interviewers is important not only to avoid any discriminatory behaviors or misunderstandings, but more importantly to identify the diverse value-added characteristics of a potential employee. Interviewers trained to decode national culture, reconcile corporate value conflicts, and utilize the internal and external dimensions of culture will be more successful. It is also important that diversity training not be a global "add-on" to some domestically designed program. Those models consistently view diversity within the limits of their national perspective and its associated biases. Neither the American model, which is rooted in "color," nor the United Kingdom model rooted in "class" is universal. Mastering and adapting the SSI Model to create your own will enable recruiting efforts to be more inclusive.

Become Skilled in Intercultural Communication

Communication skills are among the most important components of any corporate interview process, particularly global companies. Review the information in Chapter 4 as it relates to communication and consider the following questions:

- Can the interviewer identify different oral communication styles that reflect different cultural preferences for directness or indirectness?
- Can the interviewer sufficiently understand the SSI profile of a candidate to create a strategy to gather and confirm information using alternative methods and communication styles?
- Does the interviewer have sufficient skills to conduct interviews with persons who are communicating in a second language?

Be Impervious to the International Halo

There is always the chance of assuming too much about a candidate because a superficial cultural impression is weighted too heavily. Does the applicant's communication style impress an interviewer because it really has depth or does the prosaic expression of the English-speaking Frenchman create the aura of insight? Does the British managing director in the American-headquartered company choose a fellow European for a position due to the commonality of Europe or does she really see professional enhancements that were not seen by the previous American director? How does the interviewer not fall captive to seduction by people of a different national culture or civilization or impugn the lack of or exaggeration of skills? Monitoring one's emotional disposition for underlying truth helps one to get beyond the seductive "halo effect." If one is experiencing the same sense of personal liking that one normally feels at a party with a friend, chances are the interview is on the wrong track.

Maintain Objectivity

Making comparisons between diverse candidates is difficult but important. Prior to the interview, identity all social and intellectual capital requirements as well as the specific global diversity perspective required in the position. Then create behaviorally based competencies to test for those requirements. What is most important is not that the person "fits the profile" but that he or she knows how to reconcile the required social and cultural dynamics related to the position. An example from South Africa highlights this challenge. Initially, many U.S. companies sent a disproportionate number of black Americans to South Africa, apparently believing that commonality of skin color was a helpful business attribute. Because race was considered a constitutive part of the assignment, it became a constitutive part of the selection process. Some black American candidates and their families supported this bias. They resisted cultural training, believing that being black was enough to crack the national code of South Africa. However, many of the selected candidates' behaviors were off-putting to South Africans. The Americans were seen not as fellow blacks but as Americans. Because hiring offices and expatriating employees looked only at one internal aspect of diversity and not the full range of candidates' social and cultural capital, they failed to reconcile their American style. Consequently, serious assignment mistakes were made. It is important to maintain objectivity and define a position well before engaging in interviews. Define the position's global diversity context and the challenges the candidate will have to reconcile. Do not rush to judgment or the seemingly obvious answer.

Observe High-Context and Nonverbal Behaviors

Have the interviewers been trained in understanding their own nonverbal communication and how they will be seen and understood by others? This may include the interviewer's amount of eye contact, where he or she sits (behind, next to, or in front of a desk) and how he or she allows or endures interruptions. How does the interviewer determine when looking the candidate in the eye is supportive, as it is in the United States, or when is it intimidating, as it is in Thailand? Is the interviewer ready to switch styles in order to test whether resistance is cultural, professional, or personal, as suggested in Chapter 4? Can an interviewer switch context—being more specific and direct in asking a question to facilitate communication with low-context candidates and being more elaborative and personal with high-context employees? The clues to change will come from reading nonverbal communication. Success will involve a shift in style.

Examine Referrals and Recommendations Carefully

Referrals from fellow employees, teachers, and professional associates differ across cultures. In the U.S., Canadian, German, Austrian, and Swiss models, the referral provides an introduction or opens the door for an opportunity. In such individualistic societies, it is expected that the referree will then follow up and earn future prospects on his or her own merits. Ongoing involvement, other than informal coaching, is not anticipated.

In Asian countries, however, the referral relationship is different. The referrer's role does not conclude at the introduction phase but continues throughout the candidate's career in that company. *"Guanxi,"* the informal business networks between individuals in the workplace in China, facilitate the continued placement of fellow classmates, students, friends, and family members in organizations. It also requires that the referring person support and monitor those candidates throughout their careers. The employee, in turn, has a sense of responsibility to the referral agent. In Japan, former graduates, or "Sempai," return to their universities to personally invite the best of the upcoming graduates, "Kohai," into their companies. When a candidate is accepted, in that company or any other company, the referral relationship remains. There is a reciprocal and respectful professional accountability. Poor performance reflects on both. In the higher context cultures of Latin America, Africa, and Asia, an introduction also means an endorsement. Interviewers can identify the depth of referrer and referee relationships by carefully examining letters of recommendation. In higher context cultures, broader and more effusive comments are customary. Interviewers and recruiters should always check the depth of relationship and the network assets they bring to the company.

Carefully Choose Questions

Cultural informants can guide interviewers in avoiding questions that, while legal, may be culturally off-putting. They can also give advice about the appropriate style for asking questions, since the formality of language and the structure of questions have an impact on the interview. Many Asian languages and the romance languages of Europe are structured to demonstrate respect and interpersonal courtesy. Although the English language is not structured with these same patterns, the interviewer can mirror equal levels of respect. Use of "Please," "Thank you," "Would you be kind enough to . . . ," and "May I please ask you another question?" are all ways of showing respect. However, other questions may be difficult. "Is there something else that you might like to share?" or "Do you have any questions about our company?" may work very well in individualistic and self-assertive societies such as the United States and the United Kingdom. In Southeast Asia, such a question would frequently be met with silence unless the person has been clued in. Direct questions may not be culturally appropriate. Statements may be more helpful in eliciting information. Using "Please describe a . . ." or "Tell me . . ." as initiators may help. Questions that have an implied answer within them may be more helpful as opening questions. Did you mean "x," "y," or "z"? After a relationship is built, interviewers can transition to questions that are more direct.

Balance Public and Personal Information

The boundaries between personal and public information are different across national and civilizational borders. Understand what is considered personal and public and what information can legally be obtained. While an American may not discuss his or her personal relationships, he or she may discuss mistakes in the workplace that would demonstrate an ability to learn. For many Asians, that information would be private. A mistake in the Asian context reflects a failure in relationship and a loss of face for both employee and manager. That is a personal matter, although a candidate may "unintentionally" mention the names of strong allies in the company.

National and regional entities such as the EU have legislated what information and questions can be asked. This Western orientation to describing employment opportunities in their strictest behavioral terms guides interviewers to ask only questions that relate to the ability to do the job as defined in the job analysis. These highly structured interviews are preferred in the United Kingdom, Germany, the Scandinavian countries, and Austria. Information related to an individual's personal situation does not enter into the interview unless it clearly relates to functioning in the position.

Be Aware of Dominance and Privilege

Dominance and privilege impact the interviewing process. Classic United States' stereotypes of privilege and dominance as white, upper or middle class, heterosexual, nondisabled, Christian, and masculine do not translate around the world. Each nation and culture has its own version of dominance and privilege. The Gandhi and Tata names in India carry the same privileges as the Kennedy and Rockefeller names do in the United States. Whether it is caste, tribal affiliation, or family hierarchy, no nation or civilization is without some aspect of privilege. Before you begin an interview, be sure to assess where you, as an individual interviewer, a corporate representative, or a national representative, fit in the power and privilege hierarchy.

Reconcile Interviewer and Interviewee Dissimilarity

An orientation to inclusivity, style change, and cultural reconciliation is the prerogative not only of management, but of all employees in a global company. Interviewer and applicant should maintain reciprocal cultural watchfulness during the interviewing process, as both may need to switch styles in order to better influence one another. If they do not use different styles, preemptive judgments are likely to occur on either side. Because it is an interviewing process, most of the responsibility falls on the manager. Interviewers frequently gravitate toward candidates with similar profiles. Interviewees gravitate to work contexts and managers who support their worldview. This reality supports subjective selection processes and a tendency to perpetuate mono-cultural or national environments. Such behaviors will not support the diversity required in a global workplace. An unreflective Japanese HR professional interviewing an American might perceive some commonality in both being female executives, but she may believe that the American's repetitive references to her accomplishments show her to be conceited. The interviewer might rate her as inappropriate for an Asian, male-dominated team environment because of her strong orientation to individualism. By the same token, the American candidate might consider the corporate culture too limiting for self-expression, creativity, and initiative, given the company's insistence on team recognition. Both interviewer and interviewee need to understand the difference in perception, style, and cultural identity. With that knowledge, they can both switch styles to clarify perceptions. To gain the best data for decision making, interviews should allow for a variety of styles, methods, and interpretations. Usually one person is working in a second language. Added complications arise when both interviewer and interviewee use a second or third language. Due to the degree of nuance and loss of primary persuasion skills, valuable data is often lost in such an interview. No one should conduct an interview unless he or she has received training in and been tested in understanding the interview implications for candidates who are using their second or third language.

Reconcile any difference between interviewer and interviewee that surfaces and brings the diversity disconnects forward. The manner in which the differences are surfaced, identified, discussed, and reconciled within the interview provides a microcosm of what may happen with that candidate in a company. The open discussion of difference brings depth to the interview and enhances the interviewer's ability to identify good candidates.

Interviewers, whether working with new hires or with internal employees, can benefit by using these categories to sharpen their skills. Use the "Global Diversity Interview Review Checklist" to reflect on your performance. If you were able to consistently implement behaviors supporting the category and received positive feedback from the interviewee, rate yourself with "high marks." If you observed yourself as introducing the category adequately, rate yourself "good." Rate yourself "OK" if you acted in ways that supported the category only occasionally. If you find the category was never used or used only once, you may need to do some work to increase your skill levels.

Suggestions for Using the "Global Diversity Interview Review Checklist"

Objectives

- To provide a quick evaluation of personal and professional effectiveness in conducing global diversity-oriented interviews

- To identify areas of competency in conducting global diversity interviews

- To discover areas of needed enhancement or training

Intended Audience

- Corporate supervisors, managers, trainers, human resource personnel, and executives exploring global diversity issues in training, interviewing, and compensation

Time

- 45 minutes

Materials

- A copy of the "Global Diversity Interview Review Checklist"

Directions

- Upon completing an interview, use the checklist to evaluate your global diversity-related interview competencies.

Global Diversity Interview Review Checklist

Directions: After completing an interview, use the following checklist to evaluate your skill levels. Consider specific behaviors that you demonstrated in the interview. When finished, review your level of competency. Then use your findings to increase your effectiveness in the next interview.

Category	High Marks	Good	OK	Needs Work
1. Implemented a global diversity and inclusive perspective				
2. Demonstrated intercultural communication skills				
3. Resisted the international halo				
4. Maintained neutrality				
5. Observed high-context and nonverbal communication				
6. Used referrals and recommendations				
7. Selected carefully chosen questions				
8. Balanced public and personal information				
9. Maintained awareness of dominance				
10. Reconciled interviewer and interviewee dissimilarity				

1. In conducting this interview, I became aware of the following behaviors:

2. What would I do differently next time?

3. What insights from this interview do I want to share with my company?

4. How can I gain the skills on which I need to work?

- Consider the specific behaviors you demonstrated during the interview. If you were able to consistently implement behaviors supporting the category and received positive feedback from the interviewee, rate yourself with "high marks." If you observed yourself as introducing the category adequately, rate yourself "good." Rate yourself "OK" if you occasionally acted in ways that supported the category. If you find the category was not used or was used only once, you will need to do some work to increase your competency levels.

- When the checklist is completed, review your level of competency and answer the four questions.

- Review your responses and create a strategy for your next interview.

DIVERSITY AND INTERNATIONAL ASSIGNMENTS

Global assignments are an important tool for establishing corporate inclusivity and supporting global diversity. They are also a key tool within the Global Diversity Capability Cycle.

A longstanding bias exists that cross-border employee exchanges should occur only at the most senior leadership or managerial levels. However, exchange at all levels is necessary to establish global diversity. Without such an exchange of nationals, it is unreasonable to imagine that any company will demonstrate global inclusiveness or reap its benefits.

Currently, most international exchanges have been for employees who manage term-limited projects, such as installing programs, accomplishing technology or corporate culture transfers, or serving as a financial link to headquarters. Global companies continue to struggle with creating a way to exchange employees at all levels. Driven by the economic constraints of the early 2000s, human resource professionals have restructured transborder employee mobility. They have created greater opportunities for short-term assignments, that is, assignments that range from one to six months. Greater interpersonal and cross-cultural damage can be done on this type of assignment because transferees do not have sufficient time to acculturate and learn appropriate behavior. Interviewing for short-term assignments demands rigor and a greater structure. Frequently, a sending manager, who has little contextual understanding of the receiving location, does the selection. Diversity performance outcomes should be tied to the sending and receiving managers' compensation to increase the likelihood that selected candidates will use the experience as a diversity learning opportunity. Short-term assignees usually receive no training or cultural briefing before departure. They are ill-prepared to either include themselves in their new work context or recognize the unique contributions their colleagues offer. They are rarely alerted to the fact that they are entering a different national context that requires personal behavioral change and diversity alertness. They will know, however, how to get to the office, the hotel, the restaurants, bargain locations for a gift for a family member, and where to go for entertainment if there is time—which there usually is. That level of cultural information is always exchanged. Short-timers do not recognize their range of assumptions about diversity forged from their home experience. Attitudes in the workplace toward race, gender, sexual orientation, ethnicity, nationality, religious orientation, and even toward work are usually carried unconsciously to new environments.

During the initial interview for a long-term or short-term assignment, diversity assignment objectives should be clearly communicated and documented. When professional or technical standards are outlined with clear outcome measures—that is, the operational goal of the assignment—global diversity goals should also be articulated. Goals that focus on inclusivity need to be a constitutive part of all selection processes. They need to be supported by the local and regional training staffs, as well as the sending and receiving managers. Global diversity objectives can be accomplished when employees are prepared for and held accountable to them. Basic goals for a short-term assignment (a two-to-six-month exchange) are

- An increased knowledge of inclusivity and discrimination within the country of assignment and of the corporation's reconciling programs and policies;
- An enhanced ability to establish and sustain a professional relationship with an employee of another national culture;
- A proven ability to switch style when working with an employee with a nationally diverse background;
- A mastery of basic greetings, polite phrases, and major proverbs and the use of unique cultural words in conversation;
- An ability to communicate a personal reflection on issues such as gender, race, ethnicity, religion, and sexual orientation for a different and equally legitimate perspective; and
- A willingness to share corporate process knowledge learned on assignment with colleagues when returned to the home country.

A structure to encourage reflection and learning is necessary. In expatriate and repatriation workshops, outgoing and homecoming employees can share lessons learned and co-coach. Globe Smart and Peer Notes, a tool being used by Rockwell, Guidant, and Kodak, is a web-based intranet application that allows employees on long-term and short-term assignments to share their perspectives of working in diverse work environments. This allows others to quickly learn what works and what does not.

Assignment assessment and selection systems must be restructured to high-light inclusivity. Most companies still maintain a corporate structure in which the staff responsible for diversity implementation is separate from the international selection and training staff. This is an unproductive disconnect. Without coordination of those two corporate functions and the conceptual expansion of diversity beyond gender, race, disability, and sexual orientation, companies will fail to leverage the broader dimensions of global diversity, that is, the interplay of national preferred business styles, the relevance of a multilingual work environment, and the cultural enhancements of organization building.

TRAINING AND DEVELOPMENT

Training and development functions differ due to the impact of their educational institutions. In the United States, training supports individual skill building and competency enhancement, enabling Americans to take control of their work environment and their future. Diversity training focuses mainly on issues related to the internal and external dimensions of diversity, that is, gender, race, ethnicity, sexual orientation, and enhanced communication. Such programs build the competency of an employee base and are primarily seen as enhancing motivation—and competency for individual employees.

Global training and global diversity expand on this foundation. In the developing economies of China, Southeast Asia, and South Asia and in regions of Latin American and Eastern Europe, corporate-sponsored training is a business requirement that assures a company that its employees have basic skills. Training is a survival need within those economies. Many of the educational institutions in developing nations are restricted to certain economic or social classes, so employees do not have easy access to education and training. A large percentage of employees cannot purchase those educational benefits on their own and want companies to provide them. While people in the United States will talk of disproportionate access to "good" education, many in the developing nations experience disproportionate access to any education.

Training Across Cultures

Many if not all of the following considerations for global diversity training apply to cross-cultural and cross-national training. In corporate training within national boundaries, the issue is the degree to which training conforms to the nationally preferred corporate style, with appropriate adjustments for the subcultural values of minority groups. Training in the United States is in English, without considering those whose preferred language is Spanish, Cantonese, or Urdu. The burden is on the person who speaks English as a second language to master the dominant culture's language. This is not as true in global companies that wish to respect diversity. "Suitcased" programs—designed, developed, and initially conducted for one specific country and culture and assumed to be transportable to anywhere in the worldwide corporate system—create a disservice to global training. However, because of limited time, staff, and funds, they will continue to be developed. Trainers and instructors supporting global diversity should ask the following questions:

- What aspects of this program's objectives, goals, activities, and processes are ethnocentric and need adjustment to provide greater service to the targeted international audience?

- Can I conduct this program in the designated language? If so, why is this so? If not, what needs to be done to change the process?

- Is my preferred communication style effective in this environment or among the people in the training group? How will I have to adjust that style to be more effective? Is it easily adjustable, or do we need to redesign?

- How does the targeted group look at training and its own involvement in the training process? Will members be interactive? Reactive? Nonactive? What is my role as trainer, teacher, and coach?

- What terms, concepts, and ideas need to be simplified, redefined, or contextualized in order to be most effective?

- What environmental and cultural context exists in the training location that would make the concepts and process ineffective? What can be done to address this incompatibility?

As we continue examining global diversity training, keep in mind your general orientation to training, as many of the things discussed have an application to domestic training with persons who are of different cultural backgrounds.

Training Department as Strategic Diversity Change Agent

Training and learning/development functions need to reflect on their responses to the concepts of globalization and inclusiveness. There is an increasing requirement to support inclusivity of opposing thoughts, divergent behaviors, and dissimilar styles of trainees. This can be in marked distinction to centralized training policies. Training departments also need to become the center point for the collection, analysis, and exchange of vital corporate intelligence, which supports the concepts of the Global Diversity Capability Cycle. Today's market can move beyond traditional educational and professional roles of classic training departments to the creation of agents who will gather, sort, and reintroduce globally diverse workplace intelligence. Diversity training has been aligned with EEO in the United States and current EU legislation as a protection from discrimination. It has not yet become a core part of a corporate strategy that promotes individual and systemic inclusiveness.

What can training departments do to help a company make the most of global diversity? Training departments have the methodology, skills, and systems to engage adult learners. They retain the expertise needed to identify national and civilizational workplace information, cross-reference it, align it with the corporation's goals, and communicate it in the workplace. This is in marked distinction to the interpersonal, intragroup, or intergroup communication models of many domestic diversity efforts. This more expansive macro view of diversity training requires a classic training department to shift away from a longstanding position as a provider of diversity "training" and its economical but limited "off-the-shelf" programs. Training departments can become business units with centers of diversity learning and divergent cultural methods, creating tools for global exchanges of intellectual capital. Domestic diversity efforts have enhanced the visual diversity of people who work in our national factories and who sit at the training tables. Training has also increased employees' ability to communicate effectively with each other. The next step is to recognize international diversity of thought, behavior, and style as a core part of global diversity research and education. Thoughtfully constructed, culturally executed, and inclusively designed programs can accomplish that goal.

Technology supports are essential for finding best practices and designing, developing, and evaluating training products. Protocols and training designs need to be rewritten for the topics that are traditionally taught in domestic locations. The following exercise illustrates the design changes that might help a traditional corporate training event incorporate strategic global diversity.

As an individual, a member of a team, or a member of a department, review the "Global Diversity Perspectives in Training Design" listings. Consider where your company has been successful and where there is room for improvement. Which items reflect your company's success in creating greater inclusivity and global diversity?

Suggestions for Using the "Global Diversity Perspectives in Training Design" Listings

Objectives

- To increase the potential of all training to support global diversity
- To expand global diversity perspectives in specific traditional training modules
- To identity which current training programs need to be redesigned to include a global diversity design

Intended Audience

- Training and development professionals, managers, and HR professionals involved in training and development policy and implementations

Global Diversity Perspectives in Training Design

Directions: The following sampling illustrates the design changes that might help a traditional corporate training event engage with strategic global diversity. As a quick review, check as many boxes as possible in the following document reflecting your company's success in creating greater inclusivity and global diversity. As an individual, a member of a team, or a member of a department, review the following list. Consider where your company has been successful, and where there is room for improvement.

Training Topics	Suggestions to Expand Global Diversity Perspectives in Training Design and Outcomes
Diversity Training	☐ Identify and coordinate different national definitions of diversity and reconcile their unique meanings and their relationship to the corporate mission and vision ☐ Utilize different national focused case studies that support diversity and identify overlaps, disconnects, and possible solutions applicable to the advancement of diversity within the company ☐ Use an internationally diverse team to facilitate all training allowing for modeling and verbalizing of their diversity dissimilarity, especially in resolving issues such as team leadership, design, and presentation skills
Manager Skills Training	☐ Expand the corporate leadership training requirements for all junior managers to include mastery of two different national leadership styles and three cross-civilizational styles for all corporate officers and demonstrate how those models collectively bring value to the corporation ☐ Script all domestic training designs, regardless of country of origin, with multinational and cross-civilizational examples of diversity, demonstrating cultural inclusivity and transfer of global learning ☐ Train managers in identifying a broad spectrum of diversity behaviors and style-switching techniques that reconcile the corporate model with various national models ☐ Provide checklists of where, when, and how to switch style in different corporate settings, for example, team meetings, conversation with subordinates, presentations to senior management, and so forth

Global Diversity Perspectives in Training Design (continued)

Training Topics	Suggestions to Expand Global Diversity Perspectives in Training Design and Outcomes
Performance Management Training	☐ Train to identify and use different patterns of national and civilizational patterns of power, status, and privilege within the manager/subordinate relationship, highlighting how they affect performance and outcome and provide processes for reconciliation
	☐ Train and evaluate all supervisors in direct and indirect communication models and provide guidelines for the appropriate style switching
	☐ Provide guidelines on different national work orientations, ranges of cultural performance tolerance, and legal requirements for warnings and dismissals
Time Management Programs	☐ Evaluate design bias to supporting a "work to live" or a "live to work" mentality and reconcile
	☐ Identify different national orientations to workplace efficiency, including the time frames for task accomplishments and collegial workplace interaction, and create process to discuss and reconcile different expectations related to corporate productivity
	☐ Provide guidelines for timing of cross-national, regional, and continental meetings, be they face-to-face, electronic, or telephony, and their consistency with the local parameters of social appropriateness of business time, home time, and personal time
Team Building	☐ Identify and communicate the different styles of team development and leadership as legitimate within different national environments, including but not limited to autocratic, democratic, and interdependent self-directed styles
	☐ Provide global diversity profiles of national political, social, and corporate leaders, listing their specific competencies that supported their success with applications to leadership and the corporate mission and vision
Supervisor Training	☐ Identify key employee motivators within varied cultures and script options for supervisors in motivating and directing subordinates in egalitarian, hierarchical, or interdependent environments as appropriate
	☐ Outline the appropriate cross-cultural feedback styles for different SSI profiles and reconcile with the corporation's preferred style

Time

- 45 minutes

Materials

- Copies of "Global Diversity Perspectives in Training Design"

Directions

- Engage participants in a discussion on the connection between global diversity and training.
- Review each training topic on the list and discuss how each of the suggested expansions broadens the concept of diversity.
- Consider each topic and check whether your company has initiated the same or similar changes in your training design and delivery.
- Form into groups and discuss your company's successes in implanting a training strategy that addresses global diversity.

Questions for Discussion/Consideration

- What types of training programs are most conducive to including a global diversity perspective?
- What types of training programs will make it difficult to include a global diversity perspective?
- Which topic areas need to be addressed immediately to bring a global diversity perspective to your company?

Caveats, Considerations, and Variations

- This exercise can be used by any trainer for a global diversity audit.
- Be sure to create a good business case for global diversity as you begin to redesign your training and development programs. Design changes can be costly, and all changes should be clearly associated with benefit to the company.

Diversity-Inclusive Training Design

Designing for flexibility and inclusiveness illustrates a respect for diversity. Use the "Globalizing the Training Design Process" checklist to identify what you might change in order to make global diversity a subtext of all corporate training.

The questions on the checklist identify traditional stages within a standard training design. Check which aspects of these items exist within your current process. Consider those that you have not checked and explore how your design teams can reconcile these other perspective with your current state to enhance your ability to design, deliver, and evaluate training for your diverse employee base. Recognize that these statements represent extremes or polarities. Which box sounds more like your company? What can you do to reconcile it with the other box?

Suggestions for Using
"Globalizing the Training Design Process"

Objectives

- To identify how current designs and programs align with a specific diversity orientation
- To approach program design from the position of a global diversity dilemma that needs to be reconciled
- To identify which phase of the global design process needs to be addressed to increase the receptivity of global participants

Intended Audience

- Training and development professionals, managers, and HR professionals involved in training and development policy and implementations

Time

- 45 minutes

Materials

- Copies of "Globalizing the Training Design Process"

Directions

- Engage participants in a discussion on the eight phases of effective training design.
- Explain that each phase has an internal design dilemma that needs to be reconciled to create a successful global diversity design. Tell participants to choose which aspect of each dilemma best expresses how your company currently functions and to place a check in the appropriate box.
- Tell them to review and prioritize the eight phases in the order in which they need to be redesigned to be more inclusive of a global diversity perspective.
- Have participants form small groups and discuss their responses and prioritization. Each group should identify three action items that will begin the process of creating inclusive global diversity designs.
- Bring everyone together for a large group discussion.

Questions for Discussion/Consideration

- What types of dilemmas are your design teams facing as you attempt to bring a global perspective into all training?
- What specific phase of training design needs to be overhauled in order to be more effective in increasing global diversity in the company?

Globalizing the Training Design Process

Directions: Review the polarities in each stage of the design process and consider your current process and its range of inclusiveness. Check off which box best describes your current and/or preferred response. Consider how you might adjust your process by reconciling the differences to become more inclusive of diverse perspectives.

1. What We Might Need (Assumed Problem)	☐ Information stems from senior managers or those who hold influential or authority positions; data-collection tools use corporate HQ language and approved categories; formats are low-context (check-off boxes, scales, and so on); limited quantifiable data collected through e-mail/pulse surveys sent off to unknown evaluators.
	☐ Information globally sought for individuals crossing levels and reflecting diversity of nations, regions, and civilizations; respondents use their first or most expressive language to communicate; high percentage of face-to-face interviews surfacing in-depth data; balance of qualitative and quantitative data; information provided to trusted staff.
2. What We Have Found (Analysis and Confirmation)	☐ Headquarters or departmental leadership directs/controls analysis; reviews data for conformity to standards of global training objectives or models; seeks universal issues facing the company and less the particularistic issues of a nation, division, or unit; convergence preferred.
	☐ Analysis process always incorporates different and broad national perspectives and regionalized objectives; divergence valued; analysis widely shared, seeking additional feedback before completion; modes of interpretation are broad; analyzed through multiple national cultures to discover nuances of similarities, differences, and specialized perspectives.
3. What We Will Do (Intervention Identification)	☐ Range of possible interventions parallel headquarters' established plan; "We don't do that type of training in this company"; issues discovered by worldwide (HQ) guidelines and lenses; fiscal restraints set by corporate; regional interventions are massaged by expatriates to conform to "back home" models, weakening local impact and supporting mono-cultural training orientation.
	☐ Identification processes balance corporate with national training needs and are open to different requirements; local resources highly valued in intervention identification and may be more valued than headquarters.'
4. How We Will Design It (Design)	☐ Designed internally or by headquarters-endorsed vendors in country other than country of delivery; driven by worldwide vendor contracts and cost containment; focus on tangible outcomes linked with economic results; reflects mandated headquarters learning style, which is seen as an absolute so that all employees are exposed to the same data and act the same way.

Globalizing the Training Design Process (continued)

	☐ Locally designed and adapted programs reflecting national or regional preferred presentation styles and their subcultural constituents; creates a both/and learning style that responds to the tools, processes, and behaviors that best enable participants to learn; adjusts to local learning style as well as components that reflect the corporate global style; uses local case studies and role plays in addition to program–appropriate global material; reconciling process of local and corporate culture always a part of the design process and in-session design.
5. How We Will Organize (Administration)	☐ Training only involves authorized training staff; walk in, set up, walk out; low-context announcements of events, e-mail needs assessments, no personal contact before training; limited prework—people are too busy; disconnected with the business.
	☐ Senior managers are present and supportive; out-of-session time (coffee time, formal meals, evening social events) as important as in-session time; interpersonal component highly valued through selective telephone interviews and personalized invitations; high-context data gathered through interviews; close alignment of sending managers and training subordinates with accountability to manager, business goals, or learning goals.
6. Who Will Do It (Staffing)	☐ Training conducted by headquarters staff in official language only or by approved consultants and vendors who have been endorsed.
	☐ Training conducted by diverse staff from multiple locations capable of communicating in the most effective language and other necessary languages.
7. What We Say About It (Reporting, Level I, II Evaluation)	☐ Reports data points fitting the needs of global training reports (headcounts, number of programs, cost per person); pictures presented in glossy training document/company newsletter that indicate what "we" did; participants report they learned what was in the training box.
	☐ Reports on global diversity intellectual capital and what was the enhanced learning from the training event; align new learnings with the global diversity context of participants, generating a spectrum of insights related to the individuals and processes in company that illustrate diversity of thought and behavior; "We learned what they wanted, but we also discovered vital leanings outside the training box because we are different and listen to each other."
8. Was It Worth It? (Level III, IV Evaluation)	☐ Training costs fit global targets; six-month outcomes show individuals using prescribed skills.
	☐ Training applied global diversity intellectual capital from another region and is being introduced in new region with positive, measurable results.

- Does your training and design function have an inherent bias that is obvious from this exercise? If so, what is it? What can be done to create a greater degree of inclusion in the workplace?

Caveats, Considerations, and Variations

- This exercise can be used by any trainer for a global diversity audit.
- Training professionals who hire vendors or purchase programs can use this exercise to discern the bias of potential providers.

COMPENSATION AND REWARDS

An inclusive organization demands a global compensation system that reflects worldwide equity for employees and travels well. Without easy explanations for and execution of the wide variables in base pay, merit pay, incentives, and cost-of-living adjustments, inequities will be thought to exist, weakening the company's potential for remaining globally inclusive. Questions such as: "Why does the expatriate Japanese plant manager in Tennessee rent an upscale home and send his kids to private school, when the duel salaries of my husband and me barely meet our needs?" can easily come up and must be answered.

An inclusive compensation system enhances a company's ability to position itself with competitors, transfer employees across borders, maintain a diverse group of strategic leaders, recognize individual contributors, and build morale.

Traditional expatriate administration provides indicators as to what a worldwide system might look like. Ideally, it includes one global policy that uses a companywide base pay, with adjustments for the local national competitive standards of similar industries. To that figure, national adjustments can be added that correct the cost-of-living variances due to the economic and social environments of nations, as well as all national compliance issues, such as social security, government health programs, workers' compensation, and so forth.

While these calculations are straightforward and formulaic, the components that relate to motivation and performance are influenced by national culture. They also allow for the greatest abuse due to favoritism, nepotism, and forms of corruption. If we are going to pay for merit, what constitutes merit? What cultural standard of merit do we use? Is it the completion of the job to the specification of the job analysis—that is, staying in the box—or the demonstration of skills and outcomes that exceed expectations? Is a lump sum dollar award more motivating to the Argentinean plant manager or would she rather receive a level advancement with incrementally increased compensation? Cultural analysis is needed to create the best system. One size does not fit all, and the imposition of headquarters' cultural model is not the most effective way to demonstrate diversity. Attention must be given to the worldwide use of stock options, restricted stock grants, stock appreciation rights, phantom stock, and cash incentives, as well as cooperative saving plans that would provide educational endowments for children or home ownership. These tools are well-accepted in many developed nations, but mechanisms have not been established to create equity among worldwide employees. Without this equity, the perception of discrimination will undercut the gains in workplace inclusion.

SUMMARY

With the rapid expansion of companies in the late twentieth century, worldwide organizations developed quickly but without sufficient consideration for inclusivity of others' cultures, behaviors, and thoughts. Corporations felt that their strong homegrown corporate culture would be sufficient to address hiring, training and development, and compensation worldwide. During the past fifteen years, many companies have experienced the downside of this assumption. What remains unclear is the degree of loss in staff, market position, and profitability when a company fails to reconcile the thoughts, structure, behavior, and systems of the workforces of other nations and civilizations. The twenty-first century may tell a different story if we begin to allow reverse diversification to occur. We can all learn from the vast array of business expertise and insight contained in the distinctive styles of our global workforce. Most global corporate systems will have to be redefined to accomplish that goal.

This chapter has provided a review of a few of the systems that affect global diversity. By beginning with these systems modifications, global diversity practitioners can begin the process of change.

Notes

1   Friedman, T.L. *The Lexus and the Olive Tree* (New York: Farrar, Straus and Giroux, 1999).

2   Fears, D. "Diverse and Divided—Black Community as Foreign-Born Population Grows, Nationality Trumps Skin Color," *Washington Post*, February 24, 2002, p. A01.

3   Wagne, C.G. "Transmigrants: Living in Multiple Cultures," *Futurist*, 2000, V18, N34, p. 5. www.meridianglobal.com

CHAPTER 8

Managing Performance
in an International Workforce

Global performance management systems (GPMS) range from "one-global-process-fits-all-nations" models—sometimes expressed as, "If we do it this way at home, it's good enough over there!"—to a set of loosely connected, dissimilar models that have no value outside of their national borders. This chapter will provide information and exercises to help companies understand global performance management systems that allow both local integrity and global inclusiveness—the key elements of a corporate initiative. We will also examine the national and civilizational dimensions of the SSI Model and their relationship to performance management.

CORPORATE CULTURE BIAS

Managers' national preferences always influence the style and structure of their performance reviews. This is true even when there is a universal, headquarters-mandated system. How many managers, international or national, complain about the headquarters model and later "do their own thing" behind their office doors? Managers, whether expatriate or local, who do not have broad cross-cultural and global diversity exposure will remain in their own cultural comfort zone and use the home-country approach. Such behaviors, unwittingly fueled by one's nationality or civilizational heritage, open the door to discrimination. Some corporate training departments have decreased rater bias through mandated training programs that align diversity, skill building in cross-cultural communication, and global awareness training. Notwithstanding these efforts, the design of performance management systems may retain cultural biases. Both the personal and the systemic issues need to be addressed.

Some companies adamantly believe that a universal and standardized performance management process guarantees fairness, a value that American and British nationals unquestionably share. This approach has been partially successful in companies where large numbers of home country expatriate managers transferred the corporate culture and implanted their performance management process. Managers installed these "foreign" systems in the "field" with only cosmetic cultural changes. This approach pushed the discriminating biases deeper. You cannot incorporate diversity into the business if you do not allow it to surface and be acknowledged. Those systems rewarded the employees whose profiles best suited the universal headquarters' profile, rather than that of the region. Unfortunately, corporations have done little to identify what they have to gain in intellectual capital if they use a performance management system that allows local and national styles to surface, be used, and ultimately be introduced in other locations or business units. Just as we transfer products across borders, a GPMS should allow for the transfer of performance capital as well as the diversity lessons of a global workforce.

A WORD OF CAUTION

Underlying these incongruities are national and civilizational orientations that define the very nature of work and the future of an individual in a corporation. The social democratic perspective of a laborer in East London is very different from the capitalistic point of view of a trader on Wall Street or the factory worker in a state-run joint venture in Shanghai. As discussed in Chapter 9, these values have a major impact on the corporation. Before designing or conducting a GPMS audit, managers and HR professionals should understand the value of work in their respective national environments by using a tool such as the "Performance Management Quick Check."

THEMES FOR RESOLVING
CULTURE AND DIVERSITY

Global diversity within a GPMS will manifest in the areas listed in the tool and described in the following text. Evaluate employee reactions to your current process to see if it reflects the appropriate levels of reconciliation.

Performance Management Quick Check

Directions: The following perspectives should be present when you conduct any performance management activity in a global company. Review the status of your own thinking before beginning the chapter.

OK	Needs Work	Performance Management Quick Review
		Balances achievement-focused and non-achievement-focused employee behavior
		Understands the influence of role and status within the manager/ subordinate relationship
		Resolves tension between an individual recognition system and group-centered acknowledgements and rewards
		Considers past performance while balancing current competency and future needs of employee and company
		Aligns accountability to self/the individual with responsibility to the company/the collective

Balancing Achievement-Focused and Non-Achievement-Focused Employee Behaviors

In performance systems, employees are measured by the successful completion of discrete activities, the fulfillment of additional requirements contained in a developmental or performance plan, and the alignment of individual productivity with appropriate global corporate targets, be they increased profitability, expanded market share, or cost reduction. Did the employees do what they were expected to do, did they do it in the time allotted, and did their performance reach the quality or service standards expected by the organization?

In the United States and England, achievement is highly valued and is fueled by a competitive work environment as well as by the ever-present measuring card of Wall Street and the City. In collective societies such as Japan, Brazil, and India, employees value interpersonal affiliation. Thoughtfulness toward fellow workers, skills for reconciling conflict and creating harmonious environments, and the ability to "fit in" and support senior management are indicators of accomplishment. The spiritual traditions of Confucian, Buddhist, and Hindu beliefs support this drive to seek harmony in the workplace. Spirited competition is secondary to collaborative cooperation.

Tools such as 360-degree feedback surface this tension in global companies. Americans on assignment in collective societies, as a rule men more than women, receive mixed performance reviews. From the U.S. headquarters' perspective, expatriates are rewarded for their individual contributions and results. From the Asian perspective, they are seen as nonresponsive and impersonal and are judged as self-serving and having little or no long-term commitment to the local organization. The expatriate is seen as declining to identify with the local group.

A performance management process requires a balance that reconciles different orientations to achievement and affiliation. Some global or international workers will be identified as "high performers" or "overachievers" since their cultural heritage or personality suggests success is attributed to exceeding expectations. Many Euro-U.S. global companies support this standard. Other employees, who respond to their more affiliated or group-oriented national business cultures, do not perform to those standards. They respond to their own cultural environment and run the risk of being seen by others as "underachievers." How do we reconcile this tension? This is a difficult impasse, since both employees function from their preferred cultural assumptions and feel the support of their national and regional environments. Both are correct. Managers in charge of career development need to carefully examine their corporation's performance management tool for its bias toward achievement or nonachievement indicators. Competencies need to reflect both achievement and affiliation.

Consider the following process to examine your performance management system:

1. *Choose three different civilizations and a nation in each of those civilizations.* Seek out a national in your company and ask him or her: "Who are three national employees that you see as successful? What qualities do they have that signal they are successful? Are they recognized and valued?" Contrast the responses from each country. What are they and how do you reconcile the differences? Does your current performance management tool bring these values to light? What changes can be made to help it do so more efficiently?

2. *Examine your corporate newsletter or magazine for profiles of the most successful employees.* What behaviors are most frequently described? Is there a consistency of style—and, if so, does it align with a specific national culture and civilization? Does this create a sense of inclusion or exclusion for other nationals? What could be done to resolve these differences?

3. *Identify a person from each of the SSI civilizations and identify one characteristic behavior that supports achievement.* What is the similarity? What does that suggest to your corporation?

Repeat the exercise, but this time explore behaviors that support affiliation. Compare your findings and discuss implications for a performance management process.

Understanding the Influence of Role and Status Within the Manager/Subordinate Relationship

National business styles parallel their "at home" social and cultural orientation to class, hierarchy, and status. For example, in the first moments of a conversation, many British professionals can identify differences in accent that can trace a person's origins to within thirty kilometers of his or her birthplace. Assumptions related to social class, education, upbringing, and religion are entrenched in those identifications. In the United States, educational institutions confer status on their graduates. For example, a young Wall Street employee received his education through the New York City community colleges. He became aware that he would never advance to the highest levels in a financial institution because he did not attend an Ivy League institution, whose alumni network could provide access to firm leadership as well as influential clients. Few organizations openly espouse status and class, yet those dynamics are present and create unequal hierarchies within the workforce. Issues of gender are very pertinent to this discussion, too, as many cultures maintain male-dominated hierarchies and networks.

Economists have also created status hierarchies by classifying nations as first-, second-, or third-world countries. Currently, business communities define the world in terms of developed and developing countries. Civilizations have extended hierarchical patterns by using ethnicity and religion as the triggers. Many Middle Easterners express allegiance first to fellow Muslims, then to any Arab, and later to non-Muslims. In China, descendants of the Han people see themselves as racially higher than other minorities in China and appreciably higher than whites or blacks. These hierarchical orientations can negatively affect employee relations. However, hierarchy can also have a value.

In Asia, South America, Central America, and Mediterranean Europe, hierarchy has a positive connotation of reciprocal accountability and responsibility that supports the business community. For example, in Asian corporations, the "tea woman," usually a female employee hired to serve refreshments to senior executives, models the social hierarchy of server and served. She attends to the managers, who in turn provide for her, displaying a paternal responsibility for her well-being. In contrast, American companies flatten this hierarchy where possible. They depersonalize the "tea service" by installing a coffee room where employees can brew their own drinks from an overengineered German-designed coffee machine. There is no longer a human touch or remnants of a reciprocal service hierarchy in this egalitarian environment. All that remains is a system that impersonally distributes the product—a double-skim latte.

Failure to recognize the implications of role, status, and hierarchy within performance reviews leads to poor and ineffectual outcomes. The greater the orientation toward hierarchy within a culture, the greater the power of a manager to control the manager/subordinate relationship. Such control can be positive or negative. When negative, the employee may never feel free to challenge a manager, or even to talk competently with a manager about issues related to performance. An Asian employee may never blow the whistle to some regulatory board when he or she sees unethical or questionable practices.

On the other hand, when role, status, and hierarchy are positive, the employee feels nurtured and well-coached. Less hierarchical cultures enable employees to communicate their thoughts without fear of reprisal from those in authority—a quality theoretically inherent in the U.S. and U.K. models. Highly egalitarian performance reviews require flexibility with regard to a different culture's orientation to status and hierarchy.

Most performance models from the United States favor an egalitarian approach to status. Transferring a GPMS based on an egalitarian perspective into a collective corporate environment creates tension. Egalitarian managers will be intolerant of behaviors that support collective and hierarchical behaviors. Hierarchical and risk-averse employees would be rated lower by their individualistic and egalitarian managers because they did not speak up during the performance management process. Giving negative or corrective feedback best illustrates the consequences when managers misjudge the impact of status and hierarchy. Subordinates hearing their manager's negative feedback may uncritically accept it, since the boss said it, and "the boss must be right." Later, the employee may resign due to the loss of face that resulted from failing to meet the expectations of a manager and the fear that others will know.

Consider the following to examine your performance management system:

1. *Who has the "status" in your corporate performance management process?* How does that status reflect the headquarters environment or a local environment's orientation to hierarchy? How does that status distribution enhance or diminish communication for employees from different civilizations and nations? What needs to change to reconcile this inconsistency?

2. *What national culture does your performance management system's structure favor?* What national culture struggles most with your current system? What needs to be reconciled to support those employees?

3. *How does your current performance management system offer flexibility so that multinationals can feel comfortable regardless of their class, status, or position in the hierarchy?* What programs and processes exist in your corporation to address the wrongful uses of class, status, and hierarchy? What design changes are required to make it more inclusive?

Resolves Tension Between an Individual-Focused System and a Group-Focused System

Western employees value recognition and acknowledgement. In Western civilization, Maslow's theory of personality development concludes in self-actualization, a quality that the psychologically oriented U.S. society looks at almost as an endowed human right. Collective societies, such as China, Japan, India, and the countries of Southeast Asia and the Middle East, consider the highest developmental level as individual integrated into a group—be it a family, a work unit, or the broader social community. This dissimilarity surfaces when structuring recognition and rewards. In China, during the late 1980s and early 1990s, it was difficult to collect the proper data in order to structure rewards. Chinese employees who worked in American joint ventures were encouraged to discuss their personal accomplishments. Managers needed to probe the Chinese subordinates to identify their contributions. They would not answer directly. They preferred to talk about what their group did. Chinese are taught from childhood not to call attention to themselves, because of the strong Confucian aversion to self-directed praise. They are trained to submerge individual achievement within the group. The state-owned communist economic model reinforced the belief that the "we" was more important than the "I."

Self-effacing behavior by a British or American employee would signal a failure in self-esteem, an inability to acknowledge personal worth, and ultimately a lack of professional confidence. The developmental plan for such an employee would mandate personal growth programs before he or she could advance to another position.

What are the ramifications for structuring a GPMS? Most performance systems focus on the identification of individual accomplishment. Collectivist managers and employees, such as those of Asia, South America, Central America, and Southern Europe, would be rated less competent than would their colleagues in individualistic environments, because they do not communicate their personal accomplishments. Their nonassertive nature does not serve them well in a self-affirming U.S. or Western European corporate culture.

The process is more difficult if a same-country national is able to "adjust" and "communicate" in an individualistic-centered style or speak impeccable English, although that employee may not demonstrate the appropriate competency to perform the job. Others wonder why that person receives a higher rating and reward. The manager does not identify the underlying performance issues because of the linguistic comfort zone or halo effect surrounding the employee who matches his or her linguistic or cultural profile. What is the diversity loss to the company? The employee who is underperforming but linguistically competent advances. Another employee, whose aptitude and knowledge could add to the global intellectual capital of the company, either plateaus or is dismissed.

The converse is also true. The overly confident employee, frequently a U.S. expatriate prone to the word "I," requires continuous probing to identify success factors that are a function of a group's behavior. From an Asian manager's perspective, this employee's developmental plan would mandate group skills training, if not humility coaching. Corporations provide managers with group skills training to resolve conflicts related to corporate culture, cross-functional disconnects, and managerial disputes. Today, corporations mandate that senior executives attend domestic diversity training, partly as protection, partly as a tool to increase competency in working with differences. Few corporations, though, train global managers in the diversity that is created by the differences in national style or the interface of civilizations.

Consider the following to examine your performance management system:

1. *Is there a bias toward individualism or collectivism within your corporation's performance management system?* What national style does that bias favor? What other national styles will be automatically excluded? What concrete actions should be taken to balance individualism and collectivism in order to enable broader inclusion of currently excluded employees? Who needs to be involved to create that change?

2. *When conducting a performance review and hearing "I" conversations, what questions should a manager ask to guide a strong individualist into seeing his or her behaviors in terms of "we"?* Within the same process, when hearing too many "we" statements, what questions could guide a strong collectivist into seeing his or her behaviors in terms of "I"? How can your corporate performance process encourage reconciliation?

3. *Do the developmental objectives of your corporate performance review have a bias toward training that supports individually focused business behaviors?* How can they be reconciled with collectively focused business behaviors? Does the developmental focus of your corporate performance review have a bias toward collectivistic business behaviors? How can they be reconciled with individualistic business behaviors?

Considers Past Performance While Balancing the Current Competency and Future Needs of Employee and Company

Human resource and personnel departments are structured differently around the world. They have dissimilar focuses, ranging from an administrative, legalistic tradition of performance appraisal to management of extensive competency-based performance systems. Appraisal systems generally focus on past performance and on how well the employee meets the corporation's operational standards—doing the job. A competency-based performance evaluation system affirms qualitative and quantitative professionalism and examines performance in light of what may be expected in the future. Many performance systems identify a percentage of employees who will be terminated because their past and present performance indicate they are unlikely to meet the company's future requirements. It is important that such employees not be excluded due to cultural bias.

Assessment systems use linear indicators of past performance—for example, number of units produced, quality standards achieved, production times met—and favor an "operational doing" point of reference. This style is highly favored in manufacturing and technically oriented corporate cultures and in low-context countries. Managers reward employees who produce tangible, verifiable, and reliable results within clear time limits.

Competency models for nontechnical positions, and for the nontechnical aspects of technical positions, focus on the innate qualities that an employee brings to the job in combination with the "doing" of the job. These models measure the intangibles that predict success, drawn from research of exemplars—employees whose past performance continually exceeded corporate expectations. Measurements may focus on the employee's ability to be "collaborative," "a proactive problem solver," or "a perspective-taking contributor." Competencies focus on the "here and now" abilities and project them into the future staffing needs of the company.

The question, "Where would you like to be in this company in two years?" demonstrates a corporate bias toward the future. In Western companies, the question is common. Future-oriented organizations want to exploit an employee's desire for advancement. At the same time, employees want to know their future. If there is not a future for them in the company, the wise employee will seek new employment.

In contrast, the Vietnamese worker in an American firm as well as many other South Asian and South and Central Americans would respond differently. The Vietnamese worker expects the *manager* to know where the next step will be. In the employee's eyes, it is the manager's role to tell the employee what is needed to be successful. In U.S. culture, managers want the individual to think creatively or "out of the box," develop competencies for the corporation's future, and set their own developmental goals. In most countries in Asia, employees receive recognition by fitting into the set plan—the box, as it were. It is a position of living in the "here and how"—a durable Buddhist ideal. Bias toward self-directed and future-focused career planning is a point of reference in the United States. Global performance systems need to balance focus on the past and leader dependence with future-focused individual independence.

Consider the following to examine your performance management system:

1. *Review your competency definitions.* Tally the number of words that describe activity, that is, the "doing" of the person, and the number of words that describe the "being" of the person. Rewrite those competencies to bring the doing and being into balance.

2. *How often do managers and subordinates talk of past performance during the interview?* How is current performance reviewed? How is future performance determined? Is it the same in other regions in your company? Where is the bias, and how can it be reconciled?

3. *Examine all corporate and regional communications that describe the company and its activities.* Using local, regional, and global viewpoints, what are the differences and similarities? Is there a bias toward the past, present, or future? Is there a correct balance that respects both the national cultural orientation to time and corporate global requirements?

Aligns Accountability to Self/the Individual with Responsibility to the Company/the Collective

By definition, culture creates social patterns and structures preferred responses. For example, few Asians perceive their personal identity outside of a relationship. When functioning in the workplace, the Asian worker is very aware that his or her actions are not unique but reflect on the manager, his or her co-workers, and the company as a whole. A group identity, established in the formative years of family and school, is extended to corporate affiliation and workplace relationships. Group harmony is a core value, and therefore conflict is averted. Unfavorable communication is guarded, and civility is encouraged.

In the United States, employees' key responsibility is to themselves, although this may be veiled under statements about the "team." For them the company is a tool for self-advancement and time-limited professional development. As parts of one of the most individualistic societies in the world, corporations in the United States spend fortunes on campaigns to secure individual commitment to the corporation. This is dramatized at the pageant-like meetings of Mary Kay employees and sales events that hire the Cirque du Soleil to motivate individuals to believe in the corporate mission. The company is seen as a group of individuals who voluntarily work together. The accountability is to the completion of the shared tasks, not to the manager, the team, or even the company. Managers and subordinates will openly communicate their ideas because doing so moves the job along. Indirectness, carefully crafted words, or fears of reprisal are generally absent. The alignment of the individual's goal with the company is more important than the interpersonal alignment of manager and subordinate that one finds in Asia and Latin America.

Many global performance systems support Western civilization's performance standard of individualism and direct communication. Be careful when global or international performance methodologies cross borders on this dimension. Missed cultural clues and misrepresentations of an employee's style can lead to inequities.

Consider the following to examine your performance management system:

1. *Review your performance management system and identify how it supports individuals or groups.* Where is the bias? Based on your findings, what would you need to change to enable it to balance accountability to the individual with a responsibility to the company as a whole? How can you have both?

2. *Review the nations where your organization works and the different national and civilizational styles of accountability to self and corporation.* Which nations are biased toward individualism? What is the value or loss to the company due to that bias? Which nationals are biased toward collectivism? What is the value or loss to the company due to that bias? What nations find it easiest to balance these two dimensions? What nations struggle to align these two dynamics?

3. *Are there specific cultural subgroups within your company that are more oriented to accountability to self or to the company?* What dimensions of the SSI Model encourage this orientation?

Each of the above dilemmas can be reconciled by identifying the underlying values that support each position. In the global context, it is not that one position is right or wrong. Through thoughtful reflection and behavior style switching, better communication can be achieved. We can promote a dialogue between the two dynamics to support the current needs of a company.

The "National and Civilizational Influences Within the Performance Management Process" exercise is structured to identify areas that need to be analyzed in your corporate performance system. By examining your corporation's programs, policies, and practices, you will be able to see your bias toward one dimension of each of the five national and civilizational perspectives discussed above. Use this tool to sketch out the areas of reconciliation in your company's performance review plan and to identify suggested action steps.

Suggestions for Using "National and Civilizational Influences Within the Performance Management Process"

Objectives

- To use five cultural perspectives to assess national and civilizational disconnects within your company's performance management system

- To apply the perspectives to current global diversity disconnects within a performance management system, policy, or local or regional standard

- To identify action steps to reconcile national and civilizational issues within your corporate performance management system

Intended Audience

- Corporate supervisors, managers, and executives exploring global diversity issues and performance management
- Any manager, facilitator, internal/external consultant, HR professional, or trainer charged with the task of creating a global diversity initiative

Time

- 75 minutes

Materials

- An overhead transparency and copies of "National and Civilizational Influences Within the Performance Management Process"
- Chart paper and markers

Directions

- Introduce the five global diversity cultural perspectives and discuss how each can be used to evaluate a company's performance management process, a specific policy, or a local or regional practice.
- Ask participants to provide one example that reflects a diversity disconnect that negatively influences the success of their company.
- Identify the core issue or values underlying those influences and how they conflict with some employees' values or professional preferences.
- Create an action step to reconcile these conflicts and create inclusion.
- Form participants into groups of five or six to share responses.
- Have a group member create a summary sheet of each influence and identify learnings to be shared with the larger group for change.
- Lead a discussion of results and make plans for needed change.

Questions for Discussion/Consideration

- What are the common disconnects within your corporation's performance management systems?
- Which global diversity cultural influences surface the greatest disconnects? In what regions of the world?
- What were some of the possible action steps suggested to reconcile the differences? What are some of the resistances to this change? What will be lost if change does not occur?

National and Civilizational Influences Within the Performance Management Process

Directions: The following five national and civilizational perspectives influence the execution and design of any global performance management process. Use them to evaluate your company's performance system, policies, and practices. Apply the questions from what you have just read and record your strongest findings in the second column. In the third column, identify the global diversity dilemma that is contained in your findings and that requires reconciliation. In the last column, list your action steps that will facilitate diversity reconciliation. Some examples are given.

National Civilizational Cultural Perspectives	Corporation's Programs, Policies, and Practices	Areas to Reconcile	Action Steps
Balance achievement-focused and non-achievement-focused employee behaviors	Managers are required to bring in a 22 percent return on investment (ROI) and exceed targets. If not, downsizing is required to meet numbers	Success is measured only in financial terms and not in terms of relationships that are primary in some cultures in building expanded market share or growth	Create regional strategies to maintain return on investment (ROI) balanced with time frames required to build increased market share through relationship building
Understanding the influence of role and status within the manager/subordinate relationship	Managers and employees are both required to complete and share performance appraisal forms, giving the illusion of equality. Belief is that managers and subordinates can openly communicate without fear of status or hierarchy		

National and Civilizational Influences
Within the Performance Management Process (continued)

National Civilizational Cultural Perspectives	Corporation's Programs, Policies, and Practices	Areas to Reconcile	Action Steps
Resolve tension between an individual-focused system and group-focused system	The more aggressive self-directed people appear to be invited into high-potential groups in contrast with people who have high people-management skills		
Considering past performance while balancing the current competency and future needs of employee and company	Some regions conduct performance appraisals (past performance) and others are focused in competencies reviews (future-focused), creating a complication in making cross-national comparisons or reference		
Aligning accountability to self, the individual with responsibility to the company, the collective	Team-based performance goals and rewards are standard and resisted by more individualistic-focused nations		

- What has been the loss to the company for not having addressed this global diversity disconnect? What will be gained by the company if one of the selected actions is carried out?

Cultural Considerations

- In high-risk-averse and high-context cultures, participants may not be comfortable in raising corporate dilemmas since they feel it will be seen as criticizing the company. If so, have participants generate issues that they know from their broader knowledge.

Caveats, Considerations, and Variations

- Instead of an individual exercise, the exercise can be done as a group. Encourage the participants to spend time understanding each cultural perspective before they begin the analysis.

- Many participants may not have international experience or experience of global diversity. Participants can use their national diversity experience. Avoid drifting into domestic diversity debates and projecting them into the global arena. Check out phrases such as "It's just like here" or "They are at the same point we were twenty years ago" for their truth as well as their inherent minimization. Do prework and prepare for this eventuality. Identify the local issues that can be rightly transitioned into global insight.

- Use cases from organizational experience and have participants analyze these using the chart.

THE FIVE-FOCUS PERFORMANCE DIALOGUE MODEL

The nucleus of a global performance review remains the real-time interaction between the manager and the employee. The Five-Focus Performance Dialogue Model takes the SSI Model of Chapter 2 and applies it to the context of a face-to-face performance review. Skill in cross-cultural communication, as outlined in Chapter 3, is fundamental for both the manager and the employee when conducting any GPMS. Each of the five areas of the Five-Focus Performance Dialogue Model will support global diversity. During each stage, the manager and employee identify parts of the diversity dialogue that will support a strong understanding of diversity.

Interpersonal Focus

The first focus acknowledges the manager and subordinate's cultures of origin and the complexity of their personal global identity, as identified in their SSI personal profile. Before a performance review, both rater and ratee should use the SSI Model to construct their own SSI profile and thus create a baseline from which they can openly acknowledge and communicate their diverse perspectives. Managers and subordinates should acknowledge their cultural dissimilarities before discussing any work-related issues. Managers frequently believe that sharing a common corporate culture precludes global diversity disconnects. They may also believe that sharing identities drawn from the internal and external dimensions of diversity, that is, sharing the same gender, race, nationality, school affiliation, and so forth, brings an immediate level of comfort. There is only limited truth to that belief. The English-speaking French manager needs to put the Korean subordinate at ease by demonstrating not only an understanding of their shared hierarchical heritages but also a respect for the differences in social behaviors between managers and subordinates. The American and the Brazilian who both received their MBAs from Wharton need to discuss a way to talk of the things they "do," that is, their performance and accomplishments—the American model in which they were both trained. They also need to talk about who they are, their "being," that is, their families and cultural interests—the Brazilian model of relationship and *jeito*.

Using appropriate greetings, monitoring the pacing of information, and setting an appropriate physical distance between manager and subordinate are a few strategies for setting the necessary tone. However, the need goes beyond external civilities. Managers and subordinates, during the opening moments of the review, need to acknowledge workplace biases and strengths that are drawn from different national performance standards. Each brings a different and valid perspective. The manager's role is to validate differences drawn from an employee's uniqueness and position them in the corporation. The employee's role is to communicate his or her experience for it to be used effectively in the company. During the initial focus of the interview, articulate and discuss the value of difference. One cannot be culturally inclusive in the global workplace without talking of difference. A tool that has been helpful is to describe a range of behaviors and state the positive outcome those behaviors have had for the company. People can communicate directly with one another whether those behaviors and outcomes are similar or different in their cultures. This type of dialogue opens the door for identifying and using differences as well as increasing the confidence of managers and subordinates to talk of difference. A manager might ask a subordinate if American directness can frequently sound like criticism in Thailand; an Indian subordinate might inquire how being quiet will be interpreted in the German-headquartered corporate culture.

Global Focus

The manager's obligation is to position the employee's work in the broader global context of the company. Many operating units and businesses have developed their own nation-centric and function-focused performance models. The best qualities of those models are frequently patched together by corporate HR in conjunction with the headquarters' model into a "global" system. Rarely do corporations have a truly global design, since the phenomenon of global companies is relatively new and little research has been done on the overall structure of global companies, much less on performance tools. Many performance management systems do not reflect the employee's contribution to the global organization per se. Instead, they emphasize the immediacy of a specific contribution to the local environment, be it a factory, a region, or a nation. This may be due to the manager's inability to identify a specific contribution or an employee's lack of interest in the importance of a contribution to the broader corporate context. When corporations fail to connect local performance with global performance, they unconsciously perpetuate intra-company regionalism and nationalism.

A manager can stimulate diversity of thought and practice. The manager first identifies a specific subordinate's contribution to the local organization. Then he or she highlights the value of that accomplishment for peers who are working in similar functions but different global settings. Doing so allows the manager and subordinate to discuss significant accomplishments, with their inherent styles, processes, and thought patterns, and consider their global application. Through this process, a manager transforms nationally generated knowledge into a potentially global intellectual resource. This is also a two-way street. The employee, by listening to other national approaches to his or her position, learns alternative performance standards that enrich the job. Applications too often stop at national borders. The inclusion of this rather simple step within a performance review will do more good than a host of global awareness programs, since it specially targets an employee's work and its transborder impact. A user-friendly data-collection system is needed to process this information across regional and national borders.

Functional Focus

The functional focus of the Five-Focus Performance Dialogue Model centers on the specifics of the employee's current position as seen in a national context. Managers who come from different cultural backgrounds or who are using material from performance management systems for promotions must understand the performance standards and styles of a specific country of operation. They must understand the context in which the performance was generated. Performance styles and outcomes are influenced not only by cultural context but also by the differences in organizational infrastructure that affect productivity. Knowing context, both hard and soft, is necessary. A line manager's projection quotas may be down, not because of management skills, but due to continued electrical outages, be they in California or Guangzhou, China. It would be unfair to label this worker "underperforming," although that's true from a numbers perspective. In actuality, the manager may have performed above the standard with limited infrastructure supports. Local managers would know this information. Global managers may not. One breakdown in global diversity thinking can occur because we assume that our home infrastructure, with its levels of education, technology, and organizational capability, exists elsewhere.

Integration Focus

The manager's goal is to highlight the way an employee has integrated his or her distinctive diversity advantage into the workplace. An open dialogue enables employees to talk about their specific contributions as expressions of their diversity. The manager and employee will discuss the most appropriate subsets of the employee's SSI profile as they relate to performance and the manager/subordinate relationship. Key to this model is the belief that one's diversity profile is an asset to the organization. The tone of the presentation is important. (Refer to Chapter 2 and the Continuum of Diversity Development.) Clearly, the manager and employee are attempting to strategically use the value of diversity in bringing out the uniqueness of the employee. The dialogue is not intended to discuss why the person's diversity has been excluded but rather to verbalize the positive assumption of inclusion. The manager encourages the employee in

- Articulating the values of the core civilization that have influenced his or her work;
- Listing effective expressions of preferred national business styles that have enhanced his or her performance;
- Communicating fulfillment of the norms and standards of the greater corporate culture;
- Linking specific skills and unique competencies learned through the employee's societal formation;
- Empowering specific social, genetic, and ethnic perspectives in the workplace; and
- Acknowledging the contributions of the employee's individual personality.

A word of caution to the manager. Before and during this focus, a manager should identify the subordinate's goals, understand the employee's SSI diversity profile, and understand where they can be reconciled within the organization. A manager is required to model and communicate commitment to global diversity. By monitoring his or her own personality, individual identification, and societal dimensions, he or she will be able to effectively engage in a performance management session.

In global companies, no one has sufficient intuitive understanding or self-knowledge. That is why being a global manager is so difficult. Managers and employees are always learning and making mistakes. They will need to rely on the constructs contained in the SSI Model to discern where biases as well as cultural strengths exist. To prepare for a performance review, each manager should identify a peer who understands the different core civilizational and national diversity of his or her subordinates. This could be a peer within the company or someone in a professional association who can serve as a coach. For example, a female Finnish white manager of a male African American employee has developed her understanding of "whiteness" based on the historical context of Nordic Europe. Before entering the performance session, she needs to speak to a white American to understand how color is understood in the United States. The Finnish manager would need to understand what "whiteness" means from the perspective of a black American before engaging in this process. Cultural context for gender would also need to be understood. For example, a Cantonese-heritaged American manager who supervises a People's Republic of China employee would need to understand why his subordinate does not consider him Asian, but rather American.

Recognition and Development Focus

Recognition mechanisms need to reflect not only national standards but also global ones. Collective societies such as Korea and Japan require group-based recognition for team members. Strongly individualistic societies such as the United States seek impersonal objective criteria for measuring success, as long as a person is recognized as succeeding or "winning." The American at a recognition meeting proudly stands to receive an award; the Chinese stands reluctantly and acknowledges the contribution of others.

Countries that are "masculine" in tone, that is, countries that are oriented toward assertiveness and materialism, such as the United States, Australia, and the U.K., encourage competitive careers and aggressive workplace performance. The employee who wins the game gets the trophy. Monetary incentives and career-advancing promotions are common recognition tools.

Countries that are more "feminine," that is, those that focus on relationship and social interdependence, such as Sweden and France, shy from competition in favor of cooperative workplace behaviors that foment stability. Rewards that support quality-of-life and work/life balance are highly valued. Flexible time, varied workplace locations, club memberships, and holiday reward trips are important. Recognition systems must be aligned with the national and cultural orientation of employees, balancing the individual and collective, masculine and feminine. Using a principle-based orientation, managers and human resource professionals need to assure the suitability of corporate reward systems.

Some nationals are comfortable with a written or oral statement of recognition and are content to manage their own development. Other employees feel affirmed when their manager sets specific goals so they know what needs to be done in a coming year. For example, a French employee may feel recognized by inclusion in an elite group, which guarantees future advancement. A Hong Kong manager may be affirmed when offered a club membership that signals to his peers that he is valued by the corporation. Employees in individualistic organizations feel rewarded by receiving higher levels of training and development that support their self-managed professional development. Employees who are collectivists value a mentoring relationship with their boss as their reward. Understanding the preferred national reward system will enable managers to provide appropriate recognition.

APPLYING GLOBAL DIVERSITY IN A PERFORMANCE MANAGEMENT SYSTEM

In the "Nordic New Co Petroleum Goes Global" case study that follows, you will meet a manager, Gunnar Halvorsen, and his direct report, Richard Chamberlain. Review the SSI Model from Chapter 2 prior to reading the case study, as knowledge of both the SSI Model and the Five-Focus Performance Dialogue Model are necessary to lead participants through the exercise that follows. By working through the exercises, participants will be able to broaden the diversity perspective that is present. Global diversity goes beyond the obvious. At play are issues that need to be reconciled, even though both "actors" in the case are middle-aged to older white males. Managers and practitioners need to develop the skills to understand much broader dimensions of diversity to determine employees' potential contributions. Equally, employees who are able to identify the unique contributions they bring are better able to support their company and enhance their careers.

Suggestions for Using the "Nordic New Co Petroleum Goes Global" Case Study

Objectives

- To determine explicit and implicit global diversity issues within a performance management session
- To apply the SSI Model as a diagnostic tool
- To assess the diversity issues operating within performance reviews
- To use the Five-Focus Performance Dialogue Model to sequence pertinent diversity insights within a performance review protocol
- To support the company in being more inclusive during performance reviews

Nordic New Co Petroleum Goes Global:
A Case Study

Directions: Read the case study below. Identify possible differences in perspectives and the reconciliation strategies that can be used in the upcoming performance review.

Richard Chamberlain was the head of an offshore unit of a larger British petroleum company that was recently acquired by Nordic New Co Petroleum (NNCP). Richard is fifty-nine and an American citizen, although he has lived in London for the past twenty-six years. He was quite successful in his career with his former British employers. Gunnar Halvorsen, a senior director for NNCP and the major architect of the acquisition, had developed a good working relationship with Richard during the due-diligence process. Richard was pleased about this relationship, as his business group was to be incorporated into Gunnar's business unit. Richard would continue as country manager and have responsibility for all of NNCP's business in the United Kingdom and Ireland. Twenty years Richard's junior, Gunnar Halvorsen has been straightforward in his approach, especially around issues of industry restructuring.

Initially, the integration process appeared to be going well. Newer EU regulations seemed to provide guidelines that facilitated major downsizing and personnel changes. After several months though, it became obvious to Richard that things were changing. The mandatory senior management meetings held monthly at the Oslo headquarters were conducted in Norwegian, although the team was multilingual. In addition, all major business communication was written in Norwegian. This limited Richard's ability to contribute, as well as to demonstrate his true value to the emerging global organization. Richard had mixed feelings when he was directed by a more senior Norwegian director to fire a British colleague in favor of a Norwegian woman expatriate. It was becoming clear that the acquiring management group was going to put its own nationals in the top positions, regardless of the experience and talents of the current staff. A senior manager also told Richard that he was not Norwegian enough, which completely dumbfounded Richard. During his years in working in Europe, no one had previously referred to his cultural style or nationality. There were also references made to his management style as "not being in line with the company." Richard was never told specifically what that meant. When Richard had breakfast with his long-time friend, Peter Fallon, the president of the American Chamber of Commerce in London, Peter commented that confronting employees with such unspecific and unclear grounds related to managerial styles could constitute discrimination.

Richard was uneasy about the way the company was developing, especially when a manager suggested the possibility of Richard taking early retirement. At the end of the month, Richard had a meeting with Gunnar for a performance review. He was worried that misunderstandings would surface in the meeting that could have significant consequences for his career and family.

Source: The material in this case is a dramatization based on data from an actual case related to Saga Petroleum of Norway.

Five-Focus Performance Dialogue Model
Nordic New Co Petroleum Goes Global

Directions: Use the following short form to practice using the Five-Focus Performance Dialogue Model. After determining the SSI profiles from the Nordic New Co Petroleum Goes Global case study, answer the following questions:

1. What are the explicit diversity issues that Richard Chamberlain will confront in his performance management session?

2. What are the hidden diversity issues that will shape Richard Chamberlain's performance management session?

3. What are the explicit diversity issues that will influence Gunnar Halvorsen's handling of Richard Chamberlain's performance management session?

4. What are the hidden diversity issues that will influence Gunnar Halvorsen's handling of Richard Chamberlain's performance management session?

5. What strategies are needed to reconcile and align diversity strengths and liabilities during a performance review?

6. How would you sequence this information in the interview?

Intended Audience

- Corporate supervisors, managers, and executives who conduct performance reviews
- Any manager, facilitator, internal/external consultant, HR professional, or trainer charged with the task of creating a global diversity initiative

Time

- 60 minutes

Materials

- An overhead transparency and handouts of the "Nordic New Co Petroleum Goes Global" case study along with copies of the "Five-Focus Performance Dialogue Model"
- Copies of the Five-Focus Performance Dialogue Model itself and the SSI Model
- Chart paper and markers

Directions

- Define each focus of the Five-Focus Performance Dialogue Model and provide examples.
- Refresh participants' knowledge of the SSI Model, highlighting the six major dimensions and associated subsets.
- Direct participants to read the "Nordic New Co Petroleum Goes Global" case study and complete the "Five-Focus Performance Dialogue Model" worksheet.
- Ask participants to form small groups to discuss questions 1 through 4 of the worksheet. Have one participant record a list of responses for each question.
- Upon completing the issue analysis (questions 1 through 4), direct participants to discuss in detail questions 5 and 6.
- Record the most comprehensive strategies that should be included in an inclusive global diversity performance review on the flip chart.
- Ask participants to use the Five-Focus Performance Dialogue Model and order the strategies as they would appear in an actual session.
- Return to the large group. Discuss their findings and the value of the Five-Focus Performance Dialogue Model.

Questions for Discussion/Consideration

- What explicit diversity issues do you anticipate within Gunnar Halvorsen's performance review of Richard Chamberlain?

- What implicit diversity issues do you anticipate within Gunnar Halvorsen's performance review of Richard Chamberlain?
- Based on the identified issues, what factors are in the best interests of NNCP, Richard Chamberlain, and Gunnar Halvorsen? Which issues should be resolved in a performance management session?
- What strategies have you formulated to resolve these issues? How should those issues be brought into a performance review?
- Using the Five-Focus Performance Dialogue Model, how would you introduce these strategies in an actual performance review?

Cultural Considerations

- The most obvious difference between Richard Chamberlain and Gunnar Halvorsen is their nationality. Participants may only wish to discuss nationality as the key diversity issue or may be limited by Richard Chamberlain and Gunnar Halvorsen being both Western white males. Help participants cross-reference these perspectives with other aspects of the SSI Model.

Caveats, Considerations, and Variations

- Participants can augment this exercise by using the "SSI Global Diversity Assessment Tool for Nordic New Co Petroleum Case Study" and the "Global Diversity Performance Management Focus Sheet," although doing so would increase the exercise's time. (Instructions for their use are given below.)
- Use the worksheet to prepare for one-on-one planning.

Suggestions for Using the "SSI Global Diversity Assessment Tool for Nordic New Co Petroleum Case Study"

Objectives

- To enhance rater analytic skills for more inclusive performance reviews
- To apply the SSI Model to a case study identifying explicit and implicit diversity issues that influence the rater and ratee relationship
- To practice resolving the most pertinent global diversity disconnects by creating inclusive strategies
- To increase inclusivity and a positive regard for global diversity in the organization

Intended Audience

- Corporate supervisors, managers, and executives who conduct performance reviews
- Any manager, facilitator, internal/external consultant, HR professional, or trainer charged with the task of creating a global diversity initiative

SSI Global Diversity Assessment Tool
for Nordic New Co Petroleum Case Study

Directions: Inclusive global diversity performance sessions begin with an accurate diversity assessment that includes all levels of the SSI Model. The following worksheet suggests how Richard Chamberlain and Gunnar Halvorsen might look at differences due to their global diversity profile.

Global Diversity Dimensions	Richard Chamberlain's (RC) Profile	Gunnar Halvorsen's (GH) Profile	Reconciling Behaviors and Styles
Civilization Orientation: (Latin American, Slavic, Orthodox, Japanese, Islamic/Judaic, Confucian/Sinic, Hindu, African, Western)			
National Identification: (Independence/Dependence/Interdependence, Inclusion/Exclusion, Functional Hierarchy, Political Structure, Social Hierarchy, Individualism/Collectivism, Distribution of Wealth, Economy, National Identity)			
Organizational Factors: (Management Status, Work Location, Union Affiliation, Division/Department, Functional Level, Seniority, Work Content/Field)			
Societal Formation: (Educational Background, Marital Status, Family Structure, Parental Status, Appearance, Recreational Habits, Personal Habits, Religion, Income, Geographic Location)			
Individual Identification: (Gender, Age, Physical Ability, Sexual Orientation, Race, Ethnicity)			

Source: Adapted from Lee Gardenswartz and Anita Rowe, *Diverse Teams at Work* (Homewood, IL: Business One Irwin, 1994); M. Loden and J. Rosen, *Workforce America!* (Homewood, IL: Business One Irwin, 1991); Samuel P. Huntington, *The Clash of Civilization and the Remaking of World Order* (New York: Simon & Schuster, 1996); and F. Trompenaars and C. Hampden-Turner, *Riding the Waves of Culture* (2nd ed.) (New York: McGraw-Hill, 1998).

Time

- 60 minutes

Materials

- An overhead transparency and a copies of the "SSI Global Diversity Assessment Tool for Nordic New Co Petroleum Case Study"
- Chart paper and markers

Directions

- Review the six diversity dimensions of the SSI Model and their subsets, identifying common examples of exclusion that might negatively influence a performance review.
- Ask participants to reread the case study.
- Introduce the "SSI Global Diversity Assessment Tool."
- Invite the participants to identify which elements of the SSI Model are most pertinent to the case study.
- Invite the participants to look through the issues related to Richard Chamberlain's global diversity profile and then those related to Gunnar Halvorsen.
- Ask them to identify specific reconciling behaviors and strategies that will facilitate an inclusive performance review and dialogue.
- Form into small groups of six and discuss participants' responses.
- Have participants identify areas of commonality and difference in their responses. Record them.
- From that list identify the three most crucial areas for reconciliation and suggested reconciling strategies.
- Return to the total group for discussion and analysis.

Questions for Discussion/Consideration

- What are the major areas of reconciliation for Richard Chamberlain and Gunnar Halvorsen?
- What are the specific diversity dimensions that should be addressed in Richard Chamberlain's performance session?
- Which dynamics are most essential to resolve for NNCP culture?
- What are the explicit and implicit dimensions of the SSI Model that will most affect an inclusive performance review?
- What specific strategies should be employed?

Cultural Considerations

- The most obvious difference between Richard Chamberlain and Gunnar Halvorsen is their nationality. Participants may wish to discuss nationality

Global Diversity Performance Management Focus Sheet
Nordic New Co Petroleum Goes Global

Directions: Based on your pre-session assessment, record in the second column the most pertinent data from the ratee's SSI profile that will affect the session. Place the information in its appropriate focus of the five-focus process. In the third column, do the same for your SSI profile. Review both columns and identify the reconciling strategy that will create a more inclusive performance management session.

Performance Review Process	Analysis of Richard Chamberlain's (RC) Environment	Analysis of Gunnar Halvorsen's (GH) Environment	Strategy to Maximize Global Diversity
1. Interpersonal Focus	Although American by birth, RC may have adopted a British style that displays itself in formality and interpersonal reserve. He could be inconsistent in communication by shifting between informality and formality.	Since manager/subordinate conversations are more open and interpersonal, GH may approach RC with a sense of egalitarian informality. While signaling Norwegian informality, behaviors may also signal a lack of respect for a professional many years his senior.	GH will begin with a formal style and respond to RC's clues of informality. Use the opening segment of the interview to model the respect for diversity of style yet encourage informality, since it aligns with NNCP's current corporate culture.
2. Global Focus	RC has strong credentials in his industry with noted success in offshore management. He has shown leadership in operating cross-culturally (U.S./U.K.) as well as directing the initial integration with NNCP of U.K. operations. RC is aware that he has contributed value to acquisition. His international experience is limited to the U.K. and the confines of the Baring Sea.	GH is recognized as the driving force in NNCP's future acquisitions as well as their overall global restructuring. He is a strategic thinker and is not afraid to make mistakes to reach a goal.	Acknowledge RC's 25-year experience in the industry and his contribution to NNCP's acquisition. Be specific. Identify several competencies. Note RC's successes that helped NNCP's global operations and expansion.
3. Functional Focus	Demonstrated managerial skills and technical competency to run an off-	Profit margins and industry conditions require reorganization in U.K. and	Affirm RC's specific contributions to the merger process. Position relevant com-

	shore business. Growing into new role as country manager for NNCP, incorporating new business units under his national direction. Becoming more comfortable with the move from more technical knowledge leadership to broader organizational managerial competency.	restructuring of all European operations under direction of Oslo HQ. Two additional acquisitions are planned for next quarter that will put pressure for an additional round of downsizing.	petencies within the emerging requirements of the U.K., highlighting RC's strengths and development areas. Identify areas of European style shifting required throughout the organization. Clarify the required style competencies for senior management leadership, regardless of national origin or location.
4. Integration Focus	Although recognized with a new position, RC is still facing changes in the requirements of the job. He has not considered retirement nor has he done any pre-retirement planning. Very unclear whether RC and wife will continue living in London or repatriate to U.S. Kids identify themselves more as British than American. Committing to NNCP's corporate culture creates a sense of starting all over with a Norwegian management group, all under forty-two.	GH is beginning to gain a reputation in NNCP for creating the emerging global strategy. He feels his contributions are being recognized. Stewarding the globalization efforts for NNCP is key to his future personal and professional success. Stimulated by working with different nationals; not married but having his first child and wants to gain some family security. Has only lived in Norway with the exception of a year's pre-university sabbatical in Thailand.	Reconcile the difference in career life cycles by seeking RC's experience. Align around family security issues. Outline the issues related to being an older executive having experienced a merger and living an extended expatriate lifestyle. Be prepared to outline outsourcing and retirement planning as well as other arrangements such as internal consulting opportunities.
5. Recognition and Development Focus	Anticipates acknowledgement of contribution as experience in former company and reviews. Feels that he has contributed to due-diligence and to initial NNCP integration. Sees self as a contributor.	Personally likes RC but not sure about long-term value in emerging organization. GH's personal compensation is aligned with NNCP's success.	Acknowledge RC's accomplishments in U.K. during initial integration. Set interim goals for personal style change for role as GM in U.K. Align RC with Norwegian management group. Define interim position with clear outcome measures. Institute intensive Norwegian language training to support communication and cultural understanding.

as the key diversity issue as well as focus on Richard Chamberlain and Gunnar Halvorsen being both Western white males. Help participants cross-reference these perspectives with other aspects of the SSI Model and other organizational dimensions such as inside/outside.

Caveats, Considerations, and Variations

- The tool can be used with the case study as a training tool for manager development.

- Guide conversation away from any discussion of cultural factoids or recitations of "do's and don'ts" related to national culture. Also, be prepared for the "national cultural expert" who makes "all-knowing" pronouncements. Continuously cross-reference national culture with other dimensions of global diversity.

GUIDELINES FOR A GLOBAL PERFORMANCE MANAGEMENT SYSTEM (GPMS)

A global performance management system must be grounded in standards of inclusiveness. It is neither a product of the country of origin nor the product of the country of operation. It does not solely focus on a national preferred orientation of its global or regional headquarters. It is much broader. A global performance management system is a distinct third entity designed to meet the needs of a global company. Its design demonstrates a tolerance for difference.

Data Collection and Analysis

Organizations cannot empower their employees if they do not know their capability. Comprehensive communication of employee data enhances diversity. The key is to reconcile the different styles that support the corporate vision.

Communication Style

Asian and Southern European employees prefer indirect communication in a performance management session. This style protects ambiguity while maintaining interpersonal face with one's manager. Their written responses will follow the cultural patterns of diffuse communication. Managers and those who review performance management documents should be trained in identifying the cultural context that is encoded in the employee's indirect written and oral communication. The fact that we speak English or German is not enough.

High-context and low-context communication patterns influence the design of data-recording devices. Employees from Japan, China, and Southeast Asia are frequently unable to comment in the "allowed" spaces or in forced-choice rating scales that are created by low-context North American or European designers. High-context communicators require additional space to include descriptive data that contextualizes their comments. Due to the manager-subordinate relationship in high-context cultures, there is a reluctance to be critical of one's superior, peers, or the organization in any written format—even when information is requested. Open-ended questions such as, "Is there anything else you would like to say" do not generate comments. "Check off" boxes or "yes—no" forced-choice ratings tend to decontextualize information. High-context communicators want to answer questions "yes" under "abc" conditions and "no" under "xyz" conditions. There is never a clear "yes" or "no" answer—always a qualification. High-context respondents do not structure thought in absolute categories, as Westerners prefer. A check box or yes—no forced-choice rating appears to their orientation as too abstract in content. Skillful managers in high-context cultures provide questions that have implied options within the question, such as, "Do you think that 'X,' 'Y,' or 'Z' best describes your attitude toward work?" By providing a series of options within the question, you can identify the truer intent of an employee.

Most Anglo-Saxon heritage European nations, the United States, Canada, and Australia, value directness. They want to get things out in the open or speak one's mind. They write their opinions so they are "on the record." Low-context people utilize small recording spaces—like Americans who excel in "bulleting" their thoughts in short, clear phrases. After all, short answers save time in writing and, as the saying goes, "Time is money!"

Rating scales contain cultural bias. In individualistic societies, employees rate everything from products to corporate morale. Pulse surveys are taken in teams and business units. These societies have a bias toward expressing personal opinion and therefore a scale, such as a Likert scale, becomes a tool for self-expression. Risk-adverse and collective societies respond differently to rating scales. They rate themselves lower, reflecting a cultural orientation to humility. They are likely to rate managers higher, following the Confucian or Latin orientation of respecting hierarchy. Cultural communication variables influence rater reliability and consequently skew worldwide tabulations favoring Western cultural bias. These scales can also be confusing to managers on a personal level. A bewildered manager once said, "Why did they love me more in Shanghai and not so much in London!"

When scales are used, it is advisable to have broader numerical ranges, like an eight-point scale, with clear behavioral descriptors for each point supporting the contextualization of each rating increment. When evaluating training programs that are "suitcased" abroad, be cautious using Likert scales. A high trainer rating in Germany may mean that the trainer demonstrated professional standards and knowledge of the subject. A high rating from Japanese participants may indicate the trainer was interpersonal and paternalistically responsive to their needs, thus fulfilling the Confucian role of teacher and student. The training may not have been helpful, but the high rating illustrates respect for the trainer as teacher. In low-context cultures, the rating will skew lower, since a person will never be seen as that first-rate.

Data-collection tools need to correct for multiple languages and dialects that exist within companies. Regardless of the level of language acquisition, employees who work in a second language require more time to prepare their thoughts. This is true in face-to-face sessions as well as in completing any written pre-work. Failure to respond rapidly does not mean a lack of professional or cognitive ability. Not all languages have the same cultural context for a word, although employees understand the meaning of the word. Race connotes skin color in the United States and contextualizes images of slavery. In Germany, the same word brings images of the Holocaust. Workers' rights mean different things in Europe, the United States, and Asia, although we can easily translate the words. However, not all words are translatable. Many concepts from American management parlance cannot be translated, such as empowerment, or even diversity.

Predistributed forms allow employees who must use a language that is their second or third language enough time to reflect on appropriate word usage or consult with others as how best to answer the questions. Responses will always be more thoughtful when the format provides space and time to respond. Before any multinational meeting, plan a session to discuss terms and questions.

How do we reconcile differences in data-collection methods and communication styles? Instrument designers should allow for variable formats as well as variable language systems to capture diversity of thought. Allow candidates to choose the language that allows the fullest expression of thought and encourage rater and ratee to struggle through the exchange. Both managers and subordinates need to adapt their oral and written styles. When managers do not acknowledge a subordinate's preferred style, they will make inaccurate judgments. When style switching is used, a manager will see that a subordinate is not withholding information but rather is being respectful.

Subordinates can also make inaccurate assumptions when they do not recognize a manager's preferred written and oral style. The employee may not understand that a manager is not expressing anger in written comments but rather is being direct and specific. Raters and ratees should consider all negative comments and search for alternative meaning and interpretation. The perceived pattern may not be negative in a ratee's cultural context and a rater can quickly address the misperceptions.

Analysis, Sorting, and Storage of Information

A performance management system supports management decisions. Comparisons are made, judgments formed, and actions taken. Bias-free information gathering and recording is essential, although it may be impossible. The French think their professionals are best since they have academic rigor. The Germans believe their certificated professionals are more technically and theoretically sound. The Americans believe their out-of-the-box or creative thinkers bring a competitive edge. Last, the Japanese believe their systems organizers provide efficiency and profit to any operation. How do we choose a standard? Is it France, Germany, the United States, or Japan? Should it be the standard of headquarters, the local region, or a third country's system? A truly global performance system brings these diverse perspectives together.

The sheer magnitude of performance-related information available from the consolidation of worldwide information is bothersome. A global standard of interpretation must include technical, interpersonal, and transcultural criteria and a system to effectively store and sort the information. Without such a standard, it is difficult to make cross-national comparisons that support the movement of staff and the development of global products. It also limits diverse contributors who can influence the growth and development of a corporation's programs, products, and policies.

Compounding this challenge are the limited number of user-friendly and multilingual technologies necessary to collect and sort this data—even if a company were able to be consistent. Do reasonable translation capabilities exist for worldwide sharing of information? Without such a system the speakers of the corporate language, be they English, German, or Japanese, become the favored candidates—a true linguistic bias. At what level and with whom is information from a performance review shared? What is the impact of excluding other levels? Answers to these questions need to be through before redesigning the infrastructure of global diversity.

Privacy issues and laws are important. National codes of privacy determine what is appropriate to share within and between national contexts, whether a paper, electronic, or verbal format. Consult with your legal department to stay current with changing rules of privacy.

Global Diversity Issues and Staffing

A company's performance management system should maintain a qualified global workforce. A question such as, "Would you like to have an international assignment?" does not have the strength of "When would you like to have your international assignment?" A global diversity-oriented performance management system requires a more comprehensive orientation to global assignments. Without a specific commitment to the deployment of nationally diverse employees in all functions of the business, a corporation institutionalizes the HQ cultural orientation or the core national cultures of the majority of the workforce in any given location. This is counterproductive to diversity. Having a nationally diverse board of directors does not make a company globally diverse; it broadens the managerial perspective of the governance group. Having expatriates managing abroad does not establish workforce diversity; it supports a diversity of perspective in the pool of potential leaders who may or may not stay in the company. Managers who integrate their experiences from another nation bring a diversity perspective to future decisions. This, however, is not the experience of most returning employees, who consistently feel their newly acquired knowledge was not valued or used. Increased opportunities for cross-national teams, multiregional projects, and short-term assignments will experientially heighten the exchange of diverse thought and styles.

Global Ethics and Performance Review

The ethics of global diversity go beyond fulfilling the legal or social requirements associated with the multiple jurisdictions in which a company operates. For collectivistic countries, ethics reflect the fulfillment of the social and reciprocal accountability between workers and the organization, managers and subordinates. The United States and continental European social democratic contracts are very different. In the U.S. model, workers value individualism and expect to have their "worker rights." In Europe, workers form work councils and sit on the board of directors to participate in mutual responsibility and collective accountability. Together, as management and labor, they resolve issues related to employment. In family-held businesses in Asia and Latin America, employees expect the senior members of the family to represent their best interests and support the workers. Ethics in such work environments reflect collective and collegial rights.

Examine the range of social contracts that exist within your firm to understand potential ethical conflicts that will arise simply because of operating in different national environments. These ethical issues surface and require resolution during many performance management sessions. How can we intentionally advocate workplace strategies in the United States to advance women to higher levels of management, yet also hire women in developing countries to function only at the lowest production levels? Lower pay or lower status in the managerial hierarchy cannot be justified by the rationale that it is not "culturally" acceptable to do otherwise. Not reconciling this issue makes performance management sessions suspect for a woman. How can we tell the Jewish man who is on assignment in Saudi Arabia to use a second passport that labels him as a non-Jewish congregant and yet, as a worldwide policy, declare that the company respects religious diversity? If this dilemma is not reconciled, any person of religious conviction and spiritual belief will suspect that the corporation does not respect religious diversity, even though it establishes prayer rooms, has religious chaplains on staff, and provides flexible time to facilitate religious observances. These fundamental ethical issues impact performance and must be reconciled.

This is never easy, nor are there facile answers. First, communicate the issues without any rush to judgment or criticism. Second, accept that ethics can be contextual or influenced by civilizational and national traditions. Try to understand why and by whom these specific behaviors are valued. Last, align these positions with the ethical system within the corporate culture. Resolution will differ across cultures. Sometimes it is just a question of additional information; other times a decision will be made to support one perspective. The "Performance Management and Ethics" sheet can be used to study some examples of corporate and local perspectives and how they can be reconciled.

Suggestions for Using "Performance Management and Ethics"

Objectives

- To increase awareness of the ethical issues consistent with global diversity performance management
- To identify major diversity disconnects that will impact a corporation's commitment to ethics and global inclusiveness
- To identify action steps to bring local and regional diversity ethical conflicts in line with the corporation's commitment to diversity

Intended Audience

- Corporate supervisors, managers, and executives who conduct performance reviews
- Any manager, facilitator, internal/external consultant, HR professional, or trainer charged with the task of creating a global diversity initiative

Time

- 60 minutes

Materials

- An overhead transparency and copies of "Performance Management and Ethics" and the SSI Model
- Chart paper and markers

Directions

- Review the SSI Model and use the worksheet to study examples of differences and some suggested strategies for resolving them.
- Identify areas where you suspect ethical disconnects exist in your corporation.
- Identify the headquarters' perspective related to these issues.
- Identify the regional or local perspective related to these ethical issues.
- Articulate the specific nature of the ethical conflict. State the issue's impact on the individuals involved, the local organization, and the company in general.

Performance Management and Ethics

Directions: Please review the SSI Model and identify areas where you suspect there is an ethical disconnect. Record what the corporation's perspective is on this issue. Next, record what the local perspective is on this issue. Identify the dilemma that needs to be reconciled. In the last column, indicate a strategy for resolution. Some examples are filled out.

Diversity Dimension	Corporate Perspective	Local Perspective	Reconciling Ethical Conflict	Strategy for Resolution
Selective hiring of black Americans to work in South Africa	Supporting international careers among black Americans; black Americans will have an easier time in adjusting; easy opportunity for advancement of black Americans	They send us black Americans because they are black but they aren't black, they are Americans	Utilizing the racial and national orientations of workers to the best interests of the company	Have clear behavioral performance criteria to determine desired business goals and how nationality and racial identity support them
Role of women in leadership roles throughout the manufacturing sectors of company	We will expatriate women to run our factories in Asian countries	Those foreign women can be plant managers since they are American but there are not any Chinese woman middle managers in the system	Identification of women at all levels of the local organization for lower or middle management positions	Review all performance data of women in the regions to identify what data prevented women from advancing and adjust

Not sending Jewish employees to Muslim countries		
Sending lesbian and partner to South America		
Intentionally sending Hispanics to Latin American countries		

PERFORMANCE MANAGEMENT AS A METAPHOR FOR GLOBAL DIVERSITY

The performance management session is a metaphor for global diversity. It rightly reflects the core of the corporate culture and its true spirit. For that reason, the competencies of the rater and the structure and style of a global performance management system must reflect global inclusiveness and cross-national respect.

Raters with a global diversity perspective should be well-prepared to meet a global standard that recognizes a proven ability to

- Mirror communication style of the ratee;
- Switch communication patterns respecting national styles in conjunction with other diversity dimensions;
- Leverage relationships to accomplish the goals of the performance session;
- Reframe questions to obtain required information;
- Provide negative feedback in a fitting manner;
- Direct corrective/developmental process for change;
- Demonstrate socially appropriate communication patterns;
- Balance individual and group acknowledgement;
- Analyze and interpret written data for cultural insight; and
- Manage others toward inclusivity and multiperspective thinking.

Session outcomes should reflect respect for and integration of diversity. Corporations can support performance management systems that will

- Recognize the diversity-enhanced contributions of employees within their national and regional context and its relationship to global success;
- Acknowledge national preferred performance patterns and how they contribute to regional success, in addition to how they enhance global programs, policies, and product;
- Communicate respect for the national pattern of communication and acknowledge how that national pattern contributes to the success of the company;
- Position the employee's unique national orientation to work and its past, present, and anticipated accomplishments within the future global development of the company; and
- Respectfully align all aspects of global diversity with the national cultures and civilizational values, allowing for regional and global cross-referencing of all societal and personal aspects of diversity, that is, race, ethnicity, gender, and sexual orientation.

We close this chapter with two exercises that should enable readers to evaluate their current skill level in conducing performance management reviews that will enhance global diversity.

Carefully evaluate your responses to the "Global Diversity Rater Competency Review" for what they can tell you about your current style and its appropriateness for others. Use the "Global Diversity Performance Review Outcome Analysis" to identity how successful you are in conducting performance evaluations that truly reflect diversity. Note your outcomes for past performance reviews and develop an action plan to increase your ability in future sessions. Although systemic change is necessary, individual change can enhance the quality and vitality of your multicultural workforce. It will create a more inclusive organization. Individual change also provides the data that will help in systems change. This type of interpersonal change agency will ultimately lead to a greater corporate spirit of inclusivity and respect.

Suggestions for Using the "Global Diversity Rater Competency Review"

Objectives

- To outline the ten most noteworthy competencies desired in an inclusive diversity performance review
- To identify the core behavioral options in each of the competencies that need to be reconciled
- To provide a self-assessment or management tool for increasing skills in managers

Intended Audience

- Corporate supervisors, managers, and executives who conduct performance reviews
- Any manager, facilitator, internal/external consultant, HR professional, or trainer charged with the task of creating a global diversity initiative

Time

- 60 minutes

Materials

- An overhead transparency and copies of the "Global Diversity Rater Competency Review"
- Chart paper and markers

Directions

- Each competency is written as a predicament that contains two descriptions that reflect the range of the diversity challenge.

Global Diversity Rater Competency Review

Directions: After a performance session, review each behavior. Check which descriptor best describes your preferred or demonstrated behaviors. Based on that data, prioritize which of the competencies will be most important to address for training or enhancement. If you feel equally competent in both behaviors, check both.

_____ 1. Mirror communication style of ratee

    _____ Able to speak in a linear, unemotional manner for low-context employees

    _____ Able to talk in metaphors, allegories, and indirectly for high-context employees

_____ 2. Switch communication patterns respecting national styles in conjunction with other diversity dimensions

    _____ Able to switch style respecting gender and religion within a national cultural pattern

    _____ Able to understand racial, sexual orientation, disability, and ethnicity implications

_____ 3. Leverage relationships to accomplish goals of performance session

    _____ Able to use formality to direct and lead hierarchically focused employees

    _____ Able to use informality with more egalitarian-focused employees

_____ 4. Reframe questions to obtain required information

    _____ Provide multiple-choice question formats to elicit responses from high risk-averse ratees

    _____ Able to express clear, focused questions for direct responses for low risk-averse ratees

_____ 5. Provide negative feedback in fitting manner

    _____ Express clear, unemotional, fact-based data for low-context employees

    _____ Demonstrate a supportive, warm, "parental" disposition when providing feedback to high-context employees

_____ 6. Direct corrective/developmental process for change

    _____ Create collaborative plan for egalitarian, individualistic, and low-context employees

    _____ Able to direct ratees who value hierarchy by setting clear objectives

_____ 7. Demonstrate socially appropriate communication patterns

    _____ Able in informal cultural environments to demonstrate familiarity and ease of appearance as equals, yet recognize different levels of accountability

    _____ Able to act in formal manner modeling cultural norms for hierarchical and leader-dependent ratees

Global Diversity Rater Competency Review (continued)

_____ 8. Balance individual and group acknowledgement

    _____ Able to identify individual accomplishments for ratees who are from collectivist-focused cultures

    _____ Able to identify collective accomplishments for ratees who are from individual-focused cultures

_____ 9. Analyze and interpret written data for cultural insight

    _____ Able to read "between the lines" for implied and understated comments of high-context communicators

    _____ Able to intuit what is "outside the lines" of linear, succinct, and low-context communicators

_____ 10. Manage others toward inclusivity and multi-perspective thinking

    _____ Able to identify personal and professional exclusion and suggest inclusive behavior modification

    _____ Able to expand monocultural perspectives in ratees to the importance of cognitive inclusion, value reciprocity, and behavioral exploration

- After each performance session, review the ten competencies and each of their two behavioral descriptors.
- Think for a moment of times in the interview when you demonstrated those behaviors.
- Check which of each pair of descriptors was your preferred behavior during the bulk of the session.
- Next, prioritize the ten competencies, beginning with 1 for your strongest in the session and going to 10 for the least-demonstrated.

Questions for Discussion/Consideration

- Which competencies were easiest for you to demonstrate? Which were not demonstrated? Why?
- Was the failure to demonstrate a behavior or competency from lack of skill or a judgment that it was inappropriate? Which competencies demonstrated this dilemma most?
- Do some of the behavior indicators favor a particular culture, subculture, or national style? What national preferred style supports those indicators? What was gained or lost during the interview by supporting those behavioral styles?

- In column two, indicate one or more examples for each objective that record positive outcomes and demonstrate inclusivity and diversity.
- Using hindsight, consider behaviors or interactions that would enable you to do something better next time.
- Consider one action that will enhance each outcome with this employee in the future or with other employees.

Questions for Discussion/Consideration

- How many objectives did you reach? Did your behavior just reach the standard or did it demonstrate true proficiency?
- Reviewing the sheet, what knowledge, skill, or competency do you need to develop to increase your ability to bring a global diversity perspective to the performance management process?
- What knowledge, skill, or competency have you demonstrated in the session that would be helpful for others to learn?

Note

1   Hamer, R. "Man Who Won Pounds 2M for Not Being a Norwegian," *Sunday Mirror*, October 15, 2000.

CHAPTER 9

You as a Tool

Leader as a Change Agent

Every concept, guideline, suggestion, and tool in this book is designed to help managers, heads of human resources, executives in charge of strategic planning, and facilitators of change move the organization toward successful management of its global efforts. Although change is inevitable, it is not always easy for people and organizations to engage in or accept. In this chapter we look at attitudes toward change in a global context, with a particular focus on national orientations to change as they may coincide or conflict with those of organizational headquarters located in a different part of the world.

Beyond reconciling national and organizational attitudes toward change, the other important objective of this chapter is to focus on the skills required to be an effective change agent. Whether one is a manager of a virtual multinational team or an executive in charge of human resources, getting employees to be truly supportive of both planned and unanticipated change is challenging. This chapter identifies the skills and competencies required to lead people successfully through changes that move the organization toward global effectiveness.

CHANGE AND HOW DIFFERENT CULTURES REACT TO IT

Whether one lives in Nepal, Peru, New Zealand, or Turkey, change is a fact of life. The speed of change and people's openness or resistance to it may vary considerably depending on cultural attitudes toward change. Regardless of the attitudes shaped by where one is reared or resides, there are a number of real-ities about the process of change that need to be acknowledged before they can be applied to moving global organizations forward.

1. Change Is the Most Basic Dynamic of Life

Change is a neutral phenomenon that is given meaning by human beings as we experience the process. The most fundamental and universal demonstration of change is the cycle of life and death, both for humans and in the natural world as well. The changing of the seasons in some parts of the world means the drop-ping of leaves, the falling of snow, or rebirth and growth of buds in the spring. Accepting change as a given in the physical world is sometimes easier for peo-ple than accepting changes that take place in organizations because these nat-ural changes are inevitable, impersonal, and beyond our control.

The manager's challenge and opportunity lie in helping employees through-out the world who are reared with different cultural attitudes toward change accept, welcome, and learn to leverage change in ways that are positive for the organization and the people who work there. At the most extreme ends of the change continuum there is the United States, a culture that is set upon fixing and tinkering with everything. Discarding the old for a better, newer version is the norm. On the other end of the continuum, Southeast Asian countries are tradition-rich. While Singapore and Shanghai, for example, continue to change and grow in dramatic fashion, their cultures still revere tradition. Regardless of one's cultural influences that shape attitudes, change is a constant presence.

2. It Is Not Uncommon for People to Have an Ambivalent Relationship with Change

Sometimes people welcome the stimulation that change brings. At other times, it is just an acceptable reality and, depending on the situation and place, loss from change can be met with deep sadness and devastation. This emotional kaleidoscope exists because human beings have conflicting needs and conflict-ing attitudes toward change and the gains and losses it brings. Life events rarely dole out only the gains without exacting some price. The couple who has a chance to relocate will undoubtedly relish the new opportunity to learn about a different culture and have a new experience. On the other hand, friends, fam-ily, and a sense of place that indicates home will change, at least for a while.

The co-existence of gains and losses, and the attempt to control more of the former and minimize the latter, are part of the reason people in the Western world often have a strong reaction to the change process. Energy is invested in shaping one's life toward improvement. Eastern philosophy, which is consis-tent with detachment and greater acceptance of life events, may have a more accepting reaction to change in general. But in Southeast Asia the importance of tradition is a certainty. Maintaining cherished customs and honoring history can make employees more wary of dealing with change in today's fast-paced world.

Managers can help employees by having conversations that shed light on the complexity inherent in change and the gains from working through it. The exercise in this chapter entitled "Actual vs. Expected Gains and Losses from Change" will help people deal with this reality and, ultimately, move forward in a healthier way.

3. Change Serves as Both an Energizer and a Stressor

Change is primarily about physiological and psychological adaptation for all human beings, no matter their culture. When people have to adapt, they expend their physical, psychological, and emotional resources, all of which increases stress. Even positive, desired changes take energy and adaptation. The job promotion that takes a person from Hong Kong to London can be a wonderful opportunity and a thrilling, rejuvenating experience, but it will still be stressful to adapt to new surroundings, people, time zones, accents, languages, and a host of other realities day in and day out.

4. Change Is Often Viewed as a Threat to Security

Whether people like their jobs and their lives or not, most have adapted to their existing reality. They know the figurative landscape. Whether that reality is glorious and fulfilling, defeating and frustrating, or a combination of experiences both positive and negative, the familiar is a known commodity and therefore comfortable. Change requires losing the comfort of the status quo and making a conscious effort to create a different reality. Creating a good balance between change and homeostasis can make the process a struggle. A major part of a manager's job is helping people deal with changes that are viewed as a threat to security, a disruption of the comfortable.

Sometimes the issues are in fact a threat. Maybe someone will lose a job and her livelihood through the proposed merger between Detroit and Stuttgart. Sometimes, just the fear of job loss produces unnecessary anxiety. In either case, a sensitive manager can help employees see the difference between perception and reality and support them to shore up their sense of security in order to accommodate to whatever ongoing change will inevitably come.

5. Change Presents Opportunity for Growth and Learning

If one can get beyond the fear of loss, the stress of disruption, and the chaos and loss of equilibrium from uncertainty, there are tremendous opportunities for development and learning at both an organizational and an individual level. The ability to move beyond fear and to develop confidence and skills is one of the biggest benefits of change.

- What information did this give you about the range of views toward change?

- What was your biggest surprise? Insight?

- What other attitudes toward change did you hear from co-workers? How can these beliefs be helpful to you?

- What will you do to help yourself, the team, and the organization through this process?

Cultural Considerations

- Pay particular attention to attitudes toward change shaped by national culture.

Caveats, Considerations, and Variations

- If done onsite, count people off in small groups and use 18" x 24" wall charts of "Actual and Expected Gains and Losses from Change." Put information up; share in small groups first and then with the whole group.

- As a facilitator, make certain that gains and losses receive equal time. You don't want to create a negative, hopeless spiral.

The process of having employees at all levels of the organization assess their gains and losses on the emotional playing field is important. What is never level are the attitudes toward change that we inherit in part because of where we were born and reared. Fons Trompenaars,[1] in *Riding the Waves of Culture,* helps us understand these different responses to change.

CORPORATE CULTURE STYLES AND CHANGE

Trompenaars categorizes responses to change by patterns of behavior that show both cultural similarities and differences. These distinctions indicate national cultural tendencies and have implications in a global environment.

The four cultures Trompenaars describes are

1. The Family;

2. The Eiffel Tower;

3. The Guided Missile; and

4. The Incubator.

While most national cultures lean toward one style more than another, they are actually more mixed than singular in style. Each of these "ideal" types has a typical response to change that can be a harbinger of what to expect regarding cultural norms of a corporate headquarters managing a global change process.

As was mentioned in the opening paragraph of this chapter, everything in this book points toward change. In prior chapters, we have presented information about cultures, how to manage global conflicts, how to build teams over distance, and how to be culturally sensitive when creating performance management systems. These and other concepts and tools were designed to help create more resilient, productive, humane organizations. What we have not done until now is look at the process of change itself and see the intersection of the individual human response to change with a national culture's predisposition. Looking at types of responses to change that one can expect in different parts of the world can help a change agent not only better understand the corporate attitude toward change, but also anticipated responses from remote locations. The Trompenaars typology provides a framework for understanding widely different responses to the change process.

As you read the "Corporate Culture Styles and Change" model, think about your company's various locations and see whether this information seems to fit.

As you look at each of the descriptions of archetypes in the model, try to get a sense of where the headquarters culture of your organization fits. Then look at some other areas of the globe where your company has operations. Think about different changes that teams, divisions, or business units have been involved in. What different attitudes toward change were present within a particular problem-solving or decision-making group? How were these different views toward change reconciled? What conflicts were caused specifically by different attitudes toward change? Fill out the "Reconciling Conflicts Based on Different Cultural Responses to Change" sheet. Doing this analysis should lend some insight into the relationship between culture and change and how it operates in your organization.

Once you have finished this quick scan of the organization's efforts at change, the next logical step is to focus on the leadership, because leadership is often the critical difference in making change happen. Why are some changes implemented and why do they work well? Why do some results seem so disappointing? What is the role of the leader in having a change effort go one way or another? What behaviors make a critical difference in creating successful change? Identifying important change agent behaviors is the next step.

ESSENTIAL CHANGE AGENT BEHAVIORS

Whether one uses an internal change agent or external, the outcomes of a change process are often linked closely to the person facilitating the change. The change agent has to be savvy enough to understand the overall culture of the organization and astute enough to realize that a multinational organization with operations in Malaysia, Ireland, and Venezuela will be dealing with multiple

As you read this chart, think about your various locations and see if this information seems to fit.

Characteristics of Type of Corporate Culture	Examples of Nationalities That Fit Here	Response to Change
Family Culture Hierarchical Strong emphasis on the personal; almost familial relationships Leader seen as caring parent who knows what's best for subordinates Strong sense of tradition, customs, "in" jokes, and family stories Hard to break into this culture	Greece Italy Spain Japan Singapore South Korea	Change in a family model culture is political, requiring the key players to create change and modification A leader who has charisma, new visions, inspiring goals, and builds real and vital relationships is apt to make change happen
Eiffel Tower Culture Emphasizes roles, functions, responsibilities, all of which are prescribed in advance Hierarchical (supervisor oversees task function and manager oversees supervisor) Each higher level has a clear and demonstrable function holding levels beneath it together Role is more important than person who holds job; people are replaceable but role is not Personal relationships not valued; they distort judgment and create favoritism, bringing too many exceptions to the rule	Germany Austria Denmark	Resists change until inevitable Change comes through changing the rules Complex and time-consuming to keep up with constant changes necessary Requires rewriting of manuals, job descriptions, procedures Eiffel Tower values constancy and stability; does not take kindly to restructuring

Corporate Culture Styles and Change

Source: Adapted from Fons Trompenaars, *Riding the Waves of Culture* (Burr Ridge, IL: Irwin Professional Publishing, 1993, 1994, pp. 152–179).

Characteristics of Type of Corporate Culture	Examples of Nationalities That Fit Here	Response to Change
Guided Missile Culture		
How one performs and what one contributes is the number one value	United States Canada United Kingdom	Change comes quickly
Egalitarian		Target moves so what one works on or what goals have been set change regularly
Impersonal		Loyalty is to field of work (architecture, science, technology), profession, or project, not company, so people have little hesitation to leave one job for another if the reasons to do so are right
Task-oriented		
Purpose behind everything is to persevere in strategic intent and reach target		
Focus on tasks typically undertaken by teams or project groups		As one goes from project to project, bonds dissolve and new ones are formed for next task
Jobs more flexible in that employees respond to what is needed at the time		Ties are not close, deep, or of long duration; there is no expectation of permanent work relationships
Draw on professionals; cross-disciplinary		
Incubator Culture		
Exists for individual fulfillment and self-expression	Sweden United States Silicon Glen in Scotland or a few other places in the English-speaking world	Cultures that thrive in startups but rarely reach maturity
Personal		Fast
Egalitarian		Spontaneous
Little to no structure		Culture of people on same wave length searching for solutions to shared problems
Sounding board for new innovative ideas		
Frees individuals from routine so they can be creative		Problem always open to redefinition
Minimal hierarchy		

Corporate Culture Styles and Change (continued)

Reconciling Conflicts Based
on Different Cultural Responses to Change

Locations Involved	Conflicts Caused by Different Attitudes Toward Change	How Conflicts Regarding Change Were Reconciled
Example: United States, Japan, and Greece	Japan and Greece will have change driven from top down and strongly influenced by ties and hierarchy; in United States, change can be driven from anywhere, even bottom up; egalitarian and quicker, more focus on task	Focus on outcomes and manipulate the system in various locations; in Japan and Greece, working with key people is critical; in the United States people matter, but speed and task completion matter more

national cultures as well. Going back to Trompenaars' descriptions of four national cultures, a consultant will have to respond very differently in a location that has a Family culture, which is strongly tied to tradition, and an Incubator culture, where every idea is open to revision and redefinition. The only "tradition" in Incubator cultures involves the lightening speed of change, while Family culture is tradition-rich and resistant to shedding rituals. In looking at the complexity of what it takes for a change leader to shepherd an organization or a functional unit through any complex transition process, identifying skills that are essential is a starting point. Be honest in your self-assessment as you read through these behaviors. Make a mental note of where you currently feel competent and where developmental opportunities exist.

The literature on change suggests that the leader, manager, CEO, or principal change agent is the most critical variable for a successful change effort. Think about change initiatives you have been involved in, ones that worked and ones that did not. On the "Leader Behaviors" chart below, make a few notes about what behaviors created successful change and which behaviors blocked it. After making the two lists, read the fifteen behaviors that follow and compare your experience with these actions that lead to successful change.

Leader Behaviors

Leader Behaviors That Helped Create Change	Leader Behaviors That Blocked Change

1. Enrolls Others in a New and Compelling Vision.   If you are going to ask employees to go through the disruption and chaos of change, it is important to show them something enticing that may well justify their efforts. In cultures that are resistant to change, this may be difficult. While you show something new and better, you will also clearly need to articulate and identify pieces of the sacred past or traditions that will remain intact and be honored. To pursue something new and better is good so long as all the pieces of the familiar are not lost. As a vision is articulated, spelling out ways it will be helpful to the world, the company, or one's particular unit is central to having people eagerly participate. Speaking to the most central points of meaning for those involved in implementing the change is a good way to make the vision compelling and enlist people's spirit.

2. Inspires Commitment for the Work Ahead.   Change journeys are long and there are untold obstacles along the way. When energy and commitment become low, which they inevitably do, the change agent who can inspire commitment will refuel the sagging spirits of employees who wonder whether all the effort is worth it. Keeping people focused on the end point and tying employees' emotional energy and drive to a goal is essential to getting through the low points. This is probably most easily done in Family cultures that rely on inspiration or Incubator cultures where change is rapid and constant.

3. Makes a Clear Case for Change with Equally Clear Benefits for All.   The change agent who can speak the language of all the stakeholders involved will gain an edge in being successful. This means really understanding what is at stake, in both potential gains and losses, for every part of the organization involved in the change. Being able to use the values, images, metaphors, and symbols that speak differently but in equally relevant ways to people on the shop floor and executives at strategic levels, or in different locations with different attitudes and degrees of openness and receptivity to change, is a critical skill that can make or break the success of a change initiative. While benefits for change can be presented in all four of the Trompenaars models, the one that most naturally fits this idea is the Guided Missile culture.

4. Understands Sources of Employee Fear and Resistance.   Human beings as a species like homeostasis. Biologically, we are not creatures who seek out disruption and discontinuity. Change, at both a conscious and subconscious level, leaves us always looking at the gain and loss continuum. The potential losses can create paralysis. For example, any employee involved in creating change that streamlines functions wonders, "If we redo our systems and create more efficiency, will I still have a job?" "If we move all of our operations in this unit to Puerto Rico because it is cheaper for the company but I live in New Jersey, will I have to move or lose my job?" A good change agent is sensitive to these fears and anticipates the resistance. The Eiffel Tower culture would make the change regardless of people's reaction and not worry so much about the New Jersey employee, nor would the methodical Guided Missile culture. In different ways, the Family culture and the Incubator culture would at least notice and care about replacement and displacement possibilities. There's a good chance that answers to the human dilemma would be found, or at least investigated.

5. Behaves Empathetically to Allay Those Fears. It is one thing for a change agent to understand the source of the fears. It is a whole different thing to actually behave to allay the fears. Empathy, the ability to understand, articulate, and acknowledge another person's reality, is a critical skill in any culture. It enables people to bond and build relationships across a lot of different realities. The case of a woman who headed an HR function in a global organization stands out. While she was not a formal change agent, she had responsibility for carrying out the downsizing function. Her job was to let employees know they were laid off. When we asked how tough a job that was, her response was memorable. She acknowledged the emotional challenges she faced giving people the dispiriting news. What made her feel better were the countless notes she received from employees who thanked her for her empathy and understanding in having to carry out a very tough job. Good change agents, internal and external, do not lose sight of the human response to very human needs.

6. Can See the View Equally from the Top Floor or the Basement. The ability to see reality from different vantage points demonstrates objectivity and makes empathy and cross-fertilization possible. The Japanese parable of *Rashomon* is the story of three different versions of the same reality. All three stories are true, depending on each seer's vantage point. A successful change agent is able to access the different views and help bridge the differences that exist due to level in the organization, function, and responsibility. Making all these different realities important in the decision-making process is essential to making good decisions and to having people feel that their views and desires are reflected in the change process. The objectivity of the Eiffel Tower and Guided Missile cultures makes these two corporate cultures quite able to do this. The lack of hierarchy in the Incubator culture makes levels less important.

7. Cultivates Key Relationships and Networks at All Levels of the Organization. Who you know can always make a difference. Good relationships influence outcomes at both a personal and a strategic level. There is no substitute for good will, respectful relationships, high trust, and bonding. If people are reluctant to embrace a particular change that is going to be implemented in hierarchical organizations, a powerful leader or manager can make a difference.

Particularly in Family cultures, the relationship makes the critical difference. In flatter organizations, often the key difference between being willing to invest in a change effort or giving up is the relationship people have with the person advocating change. This is not uncommon in Incubator cultures. People on the same wave length listen to one another and can be influenced by each other. While personal relationships are less relevant in Eiffel Tower and Guided Missile cultures, they nevertheless do matter because relationships influence results and results matter. There is no place in the world where having good relationships is not helpful. They are always a competitive advantage. A strategic thinker in the Guided Missile culture knows this.

8. Demonstrates Courage in Telling the Truth Even If the News Is Bad. Having the courage to be real and honest with people about organizational realities is central to creating long-term, trusting relationships. One need only look at organizations like Enron or Tyco International to see the damage that a lack of honesty and transparency creates. In relationship-driven cultures, coming through on commitments and having words and deeds match cements bonds. Even in the Eiffel Tower or Guided Missile cultures, where relationships are less central, trust and honesty count. Being courageous enough to tell the truth can sometimes create short-term pain, but the long-term gain is worth it. There will be different ways to give this feedback and share information, as was indicated in Chapters 4 and 8. Adapting methods of giving feedback to be culturally appropriate is important if one wants to be heard. Telling employees what they need to hear, not necessarily what they want to hear, demonstrates respect for an employee's ability to come through and is also a way of indicating that the employee is valued enough to hear the straight story. Not talking down to people or treating them as though they can't handle the truth is a way of having them rise to the highest expectations. This communication can be managed, albeit differently, everywhere.

9. Is Open to and Invites Alternative Ideas and Viewpoints. The idea of exploring many options and having a change agent or manager actually solicit these various points of view works best in an Incubator culture. It can work in a Family culture where there is new vision, but in a more limited way, because the person in authority rallies people to a particular viewpoint. An effective change agent or manager in an Eiffel Tower or Guided Missile culture focuses on outcomes and accomplishment. If new ideas produce better results and the task is accomplished in a satisfactory way, these new ideas and options will be welcome.

10. Anticipates the Consequences of Change and Is Proactive in Mitigating Negative Outcomes. Thinking ahead leads to accomplishing results that leave the organization better after the change than before the process started. The Sierra Leonean proverb "He who upsets a thing should know how to rearrange it" comes to mind. The impact of change should be a clear plus for the organiza-tion and as much as possible for the people who work there as well.

Sometimes the organization's goal to increase profits, for example, conflicts with a union's goal in some parts of the world to give substantial increases in salary and benefits to employees. If unions are paramount in Germany but nonexistent in South Carolina, any change that impacts both locales has to be thought out very carefully. While they have different interests at stake, to come to a mutually satisfying outcome it is necessary to anticipate the problem issues, work with the people in your network, call on all those relationships built over time, and work together to minimize the negatives. The strategic thinking of the Guided Missile culture meshes with this approach.

11. Is Politically Savvy. The most overtly political culture is the Family culture in Trompenaars' model. Relationships and history dominate the culture. Who knows whom, who affiliates with whom, who feels included, and who is excluded are all part of this strongly relational, very political organizational cul-ture. In the Eiffel Tower and Guided Missile cultures, task, productivity, and pro-ject completion are primary, but people still influence these processes. Who has the necessary information, who shares it and who holds it close, who is picked for an exciting new project or held back on an old one—all can be highly polit-ical. A savvy manager or change agent will pay attention to all the unstated dynamics and watch the informal networks. Who is in favor, who is out of favor, and the difference this information makes to accomplishing the change takes an astute observer of interpersonal dynamics. It also helps to have inter-nal employees who will share organizational history.

12. Uses Facilitation Skills Effectively. The ability to work skillfully with human dynamics, how people behave together in groups, is a subtle but very important skill. Successfully orchestrating these dynamics for task accomplish-ment is no small feat. Managing the interpersonal interactions through processes and agenda design is a useful skill for achieving desired outcomes in a plural-istic environment. The ability to structure processes that help people organize, gather, and disseminate information, give and receive feedback, solve problems, make decisions, and implement change while evaluating and monitoring the new structure is enhanced by a facilitator who can create interaction, run effec-tive meetings, and maintain objectivity.

Facilitation involves not only breaking the change process down into steps, but also means detecting the unspoken thoughts or feelings that employees may be reluctant to surface. Good facilitation is an essential skill in creating a feel-ing of buy-in and harmony at the end of the process. While the personal rea-sons for paying attention to good facilitation will be less compelling in Guided Missile or Eiffel Tower cultures, effectively utilizing and leveraging the talents and skills of employees always adds value.

13. Manages Own Biases and Assumptions.   Every human being has biases and makes assumptions. Some have an Eastern civilization view of the world, while others have a Western orientation. Some people may have a spiritual bent to life that is Buddhist, while others may favor a Christian spirituality. Some people may feel safe and comfortable with anyone who speaks their language, no matter where they are from, while others may make negative assumptions and feel frustrated by people who speak their language with an accent. These and many more cultural biases and preferences exist.

In addition to our biases, we make assumptions about people based on the meaning we assign to their behavior. The problem here is that we can be very wrong in our interpretations. The Dutch and the Swiss are very direct in communication style. If company headquarters are in the Netherlands and a senior manager from the Hague makes it to Brazil once a year, his directness could be difficult for Brazilians to bear. From that limited experience, Brazilian employees may make assumptions about the Dutch in general. The reliability of these assumptions is open to question based on such limited experience. A good change agent knows that his or her assumptions influence behavior and knows further that the best way to make certain they do not exert inappropriate influence is to be aware of and manage them.

14. Is Flexible and Adaptable.   A change agent has to be willing to model the change he or she advocates while helping the group implement a change process. If a change agent is facilitating a well-designed session and unplanned issues boil up to the surface, the emerging and pressing issue takes precedence. The agenda has to be modified to suit the real issue. If a group is embarking on one path and receives new information that causes a change in direction or a rethinking of a problem definition, an effective change agent changes course. This new view will not pose a problem for an Incubator organization but could be more difficult for others, particularly one steeped in tradition.

A good change agent, in addition to being flexible, understands the culture of the organization. For example, when working with a global entity steeped in tradition, a change agent demonstrates adaptability by building on that tradition and acknowledges its strengths as he or she leads people through a process of finding areas where adaptation would be beneficial. Through language and metaphors, using examples, and designing agendas, change can be gracefully implemented. Being fluid is essential in global organizations.

15. Has Clear Expectations Around Accountability and Rewards.   If one is managing change, at the outset, a good manager lets the team or task force know what their charge is, what the stakes are, and for what and by when they will be held accountable. The rewards and consequence will also be spelled out. Sometimes rewards are a celebratory dinner, comp time for people over the next six months, complimentary letters in a file, or compliments in the company newsletter or intranet. Many options are available. Rewards should be tailored to the people and location, not be one-size-fits-all.

The change agent needs enough clarity to help the group meet its expectations. He or she also needs enough knowledge about culture in general, the organization in particular, and the specifically involved individuals to suggest appropriate rewards. In Eiffel Tower and Guided Missile cultures, the change agent will need to be vigilant in acknowledging and rewarding well-met expectations in appropriate ways.

As you review these fifteen change agent behaviors, which are your biggest strengths? Which are your biggest areas for development? Most successful change agents can access all fifteen of these behaviors in certain circumstances. Take an honest look at how skillfully and frequently you administrate each by responding to the "Essential Change Agent Behaviors" checklist. The idea is to identify areas for your own growth and development. It may be helpful to ask for feedback from someone who has seen your work as a change agent. Comparing your self-assessment with another person's picture of you adds dimension and depth to the diagnosis.

Suggestions for Using "Essential Change Agent Behaviors"

Objectives

- To identify critical change agent skills and behaviors
- To assess one's own growth and development regarding these behaviors
- To determine areas ripe for growth and development
- To consider necessary style switches, depending on what national cultures you are working with and their orientations toward change

Intended Audience

- Change agents, managers, facilitators, and consultants responsible for shepherding global change

Time

- 45 minutes

Materials

- Copies of "Essential Change Agent Behaviors" for all participants

Directions

- Distribute the questionnaire online or face-to-face to personnel assessing their effectiveness in change agent roles.

Essential Change Agent Behaviors

Directions: Read each of the behaviors below. Place a check in the box that most accurately describes the frequency with which you demonstrate each of these behaviors.

Behaviors	Almost Never	Rarely	Sometimes	Frequently	Almost Always
1. Enrolls others in a new and compelling vision					
2. Inspires commitment for the work ahead					
3. Makes a clear case for change with equally clear benefits for all					
4. Understands sources of employee fear and resistance					
5. Behaves empathetically to allay these fears					
6. Can see the view equally from the top floor or the basement					
7. Cultivates key relationships and networks at all levels of the organization					
8. Demonstrates courage in telling the truth, even if the news is bad					
9. Is open to and invites alternative ideas and viewpoints					
10. Anticipates the consequences of change and is proactive in mitigating negative outcomes					
11. Is politically savvy					
12. Uses facilitation skills effectively					
13. Manages own biases and assumptions					
14. Is flexible and adaptable					
15. Has clear expectations around accountability and rewards					

Scoring

Almost Always = 5 points
Frequently = 4 points
Sometimes = 3 points
Rarely = 2 points
Almost Never = 1 point

Add the number of points in each category.

Points

69 to 75   High marks for change agent behavior
62 to 68   On the right track; select a few areas for development
56 to 61   Does some things well but not often enough; be more intentional in a few areas
48 to 55   Need some work; ask for feedback and coaching
15 to 47   Determine whether or not this is the line of work for you; it may not be

- Explain that these behaviors all matter at some point in the change process. Ask each participant to assess himself or herself and then assign points to the results.

Questions for Discussion/Consideration

- What does your score tell you about your strengths? Where do you need to improve?
- How does your behavior change depending on the national culture of the group?
- Identify a current group you are working with. What behavior do you need more of? Less of?

Caveats, Considerations, and Variations

- Discuss national style in response to change according to Trompenaars with regard to various locations within the organization. Determine which change agent behaviors are most critical in each location.

STEPS TO HELP GLOBAL EMPLOYEES DEAL WITH CHANGE

Once change leaders have a sense of their own skills, there are specific ways they can help work groups get through a global change process in a productive and unifying way. It is critical for managers leading change in global organizations to maximize their impact using both high tech and high touch. Use the following suggestions to embark on such a journey.

1. Spend More Time with People, One-on-One or in Groups. Being visible when you are onsite, accessible, and available counts a great deal in a time of change. When you lead people through the chaos of change, they need to understand why it matters, that is, how it will improve things, and they must believe they can impact the outcome. In part, that belief is tied to having a connection with a change agent who is seen as understanding, caring, empathetic, and available. Availability on remote teams is possible if someone is determined to be responsive. Getting back to people promptly on e-mail or whatever methods a group chooses can have a very positive effect on a group.

2. Do Not Underestimate the Usefulness of Technology as a Communication Tool. When in-person contact is limited by time and distance, technology can be an ally. Use an intranet website where employees have twenty-four-hour access to information about the change, giving answers to the most frequently asked questions, for example. Set up an anonymous hot line where people can express their views, voice frustrations, and make requests. Use chat rooms for a discussion arena where people can find support and help one another in moving productively through change.

3. Keep Walking in Other People's Shoes. There is no substitute for sensitivity, empathy, and understanding when nudging employees through a change process. Sometimes it takes patience to listen to people's fears, frustrations, and aggravations. Showing empathy and understanding is a labor-intensive exercise, but frequently, in the subtle and not so subtle resistance that often accompanies change, the ability to articulate the feelings of others is what allows many people to let go of their resistance and move forward. People need to feel understood and supported. Empathy and understanding go beyond arguments for why change is beneficial. It helps people at the emotional or heart level, and this level is where energy for change can be effectively generated.

4. Engage in Processes That Enlarge People's Perspectives. It is not uncommon for human reactions to change to be mostly negative. One of the things a good change agent can do in person or online is help an employee see both the upside and downside. Yes, there will undoubtedly be loss in the transaction. There always is with change, but there are always gains as well. Using the sheet "Actual and Expected Gains and Losses from Change" presented earlier in this chapter, or any process that encourages exploration of the complex outcomes of change, will be helpful. Having people actually identify what they, the team, and the organization stand to gain is often a very good antidote to the almost reflexive resistance that occurs.

5. Be Mindful of the Larger Context in Which the Change Is Taking Place. Change never occurs in a vacuum. What is going on in an industry, in the world geopolitically, or at various geographic locations in a global organization can all impact receptivity to proposed changes the organization is trying to implement. If the economy is fragile, if unions are active, if religious intolerance is spreading, the attitudes of employees in different parts of the world may be more or less open or more or less engaged. As a change agent, there is little you can control. Most of the macro issues that impact organizations and relationships across borders are well beyond the purview of a change agent. But change agents have to be aware of these realities. Sometimes, this means the launching of an initiative has to change, perhaps temporarily be put on hold. Sometimes, how it is pitched to others has to change. The point is, to paraphrase the English poet John Donne, no organization is an island. The successful change agent notices all the background noise.

6. Be the Change Agent You Want to Create. This phrase borders on being a cliché, but the idea of being authentic and modeling the behavior others are asked to follow is not a cliché at all. There is no substitute for practicing what one preaches. There is no culture or nationality that does not recognize the hypocrisy of a double standard. A change agent, leader, or manager who is asking others to adapt to new global realities had better be the first one doing the adapting. Being bold in living the desired change will get people's attention. From watching leader behavior that models the change, others will climb on board with less fear and more confidence. They will see that leadership has faith in and believes in what they are asking of others. Modeling the desired change one sees has an unmistakable air of integrity. There is no substitute for boldly being that change.

This book has been written to help global leaders, managers, and HR professionals deal with the complexity of change in their many different locations and realities around the world. *The Global Diversity Desk Reference: Managing an International Workforce* has provided a model (the SSI Model) for viewing complex global organizations. Further, it has offered information about culture and specific managerial functions in global operations. The specific tools to use onsite or at remote locations will help teams and work groups function well in a dispersed world. You as the manager, HR professional, or change agent have enormous capacity to influence and shape the process of cultural integration and reconciliation as different world views operate across borders on the same teams in the same organizations. The task could be daunting, but while it is demanding, it is also full of opportunity. Diversity can be leveraged, change can be harnessed—a person and a team at a time. The tools in this book are your allies. They will help you forge conversations and dialogue that enhance respect, encourage relationship building, and ensure accomplishment of the organization's objectives. The breadth of knowledge, information, and interpersonal skills required to do this work well can be humbling. The possibilities are also exhilarating. By intentionally and strategically using your knowledge and experience and by adding information and strategies from this book to your repertoire of skills, you can make a very positive difference in the demanding and exciting challenge of global business.

Note

1 Trompenaars, Fons. *Riding the Waves of Culture* (Burr Ridge, IL: Irwin Professional Publishing, 1993, 1994, pp. 152–179).

PART FOUR

RESOURCES AND APPENDIX

RESOURCES FOR MANAGING GLOBAL DIVERSITY

Books

Global Diversity Management

Adler, Nancy. *International Dimensions of Organizational Behavior* (3rd ed.) (Cincinnati, OH: South-Western, 1998).

Bartlett, Christopher, and Sumantra Ghoshal. *Managing Across Borders: The Transnational Solution* (2nd ed.) (Cambridge, MA: Harvard Business School Press, 1998).

Baytos, Lawrence. *Designing and Implementing Successful Diversity Programs* (Englewood Cliffs, NJ: Prentice Hall, 1995).

Berge, Zane L. (Ed.). *Sustaining Distance Training: Integrating Learning Technologies into the Fabric of the Enterprise* (San Francisco, CA: Jossey-Bass, 2001).

Black, Jay, Allen Morrison, and Hal Gregersen. *Global Explorers* (New York: Routledge, 1999).

Brake, Terence, Danielle Medina Walker, and Thomas Walker. *Doing Business Internationally: The Guide to Cross-Cultural Success* (Burr Ridge, IL: Irwin Professional Publishing, 1995).

Duarte, Deborah L., and Nancy Tennant Snyder. *Mastering Virtual Teams: Strategy, Tools and Techniques that Succeed* (2nd ed.) (San Francisco, CA: Jossey-Bass, 2001).

Elashmawi, Farid. *Competing Globally: Mastering Cross-Cultural Management and Negotiations* (Houston, TX: Gulf, 2001).

Elashmawi, Farid, and Philip R. Harris. *Multicultural Management: New Skills for Global Success* (Houston, TX: Gulf, 1993).

Elashmawi, Farid, and Philip R. Harris. *Multicultural Management 2000: Essential Cultural Insights for Global Business Success* (Houston, TX: Gulf, 1998).

Fatehi, Kamal. *International Management: A Cross-Cultural and Functional Perspective* (Englewood Cliffs, NJ: Prentice Hall, 1996).

Ferraro, Gary P. *The Cultural Dimension of International Business* (3rd ed.) (Englewood Cliffs, NJ: Prentice Hall, 1997).

Friedman, Thomas. *The Lexus and the Olive Tree: Understanding Globalization* (New York: Anchor Books, 2000).

Gardenswartz, Lee, and Anita Rowe. *Managing Diversity: A Complete Desk Reference and Planning Guide* (2nd ed.) (New York: McGraw-Hill, 1998).

Gardenswartz, Lee, and Anita Rowe. *Diverse Teams at Work* (Alexandria, VA: Society for Human Resource Management, 2003).

Gorman, Carol Kinsey. *Managing in a Global Organization: Keys to Success in a Changing World* (Los Altos, CA: Crisp Publications, 1994).

Hallenbeck, George, and Morgan McCall, Jr. *Developing Global Executives: Value Systems for Creating Wealth* (Boston, MA: Harvard University Press, 2002).

Hampden-Turner, Charles, and Fons Trompenaars. *The Seven Cultures of Capitalism* (New York: Currency/Doubleday, 1993).

Harris, Philip, and Robert Moran. *Managing Cultural Differences* (5th ed.) (Houston, TX: Gulf, 2000).

Hofstede, Geert. *Culture's Consequences: International Differences in Work-Related Values* (Thousand Oaks, CA: Sage, 1984).

Hofstede, Geert. *Cultures and Organizations: Software of the Mind* (New York: McGraw-Hill, 1991).

Huntington, Samuel P. *The Clash of Civilization and the Remaking of World Order* (New York: Simon & Schuster, 1996).

Katsioloudes, Mareos, I. *Global Strategic Planning: Cultural Perspectives for Profit and Non-Profit Organizations* (Oxford, England: Butterworth-Heinemann, 2001).

Lewis, Richard D. *When Cultures Collide: Managing Successfully Across Cultures* (rev. ed.) (Yarmouth, ME: Intercultural Press, 2000).

Lewis, Richard D. *The Cultural Imperative* (Yarmouth, ME: Intercultural Press, 2002).

Marx, Elizabeth. *Breaking Through Culture Shock: What You Need to Succeed in International Business* (Yarmouth, ME: Intercultural Press, 2001).

Mead, Richard. *International Management: Cross-Cultural Dimensions* (Cambridge, MA: Blackwell Business, 1994).

Mockler, Robert J., and Dorothy G. Dalogite. *Multinational Cross-Cultural Management: An Integrative Context-Specific Process* (Westport, CT: Quorum, 1997).

Moran, Robert T., David O. Braaten, and John Walsh. *International Business Case Studies for the Multicultural Marketplace* (Houston, TX: Gulf, 1994).

Moran, Robert, Philip R. Harris, and William G. Stripp. *Developing the Global Organization* (Houston, TX: Gulf, 1993).

Moran, Robert, and William G. Stripp. *Dynamics of Successful International Business Negotiations* (Houston, TX: Gulf, 1991).

Morosini, Piero. *Managing Cultural Differences: Effective Strategy and Execution Across Cultures in Global Corporate Alliances* (Oxford, England: Pergamon, 1998).

Neal, Mark. *The Culture Factor: Cross-National Management and the Foreign Venture* (Basingstoke, Hampshire, England: Macmillan Business, 1998).

Odenwald, Sylvia B. *Global Training: How to Design a Program for the Multinational Corporation* (Alexandria, VA: American Society for Training and Development, 1993).

O'Hara-Devereaux, Mary, and Robert Johnsen. *Global Work: Bridging Distance, Culture, and Time* (San Francisco, CA: Jossey-Bass, 1994).

Phillips, J.J. *HRD Trends Worldwide: Shared Solutions to Compete in a Global Economy* (Improving Human Performance Series) (Oxford, England: Butterworth-Heinemann, 1998).

Phillips, Nicola. *Managing International Teams* (Philadelphia, PA: Trans-Atlantic, 1992).

Rhinesmith, Stephen H. *A Manager's Guide to Globalization: Six Skills to Success in a Changing World* (2nd ed.) (Alexandria, VA: The American Society for Training and Development, 1996).

Ricks, David A. *Blunders in International Business* (Cambridge, MA: Blackwell, 1993).

Rosen, Robert, Patricia Digh, Marshall Singer, and Carl Phillips. *Global Literacies: Lessons on Business Leadership and National Cultures* (New York: Simon & Schuster, 2000).

Schell, Michael S., and Charlene M. Solomon. *Capitalizing on the Global Workforce: The Strategic Guide for Expatriate Management* (Burr Ridge, IL: Irwin Professional Publishing, 1994).

Schneider, Susan C., and Jean-Louis Barsoux. *Managing Across Cultures* (Englewood Cliffs, NJ: Prentice Hall, 1997).

Schreiber, Deborah A., and Zane L. Berge (Eds.). *Distance Training: How Innovative Organizations Are Using Technology to Maximize Learning and Meet Business Objectives* (San Francisco, CA: Jossey-Bass, 2001).

Simons, George F. *Eurodiversity* (New York: Butterworth-Heinemann, 2002).

Simons, George F., Carmen Vasquez, and Philip R. Harris. *Transcultural Leadership: Empowering the Diverse Workforce* (Houston, TX: Gulf, 1993).

Tayeb, Monir H. *The Management of a Multicultural Workforce* (New York: John Wiley & Sons, 1996).

Terpstra, Vern. *International Dimensions of Marketing* (3rd ed.) (Belmont, CA: Wadsworth, 1993).

Tesoro, F., and J. Tootson. *Implementing Global Performance Measurement Systems* (San Francisco, CA: Jossey-Bass, 1999).

Thiederman, Sondra. *Bridging Cultural Barriers for Corporate Success: How to Manage the Multicultural Work Force* (Lexington, MA: Lexington Books, 1990).

Torp, Jens Erik, Martine Cardel Gertsen, and Anne Soderberg (Eds.). *Cultural Dimensions of International Mergers and Acquisitions* (Berlin: Walter De Gruyter, 1998).

Trompenaars, Fons, and Charles Hampden-Turner. *Riding the Waves of Culture: Understanding Cultural Diversity in Global Business* (New York: McGraw-Hill, 1998).

Cross-Cultural Communication

Bennett, Milton (Ed.). *Basic Concepts of Intercultural Communication* (Yarmouth, ME: Intercultural Press, 1998).

Berger, Mel (Ed.). *Cross-Cultural Team Building: Guidelines for More Effective Communication and Negotiation* (New York: McGraw-Hill, 1996).

Blumer, J.G., J.M. McLeod, and K.E. Rosengren (Eds.). *Comparatively Speaking: Communication and Culture Across Space and Time* (Thousand Oaks, CA: Sage, 1998).

Brett, Jeanne M. *Negotiating Globally* (San Francisco, CA: Jossey-Bass, 2001).

Fisher, Glen. *International Negotiations: A Cross-Cultural Perspective* (Yarmouth, ME: Intercultural Press, 1980).

Fisher, Glen. *Mindsets: The Role of Culture and Perception in International Relations* (2nd ed.) (Yarmouth, ME: Intercultural Press, 1997).

Fowler, Sandra (Ed.). *Intercultural Sourcebook* (Yarmouth, ME: Intercultural Press, 1995).

Gesteland, Richard R. *Cross-Cultural Business Behavior: Marketing, Negotiating and Managing Across Cultures* (Copenhagen: Handelshjikolensforlag, 1996).

Gudykunst, William B. *Bridging Differences: Effective Intergroup Communication* (Thousand Oaks, CA: Sage, 1991).

Gudykunst, William B., and Bella Moody. *Handbook of International and Intercultural Communication* (2nd ed.) (Thousand Oaks, CA: Sage, 2001).

Gudykunst, William B., Lea P. Stewart, and Stella Ting-Toomey (Eds.). *Communication, Culture, and Organizational Processes* (Thousand Oaks, CA: Sage, 1985).

Guirdham, M. *Communicating Across Cultures* (London: Macmillan Press Ltd., 1999).

Hall, Edward T. *The Hidden Dimension* (New York: Anchor/Doubleday, 1969).

Hall, Edward T. *The Silent Language* (New York: Anchor/Doubleday, 1973).

Hall, Edward T. *Beyond Culture* (New York: Anchor/Doubleday, 1989).

Hampden-Turner, Charles M., and Fons Trompenaars. *Building Cross-Cultural Competence: How to Create Wealth from Conflicting Values* (New Haven, CT: Yale University Press, 2000).

Hendon, Donald W., Rebeca Angeles Hendon, and Paul Herbig. *Cross-Cultural Business Negotiations* (Westport, CT: Quorum, 1996).

Hepworth, Janice. *Intercultural Communication: Preparing to Function Successfully in the International Environment* (Denver, CO: University Centers, 1991).

Hess, Melissa Brayer, and Patricia Linderman. *The Expert Expatriate: Your Guide to*

Successful Relocation Abroad—Moving, Living, Thriving (Yarmouth, ME: Intercultural Press, 2002).

Hodge, Sheida. *Global Smarts: The Art of Communicating and Deal Making Anywhere in the World* (New York: John Wiley & Sons, 2000).

Hofstede, Jon, Paul B. Pedersen, and Geert H. Hofstede. *Exploring Culture: Exercises, Stories and Synthetic Cultures* (Yarmouth, ME: Intercultural Press, 2002).

Kenton, Sherron B., and Deborah Valentine. *Crosstalk: Communicating in a Multicultural Workplace* (Upper Saddle River, NJ: Prentice Hall, 1997).

Kohls, L. Robert. *Survival Kit for Overseas Living: For Americans Planning to Live and Work Abroad* (Yarmouth, ME: Intercultural Press, 2001).

Leaptrott, Nan. *Rules of the Game: Global Business' Protocol* (Pinehurst, NC: Nan Leaptrott Books, 1996).

Lewis, Richard D. *Cross Cultural Communication: A Visual Approach* (Yarmouth, ME: Intercultural Press, 1999).

Maddox, Robert C. *Cross-Cultural Problems in International Business: The Role of the Cultural Integration Function* (Westport, CT: Quorum, 1993).

Mead, Richard. *Cross-Cultural Management Communication* (New York: John Wiley & Sons, 1990).

Mole, John. *Mind Your Manners: Managing Business Cultures in Europe* (Yarmouth, ME: Intercultural Press, 1997).

Nolan, Riall W. *Communicating and Adapting Across Cultures: Living and Working in the Global Village* (Westport, CT: Bergin & Garvey, 1999).

O'Sullivan, Kerry. *Understanding Ways: Communicating Between Cultures* (Sydney, NSW: Hale & Iremongerr, 1994).

Salacuse, Jeswald W. *Making Global Deals: What Every Executive Should Know About Negotiating Abroad* (New York: Random House, 1991).

Samovar, Larry A., and Richard E. Porter. *Intercultural Communication: A Reader* (Belmont, CA: Wadsworth, 1976).

Singer, Marshall R. *Perception and Identity in Intercultural Communication* (Yarmouth, ME: Intercultural Press, 1998).

Sorti, Craig. *Cross Cultural Dialogues: 74 Brief Encounters with Cultural Difference* (Yarmouth, ME: Intercultural Press, 1994).

Sorti, Craig. *Figuring Foreigners Out: A Practical Guide* (Yarmouth, ME: Intercultural Press, 1999).

Sorti, Craig. *The Art of Crossing Cultures* (Yarmouth, ME: Intercultural Press, 2001).

Summerfield, Ellen. *Survival Kit for Multicultural Living* (Yarmouth, ME: Intercultural Press, 1997).

Tanno, Dolores V., and Alberto Gonzalez (Eds.). *Communication and Identity Across Cultures* (Thousand Oaks, CA: Sage, 1997).

Thiederman, Sondra. *Profiting in America's Multicultural Marketplace: How to Do Business Across Cultural Lines* (Lexington, MA: Lexington Books, 1991).

Ting-Toomey, Stella, and Felipe Korzenny (Eds.). *Cross-Cultural Interpersonal Communication* (Thousand Oaks, CA: Sage, 1991).

Ting-Toomey, Stella, and John G. Oetzel. *Managing Intercultural Conflict Effectively* (Thousand Oaks, CA: Sage, 2001).

Turkewych, C., and H. Guerrero-Klenoraski. *Intercultural Interviewing: The Key to Effective Hiring in a Multicultural Workforce* (Halle, Quebec: International Briefing Associates, 1992).

Varner, Iris, and Linda Beamer. *Intercultural Communication in the Global Workplace* (Boston, MA: Irwin/McGraw-Hill, 1995).

Weaver, Gary (Ed.). *Culture Communication and Conflict: Readings in Intercultural Relations* (Yarmouth, ME: Intercultural Press, 1998).

Wederspahn, Gary M. *Intercultural Services: A Worldwide Buyers Guide and Sourcebook* (Managing Cultural Differences Series) (Oxford, England: Butterworth-Heinemann, 2000).

Wiseman, Richard L. (Ed.). *International Communication Theory* (Thousand Oaks, CA: Sage, 1995).

Culture-Specific Information

Althen, Gary. *American Ways: A Guide for Foreigners in the United States* (Yarmouth, ME: Intercultural Press, 1988).

Andres, Tomas. *Understanding Filipino Values: A Management Approach* (Quezon City, Philippines: New Day, 1981).

Asselin, Gilles, and Ruth Mastron. *Au Contraire! Figuring Out the French* (Yarmouth, ME: Intercultural Press, 2001).

Axtell, Roger E. (Ed.) *Do's and Taboos Around the World* (3rd ed.) (New York: John Wiley & Sons, 1993).

Axtell, Roger E., et al. *Taboos Around the World for Women in Business* (New York: John Wiley & Sons, 1997).

Broome, Benjamin J. *Exploring the Greek Mosaic: A Guide to Intercultural Communication in Greece* (Yarmouth, ME: Intercultural Press, 1996).

Clarke, Clifford H., and G. Douglas Lipp. *Danger and Opportunity: Resolving Conflict in U.S.-Based Japanese Subsidiaries* (Yarmouth, ME: Intercultural Press, 1998).

Condon, John C. *With Respect to the Japanese: A Guide for Americans* (Yarmouth, ME: Intercultural Press, 1984).

Condon, John C. *Good Neighbors: Communicating with the Mexicans* (Yarmouth, ME: Intercultural Press, 1997).

Condon, John C. (Carmen DeNeve with Paula Heusinkveld, trans.). *Buenos Vecinos: Communicandose Con los Mexicanos* (Yarmouth, ME: Intercultural Press, 1998).

Fadiman, Jeffrey A. *South Africa's "Black" Market: How to Do Business with Africans* (Yarmouth, ME: Intercultural Press, 2000).

Fieg, John Paul, and Elizabeth Mortlock. *A Common Core: Thais and Americans* (Yarmouth, ME: Intercultural Press, 1989).

Fron, Tina (Ed.). *China Practical Staff Employment Manual* (Hong Kong: Pearson Professional Publishing, 1997).

Gannon, Martin, J. *Understanding Global Cultures: Metaphorical Journeys Through 23 Nations* (2nd ed.) (Thousand Oaks, CA: Sage, 2001).

Gao, Ge, and Stella Ting-Toomey. *Communicating Effectively with the Chinese* (Thousand Oaks, CA: Sage, 1998).

Gochenour, Theodore. *Considering Filipinos* (Yarmouth, ME: Intercultural Press, 1990).

Hall, Edward T., and Mildred Reed Hall. *Understanding Cultural Differences: Germans, French & Americans* (Yarmouth, ME: Intercultural Press, 1989).

Henderson, George. *Our Souls to Keep: Black-White Relations in America* (Yarmouth, ME: Intercultural Press, 1999).

Hill, Richard. *Euromanagers and Martians: Business Cultures of Europe Trading Nations* (2nd ed.) (Yarmouth, ME: Intercultural Press, 1994).

Irwin, Harry. *Communicating with Asia: Understanding People and Customs* (St. Leonards, NSW: Allen & Unwin, 1996).

James, David L. *The Executive Guide to Asia-Pacific Communications: Doing Business Throughout Asia and the Pacific* (St. Leonards, NSW: Allen & Unwin, 1995).

Kim, Eun Y. *The Yin and Yang of American Culture: A Paradox* (Yarmouth, ME: Intercultural Press, 2001).

Kras, L. Eva. *Management in Two Cultures: Bridging the Gap Between U.S. and Mexican Managers* (rev. ed.) (Yarmouth, ME: Intercultural Press, 1995).

Kohls, L. Robert. *Learning to Think Korean: A Guide to Living and Working in Korea* (Yarmouth, ME: Intercultural Press, 2001).

Lanier, Alison R. *Living in the USA* (Yarmouth, ME: Intercultural Press, 1988).

Lasserre, Philippe, and Hellmut Schutte. *Strategies for Asia Pacific: Beyond the Crisis* (rev. ed.) (South Yarra, Victoria: Macmillan Education, 1999).

Matsumoto, David. *The New Japan: Debunking Seven Cultural Stereotypes* (Yarmouth, ME: Intercultural Press, 2002).

Morrison, Terri; George A. Borden, and Wayne A. Conaway. *Kiss, Bow or Shake Hands: How to Do Business in Sixty Countries* (Yarmouth, ME: Intercultural Press, 1994).

Nees, Greg. *Germany: Unraveling an Enigma* (Yarmouth, ME: Intercultural Press, 2000).

Nishiyama, Kazuo. *Doing Business with Japan: Successful Strategies for Intercultural Communications* (Honolulu, HI: University of Hawaii Press, 2000).

Nydell, Margaret K. *Understanding Arabs: A Guide for Westerners* (Yarmouth, ME: Intercultural Press, 1987).

Olivera, Jacqueline. *Brazil: A Guide for Businesspeople* (Yarmouth, ME: Intercultural Press, 2001).

Renwick, George W. *A Fair Go for All: Australian and American Interactions* (Yarmouth, ME: Intercultural Press, 1991).

Renwick, G., P. Pedersen, and K. Smith. *Communicating with Malaysians* (Yarmouth, ME: Intercultural Press, 2000).

Richmond, Yale. *From Da to Yes: Understanding the East Europeans* (Yarmouth, ME: Intercultural Press, 1992).

Richmond, Yale. *From Nyet to Da: Understanding the Russians* (Yarmouth, ME: Intercultural Press, 1992).

Richmond, Yale. *Into Africa: Intercultural Insights* (Yarmouth, ME: Intercultural Press, 1998).

Robinowitz, Christina Johansson, and Lisa Werner Carr. *Modern-Day Vikings: A Practical Guide to Interacting with the Swedes* (Yarmouth, ME: Intercultural Press, 2002).

Rosener, Judy B. *America's Competitive Secret: Utilizing Women as a Management Strategy* (New York: Oxford University Press, 1995).

Schneiter, Fred. *Getting Along with the Chinese for Fun and Profit* (Hong Kong: Asia 2000, 1992).

Sears, Woodrow, and Audrone Tamulionyte-Lentz. *Succeeding in Business in Central and Eastern Europe: A Guide to Cultures, Markets, and Practices* (Oxford, England: Butterworth-Heinemann, 2001).

Shahar, Lucy, and David Kurz. *Border Crossings: American Interactions with Israelis* (Yarmouth, ME: Intercultural Press, 1996).

Sheppard, Pamela, and Bénédicte Lapeyhe. *Business Across Borders: Negotiate in French and English* (London: Nicholas Brealey, 1992).

Sheppard, Pamela, and Bénédicte Lapeyhe. *The Office in French and English* (London: Nicholas Brealey, 1992).

Sheppard, Pamela, and Bénédicte Lapeyhe. *Speeches and Presentations in French and English* (London: Nicholas Brealey, 1996).

Sorti, Craig. *Old World/New World Bridging Cultural Differences: Britain, France, Germany and the U.S.* (Yarmouth, ME: Intercultural Press, 2001).

Steidlmeier, Paul. *Strategic Management of the China Venture* (Westport, CT: Quorum, 1995).

Stephenson, Skye. *Understanding Spanish-Speaking South Americans: Bridging Hemispheres* (Yarmouth, ME: Intercultural Press, 2002).

Stewart, Edward C., and Milton Bennett. *American Cultural Patterns: A Cross Cultural Perspective* (rev. ed.) (Yarmouth, ME: Intercultural Press, 1991).

Tannen, Deborah. *You Just Don't Understand: Women & Men in Conversation* (New York: William Morrow, 1991).

Tannen, Deborah. *Talking from 9 to 5: How Women's & Men's Conversational Styles Affect Who Gets Heard, Who Gets Credit & What Gets Done at Work* (London: Virago, 1995).

Tingley, Judith. *Genderflex: Men and Women Speaking Each Other's Language at Work* (New York: AMACOM, 1994).

Wallace, Paul. *Agequake: Riding the Demographic Rollercoaster Shaking Business, Finance and Our World* (Yarmouth, ME: Intercultural Press, 2001).

Wang, Mary Margaret, Richard W. Brislin, Wei-Zhong Wang, David Williams, and Julie Haiyan Chao. *Turning Bricks into Jade: Critical Incidents for Mutual Understanding Among Chinese and Americans* (Yarmouth, ME: Intercultural Press, 2000).

Wattley Ames, Helen. *Spain Is Different* (Yarmouth, ME: Intercultural Press, 1999).

Wenzhong, Hu, and Cornelius L. Grove. *Encountering the Chinese: A Guide for Americans* (Yarmouth, ME: Intercultural Press, 1991).

Winfeld, Liz, and Susan Spielman. *Straight Talk About Gays in the Workplace: Creating an Inclusive Environment for Everyone in Your Organization* (New York: American Management Association, 1995).

Articles

Adler, N., and S. Bartholomew. "Managing Globally Competent People," *Academy of Management Executive*, 1992, V6, N3.

Borkowski, S.C. "International Managerial Performance Evaluation: A Five Country Comparison," *Journal of International Business Studies*, 1999, V30, N3, pp. 533–555.

Buzzanell, P.M. "Tensions and Burdens in Employment Interviewing Processes: Perspectives of Non-Dominant Group Applicants," *Journal of Business Communication*, 1999, V36, N2, pp. 134–162.

Davidson, Sue Canney. "Creating a High Performance International Team," *Journal of Management Development*, 1994, V13, N2, pp. 81–90.

Digh, Patricia. "Crossing Borders: Thinking About Domestic and Global Diversity," *Cultural Diversity at Work*, November 1997.

Digh, Patricia. "Capitalizing on New Markets," *Executive Update*, August 1998, pp. 70–82.

Digh, Patricia. "Diversity Goes Global," *Mosaics*, January/February 2000.

Don, Wei-lin, and George William Clark, Jr. "Appreciating the Diversity in Multicultural Communication Styles," *Business Forum*, Summer 1999, V24, N3/4, pp. 54–61.

Ferner, A.Q., J. Matthias, and M.Z. Varul. "Country-of-Origin Effects, Host-Country Effects, and the Management of HR in Multinationals: German Companies in Britain and Spain," *Journal of World Business*, 2001, V36, N2, p. 107.

Gezo, T., M. Oliverson, and M. Zick. "Managing Global Projects with Virtual Teams," *Hydrocarbon Processing* (int'l ed.), January 2000, V79, N1, pp. 112C–112F.

Hambrick, Donald C., Sue Canney, Scott A. Snell, and Charles E. Snow. "When Groups Consist of Multiple Nationalities: Towards a New Understanding of the Implications," *Organizational Studies*, Spring 1998, V19, N2, p. 181.

Higgs, Malcolm. "Overcoming the Problem of Cultural Differences to Establish Success for International Management Teams," *Team Performance Management*, 1996, V2, N1, pp. 36–43.

Hofstede, G., and M.H. Bond. "The Confucius Connection: From Cultural Roots to Economic Growth," *Organizational Dynamics*, 1988, V14, pp. 5–24.

Kovach, R.C., Jr. "Matching Assumptions to Environment in the Transfer of Management Practices: Performance Appraisal in Hungary," *International Studies of Management & Organization*, 1994, V24, N4, pp. 83–100.

Lattimer, Robert L. "The Case for Diversity in Global Business," *Competitiveness Review*, 1998, V8, N2, 1998, pp. 3–17.

Lindholm, N. "National Culture and Performance Management in MNC Subsidiaries," *International Studies of Management and Organization*, 1999, V29, I4, pp. 45–66.

McDermott, Lynda, Bill Waite, and Nolan Brawley. "Putting Together a World Class Team," *Training & Development*, January 1999, V53, N1, pp. 46–51.

Mendonca, M., and R.N. Kanungo. "Impact of Culture on Performance Management in Developing Countries," *International Journal of Manpower*, 1996, V17, N4–5, pp. 65–76.

Miller, E.K. "Diversity and Its Management: Training Managers for Cultural Competence Within the Organization," *Management Quarterly*, 1994, V35, N2, pp. 17–24.

Neelankavil, J.P., A. Mother, and Y. Zhang. "Determinants of Managerial Performance: A Cross-Cultural Comparison of the Perceptions of Middle-Level Managers in Four Countries," *Journal of International Business Studies*, 2000, V31, N1, pp. 121–140.

Palich, Leslie E., and Luis R. Gomez-Mejia. "A Theory of Global Strategy and Firm Efficiencies, Considering the Effects of Cultural Diversity," *Journal of Management*, 1999, V25, N4, pp. 587–606.

Petrick, J., R. Scherer, J. Brodzinski, J. Quinn, and F. Ainina. "Global Leadership Skills and Reputational Capital: Intangible Resources for Sustainable Competitive Advantage," *Academy of Management Executive*, 1999, V13, N1, pp. 58–69.

Richard, Orlando C. "Cross-National Human Resource Diversity as Value Added: The Contingent Role of International Strategy," *Mid-Atlantic Journal of Business*, June 1997, V33, N2, p. 93.

Salk, Jane E., and Mary Yoko Brannen. "National Culture, Networks, and Individual Influence in a Multinational Management Team," *Academy of Management Journal*, April 2000, V43, N2, pp. 191–202.

Saphiere, Dianne Hofner. "Productive Behaviors of Global Business Teams," *International Journal of Intercultural Relations*, Fall 1996, V4.

Spence, L.J., and J.A. Petrick. "A Multinational Interview Decisions: Integrity Capacity and Competing Values," *Human Resource Management Journal*, 2000, V10, N4, pp. 49–67.

West, L.A., and W.A. Bogunul. "Foreign Knowledge Workers as a Strategic Staffing Option," *Academy of Management Executive*, 2000, V14, N4, p 17.

Structured Experiences and Training Materials

An Alien Among Us: A Diversity Game. Richard B. Powers. Intercultural Press, P.O. Box 700, Yarmouth, ME; (800) 370–2665. This 90-minute simulation challenges assumptions people hold about others.

Bafa Bafa: Cross-Cultural Orientation. Gary R. Shirts. P.O. Box 910, Del Mar, CA 92014; (619) 755–0272. This experiential activity simulates the contact between two very different cultures, Alpha and Beta. The activity is structured so that participants learn through direct simulated experience and then apply that learning to real-life situations.

Barnga: A Simulation Game on Cultural Clashes. Sivasailam Thiagarajan. Intercultural Press, P.O. Box 700, Yarmouth, ME 04096; (800) 370–2665. Through playing a simple card game in small groups, participants experience the effect of simulated cultural differences on human interaction. This activity is easy to run in a relatively short time.

Diversity Tool Kit. Lee Gardenswartz and Anita Rowe (New York: McGraw-Hill, 1995). This training kit in a box provides over one hundred diversity training activities in reproducible format with directions for trainers. Exercises designed to build awareness, knowledge, and skills are categorized by topic such as stereotypes and prejudice, culture, communication, and team building.

Ecotonos. Nipporica Associates and Dianne Saphiere. Intercultural Press, P.O. Box 700, Yarmouth, ME; (800) 370–2665. This simulation deals with problem solving and decision making in multicultural groups.

The Global Diversity Game. Quality Educational Development, Inc., 41 Central Park West, New York, NY 10023; (212) 724–3335. This board game is played by teams answering questions focusing on demographics, jobs, legislation, and society related to the global business environment. Cross-cultural and transnational information is highlighted, stimulating a dynamic exchange of knowledge and experience between participants.

Living and Working in America. American Media Incorporated; (800) 262–2557. This three-volume audiovisual series trains non-native speakers of English in communication skills for managing a multicultural workforce. Set includes video scenes, textbook, audiotapes, instructor's manual, and experiential activities.

The Managing Diversity Survival Guide. Lee Gardenswartz and Anita Rowe (Burr Ridge, IL: Irwin Professional Publishing, 1994). This resource provides over eighty reproducible checklists, questionnaires, and worksheets for raising awareness and building knowledge about diversity. Directions for trainers, sample agendas, and transparency masters are also included.

Multicultural Customer Service: Providing Outstanding Service Across Cultures. Leslie Aguilar and Linda Stokes (Burr Ridge, IL: Irwin Professional Publishing, 1995). This skills training handbook provides worksheets, quizzes, and case studies to train customer service staff.

Randömia Balloon Factory: A Unique Simulation for Working Across the Cultural Divide. Cornelius Grove and Willa Hallowell (Yarmouth, ME: Intercultural Press, 2001). This three-hour business simulation helps participants understand the dynamics of doing business with people who have different values.

Redundancia. Dianne Hofner-Saphiere and Nipporica Associates; (913) 901–0243. This short, effective simulation helps people understand the challenges faced by people attempting to communicate in a second language.

Assessment Tools and Instruments

The Cross-Cultural Adaptability Inventory. Colleen Kelley and Judith Meyers. (858) 453-8165.

Cultural Context Work Style Inventory. Claire B. Halverson. School for International Training, Experiment in International Living; (802) 254–6098.

The Diversity Management Survey. Cresencio Torres. HRD Press; (800) 822–2801.

Global Awareness Profile (GAP test). Nathan Corbitt. Intercultural Press; (800) 370–2665.

Intercultural Development Inventory. M.J. Bennett and M. Hammer. (503) 297–4622.

International Assessment Interview Procedures. Selection Research International; (314) 567–6900.

International Assignment Exercise. Selection Research International; (314) 567–6900.

International Candidate Evaluation. Tucker International; (303) 786–7753.

Overseas Assignment Inventory (OAI). Prudential Intercultural; (800) 257–4092.

The Questions of Diversity: Assessment Tools for Organizations and Individuals. George Simons. ODT; (800) 736–1293.

Videos/Films

Better Together than A-P-A-R-T: Intercultural Communication: An Overview. Intercultural Resource Corporation, 1997. This video features Milton Bennett outlining fundamental concepts of intercultural communication in a scholarly and entertaining style.

Building a Diverse Workforce Series. Big World Media; (800) 682–1261. This multi-part series includes videos on topics such as cultural conflicts in the EU, language and culture in evaluations, cross-cultural conflicts in global recruiting, and performance evaluations.

Chinese Cultural Values: The Other Role of the Human Mind. Intercultural Resource Corporation, 1996. In this video, George Renwick interprets the personal account of a Chinese woman and presents an analysis of four basic dimensions of Chinese culture.

Cold Water. Noriko Ogami. Intercultural Press, 1987. This forty-eight-minute video contains interviews with foreign university students and cross-cultural specialists about cross-cultural adaptation and culture shock.

The Cross Cultural Conference Room. Jaime Wurzel; info@irc-international.com. This video, DVD, CD combination presents U.S.-Americans, Japanese, and Argentineans each problem solving a case study demonstrating the cultural differences at play.

Cultural Diversity: At the Heart of the Bull. H.N. Bull Information Systems, Intercultural Press, 1992. This twenty-five-minute video, focusing on French and American employees, is designed to inform and assist in dealing with cultural diversity in the workplace.

Doing Business in China Series; Working with China Series; and *Managing in China Series.* Big World Media; (800) 682–1261. These three multi-part sets provide information on conducting business, working, and managing in China.

Doing Business in Russia Series. Big World Media; (800) 682–1261. This two-part series provides information about the why and how of doing business in Russia.

Global Scenarios Series. Big World Media; (800) 682–1261. This four-part series includes *Managing Across Cultures, The Virtual Team, The Middle East,* and *The Multicultural Meeting.*

Globally Speaking Series: Skills and Strategies for Success with Asia. Big World Media; (800) 682–1261. This series provides information on aspects such as communicating across technology, intercultural team formation, systems and meetings, and leadership when working in Asia.

Globally Speaking: Skills and Strategies for Success in Asia. Meridian Resource Associates, 1997. This six-video series focuses on building specific communication skills critical to the success of multinational organizations operating in Asia.

Going International Series. Big World Media; (800) 682–1261. This series provides information on topics such as bridging the culture gap, managing the overseas assignment, and skills for global management.

Living and Working in Singapore Series. Big World Media; (800) 682–1261. This three-part series provides information on the country, business environment, and expatriate life.

Managing in China. Meridian Resource Associates, 1997. This in-depth video series offers practical advice from over forty experienced managers sharing best practices for management and human resources in China.

Video Learning Programs. Big World Media; (800) 682–1261. This series includes programs on cross-cultural understanding, inter-cultural communication and negotiation, and doing business in Argentina, Brazil, Chile, Indonesia, Malaysia, Mexico, and Singapore.

West Meets East in Japan. Pyramid Film & Video; (800) 421–2304. This video lets the viewer experience Japanese culture from the point of view of the outsider learning the norms of Japanese etiquette.

Working with Japan Series. Big World Media; (800) 682–1261. This six-part series provides information on topics such as business entertaining, negotiating, and women in business.

Websites and Other Resources

International Survey Reports and HR References. Watson Wyatt Data Services, 218 Route 17 North, Rochelle Park, NJ 07662; (201) 843–1177. Over sixty reports with country-specific information on compensation, benefits, and employment terms.

Multicultural Resource Calendar. Amherst Educational Publishing, 30 Blue Hills Road, Amherst, MA 01002; (800) 865–5549. This award-winning calendar educates staff, highlighting the contributions of people of over thirty-five different backgrounds and the holidays of over thirty-five groups.

www.interculturalpress.com. This publisher offers a multitude of resources for understanding and managing cultural differences.

CD-ROMs

CultureGrams™ 2002 (standard ed.). CultureGrams, 1305 North Research Way, Building K, Orem, UT 84097; (800) 528–6279. One hundred seventy-seven four-page cultural reports describing each country's people, customs, lifestyle, and society, including political, economic, and cultural changes.

Global Business Navigator Series. Big World Media; (800) 682–1261. This series provides information on Brazil, China, France, Germany, Hong Kong, Japan, Italy, Mexico, Singapore, South Africa, Switzerland, the United Kingdom, and the United States.

USA CultureGrams™ for the International Visitor. CultureGrams, 1305 North Research Way, Building K, Orem, UT 84097; (8000) 528–6279. This resource, available in five languages, is designed to help visitors understand the culture and people of the United States.

APPENDIX

In order to make the most effective use of the tools and activities included in each chapter, the following matrix provides a cross-referencing of them by audience and purpose/use. For example, a tool found in Chapter 3, Communicating Effectively Across Cultures, may also be useful as a team-building activity or as a strategic organizational change intervention.

GUIDE TO TOOLS AND ACTIVITIES
FOR USE IN GLOBAL ORGANIZATIONS

Tool/Activity	Audience				Purpose/Use					
	Executives	Managers	Employees	HR Professionals	Assessment	Team Building	Training	Communication	Organizational Strategy	Coaching/Mentoring
Chapter 1										
What Do You Need to Know?	✓	✓	✓	✓	✓	✓	✓	✓	✓	✓
Diversity Values: How Well Do They Translate?	✓	✓		✓			✓		✓	✓
Global Diversity Strategy Audit	✓			✓	✓				✓	
You as a Culturally Diverse Entity	✓	✓	✓	✓		✓	✓	✓		✓
Three Cultures Model at Work	✓	✓	✓	✓	✓		✓	✓		✓
Building Your Own Business Case	✓	✓		✓	✓		✓		✓	
Chapter 2										
Global Assessment for Inclusivity	✓	✓	✓	✓	✓		✓	✓	✓	
Personal Assessment for Inclusivity	✓	✓	✓	✓			✓	✓		✓
Stages of Corporate Development and Global Diversity	✓	✓		✓	✓				✓	
Legal Drivers and Implications for Global Diversity	✓	✓		✓	✓				✓	
Global Performance Management Audit	✓			✓	✓				✓	
Identify Global Diversity Exemplars	✓	✓		✓					✓	
Global Diversity Corporate Assessment Tool	✓	✓		✓	✓				✓	

Tool/Activity	Audience					Purpose/Use				
	Executives	Managers	Employees	HR Professionals	Assessment	Team Building	Training	Communication	Organizational Strategy	Coaching/Mentoring
Chapter 3										
Cultural Orientation Questionnaire/Profile	✓	✓	✓	✓	✓	✓	✓	✓		✓
Cross-Cultural Communication Style Inventory	✓	✓	✓	✓		✓		✓		✓
Global Communication Effectiveness Checklist	✓	✓		✓	✓			✓	✓	
Global Communication Analysis	✓	✓		✓		✓		✓	✓	
Use of Interpreters Checklist	✓	✓	✓	✓				✓		✓
Considerations in Planning Presentations	✓	✓	✓	✓				✓		✓
Chapter 4										
The Impact of Culture on Global Team Performance		✓	✓	✓		✓	✓	✓		✓
Factors That Enhance Effective Global Teams		✓	✓	✓		✓	✓	✓		✓
Achieving Task and Relationship Balance on a Global Team		✓	✓			✓	✓	✓		✓
Expanding Views on a Global Team		✓	✓			✓	✓	✓		✓
Framework for Developing a High-Performance Global Team		✓	✓	✓		✓	✓	✓		✓
Leadership on a Global Team		✓	✓			✓	✓	✓		✓
Chapter 5										
What's the Source of the Conflict?		✓	✓	✓	✓	✓	✓	✓		✓
Dimensions of Conflict		✓	✓	✓		✓	✓	✓		✓
What's Your Conflict Style?		✓	✓	✓		✓	✓	✓		✓
Conflict Information-Gathering Checklist		✓	✓	✓	✓		✓	✓		✓
Assessing Your Conflict Competencies		✓	✓	✓		✓	✓	✓		✓

Tool/Activity	Audience				Purpose/Use					
	Executives	Managers	Employees	HR Professionals	Assessment	Team Building	Training	Communication	Organizational Strategy	Coaching/Mentoring
Chapter 6										
Cultural Adaptability Assessment		✓	✓			✓	✓	✓		
Problem-Solving Response Sheet		✓	✓			✓	✓	✓		
Blocks to Problem Solving		✓	✓				✓	✓		
Essential Characteristics of an Effective Member on a Global Problem-Solving Team		✓	✓			✓	✓	✓		
Influencing Others: Unimundo Case Study	✓		✓	✓		✓	✓	✓		✓
Group Experience Rating Form		✓	✓			✓	✓	✓		
Chapter 7										
Using Social and Professional National Competencies		✓		✓	✓		✓			✓
Global Diversity Trend Assessment	✓	✓		✓	✓				✓	
Global Diversity Capability Cycle Appraisal System		✓		✓			✓		✓	✓
Interview Preparations and Analysis		✓		✓				✓		✓
Interviewing Techniques Chart		✓		✓				✓		✓
Global Diversity Interview Review Checklist	✓	✓		✓				✓		✓
Global Diversity Perspectives in Training Design		✓		✓			✓	✓		
Globalizing the Training Design Process				✓			✓			

Tool/Activity	Audience				Purpose/Use					
	Executives	Managers	Employees	HR Professionals	Assessment	Team Building	Training	Communication	Organizational Strategy	Coaching/Mentoring
Chapter 8										
Performance Management Quick Check		✓		✓			✓			✓
National and Civilizational Influences Within the Performance Management Process	✓	✓		✓	✓				✓	
Five-Focus Performance Dialogue Model	✓	✓		✓	✓				✓	
SSI Global Diversity Assessment Tool for Nordic New Co Petroleum Case Study	✓	✓		✓	✓		✓	✓		✓
Global Diversity Performance Management Focus Sheet	✓	✓	✓	✓			✓	✓		✓
Performance Management and Ethics	✓	✓		✓			✓	✓		✓
Global Diversity Rater Competency Review	✓	✓		✓				✓	✓	
Global Diversity Performance Review Outcome Analysis	✓	✓		✓			✓	✓		✓
Chapter 9										
Actual and Expected Gains and Losses from Change	✓	✓	✓	✓		✓	✓		✓	
Corporate Culture Styles and Change										
Reconciling Conflicts Based on Different Cultural Responses to Change	✓	✓		✓					✓	
Leader Behaviors	✓	✓		✓					✓	
Essential Change Agent Behaviors	✓	✓		✓			✓			✓

SAMPLE AGENDAS FOR
TRAINING AND DEVELOPMENT SESSIONS

In order to help leaders, managers, and employees at all levels make the best use of global diversity, it is often useful to structure education, training, discussion, and planning sessions.

Following are a few sample agendas for sessions to suit various groups and purposes. These provide examples of how to sequence tools and activities to create training and developmental experiences and strategy discussions that increase competence in managing global diversity.

Managing Global Diversity: Half-Day Agenda
for Senior Leaders and/or HR Managers

Time	Focus	Activity/Tool	Method
5 min	Introduction	Welcome, purpose, and introduction of participants (if necessary)	Lecturette
5 min	Objectives	To increase understanding of global diversity and its impact on the organization To identify areas needing to be addressed to increase effectiveness	Lecturette
10 min	Warmup	Global diversity: greatest opportunity, greatest challenge	Individual response or paired sharing
30 min		"Global Diversity Corporate Assessment Tool" (Chapter 2)	Small group activity
45 min		"Stages of Corporate Development and Global Diversity" (Chapter 2)	Small group activity
15 min	Break		
40 min		Six Spheres of Inclusivity (SSI) (Chapter 2)	Lecturette
45 min		"Global Assessment for Inclusivity" (Chapter 2)	Small group activity
5 min	Summary		Lecturette
10 min	Closure	Top priorities for our global diversity management process	Individual response

Communicating Globally: Tools for Effectiveness
Full-Day Session for Managers

Time	Focus	Activity/Tool	Method
5 min	Introduction	Welcome, purpose, and introduction of participants (if necessary)	Lecturette, individual response
5 min	Objectives	To increase awareness and understanding of factors impacting communication in a global organization To gain tools and methods to increase effectiveness in global communication	Lecturette
15 min	Warmup	My greatest strength as a global communicator My biggest frustration in communicating with global staff	Individual response or paired sharing
20 min		Dealing with Verbal and Nonverbal Aspects of Cross-Cultural Communication (Chapter 3)	Lecturette
45 min		"Cross-Cultural Communication Style Inventory" (Chapter 3)	Paired sharing
15 min	Break		
45 min		"Essential Characteristics of an Effective Member on a Global Problem-Solving Team" (Chapter 6)	Small group activity
60 min	Lunch		
45 min		Using Interpreters in a Global Organization (Chapter 3)	Small group activity
45 min		"Preferences for Corporate Presentations" (Chapter 3)	Lecturette/ discussion
15 min	Break		
30 min		"Influencing Strategies and Presentation Expectations" (Chapter 3)	Lecturette/ discussion
30 min		"Considerations in Planning Presentations" (Chapter 3)	Paired sharing

Time	Focus	Activity/Tool	Method
5 min	Summary		Lecturette
10 min	Closure	One thing I can do to increase my effectiveness in communicating with my global staff . . .	Individual response

Team-Building
Half-Day Session for Work Groups, Functional Teams, or Task Forces

Time	Focus	Activity/Tool	Method
5 min	Introduction	Welcome, purpose, and introduction of participants (if necessary)	Lecturette individual response
5 min	Objectives	To understand the framework for building a high-performing team To assess strengths and areas for development as a team To identify behaviors that individuals can engage in to style switch more readily	Lecturette
15 min	Warmup	Our greatest strength as a team is . . . One cultural norm I have difficulty with is . . . because . . .	Individual response
15 min		Creating a Framework for Developing High-Performance Teams (Chapter 4)	Lecturette
45 min		"The Impact of Culture on Global Team Performance" (Chapter 4)	Group activity
15 min	Break		
45 min		"Expanding Views on a Global Team" (Chapter 4)	Group activity
45 min		"Essential Characteristics of an Effective Member on a Global Problem-Solving Team" (Chapter 6)	Small group activity
5 min	Summary		Lecturette
10 min	Closure	One thing I can do differently to increase effectiveness on the team is . . .	Individual response

Global Performance Management
Full-Day Session for Managers

Time	Focus	Activity/Tool	Method
10 min	Introduction	Welcome, purpose, and introduction of participants (if necessary)	Lecturette, individual response
5 min	Objectives	To increase understanding of the cultural influences in performance management To gain knowledge and skill in conducting effective performance appraisals To use tools to increase effectiveness in appraising employee performance	Lecturette
30 min	Warmup	"Performance Management Quick Check" (Chapter 8)	Paired sharing
25 min		"National and Civilizational Influences Within the Performance Management Process" (Chapter 8)	Lecturette
45 min		"Five-Focus Performance Dialogue Model" (Chapter 8)	Small group activity
15 min	Break		
45 min		"SSI Global Diversity Assessment Tool for Nordic New Co Petroleum Case Study" (Chapter 8)	Individual worksheet/ group discussion
30 min		"Global Diversity Performance Management Focus Sheet" (Chapter 8)	Individual review
60 min	Lunch		
20 min		"Global Diversity Rater Competency Review" (Chapter 8)	Lecturette
45 min		"Global Diversity Rater Competency Review Outcome Analysis" (Chapter 8)	Individual worksheet/ paired sharing
5 min	Summary		Lecturette
10 min	Closure	Individual commitment to action to increase effectiveness in managing performance of global employees	Individual response

INDEX

ABOUT THE AUTHORS

Lee Gardenswartz, Ph.D., is a partner, with Anita Rowe, in the management consulting firm of Gardenswartz & Rowe of Los Angeles, California. Since 1980, Gardenswartz & Rowe has specialized in shaping corporate culture for clients across the country. Their particular expertise is in creating inter-cultural understanding and harmony in the workplace.

Among Gardenswartz & Rowe's clients are Harvard Medical School, Sempra Energy, Progress Energy, Cox Communications, the IRS, the *Los Angeles Times,* Home Depot, Kaiser Permanente, National Atmospheric and Oceanographics Administration, Mattel, Walt Disney World, State of California Department of Health Services, British Telecommunications, and Prudential. Anita and Lee have lectured widely, giving keynote speeches, facilitating team-building retreats, and teaching seminars across the country. They have made guest appearances on such programs as "Mid-Morning LA," CNN's "News Night," "Sun Up San Diego," "AM Northwest," "Crier and Company," and "The Michael Jackson Show." Gardenswartz & Rowe's principals also continue to teach about diversity, not only through training in client organizations, but also through institutions such as the National Multicultural Institute and the Intercultural Communication Institute in Portland, Oregon.

Lee Gardenswartz earned her doctorate of human behavior from the United States International University in 1981. She wrote her dissertation on organizational stress and what a company can do to minimize its negative effects. For additional information see our website: www.gardenswartzrowe.com.

Anita Rowe, Ph.D., partner in Gardenswartz & Rowe, has been consulting with organizations regarding diversity since 1977, helping them manage culture change, build productive and cohesive work teams, and create inter-cultural understanding and harmony in the workplace. Anita holds a doctorate of human behavior from the United States International University.

Lee and Anita have co-authored a series of articles and numerous books: *Beyond Sanity and Survival,* a stress management workbook; *What It Takes,* a new model for success and achievement; and *Managing Diversity: A Complete Desk Reference and Planning Guide,* which has served as a primary guide to organizations in structuring their diversity initiatives, providing not only conceptual information but techniques and tools as well. In addition to *Managing Diversity,* which received the book of the year award from the Society for Human Resource Management (SHRM), they have co-authored *Managing Diversity Survival Guide* (1994), *The Diversity Tool Kit* (1994), *Diverse Teams at Work* (1995), *Lending and Diversity Handbook, Lending and Diversity Workbook* (1996), *Managing Diversity in Health Care* (1998), and *Managing Diversity in Health Care Leader's Guide* (1999). They also write a regular column in *Managing Diversity* and *Mosaics* newsletters, have written articles on diversity for publications such as *Physician Executive, College and University Personnel Journal,* and *Cultural Diversity at Work,* and have been featured in *Personnel Journal.*

Patricia Digh's first book, *Global Literacies: Lessons on Business Leadership and National Cultures* was named a *Fortune* magazine best business book for the year 2000. Patti's comments about diversity and globalization have appeared on PBS and in the *Wall Street Journal, Fortune, The New York Times, USA Today, The Washington Post,* and *The London Financial Times,* among other national and international publications. She serves on the faculty of the Summer Institute for Intercultural Communication and has lived, worked, and traveled in over sixty countries. Her clients have included DaimlerChrysler, Avaya Communications, PBS, Discovery Communications, PepsiCo, Shell Oil Company, the American Psychological Association, and many others. For more information see www.realwork.com.

Patti was formerly the vice president of international and diversity programs for the Society for Human Resource Management (SHRM), the world's largest HR organization, representing over 150,000 members. While there, she established the Institute for International Human Resources and the award-winning SHRM Diversity Initiative. She also launched international education programs such as the International HR Certificate Program, the Managing Diversity Forum, the Diversity Train-the-Trainer Certificate Program, and the National Diversity Conference as well as the award-winning diversity newsletter, *MOSAICS.*

Patti is currently exploring organizations as storytelling systems, the symbol-bearing aspects of organizational life, and methods for constructive effective individual and shared stories for different organizational purposes.

Martin F. Bennett is a principal in Bennett Consulting, a training and management consultancy that focuses on nationality, ethnicity, and spirituality in the workplace. Martin was a co-founder of Bennett Associates, a worldwide international training and consulting firm formed in 1990 and acquired by Cendant Corporation in 1996. He has over twenty-nine years of experience in the field of cross-cultural management training and development for corporations, organizations, and educational centers in North and South America, Europe, and Asia. He has served as a consultant and developed management, cross-cultural training programs, presentations, and consulting engagements for Fortune 500 companies such as P&G (United States, United Kingdom, and China), Motorola (United States, China, and Singapore), Nokia (Singapore and India), UBS (Switzerland, Germany, Japan, and United Kingdom) and CEMEX (United States, Spain, and Mexico). In addition, he was a consultant to the United Nations on cultural implications within assessment and senior executive selection.

In 1975 Martin founded and directed the Institute of Human Relations, Hong Kong, Ltd., an enterprise that developed intercultural communication training programs for Chinese and Western corporations, institutions, and educational centers in Hong Kong, PRC, and Macao. He also served as a lecturer in the Extramural Department of Hong Kong University and was on the board of APACE, the Association of Psychological and Educational Counselors of Asia. The author of *Update: Hong Kong,* Mr. Bennett is also featured in a recent six-part video series entitled "Working in China."

Since 1982, he has served as a private and corporate consultant to both corporate and nonprofit organizations. Martin's key contributions to the field of international human resource management have been in the areas of international assignment management, candidate assessment, expatriate training, international management development, cross-national coaching, and career development processes for integration of transnational business competencies. He has been quoted frequently and contributed to articles in *HR World, Global HR, Mobility,* and *Journal of International Human Relations.* He has co-authored a chapter on the Intercultural Implications of Occupational Medicine related to cross-cultural issues and was awarded the ERC Meritorious Service Award in 2000 in recognition of his contributions to the industry.

He has served since 1993 on the faculty of the Summer Institute for Intercultural Communication in Portland, Oregon, and participated in the Executive Education Programs at Case Western Reserve University, the Wharton School of Business, and the J. L. Kellogg Graduate School of Management. He is a member of SIETAR International (Society for Intercultural Education, Training, and Research) and a clinical member of the American Association of Marriage and Family Therapists.

Martin is a founding member of the Global Diversity Roundtable, whose aim is to provide a confidential forum for senior executives on the exchange of leading edge practices, strategies, and methodologies in global diversity. He has conducted global diversity training and corporate research in Singapore, Hong Kong, United Kingdom, and North America for Lucent, Morgan Stanley, Infineum, and Capital One Financial Group. His diversity interests focus on the role of corporate leadership in the reconciliation of the cultural values and forces drawn from the major global civilizations and national cultures with the internal and external dimensions of individual employee identity (race, gender, ethnicity, sexual preference).

Martin completed his B.S. degree at Georgetown University in Washington, D.C., and earned an M.A. in theology at the University of the State of New York. He later went on to complete a second master's degree at the University of Chicago's School of Social Service Administration, along with a two-year China Studies Program at the University of Hong Kong, where he developed fluency in Cantonese.

HOW TO USE THE CD-ROM

System Requirements

WINDOWS PC

- 486 or Pentium processor-based personal computer
- Microsoft Windows 95 or Windows NT 3.51 or later
- Minimum RAM: 8MB for Windows 95 and NT
- Available space on hard disk: 8MB Windows 95 and NT
- 2X speed CD-ROM drive or faster
- Microsoft Word 97 or higher

MACINTOSH

- Macintosh with a 68020 or higher processor or Power Macintosh
- Apple OS version 7.0 or later
- Minimum RAM: 12MB for Macintosh
- Available space on hard disk: 6MB Macintosh
- 2X speed CD-ROM drive or faster
- Microsoft Word 98 or higher

NOTE: This CD-ROM requires Netscape 4.0 or MS Internet Explorer 4.0 or higher.
NOTE: This CD-ROM also requires the free Acrobat Reader.
You can download these products using the links on the CD-ROM Help Page.

Getting Started

Insert the CD-ROM into your drive. The CD-ROM will usually launch automatically. If it does not, click on the CD-ROM drive on your computer to launch. After you click to agree to the terms of the Copyright Page, the Home Page will appear.

Moving Around

Use the buttons at the left of each screen or the underlined text at the bottom of each screen to move among the menu pages. To view a document listed on one of the menu pages, simply click on the name of the document. To quit a document at any time, click the box at the upper right-hand corner of the screen.

To quit the CD-ROM, you can click the "Exit" button or hit Alt-F4.

To Download Documents

Open the document you wish to download. Under the File pull-down menu, choose Save As. Save the document onto your hard drive with a different name. It is important to use a different name; otherwise the document may remain a read-only file.

You can also click on your CD drive in Windows Explorer and select a document to copy it to your hard drive and rename it.

In Case of Trouble

If you experience difficulty using this CD-ROM, please follow these steps:

1. Make sure your hardware and systems configurations conform to the systems requirements noted in the "Systems Requirements" section.

2. Review the installation procedure for your type of hardware and operating system. It is possible to reinstall the software if necessary.

3. Have a question, comment, or suggestion? Contact us! We value your feedback, and we want to hear from you.

For questions about this or other Pfeiffer products, you may contact us by:

E-mail: customer@wiley.com
Mail: Customer Care Wiley/Pfeiffer
        10475 Crosspoint Blvd.
        Indianapolis, IN 46256
Phone: (U.S.) 800-274-4434 (Outside the U.S. 317-572-3985)
Fax: (U.S.) 800-569-0443 (Outside the U.S. 317-572-4002)

To order additional copies of this product or to browse other Pfeiffer products visit us online at www.pfeiffer.com.

To speak with someone in Product Technical Support, call 800-762-2974 or 317-572-3994 Monday through Friday 8:30 a.m. to 5 p.m. (EST). You can also contact Product Technical Support and get support information through our website at http://www.wiley.com/techsupport

Before calling or writing, please have the following information available:

- Type of operating system
- Any error messages displayed
- Complete description of the problem

It is best if you are sitting at your computer when making the call.

Pfeiffer Publications Guide

This guide is designed to familiarize you with the various types of Pfeiffer publications. The formats section describes the various types of products that we publish; the methodologies section describes the many different ways that content might be provided within a product. We also provide a list of the topic areas in which we publish.

FORMATS

In addition to its extensive book-publishing program, Pfeiffer offers content in an array of formats, from fieldbooks for the practitioner to complete, ready-to-use training packages that support group learning.

FIELDBOOK Designed to provide information and guidance to practitioners in the midst of action. Most fieldbooks are companions to another, sometimes earlier, work, from which its ideas are derived; the fieldbook makes practical what was theoretical in the original text. Fieldbooks can certainly be read from cover to cover. More likely, though, you'll find yourself bouncing around following a particular theme, or dipping in as the mood, and the situation, dictates.

HANDBOOK A contributed volume of work on a single topic, comprising an eclectic mix of ideas, case studies, and best practices sourced by practitioners and experts in the field.

An editor or team of editors usually is appointed to seek out contributors and to evaluate content for relevance to the topic. Think of a handbook not as a ready-to-eat meal, but as a cookbook of ingredients that enables you to create the most fitting experience for the occasion.

RESOURCE Materials designed to support group learning. They come in many forms: a complete, ready-to-use exercise (such as a game); a comprehensive resource on one topic (such as conflict management) containing a variety of methods and approaches; or a collection of like-minded activities (such as icebreakers) on multiple subjects and situations.

TRAINING PACKAGE An entire, ready-to-use learning program that focuses on a particular topic or skill. All packages comprise a guide for the facilitator/trainer and a workbook for the participants. Some packages are supported with additional media—such as video—or learning aids, instruments, or other devices to help participants understand concepts or practice and develop skills.

- *Facilitator/trainer's guide* Contains an introduction to the program, advice on how to organize and facilitate the learning event, and step-by-step instructor notes. The guide also contains copies of presentation materials—handouts, presentations, and overhead designs, for example—used in the program.

• *Participant's workbook* Contains exercises and reading materials that support the learning goal and serves as a valuable reference and support guide for participants in the weeks and months that follow the learning event. Typically, each participant will require his or her own workbook.

ELECTRONIC CD-ROMs and web-based products transform static Pfeiffer content into dynamic, interactive experiences. Designed to take advantage of the searchability, automation, and ease-of-use that technology provides, our e-products bring convenience and immediate accessibility to your workspace.

METHODOLOGIES

CASE STUDY A presentation, in narrative form, of an actual event that has occurred inside an organization. Case studies are not prescriptive, nor are they used to prove a point; they are designed to develop critical analysis and decision-making skills. A case study has a specific time frame, specifies a sequence of events, is narrative in structure, and contains a plot structure—an issue (what should be/have been done?). Use case studies when the goal is to enable participants to apply previously learned theories to the circumstances in the case, decide what is pertinent, identify the real issues, decide what should have been done, and develop a plan of action.

ENERGIZER A short activity that develops readiness for the next session or learning event. Energizers are most commonly used after a break or lunch to stimulate or refocus the group. Many involve some form of physical activity, so they are a useful way to counter post-lunch lethargy. Other uses include transitioning from one topic to another, where "mental" distancing is important.

EXPERIENTIAL LEARNING ACTIVITY (ELA) A facilitator-led intervention that moves participants through the learning cycle from experience to application (also known as a Structured Experience). ELAs are carefully thought-out designs in which there is a definite learning purpose and intended outcome. Each step—everything that participants do during the activity—facilitates the accomplishment of the stated goal. Each ELA includes complete instructions for facilitating the intervention and a clear statement of goals, suggested group size and timing, materials required, an explanation of the process, and, where appropriate, possible variations to the activity. (For more detail on Experiential Learning Activities, see the Introduction to the *Reference Guide to Handbooks and Annuals*, 1999 edition, Pfeiffer, San Francisco.)

GAME A group activity that has the purpose of fostering team sprit and togetherness in addition to the achievement of a pre-stated goal. Usually contrived—undertaking a desert expedition, for example—this type of learning method offers an engaging means for participants to demonstrate and practice business and interpersonal skills. Games are effective for team-building and personal development mainly because the goal is subordinate to the process—the means through which participants reach decisions, collaborate, communicate, and generate trust and understanding. Games often engage teams in "friendly" competition.

ICEBREAKER A (usually) short activity designed to help participants overcome initial anxiety in a training session and/or to acquaint the participants with one another. An icebreaker can be a fun activity or can be tied to specific topics or training goals. While a useful tool in itself, the icebreaker comes into its own in situations where tension or resistance exists within a group.

INSTRUMENT A device used to assess, appraise, evaluate, describe, classify, and summarize various aspects of human behavior. The term used to describe an instrument depends primarily on its format and purpose. These terms include survey, questionnaire, inventory, diagnostic, survey, and poll. Some uses of instruments include providing instrumental feedback to group members, studying here-and-now processes or functioning within a group, manipulating group composition, and evaluating outcomes of training and other interventions.

Instruments are popular in the training and HR field because, in general, more growth can occur if an individual is provided with a method for focusing specifically on his or her own behavior. Instruments also are used to obtain information that will serve as a basis for change and to assist in workforce planning efforts.

Paper-and-pencil tests still dominate the instrument landscape with a typical package comprising a facilitator's guide, which offers advice on administering the instrument and interpreting the collected data, and an initial set of instruments. Additional instruments are available separately. Pfeiffer, though, is investing heavily in e-instruments. Electronic instrumentation provides effortless distribution and, for larger groups particularly, offers advantages over paper-and-pencil tests in the time it takes to analyze data and provide feedback.

LECTURETTE A short talk that provides an explanation of a principle, model, or process that is pertinent to the participants' current learning needs. A lecturette is intended to establish a common language bond between the trainer and the participants by providing a mutual frame of reference. Use a lecturette as an introduction to a group activity or event, as an interjection during an event, or as a handout.

MODEL A graphic depiction of a system or process and the relationship among its elements. Models provide a frame of reference and something more tangible, and more easily remembered, than a verbal explanation. They also give participants something to "go on," enabling them to track their own progress as they experience the dynamics, processes, and relationships being depicted in the model.

ROLE PLAY A technique in which people assume a role in a situation/scenario: a customer service rep in an angry-customer exchange, for example. The way in which the role is approached is then discussed and feedback is offered. The role play is often repeated using a different approach and/or incorporating changes made based on feedback received. In other words, role playing is a spontaneous interaction involving realistic behavior under artificial (and safe) conditions.

SIMULATION A methodology for understanding the interrelationships among components of a system or process. Simulations differ from games in that they test or use a model that depicts or mirrors some aspect of reality in form, if not necessarily in content. Learning occurs by studying the effects of change on one or more factors of the model. Simulations are commonly used to test hypotheses about what happens in a system—often referred to as "what if?" analysis—or to examine best-case/worst-case scenarios.

THEORY A presentation of an idea from a conjectural perspective. Theories are useful because they encourage us to examine behavior and phenomena through a different lens.

TOPICS

The twin goals of providing effective and practical solutions for workforce training and organization development and meeting the educational needs of training and human resource professionals shape Pfeiffer's publishing program. Core topics include the following:

Leadership & Management

Communication & Presentation

Coaching & Mentoring

Training & Development

E-Learning

Teams & Collaboration

OD & Strategic Planning

Human Resources

Consulting